W9-ASJ-673

RAVES FOR GINGER FRIEDMAN:

"There are a lot of good actors out there, but they just don't know how to audition. They desperately need Ginger Friedman."—Emanuel Azenberg, Tony Award–winning producer

"There is no doubt, the theatre is Ginger's domain. Her classes are electrifying!"—Alexander H. Cohen, Broadway producer

"Ginger Friedman is the most influential force in today's casting market. She trains them! We hire them!" —Bruce Jay Friedman, Oscar–nominated screenwriter

"Ginger Friedman is one of the most innovative and important acting teachers of our time."—Jerry Orbach, Tony Award–winning actor

Nobody knows more about the casting business than Ginger Friedman. And *The Perfect Monologue* is a *must* read for any performer serious about getting that first big break. You'll learn:

* The importance of physical movement in your audition
* Why you shouldn't choose a monologue on the basis of your age
* Why you should never perform a Sam Shepard monologue for an Arthur Miller play
* Why you shouldn't choose monologues that address the past
* And much, much more!

The PERFECT MONOLOGUE

GINGER FRIEDMAN
With a Foreword by Michael Shurtleff

I.C.C. LIBRARY

BANTAM BOOKS
NEW YORK · TORONTO · LONDON · SYDNEY · AUCKLAND

THE PERFECT MONOLOGUE

A Bantam Book / September 1990

ISBN 0-553-28391-X

Published simultaneously in the United States and Canada

*Bantam Books are published by Bantam Books, a division of
Bantam Doubleday Dell Publishing Group, Inc. Its trademark,
consisting of the words "Bantam Books" and the portrayal of a
rooster, is Registered in U.S. Patent and Trademark Office and
in other countries. Marca Registrada. Bantam Books, 666 Fifth
Avenue, New York, New York 10103.*

ACKNOWLEDGMENTS

The Owl and the Pussycat by Bill Manhoff. Copyright © 1965 by Tapaz Productions, Inc. Reprinted by permission of International Creative Management, Inc., 40 West 57th Street, New York, N.Y. 10019.

The Prisoner of Second Avenue by Neil Simon. Copyright © 1972 by Nancy Enterprises, Inc. Reprinted by permission of Random House, Inc.

Steambath by Bruce Jay Friedman. Copyright © 1971 by Bruce Jay Friedman. Reprinted by permission of the author.

Norman, Is That You? by Ron Clark and Sam Bobrick. Copyright © 1969 by Sam Bobrick and Ron Clark as an unpublished play under the title of *Normie*. Copyright © 1977 (revised and rewritten), by Ron Clark and Sam Bobrick. Reprinted by permission of the authors.

P.S. Your Cat Is Dead! by James Kirkwood. Copyright © 1976, 1979 by Elyria Productions, Inc. Reprinted by permission of William Morris Agency.

Same Time, Next Year by Bernard Slade. Copyright © 1975 by Bernard Slade. Reprinted by permission of Jack Hutto, Hutto Management, Inc., 405 West 23rd Street, New York, N.Y. 10011.

Oh Dad, Poor Dad, Mamma's Hung You in the Closet and I'm Feelin' So Sad by Arthur L. Kopit. Copyright © as an Unpublished Work, 1959 by Arthur L. Kopit. Copyright © 1960 by Arthur L. Kopit. Reprinted by permission of International Creative Management, Inc., 40 West 57th Street, New York, N.Y. 10019.

Plaza Suite by Neil Simon. Copyright © 1969 by Nancy Enterprises, Inc. Reprinted by permission of Random House, Inc.

The West Side Waltz by Ernest Thompson. Copyright © 1982 by Ernest Thompson. Reprinted by permission of the author and Graham Agency, New York City.

Bad Habits by Terrence McNally. Copyright © 1974 by Terrence McNally. Reprinted by permission of the author.

The Children's Hour by Lillian Hellman. Copyright © 1934 by Lillian Hellman Kober and renewed 1962 by Lillian Hellman. Reprinted by permission of Random House, Inc.

Orphans by Lyle Kessler. Copyright © 1983, 1985 by Lyle Kessler. Reprinted by permission of Agency For The Performing Arts, Inc., 888 Seventh Avenue, New York, N.Y. 10106.

'Night, Mother by Marsha Norman. Copyright © 1983 by Marsha Norman (Acting Edition). Copyright © 1983 by Marsha Norman. Reprinted by permission of the author.

The Rainmaker by N. Richard Nash. Copyright © 1954, 1955, 1982, 1983 by N. Richard Nash. Reprinted by permission of the author.

The Shadow Box by Michael Cristofer. Copyright © 1977 by Michael Cristofer. Reprinted by permission of the author.

Mrs. Dally Has a Lover by William Hanley. Copyright © 1963 by William Hanley. Copyright © 1962 by William Hanley (as unpublished dramatic compositions). Reprinted by permission of the author.

For
Josh and Peggy, Drew and Kathy,
Kipp and Anne and Max

———————

My heartfelt thanks and appreciation to Linda Loewenthal and Becky Cabaza for their vast editorial assistance and loving guidance.

Contents

SCENES
Comedy

SCENES
Drama

MONOLOGUES
Male
Comedy

MONOLOGUES
Male
Drama

MONOLOGUES
Female
Comedy

MONOLOGUES
Female
Drama

Foreword

Like most venerable institutions, the theater has its share of mysterious traditions: Don't whistle in the dressing room; never say "good luck" to an actor on opening night because theater tradition decrees you must say "break a leg"; never appear in *Macbeth* or bad luck will trail your career thereafter. But most bewildering and confounding is the experience known as the monologue. It brings terror to the heart of the actor who must perform it and dread depression to the auditors—directors, producers, casting directors, playwrights—who must watch. Yet we who work in the theater go on gravely year after year watching monologues, and actors go through their own private hells finding monologues on which to risk their lives, and then the further torture of preparing them for presentation. As a Broadway casting director and teacher, through the decades the question I have most often been asked is "What should I do for a monologue?"

Until now, no one has found a solution to what has seemed an insurmountable problem. But hallelujah, help is at hand for us all! In her invaluable book, Ginger Friedman has at last put between covers the good, sound advice of a sensible, nonconventional theater thinker, which will finally give some usable aid to actors faced with the dismaying prospect of having to perform a monologue.

Where did this dreadful concept of performing monologues come from? For a couple of years I handled the New York auditions for Zelda Fichandler and her remarkable Washington, D.C., Arena Stage, probably the finest of the regional theaters. We started out doing the usual monologues that are *de rigueur* for regional theater: a two-minute classical monologue, dramatic or comic; a two-minute contemporary monologue, contrasting with the choice made for the classical. They were sheer torture to watch—monologues always are. If you actors think performing a monologue is a nightmare, try sitting there all day long watching the damn things. It is enough to make you jump in front of the nearest subway to take you away from theater forever.

When I told Zelda that monologues were intolerable, she smiled wisely (she was a very wise lady as well as fascinating, dedicated, and extremely mysterious) and said, "What would you like to do?"

I said, "Ask them to bring a partner and do a three-minute scene." She nodded, with a look of patient "you'll see" in her eyes.

I did see: When the day came for the actors to present their scenes, forty percent of them canceled out because their partners had let them down, suddenly discovering they had to pick Mother up at the airport. (How many times have I been told that an actor has to pick Mother up at the airport? They must spend more time at airports than they do at acting.) Or they had to take the dog to the vet or they had the flu or a sore throat or couldn't talk or had to go to the dentist before they lost all their teeth. Since it wasn't their audition, the partners felt no regrets at canceling out for such very important reasons, leaving the auditionee stranded and partnerless.

"Now you know, my dear Michael," said dear Zelda, "why we have to go on with these damnable monologues." She had accepted this awful situation as a fact of theatrical life; I never have. I refuse to listen to monologues anymore. I've had enough. Monologues invariably present actors at their very worst. I can never tell a thing about the actors from monologues; I have to have a long chat with them after the cursed monologues are over. Usually I ask them to tell me a sad or a funny experience from their own lives, so that I can find out *who* they are: The monologues never tell me that. Theaters do monologue auditions as a way of *eliminating* actors rather than as a way of finding them.

But not everyone has made the choice I have of refusing to hear monologues. Regional theaters, never realizing where the dreaded practice came from, are devoted to hearing them. Ginger Friedman has very wisely addressed herself to the only sensible solution to the problem. Ironically enough, it is a solution that no actor has ever dreamed of, and that none of the people who run auditions requiring a monologue seem to realize is the solution that will teach them something about the actor, instead of merely being a device to turn actors away. Many a fine actor has fallen through the cracks because of doing monologues. It is the theater's loss, not merely the actors', that judgments are made of actors based on material that is guaranteed to show them at their worst: the section lifted from a play because it is a long speech in one place and published in those pamphlet-books of monologues which I advise every actor to burn immediately.

At last in this much-needed book, Ginger teaches actors how to choose material that will express themselves. I think I have seen about three impressive monologues in my entire life in the theater. If actors follow Ginger's method, watching the performance of monologues might even turn into a pleasure, for it will enable the auditors to see an actor at work creating a relationship. Since acting is the creation of relationships (not doing one-man shows unless you are Lily Tomlin—and the reason her work is so extraordinary is that she creates such beautifully convincing relationships with her characters; she is never talking to herself), a monologue in which you are talking to no one but your inner self, which turns you inward and self-involved, is patently self-defeating. The process of acting is the giving and receiving of meaningful communications from another human being. Knowing this full well, Ginger has devised a way whereby the actor can achieve the creation of relationships while doing a monologue.

Every actor who has to do a monologue should study this book from page one clear through to the end, and then start on his quest to create for himself monologues from plays that will connect with his own personal fantasies and real life, and thus express to the auditors who he is: the person who dreams of glory, who desires love, who wants to give love, who celebrates life, and finds joy (and sorrow) in coming together with another person. The goal of life is no different from the goal of acting. Ginger tells the actor, for the first time, how to achieve this. Listen to her.

Finally someone of knowledge and experience, someone sensitive to the actor's problem and yet fully aware of the auditor's problem, has come up with a real solution to the problem of monologues. Actors: Use it. Stop doing those long speeches from plays which show you at your most deadly and construct your own monologues. In this book, Ginger Friedman shows you how.

This could revolutionize the practice of using monologues for auditions, and turn what is now a dreaded, loathsome, highly *inaccurate* experience for auditors into a process they might actually enjoy—and might for the first time learn something meaningful about the actors from watching them do monologues. And for actors, it could turn the nightmare of monologues, which is tantamount to self-immolation, into an experience they could not only feel good about but actually look forward to. These were undreamed-of possibilities until the appearance of this remarkable book.

—MICHAEL SHURTLEFF

Introduction

Finding, preparing, and performing a monologue has always been an enigmatic situation for the actor—and with little wonder. Actors have had to rely on monologue books that dispense cookie-cutter speeches from dramatic literature. Well-intentioned but misguided friends and even acting teachers—many of whom are ill-informed about auditioning techniques—recommend the same, overused speeches. College professors advise their acting students to write their own monologues and ignore the wealth of dramatic literature at their disposal.

Rarely does the actor read whole plays for the purpose of being entertained and attaining a knowledge of and appreciation for dramatic literature and the playwright. Seldom does he read the full play in search of fresh, vibrant events that could be developed by the student into a monologue. Few are the times when an actor will appear at the audition with a dynamite piece of material that is working for him and not against him.

I have seen the outcome of actors' preparations for monologue auditions thousands of times throughout my career, and I must report that the situation is indeed a sad one for both the actors and the auditors (directors, casting directors, playwrights, and producers). Most actors fail at the monologue audition. They have simply not mastered the technique—a situation I hope this book will correct.

I have had the advantage of observing auditions from the point of view of director, casting director, playwright, and teacher. When I function in the first three roles, I look for and expect a single result: a finished opening-night performance. But as a teacher, I help actors learn the process that leads to that result. I have directed plays in theater and my own one-act plays on cable television. My play, *Nice Girls*, which I coauthored with Ilene Lasker, was produced Off-Off Broadway. I have been teaching professional actors audition and rehearsal technique for more than fourteen years in New York and Los Angeles. I conduct audition and rehearsal seminars and workshops in college theater departments and work with gifted teenagers in a New York State–funded program in the arts. My videotapes on audition technique are used in university theater departments in more than forty-six states.

But I, too, was an actress before becoming a casting director and acting coach, and I must confess I often failed at auditioning. After completing two years of training with one of America's foremost acting teachers, I set out on my auditions eager and ready to conquer the world, which to me existed only on the stage. However, my first audition was for a commercial. I was handed my copy and put before a camera. My acting training was deeply rooted in the Stanislavsky System, which, of course, is based on truth and realism. The very last instruction I received from my teacher was, "Now when you audition, you must make sure they can hear you in the last row." Indeed this was the *only* audition instruction I received. I clung to this advice as I began my voracious reading on the merits of soap powder, making damn sure I could be heard in the last row of the Palace Theatre! The man working the audio suddenly flung the earphones from his ears to the floor, shrieking loudly in obvious discomfort. I was quickly escorted to the door.

This was a time when audition technique was not yet being taught. I had fine acting instruction from a first-rate teacher, but I was doing poorly at my auditions. I was one of the many actors who simply could not audition no matter how intelligent we might be during the rehearsal and performance. During rehearsals we have the luxury of experimenting, developing character, analyzing the script, taking direction, working with the ensemble, correcting mistakes, making discoveries along the way, and gradually growing into the part. But the guidelines of scene study and rehearsal simply do not apply to the audition process. At the audition auditors need to see open, honest, intelligent, and appealing work. The actor who is not proficient at audition technique, does not get to the rehearsal. And there is never an opening night.

Up until just a few years ago, monologues were not a major part of the audition process. Actors were given a few pages out of the play (which are called sides). These auditions are referred to as cold readings. The actor has little time to read and prepare for them before the scheduled audition. Although the cold reading audition is alive and well, more monologues are being requested today by directors, agents, and casting directors than ever before. Monologues are also requested by resident companies, college theater departments, and production companies who once or twice a year expand their files of actors. (This kind of audition, which is not for a specific play, is called a "general.")

Because of an increase in the number of available actors and a decrease in productions, monologues often save time and money for directors and producers. When the monologue is the first audition and the cold reading is the call-back, there is less initial paperwork. A different actor can be seen every two minutes throughout the day instead of every five, seven, or ten minutes, the time usually spent on a cold-reading audition. The auditors then have the opportunity to see the maximum amount of candidates before beginning the process of elimination. Only those deemed interesting, appealing, and real will then be called back to read from the script.

I have been involved in casting plays, film, and television for the last seventeen years. Representing a production as a casting director is an awesome and wondrous way to make a living. I have observed magnificent and outlandish auditions. I have been moved and appalled, thrilled and bored, uplifted and thrown into the lowest depths. I have laughed uproariously and I have cried and felt tenderly toward some, while being enraged at others.

As an auditor, I am unimpressed by the actor who recites a remembrance from a long-ago past instead of choosing material in the here and now, which includes the other character(s) in the scene.

It is not unusual for the auditors to have to sit through the exact same monologue three or five or even ten times in one day. You do not want to be one of the actors who elicit from the auditors moans and words such as, "Oh, no! Not again!" Always keep in mind that you will be compared to the others. And lack of originality and resourcefulness will be counted against you.

Actors often ask me which monologues are overdone. My reply is, "*Any* speech in *any* play!" But with some creative effort, you can develop a monologue that will gratify you and show your strengths as an actor.

Monologue selection is a highly personal business. For me or anyone to give you your monologue would be tantamount to telling you with whom you should fall in love or dictating your future food intake without considering your personal tastes.

You've got to *own* the material. And you've got to have passion for the material you choose or you will just be adequate, which is what we see too much of at auditions—thunderously adequate performances. And adequacy does not get you a call-back and we are talking call-backs here! That is what this book is all about: getting call-backs and getting the part. By the time you finish your preparation and rehearsals, you should feel that monologue was written just for you!

Your choice of monologues should be based on a strong emotional identification with the character's words. It is not necessary for you to have experienced the same event as the one taking place on the page, but you should relate to the character's emotions; you should feel as if you might even say the same words in the same situation.

It is important for you to know what a monologue truly is, what a monologue should be *doing for you*, and what we, the auditors, look for in your monologue auditions. You must know the elements of the kind of monologues that are going to help you get the call-back.

Until now, there has been a vast lack of astute counsel on this subject for the actor. Because of misconceptions and bad advice, many actors present themselves at their monologue auditions in a variety of ludicrous ways.

I remember well the day that an actor did a Sam Shepard monologue with a real gun pointed at my head throughout his entire speech. All I could think of was that gun and whether or not it was loaded. He chose me to be the other character in his scene and he was threatening my life. I couldn't wait to get him out of there.

Then there was the actor who did the son's speech from *House of Blue Leaves*. He lit the fuse of what appeared to be a real bomb. We silently and hypnotically stared at that fuse burning down while totally ignoring the actor, fearful that our last few moments on earth were approaching fast.

There was another actor who arrived dressed in his under-shorts and one sock, tied up in a straitjacket! I don't remember what monologue he did and don't think I was aware of it even then. One day a zippy actor cartwheeled into my office, did his speech, and cartwheeled right on out. Another day, a young man pulled a chair up to my desk alongside of me, spat his speech into my face, got up, and left.

I'll never forget the actor who was ushered onto the stage at an open Actor's Equity call. It was clearly stated in *Back Stage*, the New York actor's trade paper, that a two-minute prepared monologue was required. He stood before us looking about and smiling. We looked at him and smiled back. His allotted two minutes were certainly being wasted. Finally the director asked him what monologue he was going to do for us. His reply was, "Oh, I don't believe in monologues."

Once a pretty young actress came out on stage, plopped onto the floor, removed one shoe and sock, and proceeded to bite off the tips of her toenails.

I could go on and on but my point is this: your goal as an actor is to delight us and surprise us. You should have a strong, magnetic stage presence. Don't come to us; make us come to you. Command our attention and win our affection with your powers. Be unpredictable. But for heaven's sake, don't scare the hell out of us. Don't disgust us and don't make us fearful that we are dealing with a recent escapee from the Bellevue mental ward.

Despite the actions of these actors and many others, I firmly believe that actors are the most normal neurotics in the world. You must be stable and well disciplined to make it in this business.

To act, is to give. You give gifts to your audience. You expose your vulnerability and share yourself, warts and all. You are giving love. You don't make up or pretend anything as an actor. We all do that enough in life. In theater, you create your reality. You make choices for your characters and you explore and find new truths. You make discoveries about yourself and come to know yourself better. This inner search for truth materializes during your preparation and rehearsals. It is this grand adventure that we will cover and explore within these pages.

In a sense an actor is a social scientist. As an actor, you change minds and attitudes. You help people to laugh and cry. "Civilians" —as theater people refer to those not in the theater—discover and uncover their own beings because of you. They expand their visions and horizons because of you.

Keep in mind that the second the curtain rises, the audience member wants to see himself up there in you. He has to recognize himself as he is, or wishes to be, or hopes never to be, or perhaps once was. He has to connect to you through your humanity and vulnerability. If you don't fully explore from deep within and communicate strongly, you will alienate yourself from him.

The auditor is your first audience. So whom do you risk alienating at the audition? That's right. Us! And if you alienate the auditor, you've blown the audition.

To be given the privilege of sharing yourself with audiences, you must first earn that privilege. That is what auditions are all about. Go to your auditions to perform for the audience, not to audition for the auditors. We are there to screen you for the paying audience, to see if you're worth the current price of $50 for a theater ticket or $7 for a film ticket. That is the bottom line. We want from you no less than you would give during a performance for a paying audience. It is my firm belief that the actor's contributions in a production are the most significant ones made, even though the production is a team effort. But when a play must close due to harsh notices or poor box office, it is never the fault of the actor. *Actors do not close shows!* Playwrights do. Directors do. Producers do. Composers do. Critics do. But not actors.

Of course, casting the right actor is essential and difficult. Often, a play will close after replacements have been made for a leading character. Perhaps the chemistry created by the first team seems to dissipate in the rehearsals and in performance. The audience knows! Or the director is no longer available and the A.D. (assistant director) takes over and cannot conjure up the fervor and zeal that existed at the beginning of the production. Sometimes an actor has been chosen solely for his box-office appeal and lacks the technique to make life and death choices for his character. Be assured, when this occurs the audience knows! On one occasion in New York, a superstar in pop music was cast in an important play and the *world* knew. This was frivolous casting, putting profit before talent.

If you desire to act because you are *looking for* acceptance, applause, adoration, and love, you probably won't get very far in the business, not as an actor anyway. You've got to give to get. If you desire to act becuase you want to *give* of yourself, share yourself unconditionally, expose your vulnerability, and *give* love, then you've got a shot. It is then and only then that you can *get* acceptance, applause, adoration, and love. When you step on a stage on opening night after you've rehearsed for all those hours for four or more weeks and the houselights dim and the stage lights come on and the curtain opens and you step out there, then you will know why you were born! If you do not subscribe to this sentiment, you probably will not become one of America's finest actors.

But to get to what I consider to be a very cherished place

you've first got to get through the audition successfully. So onward; there is a lot for you to learn.

On these pages, I hope some myths will finally be dispelled, wrongs will be righted, questions will be answered. I will explain specifically why extracting speeches from plays is death to your performance and for your chances for a call-back, why you *must* select your *own* monologue and why you should *not* write your own monologue. I will guide you through monologue rehearsal and the actual audition and I will demonstrate, using scenes from many plays, the most intelligent, pragmatic, and creative way to look for, find, choose, adapt, create, develop, rehearse, present, and perform *The Perfect Monologue*.

What Is a Monologue?

A monologue is a 2-, 3-, or 1,000-character scene. The other character or characters to whom you are talking happen not to be saying anything for a minute or two. You are doing the talking; they are doing the listening.

Your monologue is not from the play you are auditioning for; therefore, you do not have the obligation to service the playwright's play fully as you must do in a cold reading. You must use the monologue as a vehicle to showcase you, the actor. It must work for you, not you for it.

The best way to look for monologues is to *not* look for monologues! For the love of Williams, Pinter, Wasserstein, and Durang, stop leafing through those pages in search of those speeches! You are cheating yourself unmercifully by overlooking rich and energetic dialogue, relationships, and events that are in the here and now and involve the other character(s) in the scene.

When you extract speeches or long blocks of dialogue out of the play, notice that by and large the dialogue consists of telling and recalling an action that took place already. The material deals with the past and not with the here and now. Moreover, this sort of piece doesn't allow you to connect with the other character(s) in the scene. You are not able to create a strong relationship because you are only telling a story. The material is essentially a memory piece.

When you are being seen by auditors you want to show as much of your ability as possible. Simply telling a story prevents this from happening and does not allow you to work with your full strengths as an actor. After such a speech, auditors turn to each other as your picture is placed on the "no" pile and say, "We don't know what this actor has to offer." I consider these words worse than saying that we didn't like your work. For all I know, you might be a very intelligent and interesting actor but with that material, how can I tell? The memory piece does not service you at all. It has no sense of immediacy, and the result is characterless and insipid.

By choosing material that consists of events that are current—meaning here and now—you have the opportunity to expose more of your abilities. You are creating a sense of urgency and emotional action. By a sense of urgency, I mean your character's need to communicate right away to the other character(s) in the scene. It is through your relationship and communication with the other character(s) that we the auditors are able to see your acting range.

There are some speeches that *do* serve you well. The only problem is that because they are perfectly written monologues, they are done by many actors. They are done to death! One such overdone monologue comes from *Chapter Two* by Neil Simon. It is the speech in Act II spoken by Jennie to her husband begging him not to end their marriage. This speech deals directly with the other person in the scene and provides an emotional "reach-out" and "immediate need." This monologue has humanity and irony. It is all in the words.

By humanity I mean exposing your true feelings of love, need, and vulnerability through honest and open communication about what is going on inside of you. By sharing it, we see and feel your humanity and out of humanity emerges humor. I don't mean comedy. I mean humor—a sense of irony and absurdity. The humor is situational and behavioral. You don't have to be a funny person to do comedy or humor. You don't have to make people fall down the steps laughing but you *must* be aware of and react to the absurdities and ironies of life.

Monologues such as Mr. Simon's contain every element needed for the perfect monologue, but I strongly suggest the following: if you find a perfect monologue written by a playwright, don't do it! You won't be original if you choose what is considered to be a tried-and-true monologue. One way or the other you will be doing yourself a disservice: either the monologue is a memory piece or it is overdone. That is why it is so important to create a monologue for yourself from already existing dramatic literature.

What the Auditor Is Looking for

We want to believe everything you are saying up there. Show us that you *want* to be there and *want* to communicate with your audience. Reveal a generosity of spirit and do not be afraid of taking charge of the stage. It belongs to you for those two minutes. It is all yours! Do not cheat yourself and us by holding back the parts of yourself that are your strengths. Allow us to be attracted to the person up there. Show us the best of you. I didn't say the nicest! Don't try to get us simply to like you. We want to see the raw edges of your personality, the offbeat and quirky parts of you. We want to see your fears and vulnerabilities.

Give us, your first audience, something to latch onto— something that we can understand. We have the same faults and insecurities. Remember, we go to the theater to see *ourselves,* not you. Ourselves, through you!

Don't be afraid to expose your inner feelings that are not on the pages. Take risks even though you might fail. If you are aware that failure is a possibility, but you don't have a *fear* of failing, you're on the right track. Chances are, if you don't care if you look foolish before us, you simply *won't* look foolish!

The irony is that under these circumstances, you will be free to observe how foolish *we*, the auditors, are. There we are, sitting before you bleary-eyed, egg salad dropping down from at least one chin, a row of tense proletarians passing your picture and résumé back and forth to each other, squirming in our seats with sore bottoms from those hard folding chairs, being overly effusive to put you at ease, or staring, zombielike at you trying to maintain a professional distance, and at the end of the day practically requiring the aid of a Seeing Eye dog on reaching the outside world until our pupils adjust once more to light.

You have to be willing to fail in order to succeed. *If you are afraid of failure, you will fail!*

You've got to be willing to get your face dirty and fall down. Go out on a limb. Be courageous. Take chances. Be outrageous. I know that you've been trained at home and in school to behave well, speak softly, and have proper manners but this kind of behavior brought to the audition stage is not interesting. It works well in life with your peers, friends, lovers, and associates but it is boring on stage. I'm not telling you to be crazy. I'm telling you not to try to be a flawless character: those are not the people playwrights write about.

It is also important to take your time delivering your monologue. Do not rush through it believing we will not have to spend so much time on you, time you feel you don't deserve. We will only be bored by you. *If you are afraid of being boring, you will be boring!* Take your time. In your mind's eye talk to the other character in the scene. Communicate. Slow down enough to be able to convey each happening, development, and discovery. You need to give yourself enough time to hear what you are saying to the other person (character) and to play off that person. You must respond to his or her nonverbal reactions. Take a breath periodically for emotional reasons, not only when you need air. Do this two or three times during the monologue. This procedure will not only help you to slow down but also contribute to an exclusive meter. You want to keep the dialogue going with a sense of urgency but certainly not at a galloping pace. If you rush through the monologue, you will be giving a line reading. You will become an acting machine dispensing words, and you will bore us.

On the other hand, the self-indulgent performance should also be avoided. This happens when the actor does his homework during the audition. Right there in front of us he searches for the inner justifications for the words. These inner feelings should have been assimilated by making choices during several rehearsals. Instead, the actor probably had no rehearsals—he just memorized lines. Therefore, what we see at the audition is a weak, empty performance. And its inevitable slow pacing will cause many auditors to stop the performance before the actor even finishes the monologue. I've seen this happen many times. The actor is very wounded but has no choice but to stop and leave.

You must remember always to have a sense of urgency. Be careful of those Pinter pauses; those long gaps between sentences. There should be very little silence emanating from the stage during the monologue audition. Keep the action and dialogue going, and don't give us a spiritless performance.

Your monologue is a vehicle to showcase *you*. You are presenting yourself in your own two-minute production. We are not auditioning the material. We are auditioning you, and we expect you to choose the best material you can find.

Here are some basic ideas to keep in mind when looking for and developing monologue material. As I said before, your character must be reaching out for something from the other character(s). Remember, the more you communicate with the other character(s), the more you are communicating with us. The material should provide you with the opportunity to make life-and-death choices. If the conflict in the words is a powerful one involving your character's happiness and future, then he or she will be fighting for his or her life. The actual words do not have to deal with life and death, literally, but the content of the material must involve strong conflict and a need to solve it immediately.

It has become tiresome to hear actors in my classes tell me that they "feel it" as I discuss the lack of communication in their performance. I say to them, "Wonderful! I'm glad someone in this theater felt something."

It is not enough simply to feel. You have to communicate these feelings to your audience. How? By making specific choices about your character's background, relationship with the other character(s), and what it is your character desperately needs from the other one(s) right now! You accomplish this by using your sense memory or emotional and memory recall powers and by personalizing and substituting. This means choosing from your own life experiences and events and making the other character in the monologue a real person from your (the actor's) life.

In some material your character will be talking about a third person, someone who is not in the scene. Be wary of this kind of scene. I'm not saying that you must avoid such material, but you must be sure there is enough dialogue concerning the relationship between the two characters, you and the one to whom you are talking. Let's say you're in love with a character offstage—make sure through the creation of your inner life that the character onstage can help you get to the other one; therefore, the character you're interacting with becomes more important to you in the here and now.

Another example is doing a monologue in which you are talking to your best friend about your mother not allowing you to see your lover. In this instance, in your preparation and rehearsals, you must make choices about your relationship with your best friend. It is this person who for the next two minutes is the most important person in your life, not your mother or your loved one. It is this person who can provide the help you so desperately need to change your mother's mind. The monologue is really about you and your friend. Because your mother and lover are not in this scene, you don't have the opportunity to play out the actions between yourself and them. You can talk about them, but the action takes place between you and your best friend.

Another important tenet of effective auditioning is to *never give us what you think we are looking for!* Give us *your* strengths. Don't try to guess our preferences, because you don't know! Even if we tell you, we are often not being realistic.

Many actors proclaim, "The auditors don't even know what they want!" How wonderful for you if that is true. This means we will be open. It also probably means we will see a variety of types and many more actors at the audition. If we really knew exactly what we were looking for, you might not even get to audition; you might not be the type. If you try to give us the type we say we are looking for, you might hold back some of your personal strengths and qualities, all based on *your* perception of what you perceive we perceive we are looking for!

Very often the playwright doesn't even know what his play is really about. You, the actor, will help him to discover its meaning. It is through the casting procedure that the playwright and director learn about the script. The way the play is cast makes a strong statement. You bring a new dimension to the script; therefore, you have great power as an actor at the audition. Please use it. Give us who you are.

When a theater director opts for type—the physical aspects of the actor that correspond to the character on the page—over talent, he will soon discover at the rehearsal that he is in trouble. The actor who gave the most intelligent, exciting, and honest audition should have gotten the part. During the rehearsal process he would have become the type. That is what rehearsals are for. That is what acting is. This is a very simple premise but one not fully grasped by shortsighted directors. What they need to learn is talent becomes type!

Directors *do* cast type in film and certainly in television. If you've got the "hair, teeth, and bone school of acting face," there's a land of television waiting for you on both coasts and in Florida.

Agents around the country tell me that they will always represent a beautiful face and body. They say that the more beautiful or handsome, the less talent required. These actors are hired for type only. They can be coached on the set before each shoot if need be and before each audition. A television director is not an actor's director. In actuality he is a technical director. He is there to tell you where to stand, which camera to play to, when to turn or sit, etc. It is the casting director who auditions and hires you. Often the director doesn't meet you until he is shooting your scene! And he will not work with you on acting problems. You may have your private coach for that and at your expense. By and large, however, you must give a decent audition to show that you have something besides that hair and those teeth. If you are not one of the world's great beauties, your audition must be terrific.

You will not be required to do monologues for television or most film auditions but you *will* have to do them for the agent *before* being submitted to the television or film casting director.

When a monologue is requested by a television auditor, be careful about which monologue you choose. Some monologues can be offensive to television casting directors and agents. They are not accustomed to hearing "raw" material; therefore, because four-letter words or sexually explicit material is not done on commercial television, you should not choose a monologue with those elements. It would be highly inappropriate and your audience could be offended. On the other hand, theater casting directors and agents are only too aware of and used to raw material and are not easily shocked.

No animal torture stories please! Please do not do a monologue dealing with the explicit details of a puppy being squashed under the wheels of a truck or of birds being killed by rocks thrown by boys, or of an old dog barely able to make it up the steps to be euthanatized by the veterinarian; all these are events in legitimate plays, but when taken out of context, they are totally inappropriate for an audition. Actors proclaim that this kind of material allows them to display strong emotion, therefore demonstrating powerful acting expertise. This may be so, but relating a horror story that concerns the grisly details of violence or pain leaves auditors very upset and saddened, and some of us admit that this sadness turns into anger toward the actor. I suggest that you keep away from any material dealing with explicit physical violence.

Do not write your own monologue unless you are a professional writer, because chances are you will not write a dramatic piece with the needed conflict. You will probably write about an incident that occurred in your life, which is fine. But you will probably write it exactly as it occurred, which is not fine. You will relay an incident that is important to you but not to anyone else, and it will then fall into the memory-piece category. Because you are not a professional writer, you will not want to nor will you have the facility to embellish the story. The truth of life does not transfer well to the truth of theater. You must create, add to, change, enhance, and dramatize the truth. How many times have you said or heard someone say something to the effect of, "The story I told you is the absolute truth and yet if I wrote about it, no one would believe it!" To these people, my retort is, "Fictionalize it and then they'll believe it." If the material lacks conflict, you will have very little to work with. Your true story will not serve you well at your audition.

I have had to contend with many actors at auditions asking me, "May I use you?" This means that the actor is asking if he may play his monologue to me by making me the other character. First of all, I do not want to be *in* your scene! Allow me to observe and evaluate your performance by not involving me in your monologue. I am your audience, and I want to maintain an audience-actor distance so that I am free to enjoy you. No auditor wants to be forced into making eye-to-eye contact with you throughout your monologue. You will feel rejected and ignored if you see that I am not looking at you or that I am whispering something to my associate or putting lipstick on or eating my sandwich (we often don't get a lunch break).

On the other hand, when you are auditioning for camera work, there are some auditors who want you to look at them and it is hoped they will communicate this to you. I say "it is hoped" because unfortunately I have heard too many reports of auditors telling the actor *after* the audition that he should have played it to the auditor. This is very frustrating for the actor and it is also unjust. I suggest that you ask the auditor if he wants you to play to him when you know the audition is for camera work.

The problem with playing to the auditor is that you must abandon your previously rehearsed choice of who the other person in the monologue is. By suddenly switching to the auditor, you could be thrown off. The way to avoid this problem if you think you will have to play to an auditor is to make sure you have faith in your choice—something that should come with many rehearsals. When the auditor wants you to play directly to him, tell yourself (as actor) that you are playing to a camera lens and (as character) that you are talking to your original character. This other character should be in your mind's eye.

Don't expect to be treated lovingly at the audition every time. The way you are treated has nothing to do with you, or it shouldn't if you arrive on time and don't make waves. Remember that auditors, like real people, can be in a foul mood. One Los Angeles casting director ends each audition by saying to the actor, "All right, get out!" I counseled my West Coast students who were recipients of this discourtesy to think of a person who treats you this way as a person who is nonorgastic and chronically constipated! Without exception, the students felt better.

The proper procedure for holding the audition is for you to be ushered into the assigned studio, theater, soundstage, office, storefront, living room, or back hall at the exact time your audition is scheduled. The auditors should already have your picture and résumé. If not, you will hand it to the director, agent, casting director, or stage manager on the way in. You will then stand before them, announce your name, the name of the play, and the name of the character. Do not "set up" the scene. In other words, do not explain what is happening in the scene or what has happened to lead up to this scene. Do not ask if we are familiar with the play. Perform for your audience. When it is over, give yourself a silent count of five to allow the "curtain to fall." Then break character, look at the auditors and say, "Thank you"—not a grateful thank-you but a courteous one.

Do not apologize when you are finished with your monologue. Too many actors do this. They shrug and giggle and look at us and say, "That's it." We get the strong feeling that they mean to say, "Sorry, but that's the best I can do and that's the only monologue I know how to do, and I know it's not really a good piece."

Avoid accents or dialects when you are auditioning for a specific play unless you know the play requires one. Do not use them for general auditions unless you are allowed to do three monologues, which is quite infrequent. But in this rare instance, your third piece certainly may have an accent or dialect. All accomplished accents and dialects should be listed at the bottom of your résumé.

Producers will mention in the character breakdown, which appears in the actors' trade paper, whether or not they are looking for accents or dialects. The character breakdown gives a short description of each character. Very often, with an English play, "authentic" English is requested, whatever that means. I suppose it means someone born and bred in Great Britain. And what kind of "authentic" English accent do they mean? There are so many, just as there are here in the United States. If an "authentic" American accent was requested, which would one choose? Of course, in Great Britain there is something called stage English. It is an English accent to us but to the natives of Great Britain, there is no noticeable accent. In America, the equivalent would be the way the natives of Chicago talk.

It is very easy to acquire an accent. Spend a day or two with someone who has the one you want. Do not listen to *anyone* else for that period of time! Or get a tape of that accent or dialect and put the earplugs in your ears for twenty-four hours. Then go to the audition. I had a student who went on an audition and found when she arrived there that they wanted her to have an Hispanic accent. She asked for an hour to prepare and was granted it. She ran to upper Broadway, which was one block away from where the audition was being held; she stopped someone whom she perceived to be Hispanic and asked her for bus directions. She listened very closely. She repeated this scenario with six more women along Broadway; then she ran back to the audition and got the part.

Imagine yourself looking at a painting. It is a landscape. There is the sky with a few clouds. In the background are hills of varying height. The foreground has trees, a meadow, a lake, birds flying, and flowers surrounding a small thatched-roof cottage with a picket fence around it. Everything in the picture is the exact same color!

Imagine listening to a symphony. Musical instruments made up of wind, string, and percussion. And every note played by each instrument throughout the entire composition is the exact same note. Repeated over and over!

This picture and symphony could take place in someone's disturbed dream.

Why, then, are so many monologues performed with one color and with one note? Why are actors not painting broader brushstrokes that are harmonious, decorous, delightful? Why are they not playing all the notes that are compatible yet unexpected, awesome, and wondrous?

The monologue is the composition and you are the artist. You are making the brushstrokes. You are playing the notes. We don't want a monochromatic or Johnny-one-note recitation. Give the composition a full life. We want all the colors and all the notes.

How to Find the
Perfect Monologue

Monologues don't start out being perfect. In fact, the perfect monologue doesn't even start out as a monologue. You must adapt, create, and develop your own personal material. You must expend a little energy, do your *own* reading and make your own choices.

Plays are the best source for monologues. Film scripts for the most part don't contain strong dialogue. Films deal with physical action, visuals, and camera angles, which are moving pictures. Dialogue is secondary. If you find good dialogue in a film script, chances are the film began as a stage play. Of course, there are exceptions, but not many. Therefore, I recommend that you concentrate on plays to find your monologues.

It is also possible to find material from novels, nonfiction, articles, poems, and songs. But remember, you need material that has a built-in relationship complete with needs and conflicts in the dialogue. You might not have problems coming across material in novels but nonfiction, articles, poems, and songs do not usually contain conversation between two people.

It is not necessary to choose characters only in your age range. In this business, you are as old as you look, not as old as you are. But for the monologue audition, you may choose a character who is *nowhere* near your age or age range! Don't limit yourself by allowing your age, gender, or race to prevent you from choosing a piece of material when the dialogue and circumstances affect you very deeply. Whatever the gender, age, or race, you will play *yourself*. Can't you relate to and identify with actual words you've heard people say who are not your gender, age, and race?

If you are a twenty-year-old male and you read dialogue spoken by a forty-year-old female and you find that you are relating to the sentiments and the emotional life, don't be afraid to use it. Make it your own. Remember, you are creating a vehicle to showcase *you!*

If within the actual *dialogue,* it is strongly indicated that the character's age is nowhere near yours, then, of course, it will not work for you. But you probably wouldn't identify with it anyway under those circumstances. If it is a very well-known character such as Maggie in *Cat on a Hot Tin Roof* and you are a forty-year-old female or a male of any age, it would not be an intelligent choice. The auditor will know the character so well that any deviation might cause him to ponder your dramatic propriety. But you don't have to limit yourself to esoteric material; indeed almost all popular work produced on Broadway and Off Broadway is eligible and available for your purposes.

If the character is black and you are white, there is no reason why you can't do it unless it is about *being* black. If the character is white and you are black, do it by all means unless it is about *being* white. If the character is a male and you are a female or the other way around, there is no reason why you should not do it as long as it is not *about* the other gender. If you really relate to the emotional content, do it.

I saw *Torch Song Trilogy* six times; it is a highly successful Broadway play written by Harvey Fierstone. I recognized myself up there on that stage in the lead character, Arnold Beckoff, a male homosexual drag queen in his twenties; none of these are characteristics I share. Nevertheless, that was me up there. I strongly identified with his pain, his humor, his vulnerability, and indeed with several of the actual events taking place in his life. I laughed throughout the play along with the entire sold-out audience, and I cried in total self-indulgence on six different occasions; it was a most enjoyable release of emotions.

A former acting student of mine (and most likely a former actor) called to ask me to recommend plays with characters that were right for him. He said he didn't want to waste his time reading just any play! This kind of thinking is not compatible with the sensibility of the serious dedicated actor.

Think back throughout your adult life to all the plays you've seen and read. Do not concern yourself with thoughts about monologues. Forget the monologue! I'm talking about plays. Are you able to recall one or more that you have loved? Have you been moved, excited, stirred, aroused, and affected by any of them? If so, then you've got the beginnings of your monologue. Something caused you to react strongly to the relationship and the words. It doesn't matter what the emotion was as long as it hit you hard! Get the plays and read them. All professionally produced plays are published either by Dramatists Play Service, Inc. or Samuel French, Inc., and can be purchased in a bookstore specializing in theater arts or can be found in some libraries.

After you've reacquainted yourself with the play, go back to the scene or scenes in which the events taking place most affected you. Read *only* the dialogue of the character to whom you relate and with whom you identify. With a pencil, underline your dialogue. What will happen eventually if not immediately is that a line will not make sense in relation to the previous one. Do *not* allow this to discourage you. Expect it to happen. After all, the other character is responding to what you just said and you will respond in turn to what he just said. Remember, because this monologue is being created by you and it is not from the play that you are auditioning for, you have the privilege, the right, and the luxury to edit and change dialogue. You obviously do not want to change the context of the material but do put to use editing skills that you will discover you possess.

When your line doesn't make sense, read the other character's dialogue immediately preceding the problem. Being aware of the other character's dialogue at this point will help you determine how to build a bridge to correct the gap. You may incorporate the other character's dialogue into yours, or leave out your line if need be, or change a statement to a question, or vice versa, or you might delete a few lines or indeed a whole chunk of dialogue. You might have to patch together dialogue over the next several pages. Whatever you do, you will be creating the bridges to link the dialogue together. Make sure all of it makes sense to you. Do not concern yourself with whether or not the material makes sense to us, the auditors. We are not auditioning the material, we are auditioning you. As long as you, the actor, can justify the bridges and patchwork through your acting choices and performance, that is good enough. In other words, if it makes sense to you, it will make sense to us.

The piece should play for one to two minutes, but don't worry if it goes over two minutes while you are still creating your monologue. You can always cut it during your rehearsals when you will more accurately be able to time the piece. You might even end up with enough material for two separate monologues and will then have a choice as to which monologue is the stronger and more interesting of the two. Don't use both at the same audition, as they are not contrasting pieces.

Then transfer your dialogue onto a sheet of paper. Test the material to be sure that there is sufficient emotional action in the words. Here are two guidelines to help you determine if the material has the elements needed to allow you to show your acting range. Using the other character's name say (as character), "'Blank' is the most important person in my life. Today is the most important day in my life." As character ask yourself, "Why is today the most important day in my life?" This question can be answered immediately without any preliminary work on the piece because the answer is the same for every audition piece you will ever do for the rest of your auditioning days. The answer is, "Today is the most important day in my life because today is the day that I've *got* to change my life. I've *got* to make it better." The change you are seeking must include the other person (character) in your life. The specific answer to the question will be dictated by the words and circumstance on the page. You have not yet connected to the material through the rehearsal process. As an actor, you are feeling a strong pull toward the material and you are testing it to make sure it will serve you well.

If the dialogue does not in any way deal with the other person, the piece will not allow you to communicate strongly. You will be unable to create a relationship because it is nowhere on the page. If it is too shallow it will not showcase you properly and should be discarded. If the material is powerful enough to expose many facets of your character, then we will see many facets of you, the actor, and you probably have found, chosen, adapted, and created a perfect monologue for you. The next step is to continue to develop and rehearse it.

Another way to look for your monologues is to always be on the lookout for material from the plays you see. Go to as many plays and productions as you can afford. Keep in mind that if the play is an original one, the published version won't be on the market until about a year into production. Also read plays by both working and long-gone playwrights. The more you read, the more plays you will fall in love with. It is from these plays that your monologues should come.

The Classics

You do not want to edit Sophocles, Euripides, Aeschylus, Plautus, Shakespeare, Molière, or others of this ilk. This is not to say that modern playwrights are inferior to classic playwrights. All writers today have a personal rhythmic pattern. The written word is to be respected. But if you edit a play, classic or modern, that is written in verse, you will inevitably destroy the meter. As an example, the following is a scene from *Tartuffe* by Molière as written by the playwright.

Valere:
    Madam, I've just received some wondrous news
    Regarding which I'd like to hear your views.
Mariane:
    What news?
Valere:
            You're marrying Tartuffe.
Mariane:
                                        I find
    That Father does have such a match in mind.
Valere:
    Your father, Madam . . .
Mariane:
                            . . . has just this minute said
    That it's Tartuffe he wishes me to wed.
Valere:
    Can he be serious?
Mariane:
                        Oh, indeed he can;
    He's clearly set his heart upon the plan.
Valere:
    And what position do you propose to take,
    Madam?

Mariane:

Why—I don't know.

Valere:

For heaven's sake—

You don't know?

Mariane:

No.

Valere:

Well, well!

Mariane:

Advise me, do.

Valere:

Marry the man. That's my advice to you.

Mariane:

That's your advice?

Valere:

Yes.

Mariane:

Truly?

Valere:

Oh, absolutely.

You couldn't choose more wisely, more astutely.

Mariane:

Thanks for this counsel; I'll follow it, of course.

Valere:

Do, do; I'm sure 'twill cost you no remorse.

Mariane:

To give it didn't cause your heart to break.

Valere:

I gave it, Madam, only for your sake.

Mariane:

And it's for your sake that I take it, Sir.

Dorine: *(Withdrawing to rear of the stage.)*

Let's see which fool will prove the stubborner.

Valere:

So! I am nothing to you, and it was flat

Deception when you . . .

Mariane:

Please, enough of that.

You've told me plainly that I should agree

To wed the man my father's chosen for me,

And since you've deigned to counsel me so wisely,

Mariane:

I promise, Sir, to do as you advise me.

Valere:

Ah, no, 'twas not by me that you were swayed.
No, your decision was already made;
Though now, to save appearances, you protest
That you're betraying me at my behest.

Mariane:

Just as you say.

Valere:

Quite so. And I now see
That you were never truly in love with me.

Mariane:

Alas, you're free to think so if you choose.

Valere:

I choose to think so, and here's a bit of news:
You've spurned my hand, but I know where to turn
For kinder treatment, as you shall quickly learn.

Mariane:

I'm sure you do. Your noble qualities
Inspire affection . . .

Valere:

Forget my qualities, please.
They don't inspire you overmuch, I find.
But there's another lady I have in mind
Whose sweet and generous nature will not scorn
To compensate me for the loss I've borne.

Mariane:

I'm no great loss, and I'm sure that you'll transfer
Your heart quite painlessly from me to her.

Valere:

I'll do my best to take it in my stride.
The pain I feel at being cast aside
Time and forgetfulness may put an end to.
Or if I can't forget, I shall pretend to.
No self-respecting person is expected
To go on loving once he's been rejected.

Mariane:

Now, that's a fine, high-minded sentiment.

Valere:

One to which any sane man would assent.
Would you prefer it if I pined away
In hopeless passion till my dying day?

Am I to yield you to a rival's arms
And not console myself with other charms?

Mariane:

Go then: console yourself; don't hesitate.
I wish you to; indeed, I cannot wait.

Valere:

You wish me to?

Mariane:

Yes.

Valere:

That's the final straw.
Madam, farewell, your wish shall be my law.
(He starts to leave, and then returns: this repeatedly.)

Mariane:

Splendid.

Valere: *(Coming back again.)*

This breach, remember, is of your making;
It's you who've driven me to the step I'm taking.

Mariane:

Of course.

Valere: *(Coming back again.)*

Remember, too, that I am merely
Following your example.

Mariane:

I see that clearly.

Valere:

Enough. I'll go and do your bidding, then.

Mariane:

Good.

Valere: *(Coming back again.)*

You shall never see my face again.

Mariane:

Excellent.

Valere: *(Walking to the door, then turning about.)*

Yes?

Mariane:

What?

Valere:

What's that? What did you say?

Mariane:

Nothing. You're dreaming.

Valere:

Ah. Well, I'm on my way.

Farewell,
(*He moves slowly away.*)
Mariane:

Farewell.

The following is the monologue created from the previous scene for Valere.

Madam, I've just received some wondrous news regarding which I'd like to hear your views. The news that you're marrying Tartuffe. That your father, madam has just this minute said that it's Tartuffe he wishes you to wed. Can he be serious and if so what position do you propose to take, madam? For heaven's sake—you don't know? Well, well! Marry the man. That's my advice to you. You couldn't choose more wisely, more astutely. And if you follow this counsel, I'm sure 'twill cost you no remorse. I gave you this counsel, madam, only for your sake and if you take it I see I am nothing to you, and it was flat deception when you said you love me. Your decision was already made, though now, to save appearances, you protest that you're betraying me at my behest. Now I see that you were never truly in love with me. Here's a bit of news: You've spurned my hand, but I know where to turn for kinder treatment, as you shall quickly learn. Forget my qualities, please. They don't inspire you overmuch, I find. But there's another lady I have in mind whose sweet and generous nature will not scorn to compensate me for the loss I've borne. I'll do my best to take it in my stride. The pain I feel at being cast aside time and forgetfulness may put an end to, or if I can't forget, I shall pretend to. No self-respecting person is expected to go on loving once he's been rejected. Would you prefer it if I pined away in hopeless passion till my dying day? Am I to yield you to a rival's arms and not console myself with other charms? You wish me to go? That's the final straw. Madam, farewell. Your wish shall be my law. This breach, remember, is of your making; it's you who've driven me to the step I'm taking. Remember, too, that I am merely following your example. Enough. I'll go and do your bidding, then. You shall never see my face again. Well, I'm on my way. Farewell, madam.

Valere has most of the dialogue so there is a minimum of sacrilege to the meter but nevertheless the piece has been thrown out of kilter.

The following is a monologue created from the scene for Mariane.

Father has a match in mind. He has just this minute said that it's Tartuffe he wishes me to wed. He is serious. He's clearly set his heart upon the plan. I do not know what position to take. Advise me, do. Marry the man? That's your advice? Thanks for this counsel; I'll follow it, of course. To give it didn't cause your heart to break. And it's for your sake that I take it, sir. You've told me plainly that I should agree to wed the man my father's chosen for me, and since you've deigned to counsel me so wisely, I promise, sir, to do as you advise me. I do not betray you and if you feel that I was never truly in love with you, alas, you're free to think so if you choose. I'm sure you'll know where to turn for kinder treatment. Your noble qualities inspire affection. I'm no great loss, and I'm sure that you'll transfer your heart quite painlessly from me to her. Go then: console yourself; don't hesitate. I wish you to; indeed, I cannot wait. Farewell.

Valere's dialogue has been interjected into her dialogue and once again the piece is off balance. The poetry has been tampered with. It may appear to be acceptable as a monologue but the rhythm and verse have been thrown off.

Many American actors cannot do their best when attempting the classics, primarily because most of us, unlike Europeans, are not taught the classics in our early education. American students practically have to major in the classics in college in order to read them. In college drama departments, the classics are suddenly thrust into the lap of the young acting student who memorizes a part meant for a person thirty to fifty years his senior. This character's life is imbued in epic and monumental events that are totally alien to the young acting student. Underneath the epic elements of the text, of course, these characters are actually struggling with issues we all can relate to, including the young acting student: love, fear, vulnerability, insecurity, greed, power, envy, jealousy, hate, conquest, lust, and just plain fighting for their very existence and lives. Style, manner, and form are often stressed in the acting class at the expense of the humanity and dynamics of the character. This gets in the way of the inner lives of the characters, and the student too often plays only what is on the page. When the actor comes to us with a classic monologue, we see a technical exercise and nothing more.

I do believe that the young college acting student should read the classics and analyze, ponder, philosophize, and get into the skin (in my classes I say "get into the shoes and underwear") of the characters. Students should try to find the characters in themselves just as they would with contemporary characters, not only by using the actual events as a guide but by exploring what is *not* on the page: the inner fear, needs, struggles, and desires of the characters. There are no villains in dramatic literature. The villain does not know he or she is one and would defend himself or herself to the death to prove it; so should the actor during the preparation for the part. Too often students concentrate on the outside negative aspects of a character instead of the inner life where the humanity is.

I believe improvisation is as essential in the classics as it is in contemporary plays. The student's own words help break through to the core, heart, and soul. The student should not start out by playing a king. He should be playing a man who happens to be a king, at least at the onset of the rehearsal. He should find the man first. The king will follow.

Impeccable diction is a fundamental necessity, accompanied by strong commitment to voice projection, physical control and agility, a fascination and thirst for history, and a fierce love of language.

If you do a classic monologue for your audition, present it as it was written by the playwright. Many of the speeches appearing in the classics are actually soliloquies, which means you are talking to yourself. There is no one there to hear you; therefore, you cannot create the needed relationship, communication, and emotional reach-out, and there is no other character for you to respond to. What you are thinking, you are saying. There are no hidden meanings, no opposite thoughts. It is the moment of truth for your character. Choose someone to hear you. This person may be God or a dead person who was important to you. But please do not address your soliloquy upward to God or downward to the deceased. You should see them in your mind's eye.

You will need one or two classic monologues for Master of Fine Arts auditions, Shakespeare festivals, some stock companies, resident companies, many Broadway and Off Broadway auditions, and, naturally, for a classic play.

Which Monologue for Which Audition

Do not do a Sam Shepard monologue when auditioning for an Arthur Miller play or Woody Allen for Tennessee Williams and so on. There are vast differences between the sensibilities of the playwrights, and it is up to you to make intelligent choices as to which piece to choose for each audition. You should have at least four monologues at your disposal at all times. You need a dramatic piece and a comic piece. If you plan to audition for the classics, then, of course, you should have a dramatic and a comedic piece in the classics.

Often the locale is the South so you should have southern material. Other plays are set in the Southwest and you certainly have enough material available to choose a piece set in this region.

Once I was casting Max Frisch's play *The Firegug*, which was written in German and translated into English. The character breakdown in the trade paper specified that the characters were urban Europeans and monologues were requested for the audition. I would say that at least 75 percent of the actors brought in southern or southwestern characters. This made no sense at all. We were looking for certain urbane qualities. Auditors are now being more explicit regarding monologues in the trade papers. At times, they actually list the playwrights whose work they want to see.

How to Rehearse Your Monologue

Actors never think in terms of rehearsing their monologues. They memorize them and "do" them a couple of times out loud; then they feel ready to perform them at the audition. Many of my private students come to me with a monologue they've found and want me to help them prepare for their upcoming audition in two days! They have not even gotten off book yet (memorized the monologue) and what they bring to me over and over are dull emotionless pieces of material.

Unlike the cold reading, you have luxuries with the monologue. You need and have the opportunity and time to give yourself hours of rehearsals. You can experiment, make mistakes and correct them, try it different ways, develop character, analyze the script, and play with it as you see fit. Plan to rehearse the piece for at least a half hour each day for at least one week. Don't go for results until your sixth rehearsal. This is the rehearsal process so take one step at a time and live with the material. Think about it and sleep on it. Each hour that you rehearse it, take one step forward toward your opening-night performance, which is your audition. Keep track of the hours spent on the preparation and rehearsal. Do not be in a rush to achieve results, and prepare by using the *character's* vocabulary, which means getting into first person immediately!

The beginning of *each* rehearsal should *not* start with the monologue! It should begin with the history and background of your character. Before you begin your first rehearsal, write down the highlights of your character's life since the day of birth. Write where you (the character) were born, what kind of parents you had, outstanding events in your life as you were growing up, including friends, lovers, school, and family matters. Be specific and use as much as you can from your own life that will not interfere with what the playwright has given to you—use only what will complement the words and events in the monologue. Don't write that you came from a middle-class family or a poor one or an upper-middle-class one. Write that your father had a small hardware store that did nicely, or he was a drunk and couldn't make a living and your mother had to take in wash, or your father was a Fortune 500 president. Write with candor the conflicts and hurts you experienced over the years. Write what your adult life has been like so far and then get to the point in your life when you met the other character in the monologue; write all the important events between the two of you leading up to the confrontation in the monologue.

The playwright might have supplied you with background and, if so, use whatever you choose to incorporate into your history. Start each rehearsal by going over this history before you start on the dialogue.

The playwright writes half a play—the writer's half! You, the actor, must write your half—the half that is going to get you the call-back. You will be creating choices for yourself as character throughout the monologue and the best choices will come from *your* head, *your* world, *your* perceptions, not the playwright's. You don't know what was in the playwright's head, world, or perception, and second-guessing will only interfere with your preparation. He did his work. Now you must do yours. He has given you all he has to give—the words. You only know what is on the page. He leaves the inner life and interpretation up to you.

What is *not* on the page is the most important part of the character and the play. You know how we sometimes do not divulge our real feelings and thoughts because we are protecting ourselves and simply cannot expose our vulnerability, well, so do the characters in plays. Sometimes the playwright has the character lie, just as we do in life at times without the help of a playwright. You need to create a play within the play. Embellish and create your reality. Write down your (the character's) thoughts, feelings, and needs. Don't forget to include the other character who is the most important person in your life.

Your character must come alive through *you:* through *your* emoions, *your* sensibilities, *your* frame of reference, *your* attitudes, *your* mannerisms, *your* idiosyncrasies, *your* character. First of all, that person on the page is only a printed word! There *is* no such person! There is no playwright still there to give you insight into your character. You are on your own.

Do not concern yourself with the physical aspects of your character for the first few rehearsals. Actors worry about what to do with their hands at the beginning of their preparation. Of course you don't know what to do with them at this stage of the development of the piece—you haven't had a chance to explore or develop the character. You don't comprehend the inner thinking and feelings of the character because you have not yet completely formulated your choices. Allow your body to do what it will during the first few rehearsals. Character development begins from within.

As you prepare, you will begin to use your body as a prop, the best prop you will ever have. Allow your body to reflect your inner feelings. Because today is the most important day of your life, you will not move about in a slow and lethargic fashion. That would oppose your inner feelings as well as the sense of urgency that should be in the words. In your rehearsals, as you develop the character from within, make deliberate and strong movements. Don't be afraid to move. Body movement is a language. You will begin to use your hands automatically almost from the beginning of your first rehearsal. One thought to keep in mind is that whenever you gesture, make sure your elbows are not touching your rib cage. Gesture all the way with a strong full movement.

Do not use a chair to be the other person in your scene, and do not place the other character in a chair. We don't want to watch you talking to an empty chair. It looks ridiculous and makes it that much more obvious that there is no one there.

And you should not plant yourself in a chair or on a stool and then just stay put for the entire monologue. You may use one as a prop to perhaps sit on for a small portion of the monologue. Then get up and use some of the space for yourself. If you sit throughout the monologue, you are folding yourself in half and become a smaller person up there. You are hiding part of yourself and sitting on your energy. You are making your two minutes inactive and you cannot use your body as a prop as effectively as when standing and walking about. You create a stronger stage presence when you are standing. The character might be sitting down according to the stage directions. Change them by creating *your* stage directions!

Don't try to make us see the other person. You know there is no one there, and we know there is no one there. If you make life-and-death choices and the other person is the most important person in your life and is the only one who can and *must* help you, we will see what we want to see.

Put the other person in the scene down right, down center, or down left, put him on your eye level, or slightly above. We want to see your eyes, not your lids. Use the fourth wall. Actors forget there is one. The fourth wall is what you are looking at when you look out above the audience's heads. For your character, it is a definite place. If you are indoors it is the fourth wall in the room you are in. If you are outdoors, there are trees, or a lake, or the backyard. Your sense of place is part of your preparation, so make choices as to what you are seeing before you.

While you are in the midst of your dialogue, you want to get many of your images from that vast place out there. Get your images from your surroundings, not directly from the other person in your monologue. Do not paste your eyes on him. It is not interesting nor is it real to focus only on the other person throughout your audition. The person doing the listening does the looking. The person doing the talking gets his images from about him. Allow your eyes to see things while you are involved in the conversation. Remember, it *is* a conversation. For one or two minutes, you are doing all the talking. You should look directly at the other person perhaps three or four times during the two minutes and only for three or four beats at a time. You do not have to establish for the auditors where the other person is. We are not concerned with the other person's location, but you must be.

I believe it is more interesting to start your monologue looking away from the other person. If he is down center, look to your left or right. Then after a few lines of dialogue at a pivotal point you should turn to him. Just see him in your mind's eye. Use a real person from your life. When you turn to him and look at him you should think, "Are you listening to me? This is my life we are talking about!" What is his reaction? The first time you address him this way his reaction should be a negative one; perhaps he is showing you that he really isn't interested in what you have been saying to him, or he has no idea what you are talking about. Incorporate his reaction into your next lines of dialogue. As you notice that he is not responding as you wish him to, you will now have to fight harder to reach him. The second time you look at him, his response should show that he is beginning to understand what you are getting at or that you are breaking through to him. This will be more positive and you will incorporate his response into your next few lines. The third time might be a totally positive response, which should precipitate a strong reaction from you. At some point you may have him try to interrupt, but you don't let him. Your inner life is "No, let me finish! This is important, you must hear me out!" All his responses to you should be nonverbal, but once in a while it might be necessary to include in your monologue a very short question or statement spoken by the other person that you are responding to. Of course, you get none of this from the playwright. You are creating a play within the play: the actor's half of the play.

Don't put a lid on your emotions. Do not ever make the choice that you don't want the other person to know how you really feel. If you make that choice, there will be no emotional reach-out and what you hide from the other person, you hide from the auditors. You will be cheating your character and therefore yourself. Turn yourself inside out and work off your inner life and vulnerabilities while you are speaking the playwright's words. You don't want to alienate the other person. If you do, you will alienate the auditors. The other person will respond to your dialogue. Allow us, the audience, to respond to your emotions. Allow us to come closer to you and to recognize ourselves in you. The playwright's words won't do it. Remember, the audience doesn't come to the theater to see you; they come to see themselves through you.

Unlike a production, there is no set. You must give yourself a strong sense of place. Your physical surroundings from audition to audition will be different each time and none of these surroundings will be the place that your character is in. Put your character in a room from your own life. If your character is in his or her living room, set your scene in your living room. If the scene is taking place in your friend's room, put the scene in your friend's room. If the scene takes place in a location, indoors or out, that is unfamiliar to you, change the locale to a familiar location. You want to substitute and personalize these places so that there will be more of *you* in the scene. By using familiar places you will feel closer to the event and more comfortable during your performance. This is all for you, not the auditors. Do not indicate where you are or where you've placed the furniture. Your awareness is enough. Put your character in this place at the beginning of each rehearsal.

When you are auditioning on a stage in a theater, even though the auditors might be sitting in the first row, please project your voice so that we know that you will be heard by those in the last row. The other person in your monologue should be across the room from where you are or if you're both outdoors, not standing right where you are. You should place him or her several feet downstage (toward the audience) right, down center or down left above the auditors' heads. Make sure that you are being heard by him or her. Communication goes beyond just making your character heard by the other person. In life that would be enough but not for theater. You have the added obligation of making sure you are being heard by an audience.

To avoid putting a strain on your vocal cords, you should be adept at using your diaphragm, a wall of muscle between the chest and abdomen. This means putting this muscle to work for you so that your voice will be emanating from deep within you instead of just from the upper end of your trachea. Too much strain will cause an inflammation of the larynx. Singers are taught how to use their diaphragms; so should actors. Indeed, professional theater actors do make proper use of their diaphragms.

I remember well a Hollywood superstar, who was cast in what was to be a major Broadway play: he lost his voice during previews and had to whisper his lines. A doctor was summoned, but the damage had been done. He had never before had to project his voice. His vocal facilities were untrained and weak, his diaphragm unused, and his breathing prowess, nil. The show closed.

In my experience, when an actor cannot be heard it is because he *does not want* to be heard! It usually has to do with personal insecurity, fear of communication, inadequate preparation, or simply shyness. Very rarely is the problem caused by something such as a sore throat. When I am directing a play and an actor cannot be heard well enough, I would not be out of line if I stated to the actor, "act louder!" It is appropriate for the director to issue result-oriented direction because he is not functioning as a teacher. In my audition class, however, I would be remiss in my duties as a teacher if I were to direct my students in this manner; classes are process oriented.

A former student of mine was loud and clear when offering feedback and critique to her fellow actors after performances in class, and she was quite audible in her conversations during class with the other students, but when it was her turn to get up on stage and perform her scene, we had to strain our ears to hear her. I usually sit in the first row, and *I* had problems hearing her. When she was stage center and on display, she froze. It was a painful experience for her. When the situation is this extreme, the acting teacher—as well as the actor—is faced with a major problem. The problem has nothing to do with acting. The actor should cope with this fear by utilizing the expertise and assistance of a therapist.

Of course most cases are not this extreme, but I am constantly confronted with the lack of communication that leads to a lack of voice commitment. If you make very strong, personal, specific, and honest choices for your character during your rehearsals, chances are that you will be heard. If you can't be heard, it is because you didn't make today the most important day in your character's life and you didn't make the other person the most important person in your character's life.

When doing a monologue in an office that is on the small

side, talk to the other person in the scene as if he is across the room. If the auditor asks you to play directly to him, speak up as if he is a few feet farther from you than he actually is. When doing your audition in a very large space with high ceilings and one that is empty of furniture, rugs, and draperies, there will be a repetition of your voice by reflection of sound waves. It will be difficult to understand what you are saying if you project at full blast. Tone down your projection. You must make sure that you do not speak quickly; otherwise one word will blend into the next as a result of the echo.

How to Handle Nervousness

Nervousness is the actor's companion. First and foremost, you must fully acknowledge your nervousness. Do not ignore it and do not deny it. This is not the way to alleviate it. Admit to yourself that you are nervous. Say it to yourself out loud as you are waiting to be called in to perform your monologue. Don't be concerned that people around you will judge you for talking to yourself. You won't be the only one doing it. You are an actor doing your last moments of rehearsing and it is considered quite appropriate to speak aloud.

Let's turn negatives into positives. The only way to achieve this is to first admit that there is a negative. Let's assume that you have created a monologue from Ibsen's *A Doll's House*. You are doing Nora. You are doing a monologue from the scene where you tell your husband that you are leaving him. The following is a suggested soliloquy for you to do after you've reviewed your character's history and background and the events leading up to today's confrontation and are waiting to be called in.

I am nervous. I am very, very nervous. My hands are shaking. My legs feel weak. I am so very nervous. This is not easy, what I am about to do, but I've got to succeed. I must not fail. I am very frightened and nervous, but I've got to do this and do it well. I've got to not let my fear stop me from doing this brilliantly. I've *got* to be able to explain to Helmer why I am leaving him. But I am so nervous and scared but I've got to be honest with him and share my feelings before I leave despite my nervousness.

You see, you have given your nervousness to your character. If you've chosen well, all your characters will have some degree of nervousness. There has to be a certain amount of nervousness when a person to whom you are talking is the most important person in the world to you. This is the only person who can give you something that you desperately need and need *now*. Do be desperate. Desperation is not negative in the way we use it. We are not saying *desolate*. We are saying *desperate*. We must fiercely strive with all our might to achieve our goals and satisfy our needs in our own lives and in the lives of our characters.

While waiting to be called in to audition, perform the entire monologue out loud and remember not to be hesitant about speaking aloud. Monitors (the person who checks you in and calls your name when it is your time to audition) and actors are used to hearing lines being read out loud. At the conclusion of your rehearsal, take the energy and high emotional pitch and bring it to the beginning of the monologue and immediately do it again. *You were not big enough the first time!* I don't mean loud enough. When you think your performance is "too big," in actuality, it is *almost* big enough! Do this as close to your scheduled audition time as possible so that you don't have to sit and wait around too long. You are now ready to audition. Take charge of that stage! It is yours for the next two minutes. It belongs to you and only you.

After you have finished your rehearsals and the monologue is ready to be performed at auditions, it doesn't mean that you automatically will be doing the monologue with regularity. Your first audition might not come about very soon and they could be few and far between. You must, therefore, keep your work alive and fresh. You must stay in touch with it and continue to be familiar with it.

When you are hired in a play, you will be performing your part eight times a week. When you have created and rehearsed your monologues, you must perform them once a day *every* day. The investment of time adds up to a few minutes a day, a very important few minutes, indeed.

Read reviews in newspapers to keep in touch with story lines and plots and character breakdowns. It will help you immensely to know which scripts to be sure to read as they become available. Spend time at theater bookstores and the library in your community. Don't confine your reading to only dramatic literature. Read novels, newspapers, and books written for the layman on personality disorders. Read case histories on vibrant, troubled, tormented, and outrageous people. These are the people dramatic literature is màde of. These are the characters you will be auditioning for.

Finally, keep this thought in your mind. After the second time you have auditioned, you have become more experienced than the average auditor is in this procedure! *You* know more than they do regarding the actor's process and how to best present yourself and perform for them!

Author's Note

Optimum benefit will be derived from this book by reading it in its entirety. This book presents to the actor and student actor precise guidelines and step-by-step guidance for monologue selection, preparation, and performance for auditioning purposes.

Scenes as written by the playwright should be read and then compared with the adapted and created monologue emerging from each one. My comments and direction follow each monologue. This is a process-oriented book that should not be used only as a source for finding and using the monologues within these pages. Scenes and monologues with characters not in keeping with the reader's age, gender, or race should nevertheless be read.

Several monologues are deliberately timed over the accepted time of two minutes and, therefore, should be cut at each actor's discretion.

I strongly recommend that actors have as a companion to this book *Audition* by Michael Shurtleff and be familiar with the "twelve guideposts."

SCENES

Comedy

THE OWL AND THE PUSSYCAT
by Bill Manhoff

pp. 6–14 (Samuel French, Inc.)

The following is the scene as written by the playwright.

Doris: Hello, Pansy—rat fink pansy!

Felix: You lied about your size!

Doris: You spider—you cockroach!

Felix: You're making a mistake. I'm afraid you have the wrong apartment.

Doris: I just wanted to get a look at you.

Felix: It's a mistake!

Doris: Oh will you listen to her! Mistake! You didn't spy on me from your window and call my landlord, huh?

Felix: I don't know you.

Doris: Well, I should have known! Any queer who peeps at girls through his window like a dirty weasel wouldn't be man enough to admit it.

Felix: You gained entry here under false pretenses—You have no right—

Doris: Was it fun? Did you wish you could do what the big boys were doing?

Felix: I have no idea what you're talking about.

Doris: "I have no idea what you're talking about." Come on, don't give me that! He told me. You're the one that called all right. "Sherman."

Felix: If you leave immediately—I won't call the police—

Doris: Call them. You said you would. You told Gould you were gonna call the police . . . you know you told him that, you slimy snail—you bedbug . . . you cockroach.

Felix: I advise you to curb your foul mouth and stop making obscenities out of God's harmless little creatures.

37

Doris: Why don't you curb your foul rotten mind? Try to be a man for once.

Felix: Now listen to me—

Doris: You're lucky I'm too refined to beat you up—the way I feel—

Felix: Will you listen to me . . . you're insane!

Doris: You're lucky I can't stand physical violence.

Felix: Now look—something has happened to you obviously—

Doris: (*Starting to get weepy.*) What has happened is that I have been thrown out of my room. At two o'clock in the morning.

Felix: He did that? That was unnecessary.

Doris: Then you admit it. You called Gould, right?

Felix: I don't have to admit anything.

Doris: (*Going to window.*) I don't know how you even saw anything this far away. You must have eyes like a vulture. Why did you pick on me? (*The flood of anger is running out, leaving her weak.*) How dare you do something like this? I get sick when I think there are people like you! I took money from a couple of gentlemen—did that hurt you?

Felix: (*Condescending.*) You must expect a certain number of people to respect the laws. That's what holds society together.

Doris: Three cheers for you! And I'm not society, huh? I don't have to get held together?

Felix: My dear woman, you were breaking the law. If you find yourself in trouble it is only—

Doris: (*She notices a pair of field glasses. She picks them up.*) So this is how you saw! Oh now it's bad enough with the naked eye—but with spyglasses—now that is just plain dirty, Mister. I'm sorry! When you work at it this hard—filthy, Mister! Filthy, filthy!

Felix: (*Defensive.*) I'm a writer. A writer is an observer. I have a right to those.

Doris: You want me to tell you what you're full of?

Felix: I wouldn't expect you to understand.

Doris: You are nothing but a dirty, filthy Peeping Tom!

Felix: Why don't you ever pull down your window shade?

Doris: I never pull down my window shade. I hate window shades.

Felix: That's your privilege, by all means.

Doris: I keep forgetting the world is full of finks. That's my trouble. I ought to get it tattooed on the back of my hand—"Watch out for Finks." (*Annoyed,* FELIX *suddenly sits at the typewriter and types rapidly on a white card which he then pins to the bulletin board.*) What are you doing? (*Reading it.*) "A rule worth making is worth keeping." What is that?

Felix: That's to remind me never to open my door after midnight.

Doris: Why don't you make one to remind you to stop being a fink?

Felix: I wish you would stop using that ugly word.

Doris: You don't like it? Too bad! Fink. Pansy fink, Queer fink, Peeping Tom fink, fink fink, you fink!

Felix: Feel better? (*He goes to the door and opens it.*) If you're sure your poison sacs are empty you can go.

Doris: Just tell me where I'm suposed to go?

Felix: Don't you have a friend you could stay with?

Doris: Not that I can move in on at two A.M.

Felix: How about a hotel?

Doris: I got seventy-two cents. The son-of-a-bitch took all of my money.

Felix: Who did?

Doris: Barney Gould, the landlord.

Felix: How could he do that?

Doris: While he was helping you hold society together with one hand—he was robbing me with the other. He said you saw me take money from a couple of—and you were gonna call the cops and if I gave him the money he'd cover up with the cops—that's how could I!

Felix: He was lying to you. All I did was ask him if he knew what was going on in his building.

Doris: Gee, that was big of you!

Felix: Well, I felt he should know. For his own protection.

Doris: Oh, sweet! You're just a big mother, aren't you? Now will you lend me five bucks so I can get a room? I'll pay you back.

Felix: I don't have any money. I got paid today and haven't cashed my check.

Doris: I never knew a fink that did have any money.

Felix: Don't you know anybody you could call? (DORIS *has fallen onto a chair. She's defeated and near tears.*) Don't you have any family? (*Looking at the couch.*) You can't stay here!

Doris: I'd rather sleep in the gutter.

Felix: It's a matter of taste, I suppose. (*On her last line,* DORIS

has gone to the door. She brings in a large suitcase and a
portable TV set.) What are you doing?

Doris: Get me a sheet and a blanket for that couch.

Felix: You're not staying here. Oh, no—no!

Doris: Naturally I'm staying. Where have I got to go?

Felix: I thought you were looking forward to a night in the
gutter.

Doris: Just get a blanket, will you please . . . and stop being so
goddam bitchy! Come on, come on.

Felix: Very well, you may stay the night.

Doris: Thanks for nothing. (FELIX *starts to answer. Changes his
mind. Goes to the bedroom.* DORIS *takes off her coat, tosses
it carelessly onto the coffee table, sets the suitcase on the
sofa and she opens it; takes a nightgown out of the suitcase
and closes it.* FELIX *comes from the bedroom with one folded
sheet, a blanket, and dumps the sheet and blanket on the
sofa. He glares at her.* DORIS *plugs in the television set.*)
What kind of reception do you get?

Felix: I wouldn't know. I've never had a television set.

Doris: Oh, that's right—you got your spyglasses! By the way,
how was I on the late, late show?

(FELIX *goes to the coffee pot and pours coffee into a plastic cup.*)

Felix: You're not planning to watch television at this hour?

Doris: (*Tucking sheet under sofa cushion.*) It's the only way I
can get to sleep—I won't play it loud—Listen—I don't want
to be here—if you had kept your mouth shut—

Felix: And if you had kept your window shade down—

Doris: You got a sweetheart in there? Some bouncy young boy
or do you dig the rough trade—

Felix: You're an alley cat, aren't you? On your back and rip out
their guts with your hind claws.

Doris: And what do you do, lover? Pull their hair and scratch
out their eyes? Give me some of that coffee . . . please. (FELIX
starts to pour cup for her.) No. A whole cup'll keep me
awake. Just give me a sip of yours. Do you ever write for
television?

Felix: No, thank you.

(FELIX *crosses to her and she takes his cup; takes two sips,
watching him.*)

Doris: What kind of a writer are you? Did I ever hear of you?

Felix: No.

Doris: Did anybody?

Felix: Voices like mine are drowned out by the clatter of the cash register. That's *two* sips—

(DORIS *gives him back the cup.* FELIX *starts to drink, switches the cup and drinks from the other side.*)

Doris: Now, what was that you just did?

Felix: What?

Doris: Drinking out of the other side like that—

Felix: Oh—I always do that—it's a reflex—

Doris: Yeah—sure it is.

Felix: Really—I'm a hypochondriac.

Doris: You make me feel like I'm a cockroach and I just crawled into your clean little house and you're trying to get up the nerve to squash me—that's the way you make me feel.

Felix: Oh my God, you're crazy!

Doris: Listen, Mister—I don't want to see that in your eyes when you look at me—I am a model. I have been in many television commercials at a time when I weighed 105, which unfortunately I don't any more. So don't you dare turn that cup around, you hear? You don't catch anything from a model—do you hear me—I may turn a trick or two but *I am a model!* (DORIS's *voice has risen hysterically. At this point there's a KNOCK at the wall.*)

Felix: Listen—you can't stay here. Why don't you try the YWCA?—

Doris: With seventy-two cents? That Christian the YWCA is not—

Felix: Will you try to be quiet—there's an old man downstairs.

Doris: And you don't want him to think you switched to girls, right?

Felix: Now look—

Doris: (*Interrupting as she exits to bathroom.*) Don't worry about it—just leave me alone. I'll try to get out of here before you wake up. (*He starts to bedroom. From offstage.*) Do me a favor—if you wake up and I'm still here, yell before you come out so I can close my eyes. I don't wanna have to look at you first thing in the morning. Where's the John? Excuse me—the jane?—the bathroom!

Felix: It's in there. Good night.
Doris: (*Off.*) Good night, fink.

(FELIX *exits to the bedroom. We hear the SOUNDTRACK of the movie clearly now.*)

Old Woman's Voice. Then you knew—all the time.
Old Man's Voice. Yes—I knew he was guilty.
Old Woman's Voice. Then why, Ben?
Old Man's Voice. Why did I let them convict me for his crime?
Old Woman's Voice. Thirty years—thirty long years—why, Ben? Why?

(DORIS *enters from the bathroom wearing her nightgown; she watches the movie for a couple of lines of dialogue.*)

Old Woman's Voice. You had so much to live for—the governorship. There were those who thought you had a chance for the White House.
Old Man's Voice. Yes—there were those who said that—
Old Woman's Voice. And you threw it all away, Ben, to save him. Why? He was a thief and a drunkard.
Old Man's Voice. Why? Because a girl with cornflower blue eyes and yellow hair loved him.
Old Woman's Voice. Oh Ben, my eyes are still cornflower blue, but my hair is all white now.
Old Man's Voice. Not to me—Alice—to me it'll always be yellow.
Old Woman's Voice. Ben—you mean—oh no!
Old Man's Voice. Then they didn't tell you? Yes, Alice—I'm blind, an accident in the prison library.
Old Woman's Voice. No, you're not blind, Ben, for as long as I live, you have two cornflower blue eyes—
Old Man's Voice. Alice—
Old Woman's Voice. Oh Ben—

(*And the MUSIC comes up for a big finish.* DORIS *crosses to the set.*)

Announcer: And that concludes the late, late show. Well—

(The voice is killed as DORIS *turns off the SET. She turns on the radio; it doesn't work; she shakes it; desperately.)*

Doris: *(Shouts.)* God damn it! Hey fink, fink!

*(*FELIX *enters)*

Felix: Now what?

Doris: My radio won't work. I must have banged it coming up the stairs!

Felix: Do you really have to—?

Doris: It's the only way I can go to sleep. You got a radio?

Felix: No.

Doris: What'll I do now? Why did I have to come up here?

Felix: Why not correct your mistake? Leave!

Doris: I should have just given a certain friend of mine a dollar to beat you up.

Felix: A dollar? Can't be much of a beating.

Doris: He's a friend. He would do it for nothing, but I make him take a dollar.

Felix: I see.

Doris: *(Calls.)* What's so goddam funny? I'll send him around tomorrow. I guarantee you won't think it's so funny. Now I'll never get to sleep.

Felix: Why can't you sleep?

Doris: I'm very high-strung.

Felix: I don't have any sleeping pills or I'd—

Doris: I don't take sleeping pills. I never take them. They're enervating.

Felix: How about a hot bath? That'll relax you.

Doris: *(Talking in a compulsive rush.)* I never take baths. They're enervating too. You know that word—"enervating"? Most people think it means just the opposite of what it really means. *(*FELIX *walks back toward the bedroom in the middle of her speech, yawning, yearning for sleep.* DORIS *raises her voice to a shout.* FELIX *stops.)* Another word that kills me is naive—I always thought it was "nave" you know. How do you pronounce it?

Felix: I never use it.

Doris: I mean I heard the word na'ive, but—

(The KNOCK is heard again.)

Felix: What's the matter with you? What are you trying to do? I got up at five-thirty this morning.

Doris: Listen, I know this sounds crazy, but will you sit here for a little while and talk to me?

The following is the monologue created from the previous scene.

DORIS: (to FELIX), Age 20s to 30s
pp. 6–14 (SAMUEL FRENCH, INC.)

Hello, Pansy-rat fink pansy! You spider-you cockroach! I just wanted to get a look at you. You didn't spy on me from your window and call my landlord, huh? Well, I should have known! Any queer who peeps at girls through his window like a dirty weasel wouldn't be man enough to admit it. Was it fun? Did you wish you could do what the big boys were doing? He told me. You're the one that called all right. You told Gould you were gonna call the police . . . you know you told him that, you slimy snail—you bedbug—. . . you cockroach. Why don't you curb your foul rotten mind? Try to be a man for once. You're lucky I'm too refined to beat you up—the way I feel. You're lucky I can't stand physical violence. (Starting to get weepy.) I have been thrown out of my room. At two o'clock in the morning. You called Gould, right? I don't know how you even saw anything this far away. You must have eyes like a vulture. Why did you pick on me? How dare you do something like this. I get sick when I think there are people like you! I took money from a couple of gentlemen—did that hurt you? It's bad enough with the naked eye—but with spyglasses—now that is just plain dirty, Mister. You want me to tell you what you're full of? You are nothing but a dirty, filthy Peeping Tom! I keep forgetting the world is full of finks. That's my trouble. I ought to get it tattooed on the back of my hand—"Watch out for Finks." Just tell me where I'm supposed to go? I don't have anyone that I can move in on at two A.M. I got seventy-two cents. The son-of-a-bitch took all of my money. While he was helping you hold society together with one hand, he was robbing me with the other. He said you saw me take money from a couple of—and you were gonna call the cops and if I gave him the money he'd cover up with the cops... Get me a sheet and a blanket for that couch. I'm staying. Where have I got to go? By the way, how was I on the late, late show? Listen, I don't want to be here—if you had kept your mouth shut... You got a sweetheart in there? Some bouncy young boy or do you dig the rough trade. What do you do, lover? Pull their hair and scratch out their eyes? Give me some of that cofee. Just give me a sip of yours. (Takes a sip and hands cup back.) Now, what was that you just did? Drinking out of the other side like that. You make me feel like I'm a cockroach and I just crawled into your clean little house and you're trying to get up the nerve to squash me—that's the way you make me feel. Listen, Mister—I don't want to see that in your eyes when you look at me—I am a model. I have been in many television commercials at a time when I weighed 105, which unfortunately I don't any more. So don't you dare turn that cup around, you hear? You don't catch anything from a model—do you hear me—I may turn a trick or two but I AM A MODEL! Just leave me alone. I'll try to get out of here before you wake up. Do me a favor—if you wake up and I'm still here, yell before you come out so I can close my eyes. I don't wanna have to look at you first thing in the morning. Where's the John? Excuse me—the Jane? The bathroom! Why did I have to come here? I should have just given a certain friend of mine a dollar to beat you up. He would do it for nothing, but I'd make him take a dollar. What's so goddam funny? I'll send him around tomorrow. I guarantee you won't think it's so funny. Now I'll never get to sleep. I'm very high-strung. I don't take sleeping pills. They're enervating. I never take baths. They're enervating too. You know that word—"enervating"? Most people think it means just the opposite of what it really means. Listen, I know this sounds crazy, but will you sit here for a little while and talk to me?

Don't be mislead by Doris's tirade against Felix. You must not play her "angry." Anger is a result of someone taking from us something we needed. Or something not given to us that we needed or wanted. Or committing an act upon us rendering us hurt, devastated, anguished, and or deprived. Anger, therefore, is loud hurt, loud devestation, loud pain, loud anguish, loud vulnerability.

Whenever it seems apparent on the page that you should be yelling and screaming in anger, go back to what caused the situation and play off the pain, which is the *true result* of the act committed against you. While you are yelling and screaming, show us how hurt you are.

Doris has been dislodged from her apartment by Felix. She is frightened, alone, broke, humiliated, unrespected, rejected, destitute, homeless, and, most of all, unloved. This indeed is a life and death situation for her. She has come to Felix to face the man who did all this to her, to regain some dignity but most of all to find refuge and to be loved and protected. The words say she is demanding things from him and that she is furious. Which she is. And of course she is yelling and screaming. But *only* because of her fears and pain. She *desperately* needs for Felix to feel sorry for what he did to her and to lovingly take care of her and make it up to her. He is the most important person in her life. She is fighting for her life. He is the only one who can save her.

THE OWL AND THE PUSSYCAT
by Bill Manhoff

pp. 36–43 (Samuel French, Inc.)

Doris: I know, but you can't insult me—It's impossible, you know why?

Felix: Why are you doing this—why don't you get out? What's it going to get you?

Doris: It's all your fault.

Felix: All right—but—

Doris: Oh, I don't mean getting me thrown out of my room. I mean it's your fault I'm in love.

Felix: You're insane.

Doris: It's true—you made me love you. *(Sings.)*
> I didn't want to do it—
> I didn't want to do it—

Felix: What do I have to do to get rid of you? I'll give you ten dollars.

Doris: Make it fifty million—that's how much it'll cost you to get rid of me—not a penny less. Hey—I thought you were going to move out and leave the vermin in possession—what happened?

Felix: No. I will not let you put me out of my home.

Doris: Good for you! I would have lost all respect for you if you left.

Felix: How long are you planning to stay?

Doris: How should I know? I'm stuck here. *(Sings.)* I'm just a prisoner of love. Notice I'm singing all the time—I always do that when I'm in love.

Felix: You're an imbecile.

Doris: Okay. Fine! See—you can't insult a person who's in love. You can't do anything to them, because they're so light—you can throw them off the roof and they'll float to the ground.

Felix: Will you stop talking about love? I've never heard such mindless drivel in my life.

Doris: Listen, I know a lot about love.

Felix: That thing you fall in and out of three or four times a week is not love. Neither is that thing you sell.

Doris: Now don't be nasty, honey. This is different. I love you in a very deep quiet way—like a river.

Felix: Like a river! *(Shouting.)* You mean like a sewer!

Doris: Now don't get worked up, darling. You tell me what love is. Go ahead, sweetheart—I'm listening. Is it when you get mad and yell at somebody like you're yelling at me?

Felix: *(Shouting.)* No it is not!

Doris: You better calm down...

Felix: *(Fighting for self-control.)* You upset me. I admit it. You're an animal. You're so foreign to anything that's important to me. Don't you understand? You personify what I hate.

Doris: You didn't hate it last night.

Felix: That's what disgusts me. All my life I fought that animal taint. It's like finding a fungus you loathe growing on your own skin!

Doris: *(Shaken badly.)* Oh, that's a disgusting thing to call somebody—"fungus"!

Felix: I didn't call you that.

Doris: Sure—I'm some slimy moldy fungus, right?

Felix: I didn't say that.

Doris: Oh yes, you did say that!

Felix: All right, I said it! I mean it! Now will you get out—will you go?

Doris: I never met anybody in my life that made me feel so cheap and dirty.

Felix: Then get out of here.

Doris: I don't understand why I love you.

Felix: Get out! I hate you!

Doris: Not as much as I hate you!

Felix: Then get out! Get out!

Doris: No! I'm gonna stay here and hate you right to your face!

Felix: All right, then I'm going.

Doris: Fine. Great. Go on.

Felix: It's the only way.

Doris: Well, go on—get out.

Felix: What do you mean, "Get out"? This is my home. I live here. Don't you tell me to get out.

Doris: Well, I'm not getting out. You can try to throw me out if you want to.

Felix: I wouldn't dirty my hands.

Doris: I wouldn't want your slimy hands on me.

Felix: I ought to turn you over to the police.

Doris: Fine. Why don't you?

Felix: That's what I should do.

Doris: Go ahead. Call them.

Felix: That's what I'll do. That's just what I'll do!

Doris: Go ahead.

Felix: That's just exactly what I'm going to do!

Doris: All right. Fine. You do that.

Felix: You bet I will. You can just bet on it!

Doris: You call the police. You do that. It's fine with me.

Felix: Don't you for a moment think I won't!

Doris: Oh, you'd do it!

Felix: You bet I would. And that's just what I'm going to do.

Doris: Fine. You turn me in. You do that. You're the man to do it.

Felix: I most certainly am, and that's what I'm going to do!

(BLACKOUT)

SCENE 3

Felix: *(On telephone. The stage is in darkness.)* Nothing serious, Victor. No—I'm a little tired. I had a very bad time last night. No—I hate to take them, they're enervating. Thank you, but I'll be fine by twelve or so. I'll come in then.

(Lights come up slowly. Morning light through the window. DORIS *stands near* FELIX *peering at him through the binoculars.)*

Doris: Ooh, look at the big man. *(He ignores her.)* Don't you love me? Oh, that's right—only in the bedroom. I forgot—it depends on what room we're in. Let's take a shower together. I want to find out how you feel about me in the bathroom.

Felix: Doris—I'm not coming back to this apartment tonight. I mean it.

Doris: Honey—what are you fighting? Why don't you take it easy? (*She tries to embrace him. He pushes her off, knocking the orange out of her hand.* DORIS *laughs, picks up the orange.*) You better bring some more oranges. We're running out.

Felix: I won't be coming back. Did you hear me?

Doris: (*Humoring a child.*) Sure. You'll be back after work to pack your things, though? (*Silence from* FELIX.) Would you like me to pack for you and have it ready?

Felix: Shut up.

Doris: I could put it all outside the door so you wouldn't even have to come inside.

Felix: Your humor is like you are—crude and clumsy.

Doris: (*Going to him—tenderly.*) Baby—why don't you stop—?

Felix: If you call me "baby" once more, I'll—(*Looks around desperately.*) I'll smash your television set.

Doris: (*Goes to him, feels his head.*) I think you've got a fever.

Felix: (*Looking to heaven.*) Oh God! Are you listening—are you laughing? She says I've got a fever.

Doris: You're not going to work today—you're getting right back into bed.

Felix: (*To heaven.*) Do you hear? The tower of my mind is crashing down—wrecked by a termite—and now the termite is putting me to bed! God—do something!

(*She's pushing and pulling him to the sofa.*)

Doris: Don't talk to God that way. He'll strike you dead.

Felix: Oh no! Not while He's having so much fun with me!

(*She pushes him down on the sofa—feels his head again.*)

Doris: Does it hurt any place?

Felix: Listen—I'm going to beg you—please—go away—please leave me alone.

Doris: (*Feeling his throat.*) Does this hurt?

Felix: You're grinding your heel in my raw soul. That is what hurts.

Doris: Wow! That's good! You ought to use that in a story.

Felix: *(Weakly.)* You must go away. Why won't you go away? Tell me why!

Doris: Because, sweetheart—I can make you happy—I do make you happy—if you'll only let me—

Felix: No—no—you make me miserable.

Doris: But, baby...

Felix: "Baby" you make happy, yes—but "Felix" you make miserable, and that's me—Felix—I am Felix. Will you listen to me? I am not "Baby." I don't want to be "Baby."

Doris: I wish you'd go to bed. Do you have a thermometer?

Felix: It's a nightmare—I'm caught in a fog—I'm screaming! But I can't make a sound!

Doris: Lie down on the sofa.

Felix: *(Limp, he flops down on the sofa.)* What's the use?

Doris: That's my boy.

Felix: Yes. That's your boy. I confess. Felix unmasked. Felix captured and brought to justice—"Baby—honey—sweetheart" alias "Felix."

Doris: Now just relax. *(She feels his forehead again.)* Does it hurt any place?

Felix: No. All the nerves have died.

Doris: Now be serious. Is your throat sore? Do you have a headache? Should I call the doctor?

Felix: That's ridiculous! The disease never calls the doctor.

Doris: Now don't say nasty things! Be nice.

Felix: *(Rising hysteria.)* Nice? You're absolutely right! Now that I have come to live in Niceville I must do as the nice people do—I must be nice. "Baby sweetheart" must be nice.

Doris: *(Beginning to be afraid.)* You're absolutely crazy. I never heard such crazy talk in my life.

Felix: You're right again. Baby must not speak the language of Felix. Felix the mind is dead. Long live Baby!

Doris: Please stop it.

Felix: Call me "Baby"—say "please stop it, Baby"—go on.

Doris: I don't want to.

Felix: Why not? That's who I am—I'm Baby.

Doris: Please, honey, you're scaring me.

Felix: Yes—yes—sorry—that's because I'm not talking Baby's language. How's this? *(Tough.)* What do you say we feed the face, Sweetie, and then we can hop into the sack and knock off a quickie. Let's ball. Let's get down in the slime and roll around in it. Let's have a little poon-tang. Let's hump.

(*As* DORIS *withdraws from him.*) That's it, hump, hump, hump.

Doris: (*Completely depressed by now.*) All right—all right, you win.

Felix: I win? What do I win?

Doris: I'm going. (*She exits to bedroom; then, from Offstage.*) I'll come back later to get my things. When you're not here.

Felix: (*Calls.*) Are you really going, Baby?

Doris: That's what you want, isn't it?

Felix: It's not my first choice. My first choice is for you never to have come. Could I have that?

Doris: You sure fooled me. I thought I had you figured.

Felix: You did—I'm the one I had fooled.

Doris: (*She opens the door.*) I'll call you tonight when I get set and let you know where I am.

Felix: Don't call.

Doris: Don't be such a baby. You can always hang up on me if you don't want to talk to me.

Felix: I won't be here.

Doris: You better take care of yourself or you're gonna be sick. You hear me?

Felix: (*Wryly.*) I'll take an aspirin.

Doris: Good idea—no—there's some fizz powder on the dresser. It gets into the bloodstream seconds faster than aspirin.

Felix: I grew up with aspirin. I refuse to believe there's a short-cut aspirin doesn't know about.

Doris: Just the same—take that powder. And I'll call you tonight.

The following is the monologue created from the previous scene.

DORIS (to FELIX), age 20s to 30s.
pp. 36–43 (SAMUEL FRENCH, INC.)

You can't insult me—it's impossible, you know why? It's all your fault. Oh, I don't mean getting me thrown out of my room. I mean it's your fault I'm in love. It's true—you made me love you. (*Sings.*) I didn't want to do it. I didn't want to do it. Fifty million—that's how much it'll cost you to get rid of me—not a penny less. Hey—I thought you were going to move out and leave me, the "vermin," in possession—what happened? I would have lost all respect for you if you left. I don't know how long I'm planning to stay. I'm stuck here. *(Sings.)* I'm just a prisoner of love. Notice I'm singing all the time—I always do that when I'm in love. You can't insult a person who's in love. You can't do anything to them because they're so light—you can throw them off the roof and they'll float to the ground. I know a lot about love. This is different. I love you in a very deep quiet way—like a river. Ooh, look at the big man. Don't you love me? Oh, that's right—only in the bedroom. I forgot—it depends on what room we're in. Let's take a shower together. I want to find out how you feel about me in the bathroom. Honey—what are you fighting? Why don't you take it easy? You're going? *(First panic, then humoring a child.)* Sure. You'll be back after work to pack your things, though? Would you like me to pack for you and have it ready? I could put it all outside the door so you wouldn't even have to come inside. I think you've got a fever. You're not going to work today—you're getting right back into bed. Does it hurt any place? I'm not going away because, sweetheart—I can make you happy—I do make you happy—if you'll only let me. I wish you'd go to bed. Do you have a thermometer? Lie down on the sofa. Does it hurt any place? Is your throat sore? Do you have a headache? Should I call the doctor? Please, honey, you're scaring me. All right—all right, you win. I'm going. I'll come back later to get my things. When you're not here. That's what you want, isn't it? You sure fooled me. I thought I had you figured. I'll call you tonight when I get set and let you know where I am. You can always hang up on me if you don't want to talk to me. You better take care of yourself or you're gonna be sick. You hear me? There's some fizz powder on the dresser. It gets into the bloodstream faster than aspirin. Take it. And I'll call you tonight.

It is the following afternoon. Felix succumbed to your charms the evening before and you both wound up in bed. When you awoke after a night of ecstatic lovemaking you are in love but he wants you to leave! He seems to be repulsed by you for some reason. Of course, you want to stay. He leaves for work hoping you will be gone by the time he returns. But there you are, eagerly awaiting his return.

Felix says some nasty things to you. On the page when it appears from your responses to him that you really haven't been insulted and hurt by his harsh words, don't you believe for a moment that his words don't sting. Hear the insult. Feel the hurt and respond with the playwright's words. Remember the playwright has you lie. So when Felix calls you "vermin," and you respond with, "You can't insult me—it's impossible, you know why?" you are pretending not to be hurt. And you are doing a good job of it. He doesn't know you are hurt. But we, the audience, must recognize that you are. The other character will respond to your dialogue. Allow the audience to respond to your emotions and feelings. You are putting on a very good act for him. You don't *want* to be hurt but you are. The opposite and your inner life where the truth lies is saying, "You really know how to hurt me, don't you?"

Your inner feelings do not negate what is on the page. You simply don't want him to talk to you that way. It isn't loving of him. You don't want to give in to the hurt. You are clinging to your strong loving feelings for him and it feels wonderful. You don't want this feeling to pass. You don't want him to take it all away. You are fighting for him to feel strong loving feelings for you. He is rejecting you all the way. He won't allow you to minister to his ills. You finally give in. "All right, all right, you win. I'm going." It hurts. Keep fighting for his love but don't deny the harsh reality. He doesn't want you there. He doesn't want you near him in any way. Be aware of the negatives but work off your positives. *You* still want *him* even if it appears as if he doesn't want any part of you. And you're not giving up just yet. Perhaps you've lost this round. You intend for there to be a next round because this is the most important day in your life. Felix is the most important person in your life and today is the day that you have *got* to change your life. It is the rest of your life that you are fighting for.

THE OWL AND THE PUSSYCAT
by Bill Manhoff

pp. 45–50 (SAMUEL FRENCH, INC.)

Felix: *(In bathroom.)* Is it still raining?

Doris: *(Still at door.)* No, it stopped.

Felix: *(Off.)* Paper said it would rain all night.

Doris: Yeah.

Felix: *(Off.)* I guess the rain doesn't read the paper. There's some scotch on the table.

Doris: Where'd you get this?

Felix: *(Off.)* Bought it.

Doris: How come?

Felix: *(Off.)* Not enough nerve to steal it, I suppose. Take your coat off. *(He enters from bedroom. His hair slicked for the occasion.)* I like your dress.

Doris: The color's good, but it flattens me out a little in the bust. You don't look so good.

Felix: I had a hard day. Listen—I wanted to talk to you, Doris. It's a little embarrassing—I wanted to apologize for my emotional behavior yesterday morning.

Doris: Forget it. It was my fault—I guess I needled you.

Felix: No. The lance is not the cause of the infection it exposes. The fact that—

Doris: *(Stopping him.)* Wait a minute— *(Thinks for a second—then triumphantly.)* You know, I understand that!

Felix: Of course—naturally. Doris, you're a bright girl. Remember I told you that soon after we met?

Doris: Yes, you did. You said I wasn't dumb.

Felix: And that's exactly what I want to talk to you about. After you left I used some good solid logic. It saved my life.

Doris: That sounds good.

Felix: Well, the fact is, I have lived almost thirty years as a logical man. My religion was the reason. The mind. It's the only thing I believe in. And it has given me a lonely life.

55

Doris: I thought you were older than thirty.

Felix: I'll be thirty in October. Fact number two—I felt a very powerful attraction to a girl—you—very powerful, all right—put the facts through the logic—there's only one answer—I had to be attracted by one thing in you.

Doris: Well, listen—

Felix: Your mind!

Doris: You're kidding.

Felix: Doesn't it sound logical?

Doris: It may be logical, but it doesn't make sense.

Felix: I realized suddenly that I'm not attracted to you at all as an animal. Don't you see—I couldn't be. It's your trapped intelligence calling out for help that drew me so strongly.

Doris: You're all excited and happy. Gee, I'm glad. You were in such bad shape yesterday, you had me scared.

Felix: That was insane grief. Premature grief for Felix the mind. I was very rough on you. I feel like dying when I think of the things I said to you. Can you forgive me? Can we be friends—nonphysical friends, of course?

Doris: Nonphysical?

Felix: I'm going to save you, Doris.

Doris: May I ask from what?

Felix: From circumstances that have kept you from using your mind. You're in a jungle. I'm going to cut through all that rotting growth and rescue you.

Doris: I feel like Sleeping Beauty with that forest around her.

Felix: Yes—yes—that's wonderful! The sleeping beauty of the mind.

Doris: Wonderful?

Felix: Without training—your unhindered natural imagination reaches for metaphor—oh, Doris—do you know how exciting that is to a man of intellect?

Doris: What's "metaphor"?

Felix: Metaphor is—no—there—*(Points to the dictionary.)* Look it up for yourself. Go—discover a word! M-e-t-a-p-h-o-r.

Doris: Not me—I hate dictionaries.

Felix: Why? You like words.

Doris: Yeah, but in the dictionary they're so, I don't know—dead.

Felix: Dead—oh, my God, of course! Laid out—dissected—by the cataloguing mind! A mortuary of words—Doris, that's wonderful!

Doris: You mean I did it again? I can't tell you how surprised I am.

Felix: I felt it in you—I sensed it, didn't I?

Doris: Yes, you did—you said something about it.

Felix: I know—I know.

Doris: *(Catching the artificial excitement.)* It was very smart of you to notice—most people don't notice—*I* never noticed! Gosh, think of all the smart things I must of said without realizing!

Felix: Yes—a flower born to blush unseen—wasting your sweetness on the desert air.

Doris: That's like poetry.

Felix: It is poetry. Famous poetry.

Doris: Hey—I spotted it, didn't I?

(As DORIS *starts to sparkle with excitement,* FELIX *is aroused.)*

Felix: Of course you spotted it. Like a thirsty root spots water—

Doris: Did I ever tell you about the essay I wrote in school?

Felix: I'd love to read it.

Doris: I lost it.

Felix: That's all right—you'll write others.

Doris: You think so?

Felix: Why not? Why not?

Doris: I used to think I had a brain. But people keep calling you stupid, you know—year after year.

Felix: Stupid people.

Doris: My goddam brother. From morning to night—"stupid-stupid-stupid." Well, after a while you figure where there's smoke there's fire—you know?

Felix: Of course. A sensitive nature like yours is no match for a bully.

Doris: Sensitive! Boy, you put your finger on it! How did you know I was sensitive?

Felix: You had to be——that's the price of a thinking mind—sensitivity.

Doris: It is?

Felix: Yes.

Doris: Well, I'm sure sensitive, all right. I cry at the drop of a hat. Well, you saw the way I carried on here yesterday—

Felix: Yes.

Doris: Over nothing at all. Did you ever see sensitive like that?

Felix: I should have known. I should have realized why I was drawn to you.

Doris: I was always ashamed of myself for crying so much. That means you're smart, huh?

Felix: It means—that's right—it means you're smart.

Doris: I always thought I was such a dope—crying over nothing.

Felix: Dopes don't cry. They have no pride. Dopes are not vulnerable.

Doris: Pride—I got a lot of that.

Felix: Of course you have.

Doris: My brother always said to me that I had too much pride.

Felix: Is that the "goddam" brother?

Doris: No—the older one.

Felix: Well, you can't have too much pride. Pride constructs dignity and lives in it.

Doris: "Pride constructs dignity and lives in it"? Poetry—right?

Felix: It's from an essay of mine.

Doris: Oh. Well, it sounds like poetry.

Felix: Thank you.

Doris: I'll bet you're a wonderful writer.

Felix: You didn't care for my short story. Remember?

Doris: When? Oh—the sun spitting in the guy's face—well, I was mad at you—I was just getting back at you.

Felix: Well, it doesn't matter.

Doris: It grows on you. I can see it, you know—

Felix: What's that?

Doris: (*Acting out the rising sun.*) The sun—like a big face. It looks up real slow over the edge of the world and it goes—pttt. (*She makes a soft spitting sound with her lips.*)

Felix: That's very imaginative of you.

Doris: Well, it's just good writing, that's all—it makes you see it.

Felix: Thank you.

Doris: Gee, I'm so excited! I'm shivering—look at me.

Felix: Would you like a drink?

Doris: I got one.

Felix: (*Putting his arm around her.*) Are you cold?

Doris: No—I don't know what it is—excitement, I guess.

Felix: I know what it is. It's the first shock of childbirth.

Doris: Bite your tongue!

Felix: (*Fondles and nuzzles her.*) No—I mean *you're* being born. *You*—

Doris: Yeah—I see what you mean—I'm being born—you know what I'm doing? I'm entering into a new world. *(He kisses her on the cheek.)* You didn't hear what I said—

Felix: What?

Doris: I'm entering into a new world.

Felix: I heard you. It's true, welcome to the world of the intellect. *(He kisses her on the neck.)*

Doris: I'm beginning to talk like you a little—did you notice—? Hey—what are you doing? I wanna talk.

Felix: *(Continuing to make love to her.)* I want to hear you talk, don't stop.

Doris: Felix—cut that out—

Felix: Talk—I'm listening.

Doris: We're intellectuals—we're nonphysicals, remember?

Felix: This isn't physical. That's what makes it so exciting—don't you see?

Doris: I don't think so.

Felix: That's what draws us together—not the attraction of bodies, but the excitement of two live—healthy—exuberant minds—calling hungrily to one another!

The following is the monologue created from the previous scene.

FELIX (to DORIS), age 20s to early 40s.
pp. 45–50 (SAMUEL FRENCH, INC.)

Is it still raining? Paper said it would rain all night. I guess the rain doesn't read the paper. There's some scotch on the table. Bought it. Not enough nerve to steal it, I suppose. Take your coat off. I like your dress. I had a hard day. Listen—I wanted to talk to you, Doris. It's a little embarrassing—I wanted to apologize for my emotional behavior yesterday morning. The lance is not the cause of the infection it exposes. I know you understand that! Doris, you're a bright girl. Remember I told you that soon after we met? And that's exactly what I want to talk to you about. After you left I used some good solid logic. It saved my life. My religion was the reason. The mind. It's the only thing I believe in. And it has given me a lonely life.

I'll be thirty* in October. Fact number two—I felt a very powerful attraction to a girl—you—very powerful, all right— put the facts through the logic—there's only one answer—I had to be attracted by one thing in you. Your mind! Doesn't it sound logical? I realized suddenly that I'm not attracted to you at all as an animal. Don't you see—I couldn't be. It's your trapped intelligence calling out for help that drew me so strongly. I was in such bad shape yesterday. That was insane grief. Premature grief for Felix the mind. I was very rough on you. I feel like dying when I think of the things I said to you. Can you forgive me? Can we be friends—nonphysical friends, of course? I'm going to save you, Doris. From circumstances that have kept you from using your mind. You're like Sleeping Beauty with that forest around her. The Sleeping Beauty of the mind. Without training—your unhindered natural imag- ination reaches for metaphor—oh, Doris—do you know how exciting that is to a man of intellect? Think of all the smart things you must have said without realizing! Yes—a flower born to blush unseen—wasting your sweetness on the desert air. It is poetry. Famous poetry. And you spotted it. Like a thirsty root spots water. A sensitive nature like yours is no match for a bully. That's the price of a thinking mind—sensitivity. I should have known. I should have realized why I was drawn to you. You're smart. You're not a dope. Dopes don't cry. They have no pride. Dopes are not vulnerable. You can't have too much pride. Pride constructs dignity and lives in it. It's from an essay of mine. Would you like a drink? Are you cold? I know what it is. It's the first shock of childbirth. It's true, welcome to the world of the intellect. (*He has become more and more excited.*) This isn't physical. That's what makes it so exciting— don't you see? That's what draws us together—not the attraction of bodies, but the excitement of two live— healthy—exuberant minds—calling hungrily to one another!

Felix, you are now allowing yourself to admire Doris's mind. You must do this to rationalize to yourself falling for such a

*Use your own age.

woman. She's *got* to have a good mind to compensate for her blatant sexuality, which is both exciting and agitating to you. You are dealing with denial and discovery. You are sexually stimulated and you allow yourself to become even more so as you discover and help to create the birthing of an original thinker of poetry. You now have permission to give in to your sexual feelings because after all, you are an intellect and the object of your desire is also an intellect! You can't just let go and enjoy, with no guilt, honest sexual feelings and sex with her. You've *got* to sell yourself on her mind and you still cannot express your true feelings to her or to yourself.

As an actor, realize that if Felix cannot express or acknowledge his true feelings, then in his reality, he doesn't know what you, the actor, know. Let him ask the questions but not know the answers. Asking the questions is enough. I don't want resolution. I want conflict and obstacles all along the way.

You have never been so sexually stimulated in your entire life. It's a wonderful discovery for you. This is, indeed, the most important day in your life.

THE OWL AND THE PUSSYCAT
By Bill Manhoff

pp. 51–57 (SAMUEL FRENCH, INC.)

Doris: Hi, sweetie.

Felix: *(Very quiet. He's holding down the lid on boiling indignation.)* Hello.

Doris: Hey, what's this? We've only been living in sin for three weeks and already you don't kiss me "hello" anymore?

Felix: I had a hard day. Have you been out?

Doris: Only for lunch. Hey, you wanna check the breakfast dishes? I'll give you a half a buck you find any dirt or any dried soap this time!

Felix: Later. I saw somebody enter the building as I got off the bus. I thought it was you.

Doris: Must have been the girl downstairs. You hungry, sweetie?

Felix: No, I've got a headache. *(Looking at her book.)* Still on chapter two?

Doris: I had an awful lot of words to look up.

Felix: *(Going to the dictionary, looks at it.)* It wasn't the girl downstairs.

Doris: Who? Oh—you want somethng for your headache?

Felix: No, thank you. I'm enjoying it.

Doris: Honest—some of the things you say sometimes.

Felix: Have you been working with your word for the day?

Doris: Oh—"impeccable"—sure—*(Sneaking a look at her pad.)* "Impeccable—without a fault—incapable of doing wrong." Now, used in a sentence—let's see. *(Looking around.)* Oh—when the typewriter got back from the repair shop, it was impeccable.

Felix: No—that's wrong.

Doris: Why?

Felix: In three weeks I don't think you've assimilated two new words.

Doris: Oh, come on—sure I have. Hey, what's the matter with you tonight?

Felix: Have you been to the dictionary today?

Doris: Sure—I told you.

Felix: Yes—(*He's been taking off his tie. He sees the radio under the coffee table. He stands up.*) Where'd you get the radio?

Doris: Oh—I picked it up at the junk shop—three bucks.

Felix: (*Going to bedroom.*) Good.

Doris: I don't even know if it works.

Felix: (*Exits to bedroom.*) It looks brand new to me.

Doris: (*Drags the set out, dumps the ashtray on it, rubs in the ashes, spits, scratches it with the ashtray as she talks.*) It's practically an antique—made in the year one. I think I got taken but I needed a radio for out here. You have to play that one in the bedroom so loud if you wanna hear it out here and my other one keeps conking out—so I figured— what the hell—I'd take a chance—sometimes these old beat-up sets play as good as a new one.

(*She abruptly drops the aging process as* FELIX *comes out of the bedroom. He has taken off his coat.*)

Felix: How many times did you say you used the dictionary today?

Doris: I don't know. What's wrong, honey?

Felix: Please go over to the dictionary and look at it closely.

Doris: (DORIS *goes and looks at the dictionary.*) What am I supposed to see?

Felix: Look at the edges—at the top—

Doris: What's this? (*Peeling off a strip of Scotch tape.*)

Felix: That is a strip of Scotch tape. It's been there for two days. Undisturbed. Where were you this afternoon?

Doris: That's such a nasty thing to do.

Felix: Where were you yesterday afternoon?

Doris: I do not care for the tone of your voice.

Felix: Where did you get the dirty but brand new radio?

Doris: I'm warning you—stop it—this warning will not be repeated.

Felix: We're not going to fight. We're going to have an honest unemotional discussion.

Doris: Yeah? So you start out by calling me a liar.

Felix: I did not call you a liar. I'm not going to lose my temper.

Doris: You might as well. I'm gonna lose mine!

Felix: Would you care to tell me what's wrong?

Doris: What's wrong? You're a creep that puts Scotch tape on the dictionary—you know that word—"creep"? Used in a sentence: "Fred Sherman is a big creep."

Felix: *(Starting at "Fred.")* What did you call me?

Doris: It's your name. Fred—Freddie—I thought that would jar your apricots! I found your yearbook from school—Fred Sherman. You didn't tell me you changed your name, did you? You creep. I'm sorry—pardon my language, but you are a creep.

Felix: It's all right—it's a step up from "fink." Congratulations—now—I'd like to hear why you feel you have to sneak out afternoons and lie to me.

Doris: I just got bored. I had to get out. Look—I tried. I tried working on hats. I tried looking for a job, right? I tried.

Felix: Have you been plying your old trade?

Doris: Have I been what? No, I haven't. I told you I was through doing that.

Felix: Where'd you get the radio?

Doris: I collected some money. Somebody owed me some money and they paid me.

Felix: I see. Why didn't you tell me that?

Doris: Because I knew you wouldn't believe it. I knew what you'd think.

Felix: I see.

Doris: Don't say, "I see," like you were looking through your lousy spy glasses. Listen—why don't you stop trying to make out like you're a human being? I mean the strain must be terrible—why don't you just relax and admit you're God and you know all about everything?

Felix: Why did you have to lie? I just want to know why you lied to me about going out and about looking up words.

Doris: Because I'm a liar, okay?

Felix: Why didn't you tell me?

Doris: Why didn't you tell me you changed your name from "Fred" to "Felix"?

Felix: *(Ignoring her question.)* I'm very sad. You had a chance to do something important for yourself and you're quitting. You're not giving yourself a chance.

Doris: I gave myself a chance—you had me going there for a while, but it's silly. I'm a dope and that's all there is to it.

Felix: You're not a dope. You're a bright girl.

Doris: Not when it comes to dictionaries and the history of philosophy, I'm not. (*Indicates the book she was reading.*)

Felix: You have a potential capacity for—

Doris: (*Interrupting.*) No, I don't have any potential anything.

Felix: (*Losing the fight against his temper.*) Don't interrupt me—who do you think is better qualified to judge mental capacity—you or I?

Doris: You—

Felix: Then why are you arguing with me?

Doris: Felix, I—

Felix: Would I be wasting my time with you if you didn't have a brain?

Doris: Felix—

Felix: Do you think an intellectual such as myself would waste his time with a dumbbell?

Doris: Felix, I know myself—you can't tell me—

Felix: I tell you you're a very intelligent girl, and you'd know it yourself if you weren't so damned stupid!

Doris: I am not stupid! I've got good healthy everyday brains. I haven't got your kind of brains and I'm glad, because I'm gonna tell you something—I think your brains are rotten!

Felix: Ah—the cat turns inevitably and bares her atavistic fangs.

Doris: To use those ugly, lonely words nobody else uses—that's all your brains are good for. To keep people away because you're scared to death of people!

Felix: She spits in inarticulate fury.

Doris: You know what your brains are good for? To make up your own lousy little language that the rest of the world can't even understand.

Felix: Well, all right—stay with the rest of the world—don't let anybody make you a foreigner there by teaching you to speak the English language!

Doris: (*Going to closet.*) What a dope I was to listen to you. (*Mimicking him.*) I'm gonna save you, Doris! (*In her own voice.*) You are such a phony, I can't believe it. You don't write for money but you keep sending your junk to magazines, don't you? And you keep getting it sent back, don't you? Meanwhile all you got is a phony job, a phony girlfriend, a phony apartment and a phony bunch of words! *(She has taken the suitcase from the closet and started to throw garments into it as she talks.)*

Felix: What are you doing?

Doris: What does it look like I'm doing?

Felix: *(Quietly.)* Now don't get washed away. Think, Doris. Try to understand one basic thing. Try to hold on to what I see in you.

Doris: *(Yelling.)* You see nothing! You don't see me at all! You don't see anything. Because even your eyes are phony! *(Knock on the wall.* DORIS *addresses the wall; yelling.)* I'll be through in a minute! *(To* FELIX.*)* You know what you see in me? You never had a girl that made you feel like a big man in bed—that's all.

Felix: Doris—

Doris: *(Interrupting.)* Well, I want to tell you something about what a hot stud you think you are in the sack—

Felix: Don't say it, Doris—

Doris: You leave me cold, Fred. You're nothing at all.

Felix: You're raising your voice.

Doris: You do nothing to me, Freddie—you only think you do. You know why?

Felix: I know—you're a great actress and to you that bed is theatre in the round—I know all about it—well, now I'm going to tell you something—I don't *leave* you cold—I *find* you cold—"frigid"—is that word in your meager stock?

Doris: Drop dead.

Felix: Sure you're an actress in bed—because you can't be a woman.

Doris: With a man I can, Fred—Freddie, it takes a man.

Felix: Sometimes. Even with fantasies, and dirty words and the guilty stink of the sewer you can only sometimes whip yourself into a parody of passion—sometimes! Isn't that right?

Doris: Stop yelling. Nobody's listening to you. *(She's closing the suitcase.)*

Felix: All right. You're lost. Goodbye. I tried.

Doris: Now try shutting up. I'll send for the TV. I'll send a man! Take a good look at him.

Felix: *(Follows her to the door.)* No matter where you go or what you do or what you call yourself—you are now and forever a whore named Doris Wilgus.

Doris: Okay. And what are you now and forever? A miserable magazine peddler named Freddie Sherman and a lousy writer and you always will be and you wanna know why—? *(Hitting him deliberately with every word.)* Because, God damn it! The—sun—does—not—spit!

The following is the monologue created from the previous scene.

DORIS (to FELIX), age 20s to 30s.
pp. 51–57 (SAMUEL FRENCH, INC.)

Hi, sweetie. Hey, what's this? We've only been living in sin for three weeks and already you don't kiss me hello anymore? Hey, you wanna check the breakfast dishes? I'll give you half a buck you find any dirt or any dried soap this time! I've been here all day. You hungry, sweetie? I had an awful lot of words to look up. "Impeccable—without a fault—incapable of doing wrong." Now, used in a sentence—let's see. Oh—when the typewriter got back from the repair shop, it was impeccable. Hey, what's the matter with you tonight? I picked up a radio at the junk shop—three bucks. I don't even know if it works. It's practically an antique—made in the year one. I think I got taken but I needed a radio for out here. You have to play that one in the bedroom so loud if you wanna hear it out here and my other one keeps conking out—so I figured—what the hell—I'd take a chance—sometimes these old beat-up sets play as good as a new one. And I'm not a liar! "Creep." Used in a sentence: "Fred Sherman is a big creep." It's your name. Fred—Freddie—I thought that would jar your apricots! I found your yearbook from school—Fred Sherman. You didn't tell me you changed your name, did you? You creep. I'm sorry—pardon my language, but you are a creep. All right, I'm sorry I have to sneak out afternoons and lie to you. I just got bored. I had to get out. Look—I tried. I tried working on hats. I tried looking for a job, right? I tried. I have not been plying my old trade! I told you I was through doing that. I collected some money to get the radio. Somebody owed me some money and they paid me. I didn't tell you because I knew you wouldn't believe it. I knew what you'd think.

Listen—why don't you stop trying to make out like you're a human being? I mean the strain must be terrible—why don't you just relax and admit you're God and you know all about everything? I'm a liar, okay? Why didn't you tell me you changed your name from Fred to Felix? I gave myself a chance—you had me going there for a while, but it's silly. I'm a dope and that's all there is to it. I'm not bright. Not when it comes to dictionaries and the history of philosophy, I'm not. I don't have any potential anything. I am not stupid! I've got good healthy everyday brains. I haven't got your kind of brains and I'm glad, because I'm gonna tell you something—I think your brains are rotten! To use those ugly, lonely words nobody else uses—that's all your brains are good for. To keep people away because you're scared to death of people! You know what your brains are good for? To make up your own lousy little language that the rest of the world can't even understand. What a dope I was to listen to you. *(Mimicking him.)* "I'm gonna save you, Doris!" *(In her own voice.)* You are such a phony, I can't believe it. You don't write for money but you keep sending your junk to magazines, don't you? And you keep getting it sent back, don't you? Meanwhile all you got is a phony job, a phony girlfriend, a phony apartment, and a phony bunch of words! You see nothing! You don't see me at all! You don't see anything. Because even your eyes are phony! You know what you see in me? You never had a girl that made you feel like a big man in bed—that's all. Well, I want to tell you something about what a hot stud you think you are in the sack. You leave me cold, Fred. You're nothing at all. You do nothing to me, Freddie—you only think you do. I'll send for the TV. I'll send a man! Take a good look at him. I may be now and forever a whore named Doris Wilgus. Okay. And what are you now and forever? A miserable magazine peddler named Freddie Sherman and a lousy writer and you always will be and you wanna know why? Because, God damn it! The—sun—does—not—spit!"

Well, of course, we are dealing with rejection here. After giving, sharing yourself, trying to please him in every way possible, you discover he has lied to you. Not a big lie, but nevertheless a lie. And naturally you are feeling guilty about the radio. You are fighting for his love all the way through this conversation. Not for his respect. Actors make that mistake.

They choose to be fighting for respect instead of love. If he loved you, he would then respect you and your feelings. He would protect you and want to be with you. Love is stronger than respect. With love comes everything else that is truly needed or wanted. But go for the love every time.

Be careful about playing the anger. Remember what anger is and play the origin of the anger. The hurt, the pain, the feelings of need. You are fighting for Felix's love. He is your life. You are fighting for your life.

THE OWL AND THE PUSSYCAT
by Bill Manhoff

pp. 61–63 (SAMUEL FRENCH, INC.)

Felix: Doris—why did you come back?

Doris: What does he mean, "counterfeit emotions and artificial images"?

Felix: He means the sun doesn't spit.

Doris: *(Reading.)* He's sorry! *(Throws down the manuscript.)* Who the hell does he think he is!?

Felix: Doris, why did you come back?

Doris: *(Looking away from him.)* I never had anybody like you in love with me before. I'll never find anybody like you again.

Felix: You mean somebody who'll try to change you and then say rotten things to you because he can't change you?

Doris: Oh, I don't care about that—I think you're a talented sweet wonderful man.

Felix: You are disgusting, do you know that?

Doris: Don't be mean to me—please.

Felix: Why not? That's what you came for. Don't you know you came back for that?

Doris: No, I didn't—

Felix: Of course you did—why else but to be insulted? "Sweet wonderful man" she calls me! Have you forgotten the things we said to each other? Didn't any of it register on your 39-cent plastic made-in-Japan brain?

Doris: Why can't we be nice to one another? We could if we tried.

Felix: Oh God, listen to her! Don't you know that you're a criminal and an animal—how can I be nice to you?

Doris: But you care for me. I know you care for me.

Felix: *(Shouting.)* That's what I'm talking about. I care for you!

Doris: You see—you said it! You said you care for me.

Felix: And you're so pleased by the words that choke me!

70

Doris: Felix, please don't talk that way. You love me and I love you. You can't control those things. It's not your fault.

Felix: No. Nature finds your level for you. You're right. I'm just shocked to see my level—excuse me.

Doris: I know I'm nothing compared to you. I know that. But that doesn't mean you're like me just because you love me.

Felix: It doesn't? Are you sure it doesn't? Doesn't your instinct tell you I'm your equal—the mate for you? Of course it tells you that!

Doris: Oh, baby— Not my equal. I'm nothing compared to you.

Felix: Nothings can only be loved by other nothings. It's axiomatic.

Doris: Don't say that. Maybe it isn't love—You could just be sorry for me—or maybe you love me the way you love a pet.

Felix: There's a thought!

Doris: Why not? A pet doesn't have any brains—you don't have anything in common with it—but you love it, don't you?

Felix: Is that what you want to be—my pet?

Doris: Now don't start twisting everything.

Felix: No, no, that sounds good—you could be my pet whore.

Doris: Felix . . .

Felix: Would you sleep in a box in the corner? Would you wear a collar? Would you run around the neighborhood nights? Yes, you probably would. Well, I could have you spayed, couldn't I? (DORIS *sits looking at him helplessly.*) Well?

Doris: Well, what?

Felix: I don't feel any reaction from you, how about it?

Doris: Don't do that, Felix.

Felix: It was your idea. Don't you even want to give it a chance? You could do it. I think you could. You're already housebroken. I'm sure you could learn a few simple tricks. Going to the market, cleaning the apartment. Give it a try. What have you got to lose? Doris . . . try it. (*Calling a dog.*) Here Doris, here girl. (*Whistles.*) Come on, Doris, come on, good girl, Doris—pretty Doris. (DORIS *starts to cry quietly.*) Damn it, I'm serious about this, you stupid bitch. Don't stand there like a human being!

Doris: I don't understand what you want me to do. If you could explain it to me, I know I'd feel better.

Felix: I want you to be a nice girl and give me your paw. Come on, give Daddy your paw.

Doris: Don't forget—I assimilated "impeccable."

Felix: If you don't give me your paw I'm going to give you away. Now give me your paw—come on.

Doris: You're scaring me. Why do you want to do that?

Felix: Do you want me to give you away? Well, do you? Answer me! Do you want me to give you to some poor family who'll beat you? Answer me—(*She shakes her head.*) Is that so hard to do?—is that such a difficult trick for a full-grown dog? Answer me! Can't you tell me—is it hard to do? (DORIS *shakes her head.*) Well, then, why won't you do it?

Doris: If I do will you stop acting like this?

Felix: We make no deals with pets here! Give me your paw, Goddamn it. (DORIS *looks at him in helpless surrender. Slowly she raises her right hand and puts it into* FELIX'S *hand. He looks at her for a moment, then he melts. He bends and kisses her`hand.*) I'm sorry—I'm so sorry, Doris. Doris, please forgive me.

The following is the monologue created from the previous scene.

FELIX (to DORIS), age 20s to 40s.
pp. 61–63 (SAMUEL FRENCH, INC.)

Doris—why did you come back? You don't want someone like me who'll try to change you and then say rotten things to you because he can't change you. If you don't care about that, you are disgusting, do you know that? That's what you came for. Don't you know you came back for that? Of course you did. Why else but to be insulted? "Sweet wonderful man" she calls me! Have you forgotten the things we said to each other? Didn't any of it register on your thirty-nine-cent plastic made-in-Japan brain? Don't you know that you're a criminal and an animal? How can I be nice to you? (*Shouting.*) And I *do* care for you! Nature finds your level for you. I'm just shocked to see my level. Doesn't your instinct tell you I'm your equal? The mate for you? Of course it tells you that! Nothings can only be loved by other nothings. It's axiomatic. Maybe I love you the way I would love a pet. There's a thought! Is that what you want to be? My pet! That sounds good. You could be my pet whore. Would you sleep in a box in the corner? Would you wear a collar? Would you run around the neighborhood nights? Yes, you probably would. Well, I could have you spayed, couldn't I? How about it? It was your idea. You could do it. You're already housebroken. I'm sure you could learn a few simple tricks. Going to the market, cleaning the apartment. Give it a try. What have you got to lose? *(Whistles.)* Come on, Doris, come on, good girl, Doris. Pretty Doris. Damn it. I'm serious about this, you stupid bitch. Don't stand there like a human being! I want you to be a nice girl and give me your paw. If you don't, I'm going to give you away. Now give me your paw. Come on. Do you want me to give you to some poor family who'll beat you? We make no deals with pets here! Give me your paw, Goddamn it! *(He melts.)* I'm so sorry. I'm sorry, Doris. Please forgive me.

Felix, you are a tormented soul. You've had your story rejected, which, of course, is a bitter disappointment to you but it is also humiliating regarding Doris because she is the first one who told you that your story was phony. You have believed all along that she is intellectually inferior to you. But you also have been discovering along the way that she has enormous intelligence and astuteness. You now are beginning to doubt yourself. You are attacking her out of your own frustration and feelings of inadequacy. You hate yourself for the harshness of your words toward her. She has been giving to you. You treat her miserably. So what is it that you desperately need from Doris right now? How would you feel if really she told you off and walked out of your life? Is that what you think you want?

These are the kinds of questions you should be asking yourself. Remember, she is the most important person in your life. You don't understand why she loves you so much when you treat her so badly. She shouldn't love you the way she does. You are the one being so loved. It is an enormous obligation for one to be loved so much. Can you handle it? It appears as if you are having a very difficult time accepting her love. You keep testing her. She loves you. She shows it. She tells you. You keep needing more proof. Yes, Felix, you are indeed confused and tormented. You're fighting for your life.

THE OWL AND THE PUSSYCAT
by Bill Manhoff

pp. 64–71 (SAMUEL FRENCH, INC.)

Felix: Listen to me. I'm going to be very calm and quiet and I want you to try to understand me—all right?

Doris: Don't use any big words.

Felix: I won't. Now listen—although you can't possibly see the reason for it—you must take my word—there's only one thing for me to do now. I've got to kill myself.

Doris: Oh, don't talk that way. You kidding?

Felix: I'm very serious.

Doris: But why? Why?

Felix: Didn't I just say you can't possibly understand why?

Doris: But sweetheart—listen—

Felix: *(Interrupting.)* Didn't I say that?

Doris: Yes—

Felix: Didn't I ask you to take my word for it? Can't you do that much for me?

Doris: But I don't—Felix, I—*(Frustrated.)* Oh, I could just kill you, sometimes!

Felix: *(Sits at typewriter—puts in paper.)* Just love me as you do, mindlessly, and see that this suicide note doesn't get lost . . . *(Thinking.)* "To Whom It May Concern" . . .

Doris: Oh, Felix—I don't want to live without you! I'll never find anybody else like you.

Felix: You'll settle for less. *(Thinking.)* "To Whom It May Concern—but never does—"

Doris: I'll never be happy. I know I won't. Didn't I try to get along without you? Why do you think I came back?

Felix: It was only a week—

Doris: It wouldn't make any difference how long it was. I know. I could see what kind of a life I would have. I couldn't stand it. Not now. Before I met you I could have stood it—

74

Felix: Will you please shut up? I'm trying to work.

Doris: Then just tell me—can I commit suicide with you?

Felix: No, you can't.

Doris: Please Felix—why not?

Felix: Because—I'm doing it alone—

Doris: Will it hurt if I do it with you?

Felix: Yes.

Doris: Why?

Felix: Because with me it's an affirmation of principle—a rebuke to the world—with you it would just be "monkey see—monkey do"!

Doris: No, it wouldn't. I would be doing it for the same reason you would.

Felix: Yours would dilute mine.

Doris: It would not!

Felix: How can I make her understand? Yours would be meaningless—you don't have a good reason.

Doris: I can't live without you.

Felix: That's a silly, sentimental suicide—that's just weakness and failure.

Doris: And what about yours?

Felix: Mine will be a proud taunting challenging suicide—a thought-provoking suicide.

Doris: Who'll know the difference?

Felix: My note will explain the difference— (*Thinking.*) Because truth is dead. (*Starting to type.*) Because moral courage is dead—I, Felix Sherman, choose to die— (*Weighing it.*) have chosen to die—

Doris: Why can't I, Doris Wheeler, have chosen to die also?

Felix: Doris, will you please shut up?

Doris: You're making me real sore now. If I want to commit suicide you can't stop me—it's a free country!

Felix: (*Very reasonably.*) That's true! I only ask that you don't louse up mine!

Doris: But I don't want to do it alone. I want to do it with you.

Felix: Well, you can't and that's all there is to it.

Doris: You're nothing but a mean selfish son of a bitch. (*She sits, angry.*) I'll fix you—I'll tear up your suicide note.

Felix: You couldn't do a thing like that.

Doris: I will unless you let me do it with you.

Felix: You couldn't be so heartless.

Doris: Look who's talking about heartless. You want to leave me all alone, don't you? You'd do that to me, wouldn't you? You don't care about me at all! Nobody does.

Felix: *(Relenting.)* Doris—darling—listen—

Doris: It feels like a hot shower when you call me darling.

Felix: My dear strange child—please try to understand why I have to do this alone—I want it to have a certain impact. I want to hit out through every morning newspaper at all—

Doris: *(Interrupting.)* You're very foolish from a newspaper standpoint.

Felix: I'm trying to force the public to think about—*(Stops.)* What did you say? The newspaper standpoint?

Doris: Certainly. What's one fellow committing suicide? You can find that in the paper any day—in the back pages—but a good suicide pact is front-page news—

Felix: *(Impressed with this. Then, discarding it.)* Oh—but it's so cheap, it's—

Doris: Cheap? Listen, what about that beautiful note you're writing? You want that mentioned on page thirty-two? "There was a piece of paper with writing on it on the jerk's body." Or you want it on the front page? "The dead lovers were both clutching a brilliant suicide note which said"—and so forth—

Felix: "Nos Morituri—Te Salutamus." I think you're right.

Doris: What is that?

Felix: We who are about to die, salute you. Latin.

Doris: Oh, Felix, really—"we"? Oh, honey, thank you!

Felix: *(At the typewriter.)* "To Whom It May Concern—we who are about to die, salute you—" Good, Doris—you're right! —you're instinctively right!

Doris: I guess it's the actress in me. How are we going to do it?

Felix: Do what? Oh—I don't know.

Doris: Sleeping pills are the nicest, but they're hard to get.

Felix: Sweetheart—please let me concentrate—

Doris: Well, I could be handling the details if you'll just give me a minute to make a decision—

Felix: Shhh—*(Writing.)* "Because truth is dead—"

Doris: I can't decide this all by myself—

Felix: *(Rises and paces.)* It needs a finish—

Doris: Why don't you knock off five minutes and we'll work this out?

Felix: Work what out?

Doris: Then I could be making the arrangements.

Felix: Arrangements?

Doris: My absent-minded professor—how are we gonna do it?—gun—knife?

Felix: Oh, no!

Doris: I couldn't agree with you more—but what then? We could never get enough sleeping pills.

Felix: No—not sleeping pills. Sleeping pills have such a neurotic connotation.

Doris: Well, we can't get them anyway—what else is nice and painless and—? Hey—right under our noses— *(Points to the stove.)*

Felix: Gas? No—

Doris: Why not?

Felix: Gas is negative. Gas is passive defeat.

Doris: Well, I give up. What do you suggest?

Felix: Hemlock is what we need!

Doris: Hemlock?

Felix: That would be perfect. It would be eloquent!

Doris: Hang ourselves from a hemlock tree?

Felix: Hang ourselves? Oh no—hemlock is the poison of Socrates.

Doris: Poison? I'm sorry—no sir! Not me!

Felix: What's your objection to poison?

Doris: Because I don't wanna burn up my insides and have cramps and like that—

Felix: You can get painless poisons.

Doris: Where—at the drugstore?

Felix: Yes, as a matter of fact. You can buy poison to exterminate pests, can't you?

Doris: *(Laughing.)* I can just see us sitting here spraying each other with bug bombs.

Felix: This is no joke, Doris.

Doris: I'm sorry—but what do we say? "Pardon me, sir—we want to kill some rats, but we don't want to hurt them, they're so cute"? Now listen to Doris—gas!

Felix: All right—I suppose it is the only sensible way—

Doris: Of course, dopey! And you were gonna do this alone!

Felix: I'll finish the note.

Doris: *(Going to the stove.)* Now how will we work this?

Felix: *(Getting a thought.)* How does this sound—?

Doris: Honey, we got problems—

Felix: What?

Doris: Only one burner works. That's not much gas.

Felix: It will work. We'll have to plug up the door. It will take time—

Doris: We can't do that—let this whole big room fill up with gas?

Felix: Why not?

Doris: We can't waste all that gas!

Felix: Damn it! If you're not serious about this, Doris—

Doris: Sure I'm serious about it.

Felix: "Waste all that gas"?

Doris: I'm sorry—it's the way I was brought up—I can't help it.

Felix: Well, we can't do it anyway, not really.

Doris: What do you mean?

Felix: Too many chinks in those old windows—too much of a draft in here—the only way gas will work in this thing is to stick your head in the oven.

Doris: I don't think it's big enough.

Felix: Yes, it is.

Doris: Not for both of us.

Felix: No, but we could take turns.

Doris: Oh, yeah? No thank you. We're doing it together. "Two-gether"—not "one gether."

Felix: But what's the difference? I'd let you go first, naturally.

Doris: Thanks a lot! And then you change your mind and I'm dead all by myself! . . . No thank you!

Felix: All right. I'll go first.

Doris: And I'm gonna sit here waiting and check you to see if you're done! . . . Forget it!

Felix: Well, maybe we can do it together. Let's see— (*They get down on their knees and try to fit their heads into the oven. There are ad-lib "Wait," "Here," "Now," "No, no, sideways," "Look out for my nose," etc. They exhaust every possible combination of positions.* DORIS *starts to giggle. Deeply hurt.*) Doris, why don't you just go home and forget all about it?

Doris: I'm sorry, honey. It just struck me funny!

Felix: You'd think you were playing some kind of a birthday party game. We're committing suicide, God damn it!

Doris: I know it, Felix—I'm sorry I laughed.

Felix: Are you sincere about this? Now really—if you're not—

Doris: Of course I am.

Felix: Are you sure? I hope you are.

Doris: I am, honey. I just wanna make sure we go together—that's all—wouldn't that be best?

Felix: I suppose so. *(Interrupting.)* Wait a minute! Oh—that's it! Of course!

Doris: What?

Felix: It combines painlessness and dramatic impact.

Doris: What, what?

Felix: A jump—hand in hand from a public building—

Doris: I don't know—a jump?

Felix: It's perfect! Talk about news value—talk about the front page—

Doris: It sounds kind of scary!

Felix: Why?—An exhilarating flight through space and then oblivion.

Doris: Well, I guess you wouldn't feel anything. *(Puts her hand between her knees.)* Except a very cold breeze.

Felix: What a gesture—what a stage setting for my note.

Doris: What building though? This one isn't high enough—

Felix: No—not this kind of a building—an office building. One of man's monuments to his false gods—one located in the center of town.

Doris: We couldn't get into an office building at this hour, could we?

Felix: No—you're right—a hotel—that's it! A hotel!

Doris: Yeah—we could check into a room on the top floor—Oh—I've got it—I've got it! Perfect—

Felix: What?

Doris: The Top of the Mark.

Felix: The Top of the Mark?

Doris: You know the bar—The Top of the Mark.

Felix: Yes, of course—look—a couple strolls in at the height of the evening's revelry. Quietly they ask for a table at the window—twenty floors above the shining city. They sit for a moment—perhaps they order a drink—the man takes an envelope from his pocket and props it against his glass. Then they rise. They turn to the noisy, laughing room. In a loud voice the man calls out: "Goodbye, Gomorrah!"

Doris: Do I say anything?

Felix: What?—You don't say anything.

Doris: It was my idea, you know.

Felix: All right—okay—you say something too—and then—

Doris: What do I say?

Felix: Whatever you want to—

Doris: Could I say what you said: "Goodbye, Tomorrow"?

Felix: "Goodbye, Gomorrah."

Doris: What does that mean?

Felix: Don't you remember Sodom and Gomorrah from the Bible?

Doris: Oh yes—the two wicked cities—sure—I get it. That's good. Hey—how about, "Farewell, cruel world."

Felix: Shut up.

Doris: Why?

Felix: Just shut up. Then together we yell—"Goodbye, Gomorrah," and before their horrified eyes we turn to the window—and, hand in hand, we jump—

Doris: We ought to kiss first and blow kisses to the whole room— (FELIX *gives her a disgusted look*.) You know—goodbye kisses . . . You know the trouble with you? You only like your own ideas.

Felix: You just don't understand this—you don't get the values involved—It's useless! I can't work with you.

The following is the monologue created from the previous scene.

FELIX (to DORIS), age 20s to 40s.
pp. 64–71 (SAMUEL FRENCH, INC.)

Listen to me. I'm going to be very calm and quiet and I want you to try to understand me. All right? Now listen. Although you can't possibly see the reason for it, you must take my word. There's only one thing for me to do now. I've got to kill myself. Just love me as you do, mindlessly, and see that this suicide note doesn't get lost. (*Thinking*.) "To Whom It May Concern . . . but never does."

I'm doing it alone. With me it's an affirmation of principle—a rebuke to the world. With you it would just be "monkey see—monkey do"! Yours would dilute mine. Yours would be a sentimental suicide. That's just weakness and failure. Mine will be a proud taunting challenging suicide. A thought-provoking suicide. My note will explain the difference. (*Thinking*.) Because truth is dead. Because moral courage is dead. I, Felix Sherman, choose to die. *(Weighing it.)* Have chosen to die.

My dear strange child. Please try to understand why I have to do this alone. I want it to have a certain impact. I want to hit out through every morning newspaper. I'm trying to force the public to think about this. *(Has a revelation.)* But a good suicide pact *is front-page news!* "Nos Morituri, Te Salutamus." We who are about to die, salute you. Latin. Doris, you're right! You're instinctively right! How are we going to do it? Not sleeping pills. Sleeping pills have such a neurotic connotation. Gas is negative. Gas is passive defeat. Hemlock is what we need! That would be perfect! It would be eloquent! Hemlock is the poison of Socrates. Wait a minute! Oh—that's it! Of course! It combines painlessness and dramatic impact. A jump—hand in hand from a public building. It's perfect. Talk about news value! Talk about the front page. An exhilarating flight through space and then oblivion. What a gesture, what a stage setting for my note. An office building. One of man's monuments to his false gods—one located in the center of town. No! A hotel—that's it. Yes, of course. Look, a couple strolls in at the height of the evening's revelry. Quietly they ask for a table at the window twenty floors above the shining city. They sit for a moment. Perhaps they order a drink. The man takes an envelope from his pocket and props it against his glass. Then they rise. They turn to the noisy, laughing room. In a loud voice the man calls out, "Goodbye, Gomorrah!" You don't say anything. And before their horrified eyes we turn to the window and, hand in hand, we jump!

(Upset.) You just don't understand this! You don't get the values involved! It's useless! *I can't work with you!*

Felix, you are fighting for you life even though you are planning to end it. You are being quite dramatic about your conflict. Actually you are being downright self-indulgent and childish. As Felix, you don't really know this. You are just in dire need of love. So as actor, enjoy doing this monologue. It's totally self-serving. And remember when you are doing comedy, you must fight even harder for what it is you are fighting for. And comedy deals with life and death just as drama does. There is no difference except the dialogue is set up to be absurd or outrageous but it is the actor who will bring in the laughs from the audience through honest life-and-death choices that deal with needs, vulnerability, humanity, and love. The more you reach out to Doris to create a relationship, the more honest your performance will be. Humor is situational and behavioral, not funny words. The more you give to the other character, the more you give to us, the auditors. We will believe you and, therefore, you have a good shot at getting a call-back.

The Prisoner of Second Avenue
by Neil Simon

pp. 12–16 (Samuel French, Inc.)

Mel: Edna! (*She stops, turns.*) Don't go!... Talk to me for a few minutes because I think I'm going out of my mind. (*She stops, looks at him, and crosses back into the room.*)

Edna: What is it?

Mel: I'm unraveling... I'm losing touch!

Edna: You haven't been sleeping well lately...

Mel: I don't know where I am half the time. I walk down Madison Avenue, I think I'm in a foreign country.

Edna: I know that feeling, Mel...

Mel: It's not just a feeling, something is happening to me... I'm losing control. I can't handle things anymore. The telephone on my desk rings seven, eight times before I answer it... I forgot how to work the watercooler today. I stood there with an empty cup in my hand and water running all over my shoes.

Edna: It's not just you, Mel, it's everybody. Everybody's feeling the tension these days.

Mel: Tension? If I could just feel tension, I'd give a thousand dollars to charity.... When you're tense, you're tight, you're holding on to something. I don't know where to grab. Edna, I'm slipping and I'm scared.

Edna: Don't talk like that. What about seeing the analyst again?

Mel: Who? Doctor Pike? He's dead. Six years of my life, twenty-three thousand dollars. He got my money, what does he care if he gets a heart attack?

Edna: There are other good doctors. You can see someone else.

Mel: And start all over from the beginning? "Hello. Sit down. What seems to be the trouble?"... It'll cost me another twenty-three thousand just to fill *this* doctor in with information I already gave the dead one.

83

Edna: What about a little therapy. Maybe you just need someone to talk to for a while.

Mel: I don't know where or who I am anymore. I'm disappearing,
Edna. I don't need analysts, I need Lost and Found.

Edna: Listen—Listen—What about if we get away for a
couple of weeks. A two-week vacation? Someplace in the
sun, away from the city. You can get two weeks sick-leave,
can't you, Mel? *(He is silent. He walks to window, glances
over at the plant.)*

Mel: . . . Even the cactus is dying. Strongest plant in the
world, only has to be watered twice a year. Can't make a go
of it on 88th and Second.

Edna: Mel, answer me. What about getting away? Can't you
ask them for two weeks off?

Mel: *(Makes himself a Scotch.)* Yes, I can ask them for two
weeks off. What worries me is that they'll ask me to take the
other fifty weeks as well. *(He drinks.)*

Edna: You? What are you talking about? You've been there 22
years . . . Mel. Is that it? Is that what's been bothering you?
You're worried about losing your job?

Mel: I'm not worried about losing it. I'm worried about keeping it. Losing it is easy.

Edna: Has something happened? Have they said anything?

Mel: They don't have to say anything. The company lost three
million dollars this year. Suddenly they're looking to save
pennies. The vice-president of my department has been
using the same paper clip for three weeks now. A 62-year-old
man with a duplex on Park Avenue and a house in Southampton
running around the office, screaming "Where's my paper
clip?" . . .

Edna: But they haven't actually said anything to you.

Mel: They closed the executive dining room. Nobody goes out
to lunch anymore, they bring sandwiches from home. Top
executives, making eighty thousand dollars a year, eating
egg salad sandwiches over the waste paper basket . . .

Edna: Nothing has happened yet, Mel. There's no point in
worrying about it now.

Mel: No one comes to work late anymore. Everyone's afraid if
you're not there on time, they'll sell your desk.

Edna: And what if they did? We'd live, we'd get by. You'd get
another job somewhere.

Mel: Where? I'm gonna be 47 years old in January. 47! They could get two 23-and-a-half-year-old kids for half my money.

Edna: Alright, suppose something *did* happen? Suppose you *did* lose your job? It's not the end of the world. We don't have to live in the city. We could move somewhere in the country, or even out west.

Mel: And what do I do for a living? Become a middle-aged cowboy? Maybe they'll put me in charge of rounding up the elderly cattle . . . What's the matter with you?

Edna: The girls are in college now, we have enough to see them through. We don't need much for the two of us.

Mel: You need a place to live, you need clothing, you need food. A can of polluted tuna fish is still eighty-five cents.

Edna: We could move to Europe. To Spain. Two people could live for fifteen hundred dollars a year in Spain.

Mel: (*Nods.*) *Spanish* people. I'm 47 years old, with arthritis in my shoulder and high blood pressure, you expect me to raise goats and live in a cave?

Edna: You could work there, get some kind of a job.

Mel: An advertising account executive? In Barcelona? They've probably been standing at the dock waiting for years for someone like that.

Edna: (*Angrily.*) What is it they have here that's so damned hard to give up? *What is it you'll miss so badly, for God's sakes?*

Mel: I'm not through with my life yet . . . I still have value, I still have worth . . .

Edna: What kind of a life is this? You live like some kind of a caged animal in a Second Avenue zoo that's too hot in one room, too cold in another, overcharged for a growth on the side of the building they call a terrace that can't support a cactus plant, let alone two human beings. Is this what you call a worthwhile life? Banging on walls and jiggling toilets?

Mel: (*Shouts.*) You think it's any better in sunny Spain? Go swimming on the beach, it'll take you the rest of the summer to scrape the oil off . . .

Edna: Forget Spain. There are other places to live.

Mel: Maine? Vermont maybe? You think it's all rolling hills and maple syrup? They have more people on welfare up there than they have pancakes. Washington? Oregon? Unemployed lumberjacks are sitting around sawing legs off chairs, they have nothing else to do.

Edna: I will go anywhere in the world you want to go, Mel. I will live in a cave, a hut or a tree. I will live on a raft in the Amazon jungle if that's what you want to do...

Mel: Alright, call a travel agency. Get two economy seats to Bolivia. We'll go to Abercrombie's tomorrow, get a couple of pith helmets and a spear gun.

Edna: Don't talk to me like I'm insane.

Mel: I'm halfway there, you might as well catch up.

The following is the monologue created from the previous scene.

MEL (to EDNA), age 40 to mid-50s.
pp. 12–16 (SAMUEL FRENCH, INC.)

Edna! Talk to me for a few minutes because I think I'm going out of my mind. I'm unraveling. I'm losing touch! I don't know where I am half the time. I walk down Madison Avenue, I think I'm in a foreign country. Something is happening to me. I'm losing control. I can't handle things anymore. The telephone on my desk rings seven, eight times before I answer it. I forgot how to work the watercooler today. I stood there with an empty cup in my hand and water running all over my shoes. If I could just feel tension, I'd give a thousand dollars to charity. When you're tense, you're tight, you're holding on to something. I don't know where to grab. Edna, I'm slipping and I'm scared. I can't even see my analyst. He's dead. Six years of my life, twenty-three thousand dollars. He got my money, what does he care if he gets a heart attack? I won't see someone else and start all over from the beginning. "Hello. Sit down. What seems to be the trouble?" It'll cost me another twenty-three thousand just to fill *this* doctor in with information I already gave the dead one. I don't know where or who I am anymore. I'm disappearing, Edna. I don't need analysts, I need Lost and Found! Even the cactus is dying. Strongest plant in the world, only has to be watered twice a year. Can't make a go of it on Eighty-eighth and Second. What worries me is if I ask them for two weeks off, they'll ask me to take the other fifty weeks as well. I'm not worried about losing my job. I'm worried about keeping it. Losing it is easy. The company lost three million dollars this year. Suddenly they're looking to save pennies. The vice president of my department has been using the same paper clip for three weeks now. A sixty-two-year-old man with a duplex on Park Avenue and a house in Southampton running around the office, screaming, "Where's my paper clip?" They closed the executive dining room. Nobody goes out to lunch anymore, they bring sandwiches from home. Top executives, making eighty thousand dollars a year, eating egg salad sandwiches over the wastepaper basket. No one comes to work late anymore. Everyone's afraid if you're not there on time, they'll sell your desk. I'm gonna be forty-seven years old in January. Forty-seven! They could get two twenty-three-and-a-half-year-old kids for half my money. And what do I do for a living? Become a middle-aged cowboy? Maybe they'll put me in charge of rounding up elderly cattle! You need a place to live, you need clothing, you need food. A can of polluted tuna fish is still eighty-five cents. I'm forty-seven years old, with arthritis in my shoulder and high blood pressure, you expect me to raise goats and live in a cave? An advertising account executive? In Barcelona? They've probably been standing at the dock waiting for years for someone like that. You think it's any better in sunny Spain? Go swimming on the beach, it'll take you the rest of the summer to scrape the oil off. Maine? Vermont maybe? You think it's all rolling hills and maple syrup? They have more people on welfare up there than they have pancakes. Washington? Oregon? Unemployed lumberjacks are sitting around sawing legs off chairs, they have nothing else to do. All right, call a travel agency. Get two economy seats to Bolivia. We'll go to Abercrombie's tomorrow, get a couple of pith helmets and a spear gun. I'm halfway insane, you might as well catch up.

This is a perfect example of survival comedy. Making jokes in a perilous situation can save your life. Mr. Simon knows this only too well. His mind works constantly with survival humor. He gives his characters this gift.

When actors ask me how to recognize humor on the page, I fear for their future in the theater. It is worth repeating. You don't have to be a funny person yourself and make people fall down the steps with laughter, but you *must* be aware of and react to the absurdities and ironies of life! You cannot be taught this! You simply have to know where the jokes are when it comes to a Neil Simon comedy. And you must be aware of the humor. If you indeed recognize humor, that means that you *have* humor! Without humor you will not be successful doing straight drama either.

Most people take life and themselves too seriously. Not only do most people not stop and smell the roses but they also don't stop and see the humor!

This play deals with a life-and-death tormenting situation for Mel. Your manhood, your earning power, your ego, your security, your future, your life is at stake. You could have a heart attack any moment. A stroke. A nervous breakdown. You could wind up institutionalized. You could lose your wife whom you love very much.

This is a comedy about fear, losing control, vulnerability, life-and-death survival. Mr. Simon has given us a character who is going through all this. He is also aware of the absurdities and ironies of life. Mr. Simon has written a character who is suffering but is also aware of these things. His character understands humor. Now, you, the actor auditioning with this piece, must understand humor.

There is nothing funny about thinking you are going out of your mind. There is nothing funny about losing touch and control, about being scared, about your analyst being dead, about losing your job, or about being forty-seven years old with arthritis and high blood pressure. And this is a comedy!

THE PRISONER OF SECOND AVENUE
by Neil Simon

pp. 14–16 (Samuel French, Inc.)

Edna: Has something happened? Have they said anything?

Mel: They don't have to say anything. The company lost three million dollars this year. Suddenly they're looking to save pennies. The vice-president of my department has been using the same paper clip for three weeks now. A 62-year-old man with a duplex on Park Avenue and a house in Southampton running around the office, screaming "Where's my paper clip?"...

Edna: But they haven't actually said anything to you.

Mel: They closed the executive dining room. Nobody goes out to lunch anymore, they bring sandwiches from home. Top executives, making eighty thousand dollars a year, eating egg salad sandwiches over the waste paper basket...

Edna: Nothing has happened yet, Mel. There's no point in worrying about it now.

Mel: No one comes to work late anymore. Everyone's afraid if you're not there on time, they'll sell your desk.

Edna: And what if they did? We'd live, we'd get by. You'd get another job somewhere.

Mel: Where? I'm gonna be 47 years old in January. 47! They could get two 23-and-a-half-year-old kids for half my money.

Edna: Alright, suppose something *did* happen? Suppose you *did* lose your job? It's not the end of the world. We don't have to live in the city. We could move somewhere in the country, or even out west.

Mel: And what do I do for a living? Become a middle-aged cowboy? Maybe they'll put me in charge of rounding up the elderly cattle... What's the matter with you?

Edna: The girls are in college now, we have enough to see them through. We don't need much for the two of us.

Mel: You need a place to live, you need clothing, you need food. A can of polluted tuna fish is still eighty-five cents.

Edna: We could move to Europe. To Spain. Two people could live for fifteen hundred dollars a year in Spain.

Mel: (*Nods.*) *Spanish* people. I'm 47 years old, with arthritis in my shoulder and high blood pressure, you expect me to raise goats and live in a cave?

Edna: You could work there, get some kind of a job.

Mel: An advertising account executive? In Barcelona? They've probably been standing at the dock waiting for years for someone like that.

Edna: (*Angrily.*) What is it they have here that's so damned hard to give up? *What is it you'll miss so badly, for God's sakes?*

Mel: I'm not through with my life yet...I still have value, I still have worth...

Edna: What kind of a life is this? You live like some kind of a caged animal in a Second Avenue zoo that's too hot in one room, too cold in another, overcharged for a growth on the side of the building they call a terrace that can't support a cactus plant, let alone two human beings. Is this what you call a worthwhile life? Banging on walls and jiggling toilets?

Mel: (*Shouts.*) You think it's any better in sunny Spain? Go swimming on the beach, it'll take you the rest of the summer to scrape the oil off...

Edna: Forget Spain. There are other places to live.

Mel: Maine? Vermont maybe? You think it's all rolling hills and maple syrup? They have more people on welfare up there than they have pancakes. Washington? Oregon? Unemployed lumberjacks are sitting around sawing legs off chairs, they have nothing else to do.

Edna: I will go anywhere in the world you want to go, Mel. I will live in a cave, a hut or a tree. I will live on a raft in the Amazon jungle if that's what you want to do...

Mel: Alright, call a travel agency. Get two economy seats to Bolivia. We'll go to Abercrombie's tomorrow, get a couple of pith helmets and a spear gun.

Edna: Don't talk to me like I'm insane.

Mel: I'm halfway there, you might as well catch up.

Edna: I am trying to offer reasonable suggestions. I am not responsible. I am not the one who's doing this to you...

Mel: I didn't say you were, Edna.

Edna: Then what do you want from me? *What do you want from anyone?*

The following is the monologue created from the previous scene.

EDNA (to MEL), age late 30s to 50.
pp. 14–16 (SAMUEL FRENCH, INC.)

Has something happened? Have they said anything? Nothing has happened yet, Mel. There's no point in worrying about it now. And what if they did? We'd live, we'd get by. You'd get another job somewhere. All right, suppose something *did* happen? Suppose you *did* lose your job? It's not the end of the world. We don't have to live in the city. We could move somewhere in the country or even out West. The girls are in college now, we have enough to see them through. We don't need much for the two of us. We could move to Europe. To Spain. Two people could live for fifteen hundred dollars a year in Spain. You could work there, get some kind of a job. What is it they have here that's so damned hard to give up? What is it you'll miss so badly, for God's sake? What kind of a life is this? You live like some kind of a caged animal in a Second Avenue zoo that's too hot in one room, too cold in another, overcharged for a growth on the side of the building they call a terrace that can't support a cactus plant, let alone two human beings. Is this what you call a worthwhile life? Banging on walls and jiggling toilets? I will go anywhere in the world you want to go, Mel. I will live in a cave, a hut, or a tree. I will live on a raft in the Amazon jungle if that's what you want to do. Just don't look at me like I'm insane. I am trying to offer reasonable suggestions. I am not responsible. I am not the one who's doing this to you. What do you want from me? *What do you want from anyone?*

So you are at your wit's end. Your husband, whom you love dearly, seems to be cracking up before your eyes. He is terrified about losing his job, and it appears as if nothing is working for him right down to the smallest thing. You are now very frightened by his behavior. This is not normal. This is not your Mel. You've seen some of this coming, but the way he is acting right now is downright nightmarish. You are fighting for the rest of your life. Mel is the rest of your life. You love him and want to do anything in the world to help him and you want to help yourself too so that you don't lose him—and this is a comedy.

THE PRISONER OF SECOND AVENUE
by Neil Simon

pp. 63–65 (Samuel French, Inc.)

Edna: *(Holding back tears.)* Well... I don't think you have to worry about that anymore, Mel... We went out of business today.

Mel: ... Who did?

Edna: We did. The business that I'm in is out of business. There is no business in that place anymore.

Mel: ... They let you go?

Edna: If *they're* not staying, what do they need me for?

Mel: You mean completely out of business?

Edna: They went bankrupt. They overextended themselves. One of the partners may go to jail. *(She starts to cry.)*

Mel: You don't go bankrupt overnight. You must have had some inkling.

Edna: *(Crying.)* I had *no* inkling... I did, but I was afraid to think about it... What's happening, Mel? Is the whole world going out of business?

Mel: *(Goes to her.)* Okay. It's alright, Edna, it's alright.

Edna: *(Sobbing.)* I thought we were such a strong country, Mel. If you can't depend on America, who can you depend on?

Mel: Ourselves, Edna. We have to depend on each other.

Edna: I don't understand how a big place like that can just go out of business. It's not a little candy store. It's a big building. It's got stone and marble with gargoyles on the roof. Beautifully hand-chiselled gargoyles, Mel. A hundred years old. They'll come tomorrow with a sledge hammer and kill the gargoyles.

Mel: It's just a job, Edna. It's not your whole life.

Edna: You know what I thought about on the way home? One thing. I only had one thing on my mind... A bath. A nice, hot bath... *(Sobs again.)* ... And now the water went out of business.

Mel: It'll come back on. Everything is going to come back on, Edna. They're not going to shut us off forever.

Edna: *(She yells.)* I want my bath! I want my water! Tell them I want my bath, Mel!

Mel: It's off, Edna. What can I do? There's nothing I can do.

Edna: *(Yells.)* Bang on the pipes. Tell them there's a woman upstairs who needs an emergency bath. If I don't sit in some water, Mel, I'm going to go crazy. Bang on the pipes.

Mel: Edna, be reasonable...

Edna: *(Screams.) I banged for you, why won't you bang for me?*

Mel: Shh, it's alright, baby. It's alright.

Edna: *(Still sobbing.)* It's *not*. It's *not* alright. Why are you saying it's alright? Are you out of your mind? Oh, God, Mel, I'm sorry. I didn't mean that. Please forgive me, Mel.

Mel: It's alright, Edna... Please calm down.

Edna: I don't know what I'm saying anymore. It's too much for me, Mel. I have no strength left, Mel. Nothing. I couldn't open my pocketbook on the bus, a little boy had to help me.

Mel: Of course you have strength.

Edna: I have anger, no strength... If something happens to me, Mel, who's going to take care of us?

Mel: I am. I always took care of you, didn't I?

Edna: But who's going to take care of us now, Mel?

Mel: Me, Edna. Me!

Edna: You, Mel?

Mel: Don't you trust me, Edna? Don't you believe in me anymore?

Edna: Let's leave, Mel... Let's give up and leave... Let them have it... Let them have their city... Let them keep their garbage and their crooks and their jobs and their broken gargoyles... I just want to live out the rest of my life with you and see my girls grow up healthy and happy and once in a while I would like to have some water and take a bath... Please, Mel... Please...

The following is the monologue created from the previous scene.

EDNA (to MEL), age 30s to 50.
pp. 63–65 (SAMUEL FRENCH, INC.)

We went out of business today. The business that I'm in is out of business. There is no business in that place anymore. If *they're* not staying, what do they need me for? They went bankrupt. They overextended themselves. One of the partners may go to jail. I had no inkling. I did, but I was afraid to think about it. What's happening, Mel? Is the whole world going out of business? I thought we were such a strong country, Mel. If you can't depend on America, who can you depend on? I don't understand how a big place like that can just go out of business. It's not a little candy store. It's a big building. It's got stone and marble with gargoyles on the roof. Beautifully hand-chiseled gargoyles, Mel. A hundred years old. They'll come tomorrow with a sledge hammer and kill the gargoyles. You know what I thought about on the way home? One thing. I only had one thing on my mind. A bath! A nice, hot bath. And now the water went out of business. I *want my bath!* I *want my water! Tell them I want my bath, Mel!* Bang on the pipes. Tell them there's a woman upstairs who needs an emergency bath. If I don't sit in some water, Mel, I'm going to go crazy. Bang on the pipes. I *banged for you, why won't you bang for me?* I don't know what I'm saying anymore. It's too much for me, Mel. I have no strength left, Mel. Nothing. I couldn't open my pocketbook on the bus, a little boy had to help me. I have anger, no strength. If something happens to me, Mel, who's going to take care of us? *You*, Mel? Let's leave, Mel. Let's give up and leave! Let them have it! Let them have their city! Let them keep their garbage and their crooks and their jobs and their broken gargoyles. I just want to live out the rest of my life with you and see my girls grow up healthy and happy and once in a while I would like to have some water and take a bath. Please, Mel. Please!

Now it is Edna's turn to be cracking up. Many actors have said to me in classes when they are doing a highly emotional scene that they don't want to take it "too far" for fear that they would be overdoing what's expected of them at the audition. They don't want to be too big. After all, they argue, if they start too big, where do they go? Of course, my answer is always, "Bigger!" Naturally you want to present yourself as character in each scene to represent the beginning, the middle, and the end of the content of the material and the conflict and needs. But when doing a monologue, you've got two minutes to show us your strengths, intelligence, and interesting qualities. Just make honest choices. Don't worry about being too big. Worry about being honest.

Some students have told me that they were advised to hold back at the audition. If they gave their all, the auditors would assume they've given all they've got to give and there isn't any more left! If you are a recipient of this incorrect advice, please immediately lay it to rest in the garbage can where it belongs.

Edna is wrought up from *before* her first line of dialogue. The important thing to remember is to communicate *very* strongly to Mel. That is the way to approach the hysteria. You need to tell Mel, your partner and lover in life. He must be there to help you. You've helped him. Now he *must* help you. Make it more important than it appears on the page. She is frightened for herself, them, and the entire country. She is afraid that Mel will not be able to take care of her. He simply must. With all her fears, she too has an awareness of the absurdities and ironies of life. So must you.

THE PRISONER OF SECOND AVENUE
by Neil Simon

pp. 66–69 (SAMUEL FRENCH, INC.)

Harry: Hello, Mel... Alright if I come in?

Mel: *(Surprised.)* Sure, Harry, sure. I didn't know you were in New York.

Harry: *(Speaks softly.)* I had some business and besides, I wanted to talk to you. How you feeling? Alright?

Mel: Don't be so solemn, Harry. It's not a hospital room. I'm alright. *(HARRY enters, MEL closes door.)*

Harry: I brought you some apples from the country. *(He opens attaché case.)* Wait'll you taste these. *(Takes out apples from case.)* You always loved apples, I remember... Are you allowed to eat them now?

Mel: Apples don't affect the mind, Harry. They're not going to drive me crazy. Thank you. That's very nice of you.

Harry: Is Edna here?

Mel: Yeah, she's in the tub. She's not feeling very well.

Harry: It's alright. She doesn't want to see me. I understand.

Mel: It's not that, Harry. She's very tired.

Harry: The woman doesn't like me. It's alright. The whole world can't love you... I feel badly that it's my brother's wife, but that's what makes horse racing. I'm only staying two minutes. I wanted to deliver this in person and then I'll go.

Mel: You came eight miles to bring me six apples? Harry, that's very sweet but it wasn't necessary.

Harry: Not the apples, Mel. I have something a little more substantial than apples. *(Reaches in pocket and takes out a check.)* Here. This is for you and Edna... The apples are separate. *(MEL takes the check and looks at it.)*

Mel: What's this?

Harry: It's a check. It's the money. Go buy yourself a summer

97

camp. (*Good-naturedly.*) Go. July and August take care of six hundred running noses. Have a good time. (*He gets up to go.*)

Mel: Harry, this is twenty-five thousand dollars.

Harry: Your sisters and I contributed equally, fifty-fifty. I'm telling them about it tomorrow.

Mel: I don't understand.

Harry: I don't understand myself. Why would anyone want to run a summer camp? But if that gives you pleasure, then this gives me pleasure...

Mel: When did Edna ask you for this?

Harry: What's the difference? It's over. Everybody got a little excited. Everyone was trying to do the right thing. Take the money, buy your crazy camp.

Mel: Harry!

Harry: Yes?

Mel: In the first place... thank you. In the second place, I can't take it.

Harry: Don't start in with me. It took me six weeks to decide to give it to you.

Mel: I can't explain it to you, Harry. But I just can't take the money.

Harry: Why don't you let me do this for you? Why won't you let me have the satisfaction of making you happy?

Mel: You already have, by offering it. Now make me happier by tearing it up. They see this much money in this neighborhood, you'll never make it to your car.

Harry: You let everyone else do things for you. You let everyone else take care of you. Edna, Pearl. Pauline, Jessie. Everybody but me, your brother. Why am I always excluded from the family?

Mel: They're three middle-aged widows, they're looking for someone to take care of. I made them a present, I got sick. What do you want from me, Harry?

Harry: I had to work when I was thirteen, years old. I didn't have time to be the favorite.

Mel: Harry, let's not go into that again. You want to be the favorite, I give it to you. I'll call the girls up tonight and tell them from now on, you're the favorite.

Harry: I'm not blaming you! I'm not blaming you. It's only natural. If there are two brothers in the family and one is out working all day, the one who stays home is the favorite.

Mel: Harry, I don't want to seem impolite. But Edna's not feeling well, we have no water and all our food is defrosting. I'm really not in the mood to discuss why you're not the favorite.

Harry: I lived in that house for thirty-one years, not once did anyone ever sing me "Happy Birthday."

Mel: *(Exasperated.)* Not true, Harry. You always had a birthday party. You always had a big cake . . .

Harry: I had parties, I had cakes, no one ever sang "Happy Birthday."

Mel: Alright, this year I'm going to hire a big chorus, Harry, and we're going to sing you "Happy Birthday."

Harry: Eleven years old I was wearing long pants. Fourteen I had a little mustache . . . At the movies I had to bring my birth certificate, they wanted to charge me adult prices . . .

Mel: I know, Harry. You grew up very fast.

Harry: Did you ever see Pearl's family album? There are no pictures of me as a boy. I skipped right over it. Thousands of pictures of you on bicycles, on ponies, in barber chairs . . . one picture of me in a 1938 Buick. I looked like Herbert Hoover.

Mel: I'm sorry, Harry.

Harry: I'm going to tell you something now, Mel. I never told this to anybody. I don't think you've got a brain for business. I don't think you know how to handle money. I don't think you can handle emotional problems. I think you're a child. A baby. A spoiled infant . . . And as God is my judge, many's the night I lay in bed envying you . . . Isn't that something? For a man in my position to envy a man in your position? . . . Is that something? What I have, you'll never have . . . But what you've got, I'd like to have just once . . . Just for an hour to see what it feels like to be the favorite.

Mel: What if I gave you a big kiss right on the mouth?

Harry: You kiss me, I'll break every bone in your body . . . I'll call you. Listen, forget what I said. I changed my mind. I don't want to be the favorite. Not if I have to be kissed by Jessie and Pauline.

The following is the monologue created from the previous scene.

HARRY (to MEL), age mid-40s to 60.
pp. 66–69 (SAMUEL FRENCH, INC.)

Hello, Mel. All right if I come in? I had some business and besides, I wanted to talk to you. How are you feeling? All right? I brought you some apples from the country. Wait'll you taste these. You always loved apples, I remember. Is Edna here? It's all right if she doesn't want to see me. I understand. The woman doesn't like me. It's all right. The whole world can't love you. I feel badly that it's my brother's wife, but that's what makes horse racing. I'm only staying two minutes. I wanted to deliver this in person and then I'll go. I have something a little more substantial than apples. It's a check for you and Edna. Go buy yourself a summer camp. Go. July and August take care of six hundred running noses. Have a good time. Your sisters and I contributed equally, fifty-fifty. I'm telling them about it tomorrow. Why would anyone want to run a summer camp? But if that gives you pleasure, then this gives me pleasure. Take the money, buy your crazy camp. It took me six weeks to decide to give it to you. Let me do this for you. Let me have the satisfaction of making you happy. You let everyone else do things for you! You let everyone else take care of you. Edna, Pearl, Pauline, Jessie. Everybody but me, your brother. Why am I always excluded from the family? I had to work when I was thirteen years old. I didn't have time to be the favorite. I'm not blaming you! It's only natural. If there are two brothers in the family and one is out working all day, the one who stays home is the favorite! I lived in that house for thirty-one years, not once did anyone ever sing me "Happy Birthday." I had parties, I had cakes, no one ever sang "Happy Birthday." Did you ever see Pearl's family album? There are no pictures of me as a boy. I skipped right over it. Thousands of pictures of you on bicycles, on ponies, in barber chairs...one picture of me in a 1938 Buick. I looked like Herbert Hoover. I'm going to tell you something now, Mel. I never told this to anybody. I don't think you've got a brain for business. I don't think you know how to handle money. I don't think you can handle emotional problems. I think you're a child. A baby. A spoiled infant. And as God is my judge, many's the night I lay in bed envying you. Isn't that something? For a man in my position to envy a man in your position? Is that something? What I have, you'll never have. But what you've got, I'd like to have just once... just for an hour to see what it feels like to be the favorite. You kiss me, I'll break every bone in your body. I'll call you. Listen, forget what I said. I changed my mind. I don't want to be the favorite. Not if I have to be kissed by Jessie and Pauline.

We have a Harry who is feeling very sorry for himself. His brother is still the center of attention. After all these years, he still takes stage center. So, Harry, you love him and you resent him. One feeling does not negate the other. Both feelings are very real. You sincerely want to help him. You wish, of course, that he did not require your help. For two reasons. One because you love him and wish him well and want only good things for him (although it would be nice if he would just fade into the wallpaper), and two because it bothers you to loan money when you feel that you probably will never see it again. And, of course, there is the power trip. You're the solvent one. You're the resourceful one. You don't ever have to go to anyone for help. You always were the serious working one. But he showed up in the snapshots! And today you are finally bringing it up and out. This is the first time you have ever mentioned your true feelings. What is it that you desperately need from Mel today? Remember Mel is the most important person in your life and today is the most important day in your life.

Do not play off bitterness. It is there and be aware of it, but play off what it is you are fighting for—love. Not acceptance or acknowledgment or approval. Those things are not strong enough choices for the actor to make. You want love—from Mel. If he loves you, he will listen to you, be sensitive to your needs and convey the love and he'll get better and he'll work hard and he'll be able to return your money to you one day soon and he'll start taking a lot of pictures of you and put them in the album to make up for the past. And he'll make sure that his wife loves you too.

STEAMBATH
by Bruce Jay Friedman

pp. 6–9 (SAMUEL FRENCH, INC.)

Oldtimer: That's really something, isn't it, when you sit down?

Tandy: It's a bitch.

Oldtimer: *(Rising, moves D.)* It don't bother me. When you're a young fellow, it bothers you, but then you develop a tough ass.

Tandy: I knew your beard got tough, but I didn't realize the other thing...

Oldtimer: It's true. I've had some wonderful sweats in my time.

Tandy: *(Taking off his shoes and socks.)* That right?

Oldtimer: Oh yeah. When the Polish came in, the union gave them a steambath down on Fulton Street. Nobody sweats like the Polish... What you're doing now?...

Tandy: *(Feeling himself.)* Yes?

Oldtimer: That's garbage. *(Sits on a small, folding stool, D. of L. wall.)* You're not sweatin'... I never exercised much, though. You see this area here. *(Pulls flesh in his lower back region.)* I always wanted to keep that nice and soft in case I got some spinal trouble. So the needle could go right in. I know guys, athletes, they're so hard you can't stick a needle into them... I figure it's a good idea to keep it soft back there. *(They sit a while longer,* TANDY *trying to read his magazine.)* How do you feel about heart attacks?

Tandy: I'm against them.

Oldtimer: Lots of people are. I'll say this for them, though. They don't mark you. On the outside. They leave you clean as a whistle. That's more than you can say for a gall bladder.

Tandy: I agree with you there.

Oldtimer: I seen guys get cut up for ulcers they got bellies look like the map of downtown Newark, New Jersey... People have always been a little too rough on heart attacks. The heart attack has always gotten a raw deal. *(An unattractive* *young* FELLOW *spits on the floor from behind the upper tier of the R. pillar.)* Hey, I saw that.

Bieberman: *(From behind the pillar.)* What?

(TANDY *rises and looks behind the pillar.)*

Oldtimer: You know what. What you did. Expectorating like that. That's disgusting.

Bieberman: What's wrong? It's a natural fluid.

Oldtimer: You're a disgrace. You got to watch him like a hawk. Probably farting back there, too. (TANDY, *starting to sit back down, sits up and moves away.)* Who the hell would ever know in a steambath?

Bieberman: I heard that. I'm not farting.

Oldtimer: Congratulations...

Bieberman: My generation doesn't do that.

Oldtimer: Your generation can kiss my ass. *(To* TANDY *who is putting on a towel found on tier R. of pillar.)* What's your line, young fella?

Tandy: I just quit my job. I was teaching art appreciation over at the Police Academy.

Oldtimer: That right? What the hell... I guess you got to do something. (TANDY *sits back down on the lower slab.)* Police, eh? Ever notice how you never get any trouble from the good people?

Tandy: Well, that's for sure.

Oldtimer: It's the bad ones you got to watch. You run the bad ones off the street that'll be the end of your crime. You got a son?

Tandy: No, I've got a little girl.

Oldtimer: You got a son, I hope he's a drunk. That'll keep him off drugs. He starts in on that dope stuff you can kiss his ass good-bye. *(From behind the R. pillar there is the loud sound of* SOMEONE *sucking on an orange.)* What's that guy doing now?

Tandy: *(Going to see, L. of pillar.)* Looks like he's eating an orange. *(Returning to the slab.)*

Oldtimer: Yeah, but what's he *doing?*

Tandy: *(Goes back to see, narrowly missing being hit by a shower of seeds.)* He's spitting out the pits.

Oldtimer: Stupid mother. *(Shouting to* BIEBERMAN.) Hey, knock it off, will you?

Bieberman: Well, what am I supposed to do with them?

Oldtimer: Hold them in your hand. Swallow them. Shove them up your ass, what do I care. Just don't spit them out. Didn't you ever hear of a person tripping on pits? (TANDY *sits back down on the slab.*) They get some crowd in here. He's probably a fag, too.

Two Young Men: (*From behind the pillar, on the lower tier, speaking in unison.*) No, we're the fags.

Oldtimer: I beg your pardon. (*More or less to himself, as* TANDY *goes to look.*) I knew there were fags in here. (*To* TANDY.) You broke a sweat yet?

Tandy: (*Sitting back down.*) I can feel one coming.

Oldtimer: You know what would go down really well now? A nice cool brew. I drank a lot of beer in my time. One thing I'll say for myself is that I never gained weight. I gained bloat. The trouble is—bloat weighs a lot, too. Most people don't realize that. Bloat can kill you.

(*An attendant, to be known as* GOTTLIEB, *enters U. with two cold glasses of beer on a tray. He wears a waiter's red jacket, with a black bow tie clipped to the lapel with gray T-shirt and pants. He gives one glass to the* OLDTIMER *and the other to* TANDY *and exits.*)

Tandy: What do you do?

Oldtimer: (*Rising.*) I done a lot of things. In my late years I took to hackin' a cab. I was terrific once I got my daily icebreaker. But until then I wasn't fit to live with. That's how I had my crash—worried sick about getting my icebreaker. I come on the job at eight in the morning, it's twelve o'clock noon I still hadn't nailed a fare. I'm so upset I drive right through a furrier's window. Into the beaver pelts. And I wound up with the car radio in my stomach. And I mean it was in my stomach, too. I had folk music coming out of my asshole. So that was it.

The following is the monologue created from the previous scene.

OLDTIMER (to TANDY), age 50s or older.
pp. 6–9 (SAMUEL FRENCH, INC.)

That's really something, isn't it, when you sit down! It don't bother me. When you're a young fellow, it bothers you, but then you develop a tough ass. It's true.

I've had some wonderful sweats in my time. When the Polish came in, the union gave them a steambath down on Fulton Street. Nobody sweats like the Polish. What you're doing now? That's garbage! You're not sweatin'. I never exercised much, though. You see this area here. (*Pulls flesh in his lower back region.*) I always wanted to keep that nice and soft in case I got some spinal trouble. So the needle could go right in. I know guys, athletes, they're so hard you can't stick a needle into them. I figure it's a good idea to keep it soft back there.

How do you feel about heart attacks? Lots of people are against them. I'll say this for them, though. They don't mark you. On the outside. They leave you clean as a whistle. That's more than you can say for a gallbladder. I seen guys get cut up for ulcers they got bellies look like the map of downtown Newark, New Jersey. People have always been a little too rough on heart attacks. The heart attack has always gotten a raw deal.

(*An unattractive young fellow spits on the floor near him.*) Hey, I saw that. You know what. What you did. Expectorating like that. That's disgusting. You're a disgrace. (*To* TANDY.) You got to watch him like a hawk. Probably farting back there, too. Who the hell would ever know in a steambath? (*To other fellow.*) Your generation can kiss my ass. (*To* TANDY.) So, you quit your job teaching art appreciation over at the Police Academy. What the hell. I guess you got to do something. Police, eh? Ever notice how you never get any trouble from the good people? It's the bad ones you got to watch. You run the bad ones off the street and that'll be the end of your crime. You got a son? You got a son, I hope he's a drunk. That'll keep him off drugs. He starts in on that dope stuff you can kiss his ass good-bye.

What's that guy doing now? Looks like he's eating an orange. He's spitting out the pits. Stupid mother. Hey, knock it off, will you? Hold the pits in your hand. Swallow them. Shove them up your ass, what do I care. Just don't spit them out. Didn't you ever hear of a person tripping on pits? They get some crowd in here. He's probably a fag, too.

You broke a sweat yet? You know what would go down

really well now? A nice cool brew. I drank a lot of beer in my time. One thing I'll say for myself is that I never gained weight. I gained bloat. The trouble is—bloat weighs a lot, too. Most people don't realize that. Bloat can kill you.

I done a lot of things. In my late years I took to hackin' a cab. I was terrific once I got my daily icebreaker. But until then I wasn't fit to live with. That's how I had my crash—worried sick about my icebreaker. I come on the job at eight in the morning, it's twelve o'clock noon I still hadn't nailed a fare. I'm so upset I drive right through a furrier's window. Into the beaver pelts. And I wound up with the car radio in my stomach. And I mean it was in my stomach, too. I had folk music coming out of my asshole. So that was it!

You're an oldtimer. You've been around. You've done a lot of things in a lot of bars around the world. Tandy is younger and has just arrived in this steambath, which you have a feeling is the last place you will ever have any kind of social confrontations. You're opening up to him. Talking about your past experiences and beliefs. He has a look about him that makes him seem like an appealing person to talk to. You need to talk to someone here and everyone else seems to be a misfit.

In this monologue there is nothing in the dialogue to indicate a strong emotional reach-out and need. Therefore, it cannot be considered to be the perfect monologue.

However, it is so outrageous, funny, and dear that you, the actor bringing your humanity and strong choices, can create a very powerful vehicle to showcase yourself. You must make choices as to your need for Tandy to listen to you, care about you, indeed save you. This may not be what the playwright had in mind. But what the playwright had in mind usually has little to do with the actor during a monologue audition. Make it work for you. But make sure that you make life-and-death choices and that Tandy is the most important person in your life. When you know that the character is really dead, still make choices for him to be fighting for the rest of your life.

STEAMBATH
by Bruce Jay Friedman

pp. 12–16 (Samuel French, Inc.)

Meredith: *(Kneeling on slab.)* Listen, if you were with the cops, could you tell me exactly where to kick someone so that he's temporarily paralyzed and can't rape you—yet at the same time doesn't feel you're an insensitive person...?

Tandy: We stayed away from that stuff in the art department....

Meredith: Well, I have to move out of the city anyway. All the men you meet here insist on dressing you up in something before they make love to you—garter belts, stiletto heels, *(Demonstrates.)* earmuffs, Luftwaffe costumes. Right in the middle of this cultural wonderland, I spend all my time dressing up for weirdos, I don't need that. I could've gotten that in St. Louis....

Tandy: What really puzzles me is that I am able to talk to you so easily.

Meredith: What do you mean?

Tandy: *(Sitting beside her.)* Well, until recently, I had a great deal of trouble talking to yellow-haired girls. I felt I had to talk to them in verse or something...maybe wear special gloves. But apparently I've gotten over that.

Meredith: You're so nice. I love meeting a nice new person like you. But look, I don't want to get involved.

Tandy: Involved?

Meredith: I just can't go through with that again....I've had that this year...the phone calls...My skin....For what it does to my skin alone, it's not worth it....Look, I just don't have the strength for another affair....Maybe around Labor Day....If it's worth anything, it'll be good then, too....Will you call me then?

Tandy: *(Thinks awhile.)* I'll give you a ring.

Meredith: You're not angry, are you?

107

Tandy: I'm not angry.

Meredith: It's got nothing to do with you personally... you seem like a very sensual person.

Oldtimer: There's a terrible stink in here. And I got a pretty good idea who's responsible for it.

Bieberman: *(From L. of L. pillar.)* I haven't done a thing recently.

Oldtimer: You'll never convince me of that. Whatever you're doing, cut it out—for my sake, for the sake of this steambath and for the sake of human decency.

Bieberman: I'm just sitting here, being natural, being myself...

Oldtimer: That's what it is? Natural... that's what you've got to stop. (BIEBERMAN *rises, crossing back to R. pillar.*)

Tandy: *(To MEREDITH.)* Listen, what do you think of this place?

Meredith: I like it.

Tandy: Notice anything peculiar about it?

Meredith: It smells a little funny.

Oldtimer: It sure as hell does.

Bieberman: *(Turning from ladder, crosses down to TANDY, L. of the pillar.)* I haven't done a thing. I've been doing a crossword puzzle. What's a six-letter word that means little red spikes of corn?

Oldtimer: How about "giggie"? Used in a sentence, it goes: "Up your giggie."

Bieberman: Lovely. *(Climbs back to upper tier of the R. pillar.)*

(The BROKER *appears U. carrying a folding convas stool. As he sits D., the lights darken and a small screen drops in. Stock quotations flash across the screen as they do in a brokerage office. The* BROKER *turns to watch them. He wears a T-shirt, boxer shorts and slippers.)*

Broker: They put that in for me.

Tandy: *(Moving D. to watch the screen.)* How's the market?

Broker: Lousy. If you own good stocks. When I went into this business, I had one piece of advice for every one of my customers: Put your money in good stuff. Stay away from shit. That's what you want, find yourself another broker. I don't touch it. So what happens in the last five years? The good stuff lays there, shit goes right through the roof. Some of my customers, they went to other brokers, they bought shit, they made fortunes....

Meredith: *(Very trusting.)* Maybe the good stuff will improve. If it's really and truly good.

Broker: Nah... it's too late for that... *(Gets up, places the stool L. of the R. pillar and exits U. The screen flies out and the lights come back up.)*

Tandy: That's the kind of thing I was talking about....

Meredith: *(Moving to TANDY.)* What do you mean?

Tandy: A guy like that... in here... watching stocks... it's strange. *(Moves L., searching overhead for screen.)*

Meredith: I just wish the numbers wouldn't go by so fast. You hardly have any time to enjoy them. Am I wrong or have you been doing pretty well lately?

Tandy: I'm doing fine. I got a divorce. I quit the police academy. I'm writing a novel about Charlemagne. And I just got involved in a charity. Helping brain-damaged welders. I was looking for a charity and that's the one I picked. They send out a terrific brochure. There are an awful lot of them... welders... with brain damage... and they're really grateful when you help them. You should see the looks on some of those welders' faces. Could break your heart.... I've been doing pretty well... I'm real close to my ten-year-old daughter.

Meredith: *(Sitting back down on slab.)* You have a ten-year-old daughter?

Tandy: Oh yeah, we just got back from Vegas.

Meredith: How did she like it?

Tandy: *(Sitting down, L. of MEREDITH.)* Well, she thought little girls were allowed to gamble out there. She insisted that somewhere in Vegas there were slot machines that little girls were allowed to play. Well, I read that you shouldn't disabuse a child of its fantasies, so I went along with the gag. So we spent four days looking for those special slot machines. Finally, at the airport, I told her that little girls were allowed to play the airport slots just before they got on the plane. She said, "I told you, Daddy." We got very close on that trip. So I've been doing pretty well lately....

Meredith: Listen, you don't think—

Tandy: What? What?

Meredith: *(Moving D.)* All I can remember is that Sheila and I were buying skirts at Paraphernalia. Then we went back to our high-rise apartment on 84th Street and, oh, yes, the Gristede's delivery boy was waiting behind the drapes, with a crazy look on his face, holding a blunt instrument. . . . (*Sits back down next to* TANDY.)

Tandy: I was in my favorite restaurant, eating some Chinese food. I ordered up a double order of Won Shih pancakes . . .

Meredith: You don't think?

Tandy: We're dead? Is that what you were going to say? That's what I was going to say. That's what we are. The second I said it, I knew it. Dead? Just like that? Christ! Bam? (*Moves L.*)

Meredith: (*Rising.*) I had it pictured an entirely different way.

Tandy: What's that?

Meredith: (*Kneeling on slab.*) Being dead. I thought dying meant that you'd have to spend every day of your life at a different Holiday Inn. Then I decided it was seeing "So Proudly We Hail" with Veronica Lake over and over for the rest of time. In a place where there were no Mounds bars.

(*A voice is heard:* "*Goobers, Raisinettes, popcorn. And no Mounds bars.*")

Tandy: Don't pay any attention. Somebody's kidding around.

Meredith: No Mounds bars.

Tandy: I don't know about you, but I'm not accepting this.

Meredith: What do you mean?

Tandy: (*Crossing to his clothes, R. of R. pillar.*) I don't like the whole way it was done. Bam. Dead. Just like that. Just like you're a schmuck or something.

Meredith: (*Moving to him.*) What are you going to do?

Tandy: (*Putting on shirt and shoes.*) I'll do something. Don't worry. I'm a doer. If you had any idea of the agony I went through to change my life around you'd see why I'm so pissed off. To be picked off like this when I haven't even started to enjoy the good stuff.

Meredith: Well, how about me? I just had my first orgasm.

Tandy: (*Stops what he's doing.*) Just now?

Meredith: No. While I was watching the David Frost Show. I was all alone, eating some Whip and Chill and I got this funny feeling.

Tandy: I'll tell you right now, I'm not going along with it. Not now. Not when I'm just getting off the ground. Another time, later on, they want me to be dead, fine. Not now. Uh-uh. (*Moving L.*)

Meredith: (*Crossing to* TANDY.)   I feel exactly the same way.

How can I die? I haven't even bought any vinyl bust
harnesses. Alexander's Mod Shop is expecting them any day.
No, I absolutely can't die. Is there something you can do?

The following is the monologue created from the previous
scene.

MEREDITH (to TANDY), age 20s.
pp. 12–16 (SAMUEL FRENCH, INC.)

Listen, if you were with the cops, could you tell me
exactly where to kick someone so that he's temporarily
paralyzed and can't rape you—yet at the same time doesn't
feel you're an insensitive person?

I have to move out of the city. All the men you meet
here insist on dressing you up in something before they
make love to you. Garter belts, stiletto heels, earmuffs,
Luftwaffe costumes. Right in the middle of this cultural
wonderland, I spend all my time dressing up for weirdos, I
don't need that. I could've gotten that in St. Louis.

You're so nice. I love meeting a nice new person like
you. But look, I don't want to get involved. I just can't go
through with that again. I've had that this year. The phone
calls . . . my skin . . . for what it does to my skin alone, it's
not worth it. . . . Look, I just don't have the strength for
another affair. . . . Maybe around Labor Day. . . . If it's worth
anything, it'll be good then too. Will you call me then?
You're not angry, are you? It's got nothing to do with you
personally . . . you seem like a very sensual person. . . . All I
can remember is that Sheila and I were buying skirts at
Paraphernalia. Then we went back to our high-rise apartment on Eighty-fourth Street and, oh, yes, the Gristede's
delivery boy was waiting behind the drapes, with a crazy
look on his face, holding a blunt instrument. . . . You don't
think . . . we're dead? I had it pictured an entirely different way. Being dead. I thought dying meant that you'd
have to spend every day of your life at a different Holiday
Inn. Then I decided it was seeing *So Proudly We Hail* with
Veronica Lake over and over for the rest of time. In a place
where there were no Mounds bars. . . . I just had my first

orgasm. Not just now! While I was watching the David Frost Show. I was all alone, eating some Whip and Chill and I got this funny feeling. . . . How can I die? I haven't even bought any vinyl bust harnesses. Alexander's Mod Shop is expecting them any day. No, I absolutely can't die. Is there something you can do?

This is a sweet, ditzy nonmental giant of a young woman who just goes on allowing words to come as they may. Her values, well, what can we say? She's simple. However, be careful not to fall into the trap and play her stupid, as unoccupied as her mind appears to be. You as Meredith do not know that you are not about to be accepted as a member of Mensa! You live your life, you have your needs, your desires, you like breastplates! But you also want and desire what everyone else does. Love, happiness, peace, and so on. And your very life is involved here. Fight for it from Tandy. You are making discoveries about what might have happened to you. You are dealing with the possibility of your own death. Make everything appear more important than it seems to be on the page. All of these things *are* very important to Meredith. They might not be to you but they are to her. Find the Meredith in you so that you will better understand how important these things can be.

This is one of the pieces for which I have to explain to actors that acting means playing parts that are *nothing* like the way we are. Acting is playing a character far removed from our own private sensibilities, who say and do things that we would *never* say or do (or so we think).

This is the kind of monologue to use when auditioning for the "dumb blond" that male playwrights used to love to write. Have fun with it.

You may substitute *So Proudly We Hail* with a film that you hated or found boring; Mounds Bars with your favorite candy bar; the David Frost Show with a contemporary television show, and Alexander's Mod Shop with a boutique or department store of your choice.

STEAMBATH
by Bruce Jay Friedman

pp. 14–25 (Samuel French, Inc.)

Tandy: I'm doing fine. I got a divorce. I quit the police academy. I'm writing a novel about Charlemagne. And I just got involved in a charity. Helping brain-damaged welders. I was looking for a charity and that's the one I picked. They send out a terrific brochure. There are an awful lot of them ... welders ... with brain damage ... and they're really grateful when you help them. You should see the looks on some of those welders' faces. Could break your heart. . . . I've been doing pretty well ... I'm real close to my ten-year-old daughter.

Meredith: *(Sitting back down on slab.)* You have a ten-year-old daughter?

Tandy: Oh yeah, we just got back from Vegas.

Meredith: How did she like it?

Tandy: *(Sitting down, L. of MEREDITH.)* Well, she thought little girls were allowed to gamble out there. She insisted that somewhere in Vegas there were slot machines that little girls were allowed to play. Well, I read that you shouldn't disabuse a child of its fantasies, so I went along with the gag. So we spent four days looking for those special slot machines. Finally, at the airport, I told her that little girls were allowed to play the airport slots just before they got on the plane. She said, "I told you, Daddy." We got very close on that trip. So I've been doing pretty well lately. . . .

Meredith: Listen, you don't think—

Tandy: What? What?

Meredith: *(Moving D.)* All I can remember is that Sheila and I were buying skirts at Paraphernalia. Then we went back to our high-rise apartment on 84th Street and, oh, yes, the Gristede's delivery boy was waiting behind the drapes, with

113

a crazy look on his face, holding a blunt instrument. . . . *(Sits back down next to* TANDY.)

Tandy: I was in my favorite restaurant, eating some Chinese food. I ordered up a double order of Won Shih pancakes . . .

Meredith: You don't think?

Tandy: We're dead? Is that what you were going to say? That's what I was going to say. That's what we are. The second I said it, I knew it. Dead? Just like that? Christ! Bam *(Moves L.)*

Meredith: *(Rising.)* I had it pictured an entirely different way.

Tandy: What's that?

Meredith: *(Kneeling on slab.)* Being dead. I thought dying meant that you'd have to spend every day of your life at a different Holiday Inn. Then I decided it was seeing "So Proudly We Hail" with Veronica Lake over and over for the rest of time. In a place where there were no Mounds bars.

(A voice is heard: "Goobers, Raisinettes, popcorn. And no Mounds bars.")

Tandy: Don't pay any attention. Somebody's kidding around.

Meredith: No Mounds bars.

Tandy: I don't know about you, but I'm not accepting this.

Meredith: What do you mean?

Tandy: *(Crossing to his clothes, R. of R. pillar.)* I don't like the whole way it was done. Bam. Dead. Just like that. Just like you're a schmuck or something.

Meredith: *(Moving to him.)* What are you going to do?

Tandy: *(Putting on shirt and shoes.)* I'll do something. Don't worry. I'm a doer. If you had any idea of the agony I went through to change my life around you'd see why I'm so pissed off. To be picked off like this when I haven't even started to enjoy the good stuff.

Meredith: Well, how about me? I just had my first orgasm.

Tandy: *(Stops what he's doing.)* Just now?

Meredith: No. While I was watching the David Frost Show. I was all alone, eating some Whip and Chill and I got this funny feeling.

Tandy: I'll tell you right now, I'm not going along with it. Not now. Not when I'm just getting off the ground. Another time, later on, they want me to be dead, fine. Not now. Uh-uh. *(Moving L.)*

Meredith: *(Crossing to* TANDY.) I feel exactly the same way. How can I die? I haven't even bought any vinyl bust harnesses. Alexander's Mod Shop is expecting them any day. No, I absolutely can't die. Is there something you can do?

Tandy: I'll check around, see if I can find out something. *(They exit U. The* BROKER *has entered U. L. He stands R. of the L. pillar, takes a shot of whiskey from a small bottle on the U. R. shelf, and begins to work a hand exerciser he takes from the D. shelf.)*

Oldtimer: *(Reading newspaper.)* Says here they got a new gas. One gallon of it'll wipe out an entire enemy country...

Broker: They got more than that. They got another one—just one drop in the water supply and the whole continent starts vomiting. *(Sits R. of pillar.)*

Oldtimer: *(Sniffing.)* They could bottle the smell around here, they don't need any gas. You hear that up there?

Bieberman: *(From behind the R. pillar.)* I'm not doing anything. I'm working on my toes.

Oldtimer: I knew it, the sonofabitch. What are you doing to them?

Bieberman: Trimming down the nails.

Oldtimer: In here? This is where you picked? Cut it out, will you, you slob, you're trying my patience.

(The TWO YOUNG MEN *move D. on the U. R. tier of R. pillar. They sit preparing pieces of fabric for tie-dyeing.* BIEBERMAN *has stretched out with his crossword puzzle U. L. tier of the pillar.)*

Tandy: *(Entering U. and coming D. R. of the R. pillar.)* Can I see you a second, Oldtimer, in private? *(Takes stool from L. of pillar and sets it D. of the shower.)*

Oldtimer: *(Taking stool from L. wall, joins him.)* What's on your mind, fella? Having trouble breathin'? *(Demonstrating.)* Suck it in through your mouth awhile.

Tandy: I was sitting over there with this girl...

Oldtimer: *(Lasciviously.)* The one with them chitty chitty bang bangs?

Tandy: That's the one. *(Sits on stool.)*

Oldtimer: Don't let her get hold of your liverwurst. They get an armlock on that they never let go. *(Sits L. of* TANDY.*)*

Tandy: I got the idea we were dead. And she agrees with me. Now I can take the dead part. That doesn't scare me. I get older, a little tired, fine. I even thought maybe later on, things go smoothly, maybe I'll knock myself off. Make it simple. But the timing's all wrong now. I'm just getting off the ground. I'm in the middle of writing an historical novel. Right in the fucking middle. (I don't talk this way in the book.) It's about Charlemagne. I've got a great new girl friend cooks me shish kebab. Bryn Mawr girl. And she still cooks shish kebab. Doesn't bother her a bit. And I never think about Wendy.

Oldtimer: Wendy?

Tandy: *(Getting up and moving R.)* My ex-wife. Wendy Tandy. Jesus, I just realized, she was Wendy Hilton. I turned her into Wendy Tandy. I probably blew the whole marriage right there. She never went for that name. Can't say that I blame her. Anyway I don't think about her anymore. Weeks at a time. She could be out fucking the whole Royal Canadian Mounties, I don't give it a thought. I forgive her. She's a little weak. It's got nothing to do with me. So, you see, I'm really just starting a wonderful new chapter of my life. And along comes this death number—I thought maybe you could help me. . . .

Oldtimer: I hardly know what to say to you, fella. You come at me like a ten-foot wave.

Tandy: Is there a guy in charge? Somebody I can talk to. E. G. Marshall? Walter Pidgeon?

Oldtimer: There's a guy comes in here. I see him I'll point him out.

Tandy: *(Sitting back down on stool.)* Thanks. You're not a bad skate. When we get out of this, maybe we can pal around together.

Oldtimer: You probably smell the sea on me. Before I took up hackin' I worked the China Coast for seventeen years. Me and my friend Ollie were the most widely respected duo west of Macao. We'd get ourselves a couple of juki juki girls, take 'em up on deck and do a little missionary work with 'em anchored in front of Bruce Wong's Monkey Meat Shop in Hong Kong Harbor. They arrested Ollie for abusing himself into the holy water fountain at the Merchant Seaman's Chapel. He died in irons and I lost the best friend I ever had. . . . *(He takes his stool U. and sits D. of the pillar.)*

Meredith: *(Enters and kneels R. of* TANDY. *She is now carrying* *the towel that had been draped over her shoulders.*) What did the old man say?

Tandy: (*Disturbed by her nudity.*) He said there's a fellow around who seems to be in charge. That he'd point him out to me. Listen, how do you feel?

Meredith: I didn't mind being nude, if that's what you mean. I just don't attribute that much importance to it.

Tandy: I know that. I can tell.

Meredith: I wouldn't want to go out and do splits or anything.

Tandy: Who asked you to do splits? Is that what you think I want—splits?

Meredith: I just like to be nude sometimes. It's very tranquil.

Tandy: You see, that's where I really got a bum steer. The fellow who first taught me about sex—very smart guy, been all over, a Socialist—he told me, "Remember one thing, kid, women feel uncomfortable about being nude." So for a long time I went around covering up nude girls. They'd say, "What the hell are you doing?" and I'd say, "C'mon, I know you're uncomfortable." And I was wrong. I covered up some gorgeous women. . . . (*Takes her hand and holds it.*)

(*A bearded* PUERTO RICAN ATTENDANT *enters U. R. and crosses to a mop and bucket U. R. He is dressed in white work pants and undershirt, with a rolled handkerchief tied around his neck and a black beret on his head. He wrings out the mop in the wringer on the bucket and crosses D. L. to the sink, as the* BROKER *rolls the bucket along after him. The* PUERTO RICAN ATTENDANT *sings as he goes. Placing the mop against the wall below the sink, he stops singing as if finished and there is a smattering of applause which he stops with a gesture. After a big finish, he gestures for applause and says, "Thank you, music lovers." He turns to the upright electric console against the U. wall of the alcove and rolls it D. As he touches it, a screen on the console lights up.*)

Oldtimer: (*Rising, signaling to* TANDY.) Psssst.

Tandy: (*Gesturing toward* ATTENDANT.) Him? (OLDTIMER *acknowledges correctness with a wink.*) You sure?

Oldtimer: Yup. . . .

Tandy: (*To* MEREDITH.) He says that's the fellow in charge.

Meredith: He's cute. (TANDY *and* MEREDITH *move to the R. pillar and sit D.*)

P. R. Attendant: (*To console.*) Hiya, baby. (*As he talks to the console, it answers in short series of electronic sounding bleeps. During the conversation he removes the wringer from the bucket, dumps the water into the sink, refills it and adds soap, finally replacing the wringer.*) San Diego Freeway. (*Bleep.*) . . . All right, first thing, I want that Pontiac moving south past Hermosa Beach to crash into the light blue Eldorado coming the other way. (*Bleep.*) Make it a head-on collision (*Bleep.*) . . . the guy in the Chevy—his wife's got her ass out the window—it's the only way they get their kicks (*Bleep.*)—they're going to jump the rail into the oncoming lane, fuck up a liquor salesman in a tan Cougar. No survivors. . . . (*Longer series of bleeps.*) All right, what's-his-name—(*Bleep.*) Perez, (*Bleep.*) the Puerto Rican schmuck from the Bronx. The one who says, "My wife and I—we are married forty years. We are born on the same hill. There can be no trouble." He comes home tonight, I want her screwing her brother. (*Bleep.*) Perez walks in, goes crazy, starts foaming at the mouth, the other tenants in the building tie him to a radiator. . . . (*Longer series of bleeps.*) All right, the guy from St. Louis (*Bleep.*) . . . bedspread salesman . . . adopted all those Korean kids. (*Bleep.*) Him they pick up in the men's room of the Greyhound Bus Terminal. Grabbing some truckdriver's schvonce. (*Bleep.*) They ask around, find out he's been doing it for years. . . . The kids get shipped back to Korea. (*Bleep.*) Now, here's one I like . . . The screenwriter flying out to Beverly Hills. Coming on with the broads. Here's what happens. Over Denver, a stewardess throws a dart in his eye. No doctor on board. He has to go all the way to Los Angeles like that. . . . (*Longer series of bleeps. He checks gauges and pipes D. L.*) The hooker—(*Bleep.*) little fat one (*Bleep.*) —been peddling her ass in Barcelona for three years—took on 4,000 sailors—she's saved up a few bucks, she's gonna go straight. Get ready. This is rough. (*Bleep.*) I want her found in a dirt pit on Montauk Highway. And if the parents really carry on, I mean really piss and moan, then go after the sister, too, the homely one. Give her an ear infection. (*Longer bleep. Sitting on the edge of the sink, he takes out a pocket knife and cleans his fingernails.*) Now, the producer up in New Haven . . . (*Bleep.*)

Never had a hit. Doing a $750,000 musical... the whole show depends on the female star. *(Bleep.)* All right. A police dog gets loose in the theater and bites her tits off. *(Bleep.)* The understudy is scared shit, but she goes on anyway. Bombsville. Next day, the guy gets out of the business. ... *(Bleeps and the console light goes off.)* Wait a minute. *(Console light back on.)* I got an idea. Back to the Freeway. *(Long bleep.)* That guy whose radiator boiled over... on the side of the road, saw the whole thing. Thought he got away clean. He gets knocked unconscious by the bare-assed broad. Never knew what hit him. That's all for now. *(He takes laundry basket from under sink, and crosses behind L. pillar.)*

Tandy: You sure that's the guy?

Oldtimer: That's him all right. He runs the show.

Tandy: What's his name?

Oldtimer: Morty.

Tandy: A Puerto Rican guy? Morty?

Oldtimer: It's Spanish. *(Pronouncing name with Spanish inflection.)* Mawwrrr-teee.

Tandy: *(To* MEREDITH.) He's sure that's the fellow in charge.

Meredith: Well, if he isn't, he certainly has a rich imagination.

Tandy: You say he hangs around here?

Oldtimer: All the time. He comes and goes.

(ATTENDANT returns to sink, puts basket down on chair, turns to console again. His voice is softer now. He sits on the edge of sink, takes off shoe and puts it back on.)

P. R. Attendant: OK, *(The screen again lights up.)* the other side of the coin. *(Bleep.)* That's the kid in the hospital in Trenton, beautiful kid, works for Carvel's. *(Bleep.)* Got his foot shot off in a stick-up. *(Bleep.)* The night nurse comes in, jerks him off under the covers. Lovely broad, little old, really knows what she's doing. ...*(Bleep.)* Give Canada a little more rain. ...*(Longer series of bleeps.)* That Indian tribe outside of Caracas. *(Bleep.)* Sick little guys, they ain't got a hundred bucks between 'em. ... Government doesn't give a shit. CBS moves in, shoots a jungle series there, throws a lot of money around. ...*(Bleep.)* The old lady with the parakeet, flies out the window, flies back in. ...*(Bleep.)* Wellesley girl, parents got a lot of dough—she's sittin' on a

ledge—36th floor of the Edison Hotel. (*Bleep.*) A cop crawls
out after her, tells her she's a pain in the ass. They go back
in, watch a hockey game on TV. (*Bleep.*) And clean up that
garbage in the lobby. It's disgusting. (*Longer series of
bleeps.*) That spade they beat up at Chicago Police head-
quarters. Got a landing strip for a head. (*Bleep.*) All right,
kill the cop who roughed him up—and then send the spade
over to Copenhagen for a vacation. (*Bleep.*) At least three
months. I don't know who picks up the tab. He's got a
cousin in the music business. Records for Decca.... All
right, that's enough good stuff. (*Crossing to exit U.*)

Voice: (*From above, fills the steambath.*) You need one more.

P. R. Attendant: Christ, I'm exhausted. Uhh...Put bigger
bath towels in all the rooms at the Tel Aviv Hilton Hotel.

Voice: Terrific!

P. R. Attendant: You kidding, buddy...? (*Exits.*)

Meredith: I liked him much more the second time.

Tandy: He's got some style. Who's he think he is?

Oldtimer: (*Rises, moves D. to shower, wipes hands on rag.*)
God.

Tandy: (*Moving to* OLDTIMER.) You believe that?

(*The* TWO YOUNG MEN, *having come down, stretch out on
towels on the floor, leaning against the D. R. wall.*)

Oldtimer: I'm not saying yes and I'm not saying no. I been
around and I seen a lot of strange things in my time. I once
stood in an Algerian pissoir urinal and watched the head of a
good friend of mine come rolling up against my size 12
moccasins like a bowling ball. Cut right off at the neck. He'd
gotten into a little scuffle with some Ghurkas. May have
called one of them a fag. Didn't know there aren't any fag
Ghurkas.

Two Young Men: That's what you think.

Tandy: (*Moving D. L.*) Well, what the hell are we supposed to
do, just stay here?

Broker: (*Going to* TANDY.) There's nothing that great out there.
The market stinks. You don't make a quarter unless you're in
pork bellies. That ain't investing. (*Returns to sit L. pillar.*)

Tandy: I'm not going along with this. For Christ's sakes, I'm in
the middle of writing an historical novel. About Charlemagne.
I got all that research to do. So far I've been going on

instinct. What the hell do I know about Charlemagne? But the book feels good.

Meredith: *(Rises.)* And I've got an appointment at the beauty parlor. To get a Joan of Arc haircut. And Sheila and I are going to make little plastic surrealistic doodads and sell them to boutiques.

Tandy: I'll get us out of this. *(Indicating D. R. door.)* Did you try the door?

Meredith: No, why?

Tandy: Don't try it. I'm pretty sure it doesn't open. If I find out for sure I'll get claustrophobia. . . . Is there another way out? What's this door? *(Referring to second door, D. L.)*

Oldtimer: You go through there.

Tandy: When's that?

Oldtimer: Hard to say. . . . We had a guy, a baker, he put him in there.

Tandy: What did he do?

Oldtimer: Not much. Beat the Puerto Rican in armwrestling.

Broker: Had a little trouble with his baking though. Everything used to burn up on him. Pastries, cupcakes . . . meat-pies . . .

Tandy: Don't tell me about cupcakes now . . . no cupcakes. When he puts you in there, does he let you out? *(The OTHERS laugh. The OLDTIMER gestures as if to say, "Are you kidding?")* And that's it, the two doors?

Oldtimer: That's it. That's the whole cheesecake.

Tandy: *(Runs to the D. R. door, tries it. It doesn't open. Tries a little harder. Still won't.)* About the way I figured. I'll get us out of here, don't worry. You with me? *(Sitting D. R. of* MEREDITH *D. of R. pillar.)*

Meredith: Are you serious? Of course. But you haven't said how.

(The TWO YOUNG MEN *stretch out on their towels D. R.)*

Tandy: I'll get us out. You'll find I do most things well. Of course, I have never been able to get out to Kennedy Airport. On my own. I can get near it, but never really in it. The Van Wyck Highway scene really throws me.

Meredith: You're sort of inconsistent, aren't you?

Tandy: You noticed that, eh? I admit it. I've got wonderful qualities, but getting out to airports is not one of them.

Don't worry, though, I'll get us out of here. By sheer strength of will and determination. I believe I can do anything if I really put my mind to it. I've always felt that even if I had a fatal illness, with an army of diseased phagocytes coursing through my body in triumph... *(TWO YOUNG MEN get up, snap their towels in disgust and disappear behind the R. pillar.)* if I really decided to, I could reverse the course of those phagocytes and push them the hell back where they belong....

Meredith: The world admires that kind of determination.

Tandy: You're damned right.

Meredith: What if we really are dead, though?

Tandy: I know. I've been trying not to think about it. No more toast. No more clams. Clams oregano.

Meredith: No more playing with Mr. Skeffington.

Tandy: Mr. Skeffington? Wait a minute, don't tell me. That's your cat.

Meredith: Yes.

Tandy: How can you compare that in seriousness to the things I'm talking about? I'm talking about big stuff. No more being under the covers. No more airline stewardesses... *Newsweek*...Jesus, no more *Newsweek*. Wait a minute, I'll get this straightened out right now.

The following is the monologue created from the previous scene.

TANDY (to MEREDITH), age 30s to 50.
pp. 14–25 (SAMUEL FRENCH, INC.)

I'm doing fine. I got a divorce. I quit the police academy. I'm writing a novel about Charlemagne. And I just got involved in a charity. Helping brain-damaged welders. I was looking for a charity and that's the one I picked. They send out a terrific brochure. There are an awful lot of them... welders... with brain damage... and they're really grateful when you help them. You should see the looks on some of those welders' faces. Could break your heart.... I've been doing pretty well.... I'm real close to my ten-year-old daughter. We just got back from Vegas. She thought little girls were allowed to gamble out there.

She insisted that somewhere in Vegas there were slot machines that little girls were allowed to play. Well, I read that you shouldn't disabuse a child of her fantasies, so I went along with the gag. So we spent four days looking for those special slot machines. Finally, at the airport, I told her that little girls were allowed to play the airport slots just before they got on the plane. She said, "I told you, Daddy." We got very close on that trip. So I've been doing pretty well lately. . . . Listen, you don't think . . . I was in my favorite restaurant, eating some Chinese food. I ordered up a double order of Won Shih pancakes . . . you don't think . . . we're dead? That's what I was going to say. That's what we are. The second I said it, I knew it. Dead? Just like that? Christ! Bam? I don't know about you, but I'm not accepting this. I don't like the whole way it was done. Bam. Dead. Just like that. Just like you're a schmuck or something. I'll do something. Don't worry. I'm a doer. If you had any idea of the agony I went through to change my life around you'd see why I'm so pissed off. To be picked off like this when I haven't even started to enjoy the good stuff. I'll tell you right now, I'm not going along with it. Not now. Not when I'm just getting off the ground. Another time, later on, they want me to be dead, fine. Not now. Uh-uh. I'll get us out of this. Don't try the door. I'm pretty sure it doesn't open. If I find out for sure I'll get claustrophobia . . . I'll get us out. You'll find I do most things well. Of course, I have never been able to get out to Kennedy Airport on my own. I can get near it, but never really in it. The Van Wyck Highway scene really throws me. I've got wonderful qualities, but getting out to airports is not one of them. Don't worry, though, I'll get us out of here. By sheer strength of will and determination. I believe I can do anything if I really put my mind to it. I've always felt that even if I had a fatal illness, with an army of diseased phagocytes coursing through my body in triumph . . . if I really decided to, I could reverse the course of those phagocytes and push them the hell back where they belong . . .

No more toast. No more clams. Clams oregano. No more being under the covers. No more airline stewardesses . . . *Newsweek* . . . Jesus, no more *Newsweek*. Wait a minute, I'll get this straightened out right now.

*   *   *

Although we know Tandy is talking to Meredith, there is no mention in his dialogue of her. You must, therefore, talk to her or to whomever you choose to be talking to. The person to whom you are talking is the most important person in your life. You've got to create the other character. She is in the play but she is not in the monologue. Technically this is not considered a perfect monologue for this reason. You must decide why you are telling her all this and what it is that you need from her. Of course, it is your life. How can she help you? You must come up with reasons why she can help you to save yourself. She is young, gorgeous, and so on, and you are trying to impress her and you want her to be saved with you so that she can be in your life. And if you cannot save your life, you need her with you wherever you are heading.

STEAMBATH
by Bruce Jay Friedman

pp. 25–42 (Samuel French, Inc.)

P. R. Attendant: *(Turning to him.)* You addressing I?

Tandy: That's right. What's the deal around here? The Oldtimer says you're God.

P. R. Attendant: Some people call me that. *(Takes bucket from floor and fills it in sink.)*

Tandy: But that's ridiculous . . . a Puerto Rican . . .

P. R. Attendant: The Puerto Ricans go back hundreds of years. Millions. There were Puerto Ricans in Greece, Rome. Diogenes—very big, very strong Puerto Rican. Too many people make fun of the Puerto Ricans. Very fine people. Lot of class. We got José Torres, Mario Procaccino . . . *(Takes soap from shelf and puts it in bucket.)*

Tandy: All right, I'll go along with you for a second. You're God. Why would you be sweeping up, a lowly job like that?

P. R. Attendant: I like it. It's therapeutic. It's easy on the nerves.

Tandy: *(Moving L. above the shower.)* God . . . a Puerto Rican steambath attendant. That'll be the day.

P. R. Attendant: *(Crossing to R. pillar with bucket and sponge.)* Look, I'll tell you what, fella. You say I'm not God. All right. You got it. I'm not God. Fabulous. You got what you want. *(Pointing to* BIEBERMAN *on U. L. tier.)* He's God.

Oldtimer: He ain't God. He's a slob.

*(*MEREDITH *moves to the R. wall out of the* ATTENDANT'S *way as he begins to rub D. R. side of pillar.)*

Bieberman: Everything doesn't pay off in cleanliness. There are other virtues.

125

Oldtimer: You stink to the high heavens.

Two Young Men: You're being much too tough on him.

Oldtimer: Don't you two ever split up?

Two Young Men: *(Seductively.)* Make us an offer.

P. R. Attendant: Mister, just don't bug me. All right? I got a lot on my mind.

Tandy: There's another one. God talking slang. How can I go along with that?

P. R. Attendant: *(Moving to L. side of pillar and wiping it down.)* I talk any way I want, man. The Lord speaks in funny ways. Remember that. You want to discuss the relativity of mass, the Lorentz Transformation, galactic intelligence, I'll give you that, too. Just don't bug me. All right? Don't be no wise ass.

Tandy: That was more like it. You had me going there for a second. I respect anyone who really knows something, my work being as transitory as it is. It's when you talk dirty...

P. R. Attendant: The way I talk, don't you see that's just a little blink of an eye in terms of the universe, the job I got to do? The diameter of an electron is one ten-trillionth of an inch. And you're telling me I shouldn't talk dirty. Let me talk the way I want. Let me relax a little. *(Crosses D. L., puts bucket in sink, turns to console again.)* All right, *(Console light goes on.)* give that girl on the bus a run on her body stocking. *(Bleep.)* And close up that branch of Schraffts.... *(Bleep.)* And send up a bacon-and-lettuce-and-tomato sandwich, hold the mayo. *(Bleep.)* You burn the toast, I'll smite you down with my terrible swift sword. *(Bleep. The console light goes out.)*

Tandy: I still don't buy it. That could be an ordinary TV screen. You could have been watching Laugh-In.

P. R. Attendant: Laugh-In? *(Turns to console. The light goes on.)* Cancel Laugh-In. *(Bleep. Pushes console back against the wall.)* There's Laugh-In. You still want to fool around?

Tandy: I don't watch Laugh-In. Only thing I watch on TV is pro football. Gets better every year. *(The ATTENDANT takes the bucket, crosses to shower pit, sits on U. edge and begins to scrub it.)* Look, you're asking me to buy a whole helluva lot. You're challenging every one of my beliefs.

P. R. Attendant: You think I care about your beliefs? With the job I got on my mind?

Tandy: *(Moving to him.)* You care. I may be one man, but there exists within me the seed of all mankind.

P. R. Attendant: *(Clapping.)* Very good. I'm going to give you a ninety on that.

Tandy: I used to tell that to my art appreciation students over at the Police Academy.

P. R. Attendant: *(Returning to scrubbing.)* Nice bunch of boys.

Tandy: You mean to tell me that you control every action on earth by means of that monitor over there? Every sneeze, every headache, every time a guy cuts himself? How can you possibly do so much?

P. R. Attendant: I go very fast. You got to move like crazy. You can't stop and talk to every schmuck who comes along. . . .

(The same attendant, GOTTLIEB, who had appeared before comes in carrying a sandwich on a plate. He now wears a different waiter's jacket.)

Gottlieb: Your BLT down. *(Places it on a shelf on U. alcove wall.)*

P. R. Attendant: Thank you. What do I owe you for that? *(Takes bucket and moves to sink.)*

Gottlieb: Are you kidding, sire?

P. R. Attendant: *(Washing hands.)* Just thought I'd ask. You don't have to get snotty about it. *(GOTTLIEB goes off.)*

Tandy: *(Moving C.)* I don't know. It's awfully hard to accept. I've heard of having your faith tested, but this is ridiculous.

P. R. Attendant: *(Sitting on edge of sink, takes out gum and sticks it on bracelet he is wearing.)* And who told you you could speak while I was eating?

Tandy: All right. I'm sorry. I beg your pardon. One minute you're casual, the next you're formal. How can I keep up with you?

P. R. Attendant: *(Takes piece of sandwich.)* Changeable, mysterious, infinite, unfathomable. That's my style. . . .

Tandy: Yeah—except that you're not God.

P. R. Attendant: *(Puts sandwich back on shelf.)* That's the conclusion you reached after all the time I spent with you? I'll tell you right now you're getting me roped off. I get roped off, watch out. Then you're really in trouble. *(Takes*

cards from shelf above sink.) All right. I'll tell you what. You
say I'm not God, right?

Tandy: Right.

P. R. Attendant: *(Spreads cards like fan, crosses to* TANDY.*)* All
right. Pick a card, any card.

Tandy: What's that gonna prove?

P. R. Attendant: Go ahead, just do what I'm tellin' you. You'll
see. (TANDY *picks a card.* MEREDITH *sits on D. R. of R.
pillar.)* You look at it?

Tandy: Yes.

P. R. Attendant: *(Crossing R.)* Okay... you got the... King of
Hearts.... Right?

Tandy: All right. You did it. So what?

P. R. Attendant: So there y'are.

Tandy: There I am what? You do a simple card trick that any
kid can do—a retarded kid can do—and I'm supposed to
think you're God.

P. R. Attendant: Can you do it?

Tandy: No, I can't do it. I can't even deal a hand of blackjack.
But there are hundreds of guys who can do that trick. In
every village and hamlet in the country. What the hell does
that prove?

P. R. Attendant: *(Taking card from* TANDY.*)* Not in the hamlets.
It's not that easy. In the villages, maybe, but not in the
hamlets. *(Crosses back R. to wall.)* All right, I show you a
trick that's not as easy as it seems, you won't buy it. Fair
enough. You're pushing me to the wall. I'm not saying a
word. *(Gives cards to* MEREDITH, *moves back to* TANDY.*)*
Now, check my pants. *(Holds out the waist of his pants.*
TANDY *reaches out to him.)* And easy on the corporeal
contact. (TANDY *begrudgingly does so.)* Anything in there?

Tandy: There's nothing in there.

P. R. Attendant: *(Turns U., reaches into the fly of his pants.)*
Now... *(With a flourish, pulls out a long, multicolored
scarf.)* How's that?

Tandy: I've seen it about a dozen times.

P. R. Attendant: Where? *(Sits D. L. of* MEREDITH, *gives her
scarf which she puts around her neck.)*

Tandy: On the Sullivan Show. These Slavic guys come over
here and do that trick. On a bicycle. Someone tells them
they can come over here and clean up. Sullivan's the only
one who'll give them a break. They make a few bucks, you

never hear from them again. They go right back to those Slavic countries. Look, I'm sorry. I don't know quite how to say this, but you are not even putting a *dent* in me. What kind of second-rate horseshit is this?

P. R. Attendant: *(Expressing great pain.)* You hurt my feelings just now, you know that, don't you?

Tandy: There's a perfect example. God with His feelings hurt. Ridiculous.

P. R. Attendant: My feelings are not supposed to get hurt? Once in a while? All right. Now I'm really going to give you one. *(Calling.)* Gottlieb. (GOTTLIEB *runs out with a footlocker kept shut by a huge padlock. Sets it down, D. C., then turns it so that the lock is U.)* Thanks, Gottlieb, I won't forget this. *(To* TANDY.*)* All right. Check the lock.

Tandy: *(Following instructions, leaving lock open and rehanging it so that the* P. R. ATTENDANT *can remove it with his teeth.)* I checked it.

P. R. Attendant. Is it strong?

Tandy: Very strong, very powerful. Big deal.

P. R. Attendant: All right. Observez-vous. *(All move D. to watch.* GOTTLIEB *takes out a piece of rope and ties the* P. R.'s *hands behind him. The* P. R. *kneels down and with his teeth, sawing away like a bulldog, chews on the lock.* GOTTLIEB *backs him by singing and tap dancing an uptempo number, and throwing paper streamers into the air. Finally, with the lock in his teeth, the* P. R. *rises and accepts their applause. He drops the lock onto the trunk.)* Voilà!

Tandy: It was okay, I admit. It was a little better than the others. At least you're showing me a little something. (GOTTLIEB *unties the* P. R.'s *hands. The* P. R. *throws the lock to the* OLDTIMER, R. *of the shower.)* Look, I don't know how to get this across to you, but you are not reaching me with this stuff. Maybe I'm crazy. Are you people impressed?

Oldtimer: Only one fella I know could do that, fella named Radio. Sneaky little bugger. Ran into him in New Guinea. Used to go crazy when he saw a radio. If you were carrying one he'd figure out a way to get it. Old Radio could have picked that footlocker with his teeth. No question about it.

(Note: During this scene a mist or fog has begun to slowly seep over the stage. It builds up till the climax of act, by which time it pervades but does not obscure the stage.)

P. R. Attendant: *(Sitting on the D. L. of the R. pillar, next to* MEREDITH.*)* There y'are. You heard what the man said. Only one other fellow could've pulled off that stunt. Radio.

Tandy: *(Stage L.)* Wonderful. Look, I can't help it. Sue me. I'm not moved. If you had made one interesting intellectual assault on my mind, maybe that would do it.

P. R. Attendant: *(Playing with cards.)* De gustibus non disputandum.

Tandy: That's it? That's the intellectual assault? Freshman English?

P. R. Attendant: Have you ever really pondered it? Savored it? Rolled it around on your tongue and really tasted of its fruit?

Tandy: That's right. I have. And it's nothing. It's garbage. It's not the kind of insight to make the senses reel.

P. R. Attendant: *(Standing on bottom tier, leaning back with arms on the top level.)* Consider the mind, an independent substance implanted within the soul and incapable of being destroyed. . . . The City of Satan, whatever its artifices in art, war, or philosophy, was essentially corrupt and impious, its joy but a comic mask and its beauty the whitening of a sepulchre. It stood condemned before man's better conscience by its vanity, cruelty and secret misery, by its ignorance of all that it truly behooved a man to know who was destined to immortality. . . . *(*MEREDITH *moves R.)* Or how about "A little philosophy inclineth man's mind to atheism, but depth in philosophy bringeth men's minds about to religion."

Tandy: *(Stage L.)* Much better. Maybe I could even chew on some of that. But you still haven't got me. All I see so far is a fairly interesting guy. For a Puerto Rican. If I ran into you at a bar—a Puerto Rican bar—maybe we could kick around a few ideas. All I'm saying is I don't see God yet. Where's God?

P. R. Attendant: You don't see God, huh? Boy, you're some pistol. Alright, here comes a little number that is going to make your head swim. You happen to be in luck, fella, because you caught me at cocktail time and I'm dry as a bone. Gottlieb . . . Now you watch this carefully . . . *(*GOTTLIEB *enters with a tray of drinks. The* BROKER *takes a stool from the L. of the R. pillar and places it C. stage. The* P. R. *sits and takes the tray.)* How many drinks you estimate are on that tray?

Tandy: Ten . . . *(*P. R. ATTENDANT *begins to knock them off, one*

at a time. TANDY *crosses R.)* . . . and you don't even have to
bother drinking them because I can name you two lushes
out there on Eighth Avenue who can do the same thing. . . . I
mean, what is this? . . . It's not even as good as the trunk.
You might have snapped off a few teeth on that one . . . but
this cheap, trivial, broken-down, ninth-rate . . . *(As he speaks,*
GOTTLIEB *drags from behind the L. pillar an enormous
whiskey sour, one that towers above* TANDY'S *head.* TANDY *is
speechless. Struggling,* GOTTLIEB *brings it D.)* Are you mad?
(He moves R.)

P. R. Attendant: *(Giving tray with remaining drinks to the*
BROKER, *who places it on the U. bench.)* Uno momento.
*(Leaps to top tier of the R. column, sits opposite rim of
glass, and takes hold of the straw.)* This is going to be
delicious. That son of a bitch mixes some drink. *(All the*
OTHERS *move in to watch. As the* P. R. ATTENDANT *begins
to sip,* GOTTLIEB, *standing L. of the drink, reaches behind
the glass and pulls a cord which allows the liquid to drain
from the glass into the empty base on which the glass sits.
The* P. R. ATTENDANT *drains the glass and bursts with
satisfaction.)* Right, what have you got to say to that, baby?
(Pulling a huge cherry from the glass.) Incidentally, you like
the cherry, go ahead, don't be embarrassed. . . .

The TWO YOUNG MEN *help* GOTTLIEB *push the huge drink
back U. of one L. pillar.)*

Tandy: *(D. of R. pillar.)* It was pretty good. All right. I take
that back. Fair is fair. It was great. My hat goes off to you. It
was really remarkable. I figure the odds were about fifty to
one against. I hardly know how to say this next thing, but
I'm still not buying it. The God routine.

P. R. Attendant: You don't buy it?

Tandy: No, sir. The fact that I just said "sir" will give you an
indication that I'm really impressed. You got a lot going for
you. But I'm not really there yet. If I said I was, I'd just be
kidding. It would be an injustice of a kind. A real sell-out.

P. R. Attendant: So you still don't buy it?

Tandy: No, sir.

P. R. Attendant: You really making me work, boy. *(Jumps down
from the pillar.)* All right. I have but one choice, my son.
(Gestures.) Shazam . . .

*(There is a crash of thunder and the lights fade to darkness.
The stage and theater suddenly fill with deafening organ
music, churchlike, ancient, soaring, almost unbearable. In
the darkness,* GOTTLIEB *unhooks the ladder from the R.
pillar and puts it on the lower tier and with* BIEBERMAN *and
one of the* TWO YOUNG MEN *pushes the pillar U.,* MEREDITH
following. The P. R. ATTENDANT *moves U. C., while the
other* YOUNG MAN, *the* BROKER *and the* OLDTIMER *move to
the L. pillar. First a beam of light is projected into the house
from the extreme D. L. Then from the extreme D. R., a
dazzling pattern of light is projected throughout the house.
U. C., the figure of the* P. R. ATTENDANT *is outlined in
multicolored shafts of light projected from U. C. through the
back wall. All but* TANDY *are discovered kneeling with head
bowed in reverential poses on or at the pillars. The voice of
the* P. R. ATTENDANT, *greatly magnified, booms out.)*

P. R. Attendant's Voice:
>   Ascribe unto the Lord,
>   Ye kindreds of the peoples...
>   Ascribe unto the Lord
>   Glory and strength....
>   Ascribe unto the Lord
>   The glory due unto his name.
>   Bring an offering
>   And come unto his courts.
>   Oh, worship the Lord
>   In the beauty of holiness.
>   Tremble before him,
>   All the earth....

*(*TANDY *looks around, observes that he is the only one
standing. He shrugs, goes to one knee, surrounded by a
circle of blue light. There is a final crash of music, the lights
fade as the curtain descends.)*

CURTAIN

At Rise: *A darkened stage. There is the sound of a television set, the voices of the* TWO YOUNG MEN *singing, and
someone jumping rope. After a moment, the lights gradually
come up, cutting through the clouds of steam.* TANDY *is*

slumped D. on the lower tier of the R. pillar with BIEBERMAN *sitting on the level above him.* BIEBERMAN *is watching a small, portable TV set. The* TWO YOUNG MEN *stand by the L. pillar, undoing and folding two pieces of tie-dyed material, while the* OLDTIMER *is stretched out on the lower L. tier of the L. pillar. The* BROKER *is jumping rope C.*

Broker: *(To* TANDY*)* You ought to try this. . . . Really gets the weight off you. . . . Look in the mirror sometime while you're doing it. *(The* TWO YOUNG MEN *hang the unknotted fabric on the pillar L., and cross to the bench U. and sit.)* Everything moves. The stuff way inside—where you have the real weight—that's moving, too. . . . *(Stops jumping.)* How much do you weigh?

Tandy: Me? Around 155 . . . 160 . . . somewhere in there.

Broker: I'm 179 myself. I'd like to lose around ten, twelve pounds. Twelve pounds I'd feel like a tiger. *(Grabbing some flesh about his waist.)* I got to lose it around here—that's where it's rough . . . 'specially when you get round my age.

Tandy: That's right.

Broker: One hundred sixty-eight. That's my perfect weight. You should see me at 168. Never seen anything like it.

Tandy: I bet you look great.

Broker: I do. I get up in the middle, high seventies, forget it. It's all gone. . . . You want to hear something else . . . ?

Tandy: Shoot.

Broker: When I'm 168, I get a beautiful bowel movement. . . . How about you? You pretty regular?

Tandy: *(Cutting in.)* I don't want to hurt your feelings or anything, but I'm really not that interested in your bowel movements. . . .

Broker: I can see that. . . . Sorry if I was presumptuous. . . .

Tandy: Perfectly all right. . . .

Broker: I once bought a stock at 168—my exact weight. . . . Fellow who recommended it said this is a stock you don't worry about. It goes off, for argument's sake, ten, twenty, fifty points, I don't care if it goes off a hundred points . . . you don't worry about this stock. So I hold it. And it *does* go off ten, twenty, over a hundred points. The stock is now selling at a fast ten points. So I call the guy. "It's down to ten," I say. "When do I start worrying?" "Never," he says. He just

wasn't a worrier. I lost every penny.... Shows you ... go
trust people.... I should've stuck to ferns.

Tandy: Ferns?

Broker: That's right. I was in the fern game for a while. A lot of
people go in for ferns, you'd be surprised. I was cleaning
up. But I couldn't take the social pressure.... Guy at a
party'd ask me what do you do, I'd say I'm in ferns. How do
you think that made me feel? I had to get out. (*Moves U. to
L. pillar, takes a miniature whiskey bottle from the top, R.
tier, drinks and sits on the lower slab.*)

Oldtimer: (*Sitting up.*) Turn off that TV set. . . .

Bieberman: (*R. of top tier, R. pillar.*) I'm watching a wonderful
movie. And it's down very low.

Oldtimer: Turn it off, I tell you. I'm trying to catch a quick
snooze. Turn it off or I'll come up there and kick you in the
bazanzas . . .

Bieberman: What are they?

Oldtimer: Never mind. You'll find out fast enough if I kick you
there.

Bieberman: Anti-Semite.

Oldtimer: (*Rises, moves to R. pillar.*) I'm an anti-stinkite. That's
what *you* got to worry about. Now turn it off, I tell you. . . .

Bieberman: (*Always a little bitter, angry when he speaks, spitting the words out deliberately.*) I suppose it never occurred
to you that every smile, every whisper, every puff of a
cigarette taken by my generation was inspired by the forties'
movie. That my generation wouldn't know how to mix a
drink, drive a car, kiss a girl, straighten a tie—if it weren't
for Linda Darnell and George Brent. . . . That the sole reason for my generation's awkward floundering in the darkness
is that Zachary Scott is gone . . . and I assure you that Dennis
Hopper is no substitute.

Oldtimer: I'll tell you what your generation needs. A movie
that instructs you on how to smell like a human being. You
can star in it. Now turn that goddam thing off. (TANDY *has
crossed U. between them and circled around the R. pillar.*)
How can you even see the screen with all this steam?

Bieberman: When it gets too dense I smear it off with a corner
of my jockey shorts.

Oldtimer: (*Moving back to L. pillar.*) I spent four years in the
Philippines. I never seen a slob like him. (*Sits.*)

Tandy: (*Sitting D., lower tier of R. pillar.*) C'mon, you guys.

Arguing about TV. That's ridiculous. You're supposed to be dead. Act like it.

(BIEBERMAN *shuts off the set and moves U. of the pillar.*)

Meredith: (*Entering from U., carrying two paper coffee cups and a handbag with knitting. Puts one cup down by* TANDY, *and sits on stool D. of shower.*) It's wonderful the way they listen to you.

Tandy: It's probably that time I spent with the cops. It really changes you. Even when you're in the art department. One day they invited me on an assault case and these two detectives, kidding around, threw me out on a fire escape with this huge, maddened transvestite. Anyway, we're on the 35th floor, we start grappling with each other, and I figure it's either me or it. So I bit him in the ear. Well, it must have turned him on because all of a sudden he confesses that he electrocuted a hippie in Vermont. Well, I told him I was kidding around, I wasn't a real dick, but he just kept confessing and I kept biting and finally they hauled us both back through the window and booked him on the Vermont thing. And me on a morals charge— (*Getting up.*) I'm just kidding. . . . I finally had to get out of the cops, it was a terrible place . . . there was one thing—you could always run up a tab at the Automat.

(MEREDITH *has put cup on floor D. of stool and taken out knitting.*)

Meredith: (*Rises, runs R.*) Oh, my God!
Tandy: What's wrong?
Meredith: I just remembered. I haven't paid my Bloomingdale's bill.
Tandy: When was it due?
Meredith: (*Moving to* TANDY.) Last Monday . . . now they'll probably send me one of those thin gray envelopes. . . . You have no idea how much I hate those envelopes.
Tandy: But it's ridiculous. You can't pay your bills now. The store will understand.
Meredith: Bloomingdale's! I don't know why they insist on making you feel so terrible. Any other store—Saks, Bendel's— if you don't pay your bill they assume you're in Acapulco.

Not Bloomingdale's. Right for the throat. "In ten days if you have not paid your bill, we are cutting off your charge account and telling your parents, friends and the principal of the first school you attended . . ."

Tandy: Look, obviously none of this has sunk in. We're in big trouble. We could be stuck in this lousy steambath forever. You're sitting around talking Bloomingdale's. You saw that Puerto Rican guy. . . . He wasn't kidding around.

Meredith: That was fun.

Tandy: What do you mean?

Meredith: The part where we got down on our knees. We used to do that at Marymount every morning, first thing, and it was freezing. It was fun getting down on a nice warm floor for a change.

Tandy: It wasn't any fun for me. I got to get out of here. *(Moving L., he kicks the cup, then circles above shower to the L. of the R. pillar.* MEREDITH *follows him and then sits on the stool L. of the shower.)* I got all this Charlemagne research to do. There's going to be a whole Charlemagne revival, I can tell. Books, movies, musical comedies. Dolls— that's right. Little Charlemagne dolls. Where is that guy? I want another crack at him. *(Exits up R.)*

Bieberman: *(Appears L. of upper tier.)* Anyone have some pimple lotion?

Oldtimer: There he goes again, the cocksucker.

Bieberman: Well, can I control my complexion, can I?

Oldtimer: *(Moving to R. pillar.)* Of course you can. Ever hear of cutting down on malteds?

Bieberman: I'll never cut down on malteds, never.

Oldtimer: Well, then, don't come to me with your pimples, you stupid bastard. *(Moves back to L. pillar.)*

Bieberman: Malteds are the marijuana of my generation.

Oldtimer: Your generation—what the hell generation is that? *(Sits, D.)*

Bieberman: It went by very quickly. . . . It was Dolf Camilli, Dane Clark, Uncle Don, Ducky Medwick and out. . . .

Oldtimer: Sounds like a real bunch of winners.

Bieberman: *(Getting up.)* We produced Norman Podhoretz.

Oldtimer: Congratulations. . . . *(To the* BROKER.*)* Who the fuck is Norman Podhoretz?

Broker: *(sitting R. of L. pillar.)* Probably some wealthy bastard who made it when you could keep it.

Tandy: *(Entering U. R., moves D. to C.)* We're all set.

Meredith: *(Crossing to him.)* What's up?

Tandy: *(Showing her.)* I've got a whole bunch of carpet tacks.

Meredith: Wow. Where did you get them?

Tandy: *(Moving R.)* They got an old carpet rolled up back there.

Meredith: *(Following him.)* What good'll they do?

Tandy: Plenty. Don't undersell them. I once saw a guy with only a handful of carpet tacks get the best of two armed cops.

Meredith: That's remarkable, overpowering two policemen that way.

Tandy: That's right. Where is that guy? *(Both sit D. of R. pillar.)* Listen, we get out, I'd like you to see my apartment. I've got big steel bars on the windows—I had a few robberies—but I've got the bars painted in psychedelic colors.

Meredith: I'd love to see your apartment.

Tandy: I'm very proud of it. I've got huge double security locks. They're in psychedelic colors too. Burglar alarm, same deal. It's not a horny thing. I won't jump on you or anything.

Meredith: Oh, I know that.

Tandy: Well, as a matter of fact, it *is* a partially horny thing. You're a very good-looking girl . . . but I'm also proud of the apartment.

Meredith: Don't you have a girl friend?

Tandy: Oh yes, I've got an ex-wife, a mistress, a mother . . . I'm covered on all sides. Now I just need a girl.

Meredith: I understand. You just want someone totally uncomplicated.

Tandy: That's right.

Meredith: It's only fair to tell you that I can only sleep with one man at a time. If I slept with you I might reach out in the middle of the night and think I was caressing Ramondo.

Tandy: Ramondo . . . ? Don't worry about it. Listen, you and your roommate don't . . . I mean . . . together.

Meredith: Make scenes? . . . Oh no . . . we don't do that.

Tandy: I hope you don't take offense . . . I was just checking.

Meredith: We don't anymore, that is. We did take a mescaline trip recently with one of my stockbroker friends. It didn't work out. It turned into a sort of business trip.

Oldtimer: Toughest sonofabitch I ever knew used to dress up

like Carmen Miranda. They found him floating five kilome-
ters outside Hamburg Harbor... all those bananas bobbing
in the water.

(P. R. ATTENDANT *comes in with* GOTTLIEB, *who has a candy salesman tray slung around his neck.*)

P. R. Attendant: OK, everybody. Let's go! Campfire time. Gottlieb, hand out those Mounds bars.

(*The* OTHERS *gather around* GOTTLIEB, *U. C. as he passes out the candy.* TANDY *motions for the* P. R. ATTENDANT *to join him D. R.*)

Tandy: Listen, I want to talk to you about getting out of here. I got a lot of deals going on the outside, a lot of things to clear up. I don't know if you know anything about Charlemagne...

P. R. Attendant: The Puerto Rican?

Tandy: Cute. Listen, I haven't mentioned it yet, but I want you to know that was very impressive stuff you did, drinking all that stuff, those lights... very good....

P. R. Attendant: I saw you on your knees.

Tandy: One knee. I just went down on one knee.... Maybe that's half-assed, I don't know. Maybe a straight solid guy—a Henry Cabot Lodge—would have either given you both knees or said the hell with it... I don't know. I figured you run the place I'll throw you one knee. A little respect. Meanwhile, I got to talk to you about getting out of here. I don't belong here, I don't need this.

P. R. Attendant: You know what I don't need. Right now. Aggravation.

Tandy: There's another hot one. God, aggravated.

P. R. Attendant: Listen, if you're God, the name of the game is aggravation. Anyway, I don't want to hear any more. You say another word, baby, I'll become wrathful and vengeance-seeking.

The following is the monologue created from the previous scenes.

P. R. ATTENDANT (to TANDY), *age 30 to 50*.
pp. 25–42 (SAMUEL FRENCH, INC.)

You addressing I? Some people call me that. God! The
Puerto Ricans go back hundreds of years. Millions. There
were Puerto Ricans in Greece, Rome. Diogenes—very
big, very strong Puerto Rican. Too many people make fun
of the Puerto Ricans. Very fine people. Lot of class. We got
José Torres, Mario Procaccino... Look, I'll tell you what,
fella. You say I'm not God. All right. You got it. I'm not
God. Fabulous. You got what you want. Mister, just don't
bug me. All right? I got a lot on my mind.... I talk any
way I want, man. The Lord speaks in funny ways. Remember that. You want to discuss the relativity of mass, the
Lorentz Transformation, galactic intelligence, I'll give you
that, too. Just don't bug me. All right? Don't be no wise
ass. The way I talk, don't you see that's just a little blink of
an eye in terms of the universe, the job I got to do? The
diameter of an electron is one ten-trillionth of an inch. And
you're telling me I shouldn't talk dirty. Let me talk the way
I want. Let me relax a little.

(*To a console lit up.*) All right, give that girl on the
bus a run on her body stocking. And close up that branch
of Schraffts... and send up a bacon-and-lettuce-and-tomato sandwich, hold the mayo. You burn the toast, I'll smite
you down with my terrible swift sword. Cancel *Laugh-In*.
(*To* TANDY.) There's *Laugh-In*. You still want to fool around?
I go very fast. You got to move like crazy. You can't stop
and talk to every schmuck who comes along... and who
told you you could speak while I was eating? Changeable,
mysterious, infinite, unfathomable. That's my style.... I'll
tell you right now you're getting me roped off. I get roped
off, watch out. Then you're really in trouble. (*Monologue
is picked up on page 42.*) You know what I don't need?
Right now? Aggravation. Listen, if you're God, the name
of the game is aggravation. Anyway, I don't want to hear
any more. You say another word, baby, I'll become wrathful and vengeance seeking.

This is a good monologue to use when you are auditioning
for a comedy where an Hispanic accent is required or desired.
You are God and you're having a hard time getting people to

believe in you. The person to whom you are talking has ridiculed your ethnicity and the way you talk. You must communicate to him that you are indeed God and have every right to be just as you are. You are very hurt and, therefore, angry with him. Make him understand the truth. You need him on your side. He is a very special person who indeed doubts. You must decide the details regarding the importance of this person to you and why today is the most important day in your life. You've taken him away from earth. Do you feel just a little bit guilty about doing that to him? What is it about him that made you bring him here now while he is still young? Why do you need him here with you?

Don't fall into the trap and play off the pages only. Create *your* play, which will deal with your inner needs.

STEAMBATH
by Bruce Jay Friedman

pp. 54–59 (SAMUEL FRENCH, INC.)

Tandy: *(Moving D. R. to C.)* Anyway, you get the idea. I've gotten my whole life on the right track for the first time. I don't hate Wendy. I'm doing this wonderful work for brain-damaged welders. You ask the welders what they think of me. And I've got a marvelous new girl who's got this surprising body. You look at her face you just don't expect all that voluptuousness. You say to yourself, she's a little girl, a quiet little girl, comes from a nice family, where did these tits come from.

P. R. Attendant: Hey, hey, there's a lady...

Meredith: Oh, that's all right. I don't mind tits. Knockers is the one I don't care for.

Tandy: All right, excuse me, but do you get the idea? I got everything bad swept out of the room. I'm closer than ever to my 10-year-old daughter. That trip to Vegas really brought us together. I'm doing work that I love. Warner Brothers saw the first hundred pages of my Charlemagne book and I understand they like it for Steve McQueen...

P. R. Attendant: Twentieth is going to buy it...for Charlton Heston...

Tandy: Then you admit...you admit I'm getting out of here.

P. R. Attendant: They're going to buy it from your estate...

(MEREDITH *and* GOTTLIEB *move to the R. pillar and sit D. tier. They try to unravel some yarn from* MEREDITH's *hand-bag. The* P. R. ATTENDANT *takes a piece of fruit from shelf above the sink, sits back down and begins to peel it with knife from pocket.)*

Tandy: *(Moving to him.)* Look, I'm all clean and straight and

141

honest. I got rid of all the garbage. Any crooked lines, I erased them and drew them straight. . . . I don't hate anybody. I love a lot of people. I'm at the goddamned starting line. I'm ready to breathe clean air. I tore myself inside out to get to where I am—and I'm not taking up anybody's space. I'm ready to cook a little. Swing. What kind of fellow is that to snuff out?

P. R. Attendant: A good fellow. But I'm snuffing him out anyway.

Tandy: Where's your compassion?

P. R. Attendant: I do plenty of good things. Half the things I do are good, maybe even a little more, that's right, maybe even a little more. Nobody notices them. I never get any credit, but I do plenty of good things. I make trees, forests, soccer fields. I let hernias get better. . . .

Tandy: But you'll wipe out a guy like me . . . and a lovely blond girl like that.

Meredith: (*L. of* GOTTLIEB, *turns to* TANDY.) Oh, listen, the blond part shouldn't enter into it, I can see that.

P. R. Attendant: (*Rising.*) I let you go, I got to let the next guy go. Pretty soon nobody's dead. You'd have people coming out of your ears. Have you seen Istanbul lately? Downtown Istanbul? Los Angeles?

Meredith: I'd never live in L.A. I don't think there's one sincere person in the whole city.

P. R. Attendant: (*Sitting back down.*) Let me ask you something. (TANDY *sits on stool R. of him.*) While you were doing all those things, unloading your old lady, you know, straightening out your head, how did you feel?

Tandy: Good. Excited . . . it was like being in a whirlpool bath. An emotional whirlpool bath. It even made my body feel good; it got springy and toughened up. (*Rises.*)

P. R. Attendant: (*Dumps peels in newspaper in basket.*) There y'are. You felt good, you had a whirlpool bath . . . a springy body . . . need I say more?

Tandy: You don't understand something. I probably never made it clear. This is very important to me. We're talking about my life. I'm not asking you for seats to a hockey game.

P. R. Attendant: (*Mocking.*) It's very important to him. Nobody else is alive.

Tandy: Is there anything I can do for you?

P. R. Attendant: You got to be kidding. *You* do something for *me?* What in the world would God want?

Tandy: A sacrifice... burnt offerings... a little lox.

P. R. Attendant: I got no time to fool around. I got to make room for the next bunch coming in here. *(Takes basket to R. pillar, begins to collect towels, moves above pillar.)*

Tandy: That's it? You're going through with this? Well, I'll tell you right now, if you're capable of wiping out a once-confused fellow who's now a completely straight and sweet guy, then I got no choice but to call you a prick. *(To* MEREDITH.*)* I'm sorry.

Meredith: Oh, that's alright. I don't mind prick. Pecker is the one I don't care for.

P. R. Attendant: *(Astonished, moves down, R. of pillar.)* God?... Did I hear you correctly?... Can I believe my ears?... Blasphemy?

Tandy: *(At L. wall.)* That's right. If you're capable of doing something like that. Taking a guy to the very threshold of marvelous things, teasing him along and then acing him out just when he's ready to scoop up one lousy drop of gravy— that is bad news, I'm sorry...

P. R. Attendant: That's bad, boy, that *is* low. Wowee. Nobody ever called me that before. That's what I call sinning, baby. You're in real trouble now. You have put your foot in it this time, fella. . . . You going to stick to what you called me?... that dirty name?... talking that way to God?

Tandy: *(Interrupting.)* Yeah, I'm going to stick to it... and you know why... because when I was in that Chinese restaurant... and I lost my breath, and I had no feelings, and I was numb and white, as white as a piece of typing paper, and I said over and over and over I don't want to die, I don't want to die, I don't want to die... and told you, in my way, how much I treasured every drop of life—you weren't impressed, you didn't hear a whisper of it.

P. R. Attendant: That right, Gottlieb? Did he do that? (GOTTLIEB *nods.)*

Tandy: *(Moving to C.)* I thought you knew everything.

P. R. Attendant: Almost everything. Once in a while there's an administrative error. Anyway, I did hear you. You came over a little weak, a little static thrown in there, but I heard you. That's why you're here. Otherwise... *(Pointing to stage L. door.)* ...you'd have gone straight in there. . . .

Tandy: Then not everybody comes here. . . .

P. R. Attendant: Neurotics, freaks . . . *(Contemptuously.)* . . . those with stories to tell.

Tandy: How was mine?

P. R. Attendant: Not bad. I heard worse.

Tandy: You were touched. . . . You just won't admit it. *(Advances, threateningly.)* Now let me out of here.

P. R. Attendant: You come near me, I'll send you back with cancer, then you'll know real trouble.

(TANDY *grabs* GOTTLIEB, *who has moved D. to pick up the cups and a stool D. L. Grabbing him from behind, he holds* GOTTLIEB *around the neck, threatening him with his other hand.* GOTTLIEB *drops the cups and stool and they fall to the floor.)*

Tandy: All right, talk, and be quick about it. Otherwise, you get these carpeting tacks right in your face. How do we get out?

P. R. Attendant: You talk, Gottlieb, and I'll see to it that you never work again. What can he do with a lousy bunch of carpeting tacks?

Gottlieb: I don't know. But I'm not taking any chances. . . . Get a mirror.

Meredith: *(Taking a compact from her bag.)* I've got one here.

Gottlieb: Shine it in his face. He can't stand that. *(She hesitates, then does.)*

P. R. Attendant: *(On the floor, cowering against the R. wall.)* Take that away. I don't want to see myself. I'm a homely guy, with pockmarks.

Tandy: *(Releasing* GOTTLIEB.*)* Wait a minute. . . . Leave him alone. . . . I can't go through with this. (GOTTLIEB *scrambles to the R. pillar, hides L. side.)*

P. R. Attendant: *(Gets himself together—then, as though feelings are really hurt.)* Et tu, Gottlieb . . .

Meredith: *(Terrified, runs to door L. Hesitates.)* Au revoir, Mr. Tandy. Did I do alright with the mirror?

Tandy: *(Having slowly gotten up.)* You did fine, kid.

(MEREDITH *turns and goes through the door.* GOTTLIEB *exits U.)*

P. R. Attendant: *(To* TANDY. *Rights the stool, picks up the cups.)*
You couldn't stand that, right, to see God get wiped out? . . . It
gave you a funny feeling.

Tandy: I don't like to see anybody get wiped out. . . . I'm notorious for breaking up fights. . . . I once threw a guy through
the window of a furniture store because somebody was
picking on him and I thought he was going to get hurt. . . .

P. R. Attendant: *(Standing on lower R. tier of R. pillar, facing*
TANDY.*)* You got a lot of nice qualities. . . . Too bad I'm filled
up, I'd let you work around here for a while. . . . Listen,
what are you giving yourself such a hard time for? . . . Suppose,
for a second, I let you out of here. . . . What would you do?

Tandy: What would I do? . . . Are you kidding? . . . What is this,
a put-on? . . . You didn't hear me go on about my new life?
My new style? The exciting world that's out there waiting
for me? . . . This terrific new quiet girl friend who practically
brings me the newspaper in her teeth—who watches me
like a hawk for the slightest sign of sexual tension—and then
whop—she's in there like a shot to drain it off and make me
feel comfortable again. . . . And if I feel like going out at four
in the morning to get some eggs—she's right there at my
side—because she comes from a tradition where the man is
like a gypsy king and the woman is someone who drags
mutton to him on her back, all the way up a hill. And all she
ever hopes for is that he'll throw her a lousy mutton bone
while she's sleeping in the dirt at his feet. . . . And this is an
intelligent girl, too, a Bryn Mawr girl. . . . When I'm alone
with her. . .

P. R. Attendant: *(Sits lower D. tier of R. pillar.)* You like this
girl?

Tandy: Like her? . . . Oh, I see what you mean. . . . Yeah . . . if
I'm so crazy about her, how come I'm constantly chasing
chicks all over the place? *(Sits on stool L. of pool.)* . . . All
right, I'll admit to you that she's a little on the quiet
side—that sometimes all that quiet drives me nuts. . . . All
right, let's face it, she's basically a dull girl. Terrific kid,
loyal, faithful, brings you mutton, but the sparks don't
fly. . . . And it did cross my mind that maybe I'll find another
girl who's got a little more pazazz. . . . I'll give you that.

The following is the monologue created from the previous
scene.

TANDY (to P. R. ATTENDANT), *age 30 to 50*.
pp. 54–59 (SAMUEL FRENCH, INC.)

I've gotten my whole life on the right track for the first time. I don't hate Wendy. I'm doing this wonderful work for brain-damaged welders. You ask the welders what they think of me. And I've got a marvelous new girl who's got this surprising body. You look at her face you just don't expect all that voluptuousness. You say to yourself, she's a little girl, a quiet little girl, comes from a nice family, where did these tits come from.

I got everything bad swept out of the room. I'm closer than ever to my ten-year-old daughter. That trip to Vegas really brought us together. I'm doing work that I love. Warner Brothers saw the first hundred pages of my Charlemagne book and I understand they like it for Steve McQueen. Look, I'm all clean and straight and honest. I got rid of all the garbage. Any crooked lines, I erased them and drew them straight. I don't hate anybody. I love a lot of people. I'm at the goddamned starting line. I'm ready to breathe clean air. I tore myself inside out to get to where I am—and I'm not taking up anybody's space. I'm ready to cook a little. Swing. What kind of fellow is that to snuff out? Where's your compassion? You'd wipe out a guy like me? You don't understand something. I probably never made it clear. This is very important to me. We're talking about my life. I'm not asking you for seats to a hockey game. Is there anything I can do for you? A sacrifice ... burnt offerings ... a little lox. That's it? You're going through with this? Well, I'll tell you right now, if you're capable of wiping out a once-confused fellow who's now a completely straight and sweet guy, then I got no choice but to call you a prick! If you're capable of doing something like that. Taking a guy to the very threshold of marvelous things, teasing him along and then acing him out just when he's ready to scoop up one lousy drop of gravy—that is bad news, I'm sorry. When I was in that Chinese restaurant ... and I lost my breath, and I had no feelings, and I was numb and white, as white as a piece of typing paper, and I said over and over and over I don't want to die, I don't want to die, I don't want to die ... and told you, in my way, how much I treasured every drop of life—you weren't impressed, you didn't hear a whisper of it!

I don't like to see anybody get wiped out... I'm notorious for breaking up fights... I once threw a guy through the window of a furniture store because somebody was picking on him and I thought he was going to get hurt. If you let me out of here there's an exciting world that's out there waiting for me. This terrific new quiet girlfriend who practically brings me the newspaper in her teeth— who watches me like a hawk for the slightest sign of sexual tension—and then whop—she's in there like a shot to drain it off and make me feel comfortable again... and if I feel like going out at four in the morning to get some eggs—she's right there at my side—because she comes from a tradition where the man is like a gypsy king and the woman is someone who drags mutton to him on her back, all the way up a hill. And all she ever hopes for is that he'll throw her a lousy mutton bone while she's sleeping in the dirt at his feet.... And this is an intelligent girl, too, a Bryn Mawr girl.... If I'm so crazy about her, how come I'm constantly chasing chicks all over the place? All right, I'll admit to you that she's a little on the quiet side—that sometimes all that quiet drives me nuts.... All right, let's face it, she's basically a dull girl. Terrific kid, loyal, faithful, brings you mutton, but the sparks don't fly.... And it did cross my mind that maybe I'll find another girl who's got a little more pazazz.... I'll give you that.

The playwright has given you much. It is obvious that it is literally your life you are fighting for. You want it back and the P. R. Attendant is the only one who can give it to you.

Tandy may have his values screwed up. He may be a chauvinist, a sexist, a victim of unresolved chaos and conflicts between him and his mother. He may be lacking a healthy father figure and be totally inappropriate in much of his actions and choices in life but he passionately wants to live and not die. He wants another chance to do a better job as a person. He is in the midst of the one and only who calls the shots. Tandy possesses many character flaws but you must make him likeable, because he is. Communicate his desire and need by exposing vulnerability. You then become one of us—the audience. And for the audition, this means the auditor. Don't forget the auditor is a person also. I need to feel for you. To root for you. I want to identify with you and find something of myself in you. That is the magic that the actor creates in theaters. That is when you touch the audience.

You don't start out by thinking of your audience. Even though they have needs and you must fulfill these needs. But they can't be fulfilled unless you begin with a history of the character leading up to today's confrontation. Read the entire play and use whatever you choose to use that the playwright has given to you that leads up to the here and now. Be aware as an actor that this is a very funny scene about the sadness of loss of life. Be aware of the absurdities of the actions and words of Tandy. If indeed you do not consider this monologue very funny, ironic, and absurd, please do not even attempt to use it as an audition piece.

Create your reality starting from the day you were born. Make personal choices from your own life. Choices that will add to and complement the playwright's choices.

NORMAN, IS THAT YOU?
By Ron Clark and Sam Bobrick

pp. 10–14 (SAMUEL FRENCH, INC.)

Ben: *(He brings in his suitcase and looks around.)* Hey, this is a nice place. *(Nods head.* GARSON *goes into the bathroom.)* You're like me. You have exquisite taste. *(Looks towards drapes.)* A little heavy on the purple, but I'm sure you're old enough to know what you're doing.

Norman: Now tell me. What are you doing here?

Ben: *(Confidentially.)* Have you heard from your mother yet?

Norman: *(Sitting down.)* No. Why should I hear from Mother? What's wrong?

Ben: *(Not realizing* NORMAN *is seated.)* Sit down, Norman. There's something I have to tell you...

Norman: Nothing happened to her? She's okay, isn't she?

Ben: She's fine.

Norman: Then what is it?

Ben: Remember Uncle Julius?

Norman: Of course I remember Uncle Julius. What happened to him?

Ben: The same thing that happened to your mother.

Norman: What are you talking about?

Ben: What am I talking about? They ran off together.

Norman: What?

Ben: That's right. They ran off together. And you're hearing it from the mouth of the injured party.

Norman: *(Suppressed laugh.)* Dad, you've gotta be kidding.

Ben: Don't laugh, Norman. It's no laughing matter. Your mother and my brother are now at this very moment cohabiting in a motel up in Canada and I hope they're freezing their asses off.

Norman: I can't believe it! Uncle Julius.

149

Ben: That's right. Uncle Julius to you. Brother Julius to me and lover Julius to your mother.

Norman: This is ridiculous.

Ben: Ridiculous, huh? I swear, Norman, it's true. And after twenty-six years of marriage.

Norman: Mother and Uncle Julius, together. What a strange combination.

Ben: I know and I've seen them both naked... on separate occasions, of course. God knows how many years they've been carrying on.

Norman: (Not laughing.) How did it happen?

Ben: How? Who knows? I tell you, Norman, the thoughts that have been going on in my mind. Not only is Uncle Julius my brother, he's also my partner, which means he's probably screwing me there too.

Norman: Maybe you need a drink.

Ben: Sure, why not? It would serve her right if I became an alcoholic. (NORMAN *goes to kitchen and brings out ice cubes and a glass and gets a bottle of liquor from the cabinet as* BEN *continues*.) You know, all night long on the bus I said to myself: should I tell Norman, shouldn't I tell Norman? Then I figure: who have I got to turn to? I can't tell your sister. She's married to that crazy chiropractor and they're hung up with that new religion. How anyone can live on lima beans alone, I'll never know. Anyway, when something like this happens, how long can a man keep it inside? Believe me, Norman, until I was downstairs in your hallway pressing the buzzer, I wasn't going to tell you.

Norman: When did you find out?

Ben: The night before last... during "Happy Days." Do you believe that? They called me from the Clair De Lune Motor Lodge in Montreal.

Norman: Montreal? Why Montreal?

Ben: They went up there to make a new life for themselves. And get this. They're registered as Mr. and Mrs. Smith. Huh? Is that Julius clever?

Norman: Why would Mother want you to know where they're staying?

Ben: You know your mother. She doesn't want me to worry.

Norman: (Handing him a drink.) Here.

Ben: Thanks. (BEN *sips it and makes a face.*) What is it?

Norman: Vodka and orange juice.

Ben: Can I have it without the orange juice? (NORMAN *prepares another drink for him.*) Ahh, what am I gonna do without that woman? How we struggled together. From nothing we built ourselves a nice respectable dry-cleaning business. In by nine, out by five. Closed Saturdays July and August. It wasn't easy for us. The first four years I had to stuff the cardboard in the shirts myself. Now look at us. Last year alone Julius and I netted over fifteen thousand dollars each. Now she's gone. What am I gonna do, huh, Norman? Who am I gonna get to replace her in front of the store?

Norman: You know, that very attitude is probably why this all happened.

Ben: What are you talking about?

Norman: Mom ran off with Uncle Julius and all you're worried about is who's going to replace her in front of the store.

Ben: You don't think that's important? Let me tell you something about your mother. She was good in front of the store. She had personality. She had a way with people. They liked her. Always a smile. Always a "Good morning." Always a "How are you? How's the baby?"... Boy, was she a phony... But that's why she was so good for my business.

Norman: But, Dad, did you love her?

Ben: (*Resentful.*) Of course I loved her. If I didn't love her do you think I would let her handle the cash register? Believe me, Norman, as God is my witness I was crazy about that woman. Sure, maybe I didn't show it but who the hell does at my age?

Norman: You know, Dad, I'll tell you the truth, I'm not surprised about Mother running away.

Ben: You knew about your mother and Uncle Julius and you didn't tell me? What kind of a son are you?

Norman: No, I didn't know about the two of them. It's just that I'm not surprised Mom decided to have herself a fling.

Ben: A fling? This is no fling. This is the real thing.

Norman: How do you know?

Ben: Believe me, I know. When she left she took the family photo album ... A woman doesn't take a bunch of old snapshots on a fling. Any man knows that ... I tell you, Norman, I'm sick about the whole mess.

Norman: Well, I guess marriage can be pretty difficult at times. Here. (*He hands* BEN *the vodka.* BEN *takes a good gulp.*)

Ben: Thanks. I'm glad I came here. I knew you'd understand.

Norman: Mom had a lot of needs that you were never concerned about.

Ben: *(Puts drink down.)* I should have gone to your sister's.

Norman: What I mean is that apparently something was missing in her life.

Ben: Don't give me that. That woman had everything. Coats, dresses, handbags, and every week at the store, I gave her Wednesdays off. I didn't have to do that. Let me tell you something about women, Norman. They're selfish, they're conniving, and I'll tell you the truth, if you don't care much for dancing you don't need them at all. *(He shakes his head sideways, while* NORMAN *nods his head up and down, agreeing with him.)* My advice to you is that if you can work it out, stay away from them.

The following is the monologue created from the previous scene.

BEN (to NORMAN), age late 40s to 60.
pp. 10–14 (SAMUEL FRENCH, INC.)

Hey, this is a nice place. You're like me. You have excellent taste. A little heavy on the purple, but I'm sure you're old enough to know what you're doing. Have you heard from your mother yet? Sit down, Norman. There's something I have to tell you. Remember Uncle Julius? What happened to him, happened to your mother. They ran off together! And you're hearing it from the mouth of the injured party. Your mother and my brother are now at this very moment cohabiting in a motel up in Canada and I hope they're freezing their asses off. Uncle Julius to you! Brother Julius to me and lover Julius to your mother. I swear, Norman, it's true. And after twenty-six years of marriage. They're a strange combination. I know. I've seen them both naked . . . on separate occasions, of course. God knows how many years they've been carrying on. I tell you, Norman, the thoughts that have been going on in my mind. Not only is Uncle Julius my brother, he's also my partner, which means he's probably screwing me there too. It would serve her right if I became an alcoholic. You know, all night long on the bus I said to myself: should I tell Norman, shouldn't I tell Norman? Then I figure: who have I got to turn to? I can't tell your sister. She's married to that crazy chiropractor and they're hung up with that new religion. How anyone can live on lima beans alone, I'll never know. Anyway, when something like this happens, how long can a man keep it inside? Believe me, Norman, until I was downstairs in your hallway pressing the buzzer, I wasn't going to tell you. I found out the night before last . . . during *Happy Days*. Do you believe that? They called me from the Clair De Lune Motor Lodge in Montreal. They went up there to make a new life for themselves. And get this. They're registered as Mr. and Mrs. Smith. Huh? Is that Julius clever? You know your mother. She called because she doesn't want me to worry. What am I gonna do without that woman? How we struggled together. From nothing we built ourselves a nice respectable dry-cleaning business. In by nine, out by five. Closed Saturdays July and August. It wasn't easy for us. The first four years I had to stuff the cardboard in the shirts myself. Now look at us. Last year alone Julius and I netted over fifteen thousand dollars each. Now she's gone. What am I gonna do, huh, Norman? Who am I gonna get to replace her in front of the store? Let me tell you something about your mother. She was good in front of the store. She had personality. She had a way with people. They liked her. Always a smile. Always a "Good morning." Always a "How are you? How's the baby?" . . . Boy, was she a phony. . . . But that's why she was so good for my business. I loved her! If I didn't love her do you think I would let her handle the cash register? Believe me, Norman, as God is my witness I was crazy about that woman. Sure, maybe I didn't show it but who the hell does at my age? When she left she took the family photo album. . . . A woman doesn't take a bunch of old snapshots on a fling. Any man knows that . . . I tell you, Norman, I'm sick about the whole mess. That woman had everything. Coats, dresses, handbags, and every week at the store, I gave her Wednesday off. I didn't have to do that. Let me tell you something about women, Norman. They're selfish, they're conniving, and I'll tell you the truth, if you don't care much for dancing you don't need them at all. My advice to you is that if you can work it out, stay away from them!

Ben needs his son more than ever before. An extension of himself as a young, virile man. His flesh and blood. Father needing son to be the father.

Fight for him to love you so much that you will lose the pain you carry with you. And the humiliation. Remember the monologue is about the person you are talking *to*, not the person you are talking *about*!

You've come to Norman because he is your son, you love him and he is the only one who can help you. He is the only person in the world who *loves* you! He has to help you to survive this terrible time you are going through. You need him to love you and give you strength to handle this situation. You need him to help you to get your wife back.

It's so easy to do just the playwright's words. It is very clear on the page what is going on. At least in this scene. What is not on the page is the humiliation, the pain of the loss and the fear for the future. That is not the playwright's responsibility. He expects the actor to provide the inner life that is both complementary to the words and opposite to them!

NORMAN, IS THAT YOU?
by Ron Clark and Sam Bobrick

pp. 26–28 (SAMUEL FRENCH, INC.)

Ben: *(Noticing the audience, he rises.)* You know what I have here? Books on homosexuals. You think it's easy to go into a strange bookstore and ask for books like these? A grown masculine man like me? And the way that salesman looked at me. Thank God I was wearing sunglasses... I couldn't believe this store. American history, two shelves. Fairies, a whole wall... And just around the corner from St. Patrick's... Here, look at these. *(He reads titles of some of the books, throwing them onto the sofa when he's finished.)* "The Homosexual in America"... "The Closet Homosexual"... "Homosexuality—For and Against"... Look at this one... "All the President's Men"... Tch. I should have known. It wouldn't surprise me if one day you pick up a copy of *Reader's Digest* and there it is in black and white... "The Most Unforgettable Homosexual I Ever Met"... I tell you, I don't know what to do. I've been reading all day and I'm more confused than ever. One says it's a mental thing. Another says it's strictly physical. One says it's natural. One says it's unnatural. One says you gotta stop it. The other one says leave well enough alone... I don't know anymore. All I know is that I had nothing to do with it. I took him to ball games, to boxing matches. When he was four I bought him a tool box... with wrenches and pliers... Maybe it's his name. Norman! Norman? I wanted to give him a real man's name. Like... Jack! When you call the name Jack a man shows up. You don't get... *(High voice and walks swishy.)* Yes, Daddy, I'm coming. *(Natural voice.)* You get... *(Deep voice.)* what is it, Dad? *(Normal voice.)* What do you do? Send him to a psychiatrist? Who needs them? All they do is blame the parents. Maybe we are to blame. I can't imagine why. As a

155

kid we always dressed him in blue... What does a father do? One out of every six! That's what one book says. One out of every six males in this country has had a homosexual relationship of some sort. One out of every six! Imagine that. *(Points to front row.)* In this row alone there could be three of you! *(Looks towards back of theatre.)* I think I see 2 sixes sitting together back there... I don't know what's happening to this world. When I was a kid there was no such thing as fairies, except for maybe little Peter Waterson. He wore glasses and got good marks, he was a hotshot in poetry and little girls used to beat him up. Nah, he couldn't have been. He married and had six kids. All boys. *(Realizes something.)* Oh-oh, poor Peter. Got himself a "one out of six" and doesn't know it. According to these books it can happen to anyone. They've got one case here... *(Picks up a book.)* A happily married man, two kids, one on the way, a home in the suburbs... bumped into the mailman one morning, their eyes met, "Goodbye, marriage"... They're now living in San Francisco and running a very successful boutique.... According to another book here, we all have homosexual tendencies. I've been trying to think all day. Did I ever feel anything like that? The only thing I remember is that in the movies I used to like Cesar Romero a lot. But once I got home that was the end of the romance... Where did it start? Where did it start with my Norman? I should have seen this coming. The high school prom. That was the tip-off. He took his mother. What kind of a kid takes his mother? And what kind of a mother accepts a date like that?... Maybe it was my fault. Maybe I kissed him too much. A daughter you can kiss forever. With Norman I should have quit at nineteen... There's only one thing to do. I'll have to be violent with him. I'll beat the crap out of him and drag him back home... where he'll meet a nice mailman and it'll start all over again... What do I do? What the hell do I do? God forbid they find out about this at the country club it's all over. The wife and Julius, that's all right. That's normal.

The following is the monologue created from the previous scene. Note the change from third person to first person.

BEN (to NORMAN), age late 40s to 60.
pp. 26–28 (SAMUEL FRENCH, INC.)

You know what I have here? Books on homosexuals. You
think it's easy to go into a strange bookstore and ask for
books like these? A grown masculine man like me? And
the way that salesman looked at me. Thank God I was
wearing sunglasses... I couldn't believe this store. American history, two shelves, fairies, a whole wall... and just
around the corner from St. Patrick's... here, look at these:
The Homosexual in America ... *The Closet Homosexual* ...
Homosexuality—For and Against.... Look at this one... *All
the President's Men*... Tch, I should have known. It wouldn't
surprise me if one day you pick up a copy of *Reader's
Digest* and there it is in black and white... "The Most
Unforgettable Homosexual I Ever Met"... I tell you, I
don't know what to do. I've been reading all day and I'm
more confused than ever. One says it's a mental thing.
Another says it's strictly physical. One says it's natural.
One says it's unnatural. One says you gotta stop it. The
other one says leave well enough alone... I don't know
anymore. All I know is that I had nothing to do with it. I
took you to ball games, to boxing matches. When you were
four I bought you a toolbox... with wrenches and pliers.
... Maybe it's your name. Norman! Norman? I wanted to
give you a real man's name. Like... Jack! When you call
the name Jack a man shows up. You don't get... *(High
voice and walks swishy)*... Yes, Daddy, I'm coming. *(Natural voice.)* You get... *(Deep voice.)*... What is it, Dad?
(Normal voice.) What do I do? Send you to a psychiatrist?
Who needs them? All they do is blame the parents. Maybe
we are to blame. I can't imagine why. As a kid we always
dressed you in blue.... What does a father do? One out of
every six! That's what one book says. According to another
book here, we all have homosexual tendencies. I've been
trying to think all day. Did I ever feel anything like that?
The only thing I remember is that in the movies I used to
like Cesar Romero a lot. But once I got home that was the
end of the romance.... Where did it start? Where did it
start with you, Norman? I should have seen this coming.
The high-school prom. That was the tip-off. You took your
mother. What kind of a kid takes his mother? And what

kind of a mother accepts a date like that? Maybe it was my fault. Maybe I kissed you too much. A daughter you can kiss forever. With you I should have quit at nineteen. . . . There's only one thing to do. I'll have to be violent with you. I'll beat the crap out of you and drag you back home . . . where you'll meet a nice mailman and it'll start all over again. . . . What do I do? God forbid they find out about this at the country club it's all over. My wife running off with my brother, that's all right. That's normal. But this!

Ben is not a bad person. He is just underinformed. We must establish immediately that this play was produced in 1970 as a comedy. Some people think this play is ridiculing gays, but what it is actually doing is being honest about a parent's discovery that there is to be a rupture in the traditional family values. He was brought up with the beliefs from the generation before him and before that. Change is frightening. Especially when it has to do with your own. So he is very confused and scared. He's trying to understand and to accept this. He's also got something of an Archie Bunker mentality, which, of course, goes hand in hand when one just follows blindly whatever it is he's been taught. It's easier and safer that way. Ben is now in a threatening situation. His own sexuality is also at stake. Especially because his wife ran off with his brother!

As Ben, you are fighting for your son to be a man! Like you! Better than you! You're not doing so terrifically yourself. You love your son. You are fighting for him to be "normal." This is a funny piece but even more it has rich irony.

NORMAN, IS THAT YOU?
by Ron Clark and Sam Bobrick

pp. 50–52 (SAMUEL FRENCH, INC.)

Ben: Well, how do you like her?

Garson: She's an animal. Just gorgeous. (*He shakes* BEN's *hand.*) Congratulations, I knew you'd find someone to make you forget your problems.

Ben: (*Looks upward.*) There goes another thirty-five bucks. (*To* GARSON.) Garson, I brought her here for you.

Garson: For me?

Mary: This is not my luckiest apartment.

(BEN *leads* MARY *to bedroom.*)

Ben: Look, Mary, why don't you go into the bedroom and get ready and let me handle the customer.

Mary: (*In bedroom doorway.*) O.K., but will you try to hurry. I have to be at the U.N. by six.

Ben: Just stay in the bedroom. (*He closes bedroom door.*)

Garson: Hey, is she the girl you brought here for Normie?

(*During the following conversation,* MARY *removes her coat and dress and sits on the edge of the bed in her slip reading a magazine.*)

Ben: (*Enthusiastically.*) Yeah. She's a smart looker isn't she?

Garson: Who said she wasn't? She's adorable... But I don't understand you. If it didn't work with Normie, what made you think it would work with me?

Ben: Because I've been watching you these past few days. You may not know this yourself, Garson, but you have a lot of... what they call... heterosexual tendencies.

Garson: (*Looking upward.*) Tch! The man is impossible!

Ben: No, I mean it, Garson. Little things that you do, like the way you dry the dishes... You don't go like this... (BEN

159

makes a very dainty, circular motion.)... You go like this... (BEN *then makes a masculine, circular motion with palm out.*) And the way you shake hands. You've got a real firm grip. You almost broke my fingers yesterday.

Garson: We weren't shaking hands, remember? You tried to push me out the window.

Ben: So what? At least you defended yourself. Garson, behind that door is a new horizon for you. A chance to go from AC to DC... to go from a three dollar bill to a ten spot. It's the big time, Garson. Think of it as opening night.

Garson: Do you mind if I lie down for a minute?

Ben: (*Points to the bedroom.*) Do me a favor. Go lie down in there.

Garson: You are so cute sometimes.

Ben: (*Imploring.*) Look, Garson, try it. What have you got to lose? I thought young people today were willing to try anything.

Garson: I know you're desperate and I'd like to help you out but what would I do with a girl?

Ben: Did you ever ride the roller coaster?

Garson: Of course.

Ben: Remember the thrill you got when you went down the first big hill?

Garson: Uh-huh.

Ben: It'll be almost as good as that.

The following is the monologue created from the previous scene.

BEN (to GARSON), age 40s to 60.
pp. 50–52 (SAMUEL FRENCH, INC.)

Well, how do you like her? She's a smart looker, isn't she? I've been watching you these past few days. You may not know this yourself, Garson, but you have a lot of... what they call... heterosexual tendencies. No, I mean it, Garson. Little things that you do, like the way you dry the dishes.... You don't go like this... (BEN *then makes a very dainty, circular motion.*)... you go like this... (BEN *then makes a masculine, circular motion with palm out.*) And the way you shake hands. You've got a real firm grip. You almost broke my fingers yesterday. I know I was trying to push you out the window. So what? At least you defended yourself.

Garson, behind that door is a new horizon for you. A chance to go from AC to DC . . . to go from a three-dollar bill to a ten spot. It's the big time, Garson. Think of it as opening night.

Look, Garson, try it. What have you got to lose? I thought young people today were willing to try anything. Did you ever ride the roller coaster? Remember the thrill you got when you went down the first big hill? It'll be almost as good as that.

You'll try anything to get Garson out of your son's life. Including getting him a prostitute. Only by reading the entire play will you understand why you are having this confrontation. If you were not to read the play but wanted to do this piece, you would have to invent and create an entire history yourself. Yours would not be as good as the playwright's history for the character. You are not a professional writer. Let him do the writing for you.

P. S. YOUR CAT IS DEAD!
by James Kirkwood

pp. 15–24 (SAMUEL FRENCH, INC.)

Jimmy: Okay... I caught you, you dirty son-of-a-bitch! Come out—hands up! *(A rattled* VITO *lifts the bedspread and peeks out timidly—but he sees* JIMMY *is facing the bathroom door and he carefully drops the spread and disappears just as: A confused and frightened* KATE *manages to open the door and appears, hands full of things, hair-dryer, etc.* JIMMY *and she are both startled, speak at once:)*

Kate: Oh—Jimmy!

Jimmy: Kate!—Oh...

Jimmy: *(Heaving a sigh.)* Oh, Kate—Ohh! God, for a second there I thought I was being ripped off again! Christ, I must be going bananas, it couldn't happen a third time! *(Another deep breath.)* Oh, wow...*(Then.)* Hey, I thought we were spending New Year's apart? *(Going to her, still holding the bar.)* Oh, lady—am I ever glad to see you. Am I ever! *(Hugs her, only then, in his confusion, does he put two-and-two together, realizing that someone indeed is packing up, glances at the articles in her hands, at the things on the bed, then back at her.)* I think I am...

Kate: *(Backing away from him slightly.)* I thought you were going right up to Claire's.

Jimmy: I was, but—something came up. I decided to... I take it you're going someplace, too. (KATE *does not reply.)* Well, aren't you? *(No reply.)* Aren't you?

Kate: *(Quietly.)* Yes...

Jimmy: *(Hit hard.)* Yes... yeah...*(Crosses downstage, leans the fox bar against the wall, goes to the coat-rack downstage entrance platform, takes off his coat, hat, hangs them up.)* Well—Oh, boy, yeah... great!... Nifty!... Neat...! *(Walks back, looks down at the TV and cassette player.)* Look, I don't mind you taking back your own Christmas present, but I bought the cassette.

Kate: *(Shocked at this accusation.)* I gave you the TV for Christmas. What a terrible thing to say! I wasn't taking either one of them.

Jimmy: *(Picking them up.)* What—they've got dates for New Year's Eve. *(Talking directly to them.)* You two stepping out again! I thought I told you about that!

Kate: Don't be ridiculous!

Jimmy: *(Crossing to counter in kitchen with them.)* I'm not in the habit of unplugging them and setting them by the door every time I go out.

Kate: I told you I wasn't taking them. Don't you believe me?

Jimmy: No, I don't believe you.

Kate: *(Continues packing.)* Oh, well I . . .

Jimmy: Oh, Kate—lookee here! *(Walking to telephone downstage end of sink.)* Whaddaya know, the *mailman's* come! *(Picks up envelope.)*

Kate: No, Jimmy, don't—not now!

Jimmy: Christ, it's addressed to me, isn't it?

Kate: Jimmy, please don't . . .

Jimmy: Please don't! You—For God's sake, you're leaving, obviously you're leaving. This is obviously—a Dear John, and you don't want me to *open* it! Who knows, I might even have a reply for once!

Kate: *(Walking to him, reaching out for the letter.)* I'd rather you read it after—

Jimmy: Well, you've been out-voted. *(He opens the unsealed envelope and reads:)* "Dear *Jimmy*"—Well, so far so good. It's not a laugh riot, but—you know, it's got a nice *homey* touch!

Kate: *(Walking away.)* You said you were going right up to Claire's from rehearsals. How did I know you weren't? How did I—

Jimmy: *(Crossing to trunk-coffee table.)* How did I know I was going to be *fired*! *(Sitting on trunk.)* I'm sorry, my plans changed. I—

Kate: Jimmy! *(Going to him, putting her hands on his shoulders.)* Oh, Jimmy! Oh, angel . . .

Jimmy: I just didn't feel like rushing up there and putting on a paper hat.

Kate: Jimmy—I had no idea. Oh, Jimmy, I'm so sorry! *(Embraces him; he does not respond.)* Jimmy?

Jimmy: Get away—please! I really don't want to cry, not in front of Miss Strength and Guts, not in front of Our Lady Photographer. If you maul me, I will! *(Rises.)* Please! *(Walking away from her.)*

Kate: And what would you be crying about? Would it be *me* or the job?

Jimmy: Oh, terrific! Can't I just play it across the board? Do I *have* to pick a category?

Kate: Jimmy, I'm sorry about the play. Why did you get fired?

Jimmy: The *why!* *(Crossing to the refrigerator in the kitchen.)* Oh, honey—you won't believe the *why!* Miss Hollywood Star wanted her boyfriend to play my part in the first place, but he was starting a picture in Spain. *(Taking out ice tray, then going to downstage counter unit.)* Yesterday, he got into an argument with the director, that English Sir Waldo-what's-his-name, on the set, in front of the entire cast and crew, and called him "a dizzy cunt!" *(Giving it a stage-reading, even a bit of "camp," he fills the ice bucket.)* "What was *that?*" asked Sir Waldo. He repeated it, with embellishments. Sir Waldo kicked him off the picture. *(Making a drink.)* Boyfriend gets on the phone to Miss Hollywood Star, Miss Hollywood Star gets on the phone to our producers and lays down the law. Know what gets me? Some flipped-out actor calls a director a "dizzy cunt" in *Madrid*—and *I* get fired in New York!

Kate: *(Crossing to sit on kitchen stool, stage right of sink unit.)* Rotten—It's rotten.

Jimmy: Well, stay tuned for the rest of the news. The soap opera's kaput, too.

Kate: Kaput?

Jimmy: *(Sitting on stool opposite her with his drink.)* Kaput!

Kate: I thought they were just writing you out while the play was out of town.

Jimmy: The ratings have been way down lately, so they made one *little* change in the storyline. Instead of writing me off on that two-month expedition up the Amazon, from which they were going to bring me back with some mysterious disease, they've decided to—just let me *drown* in the goddam Amazon! *(Downs drink in one gulp, holds his glass up.)* Drink?

Kate: *(Shaking her head: no.* JIMMY *walks to bar-counter.)* But, Jimmy, I thought you signed a three-year contract.

Jimmy: *(Making another drink.)* It can be cancelled every thirteen weeks.

Kate: So how can it be a three-year contract?

Jimmy: The network can cancel, but not the performer.

Kate: Great! What kind of clause is that?

Jimmy: *(Walking back to sink unit.)* We call that—the Fuck-You Clause!

Kate: Ohh! Acting—what a tacky business!

Jimmy: *(Crossing around, upstage of* KATE, *kneading her shoulders with his hands.)* At least it solves our problems, doesn't it? You won't have to put up with all of that jazz: No more soap opera, no more learning lines every night, no more working on the book, even. Now we can really *play house.*

Kate: Jimmy, stop it—you're being mean.

Jimmy: *I'm* being mean? Who's walking out on who New Year's Eve?

Kate: *(Breaking away from him to up right of sofa.)* I picked tonight because I knew you'd be at Claire's, also because I thought you'd be so tied up with the play it wouldn't matter that much. Oh, Jimmy, it's not as if it were news. We both knew it was coming. We said we'd skip New Year's and—

Jimmy: *(Pointing a finger at her.)* You said, you said, *you* said! You were the one who said we'd spend New Year's apart. You were invited, same as last year.

Kate: To sit around with that back-biting aunt of yours and watch her dangle you on a string? "You're my only family, Jimmy, and when I die..." and on and on. Promises, promises. Wind the Aunt Claire Doll up and it promises to die—but doesn't!

Jimmy: Let's not get into that again.

Kate: Because it's the worst possible form of blackmail; it's disgusting and demeaning. And you know it. You know what the annoying thing is about you?

Jimmy: *(Big.)* Whoa-hoh! You've been holding back? You mean there's some *ONE* thing you haven't told me? *(Crossing down right.)*

Kate: Yes, about a dozen, if you really want to know.

Jimmy: I don't. *(Sits on sofa.)*

Kate: Good, I'll tell you. You're thirty-eight years old and maybe you're really a good actor—I mean, could be if—

Jimmy: That's the most encouraging thing you've ever said.

Kate: But you play it so almighty safe! All right, I'm going to tell you something else—

Jimmy: *(Hands to his head.)* Oh, Jesus...

Kate: Yes, well, oh Jesus, I am. Two people were talking about you at a party once, and one of 'em said, "That Jimmy Zoole, he's such an attractive guy. Say, are his front teeth capped?" You know what the other one said? *"Jimmy Zoole's whole life is capped!"*

Jimmy: *(Laughs, then does a take.)* What does that mean?

Kate: It means you have absolutely no imagination, not a fresh idea in your head about how to present yourself. You're always so busy playing "Good Dog" for everybody. You roll over, sit up and bark! An actor? Honey... you conduct yourself like some dried-up ad agency squeak! *(Walking to the bed to finish packing.)* You won't even take any chances. You cling to the safe things: that tired soap opera, your occasional summer tour in—God help us!—"Call Me Madam"!

Jimmy: *(Walking up near her.)* I'm sorry, I don't get offered every choice role that comes along on Broadway, you know.

Kate: Then you must be doing something wrong! For God's sake, Jimmy, you're attractive, you're bright, you're—

Jimmy: And you are an All-American, three-dimensional, supreme pain in the ass! *(Does a proud take for this assertion, cocks his head, almost struts downstage, sits once again on the sofa, pleased with himself.)*

Kate: *(After a beat.)* Funny, that's just what my horoscope said today. Let's leave it at that, shall we? *(Walks to the bed, begins to zip her packed suitcase, then suddenly wheels, steps down toward* Jimmy.*)* And one more stupid thing: two consenting adults in 1978 keeping separate apartments. And don't think I don't know why—Aunt Claire would have changed her will if we'd have—

Jimmy: *(Standing, shouting.)* Stop it, stop it, stop it! Level with me, do you have *one*, just *one*, un-uttered opinion?

Kate: *(Silenced for a moment.)* Uhhhh, no—I guess I don't. *(Then, crossing to the counter-bar in the kitchen.)* Oh, what the heck. One for the breakup. *(Pouring whiskey into setup glass.)* Here's to the good times. We had some rocky ones, but we had some good ones, too. *(Walking to the chair opposite the sofa.)* Funny, for anyone as basically old-fashioned, filled-to-the-brim with the Puritan Ethic, you really do make the wildest—hugglebunnyburgers. *(Sits in the chair.)*

Jimmy: *(Laughing.)* Jesus, that is brutal. Who made that up? Did you?

Kate: No, my angel, you did. Actually, I've grown rather fond of it.

Jimmy: Hugglebunnyburgers! *(Then.)* Were they really that good?

Kate: Tops in town. Actually, I think that's what hooked me on you, least at first. I mean when we'd be out, you're so—oh, opening doors, Boy Scoutish, helping old women and blind people across streets, never giving a cab driver back any of the lip they give out. Then we'd get home and... Wow, it was like some dusty Italian workman.

Jimmy: *(After a long pause.)* Really?

Kate: Really. *(Then.)* Jimmy, all those unuttered opinions were uttered... because I care about you. Don't you know that? Listen, I realize it's a sore point, but I hope you'll get back to your book. It was so good.

Jimmy: To start all over again! It's hard to get steam up.

Kate: But please don't give up on it, just because—

Jimmy: *(Reaching for her hand.)* Listen, you can move your things back to your place, but—why don't we spend New Year's together? I'll call Claire up and tell her I can't make it.

Kate: No, I can't, Jimmy. Honestly, I—if I'd known that all this, I mean—but it was agreed we'd spend New Year's apart and—well, I made other... plans.

Jimmy: Plans?

Kate: Yes.

Jimmy: Oh, you made *plans.* Well, that's different. *(Stands up.)* Plans, huh? Would these be *Johnnie Plans?* Or *Joe* Plans?

Kate: I'm—we're going to a party tonight, then tomorrow up to Vermont for some skiing... *(Rises, crosses up toward the desk.)*

Jimmy: You mean, you made a date with some guy, then you suggested we skip New Year's so—

Kate: No, it didn't happen like that! Please, baby—give me that much credit!

Jimmy: Please, baby, my ass! *(As KATE goes to sink unit, snatches up vitamin bottles and then crosses up to her* *suitcase.*) No wonder Claire was catching such hell. You had to dump it on someone. You're probably in the middle of your next affair. Why the hell didn't you just tell me, instead of letting me beg and—

Kate: Jimmy, I was just doing a foto lay-out up at—

Jimmy: Umm—layout. *Lay-out!* I'll bet!

Kate: —up at Columbia, it's only someone I met through work and he asked me and I—

Jimmy: And you just—Oh, get out!

Kate: Jimmy, stop it! (*Walking to the bed.*)

Jimmy: Just—get out! (*Crossing down toward the sink.*)

Kate: (*Picks up coat from bed, begins putting it on.*) I will, I will!

Jimmy: (*Grabbing letter from the sink, heading toward the bathroom as he tears it into little pieces.*) Christ, I'd rather read the entire collected works of Harold Robbins! (*Exits into bathroom;* KATE *gathers up her things as we hear the toilet flush. When* JIMMY *emerges from bathroom, he carries a small blue plastic case,* KATE'S *diaphragm, holds it up.*) Here—you'd better take your "equipment." (*Tosses it on the bed, walks down toward sink unit.*)

Kate: (*Hurt.*) Keep it, I won't be needing it. (*Beat.*) I bought a new one.

Jimmy: Please leave!

Kate: (*Walking toward the door.*) Goodbye, I'm sorry we had to have this little squabble, I wish—

Jimmy: If you'd just been honest with me from the beginning, we wouldn't have. What a dirty, sneaky, low-down—

Kate: Enchanting! (*She walks back, puts the keys to the apartment down on the trunk, then heads for the door with her things. She turns;* JIMMY *and* KATE *look at each other, then:*) Goodbye. (*She exits.*)

Jimmy: Good luck. (*Tips a small salute with a hand to her. After a moment, he rushes to the door, opens it, looks down the steps after her.*) Skiing, huh? As we say in the theatre, break a leg! Break both of them! That way you'll have an excuse for staying on your back! (*Slams the door, steps back into the room; suddenly a hand goes to his head in reaction to what he's said.*)—Oh, my God . . . (*Still, after a moment, he rushes back to the door, opens it again and shouts:*) Mazeltov! (*Slams the door shut once more, steps back into the apartment. Glancing around, he spots the diaphragm on*

*the bed, runs to it, picks it up, then hurries to the window
in the kitchen, opens it, glances out and to his left, waits a
moment for* KATE *to appear in sight to him.*) Kate? . . . Oh,
Kate??? May all your orgasms turn to stone!

The following is the monologue created from the previous
scene.

JIMMY (to KATE), age 20s to 40s.
pp. 15–24 (SAMUEL FRENCH, INC.)

Okay . . . I caught you, you dirty son-of-a-bitch! Come out—
hands up! . . . Oh, Kate—Ohh! God, for a second there I
thought I was being ripped off again! Christ, I must be
going bananas, it couldn't happen a third time! Hey, I
thought we were spending New Year's apart? Oh, lady—
am I ever glad to see you. Am I ever! (*Realizes she is
packing.*) I think I am . . . I take it you're going someplace.
Yes . . . yeah . . . well—Oh, boy, yeah . . . great! Nifty! . . .
Neat . . . ! Lookee here! Whaddaya know, the mailman's
come! Christ, it's addressed to me, isn't it? You—for God's
sake, you're leaving, obviously you're leaving. This is
obviously a Dear John. Who knows, I might even have a
reply for once! "Dear Jimmy"—Well, so far so good. It's
not a laugh riot, but—you know, it's got a nice homey
touch! . . . Do you know that I've been fired? . . . Get away
please! I really don't want to cry, not in front of Miss
Strength and Guts, not in front of Our Lady Photographer.
If you maul me, I will! Please! Oh, honey—you won't
believe why I've been fired. Miss Hollywood Star wanted
her boyfriend to play my part in the first place, but he was
starting a picture in Spain. Yesterday, he got into an
argument with the director, that English Sir Waldo what's-
his-name, on the set, in front of the entire cast and crew,
and called him "a dizzy cunt"! (*Giving it a stage reading,
even a bit of camp.*) "What was that!" asked Sir Waldo. He
repeated it, with embellishments. Sir Waldo kicked him off
the picture. Boyfriend gets on the phone to Miss Hollywood
Star, Miss Hollywood Star gets on the phone to our
producers and lays down the law. Know what gets me?
Some flipped-out actor calls a director a "dizzy cunt" in

Madrid—and I get fired in New York! Well, stay tuned for the rest of the news. The soap opera's kaput, too. The ratings have been way down lately, so they made one *little* change in the storyline. Instead of writing me off on that two-month expedition up the Amazon, from which they were going to bring me back with some mysterious disease, they've decided to just let me *drown* in the goddamn Amazon! I may have a three-year contract but it can be canceled by them and not by me every thirteen weeks. We call that the Fuck-You Clause! At least it solves our problems, doesn't it? You won't have to put up with all that jazz. No more soap opera, no more learning lines every night, no more working on the book, even. Listen, you can move your things back to your place, but—why don't we spend New Year's together? Oh, you made *plans*. Well, that's different. Plans, huh? Would these be *Johnnie Plans*? Or Joe Plans? You're probably in the middle of your next affair. Why the hell didn't you just tell me, instead of letting me beg? Christ, I'd rather read the entire collected works of Harold Robbins than read your Dear John letter. Please leave! *(Screaming after her.)* Skiing, huh? As we say in the theater, break a leg! Break both of them! That way you'll have an excuse for staying on your back! May all your orgasms turn to stone!

We're dealing with rejection. A lot of it. The film, the soap opera, and, worst of all, Kate's rejection. At least that is the choice that you should be making for your character. Kate is the most important person in your life. You love her and need her more now than ever before. On top of all this, you've been burglarized twice. That is a very personal assault. So it appears as if you've got nothing going for you. You are suffering because you know that Kate is leaving you and might be having a relationship with another man. She probably has cheated on you many times. You are striking out in pain. Remember all that yelling and cursing and damning is coming from your hurt and pain that she is causing you. Fight to keep her. Fight for her to magically change her mind and realize on the spot that it is you she truly loves and she will never leave you. Fight for what you want, not what you think you must settle for.

P. S. YOUR CAT IS DEAD!
by James Kirkwood

pp. 18–22 (Samuel French, Inc.)

Kate: *(Crossing to sit on kitchen stool, stage right of sink unit.)* Rotten—It's rotten.

Jimmy: Well, stay tuned for the rest of the news. The soap opera's kaput, too.

Kate: Kaput?

Jimmy: *(Sitting on stool opposite her with his drink.)* Kaput!

Kate: I thought they were just writing you out while the play was out of town.

Jimmy: The ratings have been way down lately, so they made one *little* change in the storyline. Instead of writing me off on that two-month expedition up the Amazon, from which they were going to bring me back with some mysterious disease, they've decided to—just let me *drown* in the goddam Amazon! *(Downs drink in one gulp, holds his glass up.)* Drink?

Kate: *(Shaking her head: no. JIMMY walks to bar-counter.)* But, Jimmy, I thought you signed a three-year contract.

Jimmy: *(Making another drink.)* It can be cancelled every thirteen weeks.

Kate: So how can it be a three-year contract?

Jimmy: The network can cancel, but not the performer.

Kate: Great! What kind of clause is that?

Jimmy: *(Walking back to sink unit.)* We call that—the Fuck-You Clause!

Kate: Ohh! Acting—what a tacky business!

Jimmy: *(Crossing around, upstage of KATE, kneading her shoulders with his hands.)* At least it solves our problems, doesn't it? You won't have to put up with all of that jazz: No more soap opera, no more learning lines every night, no more working on the book, even. Now we can really *play house.*

Kate: Jimmy, stop it—you're being mean.

171

Jimmy: *I'm* being mean? Who's walking out on who New Year's Eve?

Kate: *(Breaking away from him to up right of sofa.)* I picked tonight because I knew you'd be at Claire's, also because I thought you'd be so tied up with the play it wouldn't matter that much. Oh, Jimmy, it's not as if it were news. We both knew it was coming. We said we'd skip New Year's and—

Jimmy: *(Pointing a finger at her.)* You said, you said, *you* said! You were the one who said we'd spend New Year's apart. You were invited, same as last year.

Kate: To sit around with that back-biting aunt of yours and watch her dangle you on a string? "You're my only family, Jimmy, and when I die . . ." and on and on. Promises, promises. Wind the Aunt Claire Doll up and it promises to die—but doesn't!

Jimmy: Let's not get into that again.

Kate: Because it's the worst possible form of blackmail; it's disgusting and demeaning. And you know it. You know what the annoying thing is about you?

Jimmy: *(Big.)* Whoa-hoh! You've been holding back? You mean there's some *ONE* thing you haven't told me? *(Crossing down right.)*

Kate: Yes, about a dozen, if you really want to know.

Jimmy: I don't. *(Sits on sofa.)*

Kate: Good, I'll tell you. You're thirty-eight years old and maybe you're really a good actor—I mean, could be if—

Jimmy: That's the most encouraging thing you've ever said.

Kate: But you play it so almighty safe! All right, I'm going to tell you something else—

Jimmy: *(Hands to his head.)* Oh, Jesus . . .

Kate: Yes, well, oh Jesus, I am. Two people were talking about you at a party once, and one of 'em said, "That Jimmy Zoole, he's such an attractive guy. Say, are his front teeth capped?" You know what the other one said? *"Jimmy Zoole's whole life is capped!"*

Jimmy: *(Laughs, then does a take.)* What does that mean?

Kate: It means you have absolutely no imagination, not a fresh idea in your head about how to present yourself. You're always so busy playing "Good Dog" for everybody. You roll over, sit up and bark! An actor? Honey . . . you conduct yourself like some dried-up ad agency squeak! *(Walking to the bed to finish packing.)* You won't even take any chances.

You cling to the safe things: that tired soap opera, your occasional summer tour in—God help us!—*Call Me Madam*!

Jimmy: *(Walking up near her.)* I'm sorry, I don't get offered every choice role that comes along on Broadway, you know.

Kate: Then you must be doing something wrong! For God's sake, Jimmy, you're attractive, you're bright, you're—

Jimmy: And you are an All-American, three-dimensional, supreme pain in the ass! *(Does a proud take for this assertion, cocks his head, almost struts downstage, sits once again on the sofa, pleased with himself.)*

Kate: *(After a beat.)* Funny, that's just what my horoscope said today. Let's leave it at that, shall we? *(Walks to the bed, begins to zip her packed suitcase, then suddenly wheels, steps down toward* JIMMY.) And one more stupid thing: two consenting adults in 1978 keeping separate apartments. And don't think I don't know why—Aunt Claire would have changed her will if we'd have—

Jimmy: *(Standing, shouting.)* Stop it, stop it, stop it! Level with me, do you have *one*, just *one*, un-uttered opinion?

Kate: *(Silenced for a moment.)* Uhhhh, no—I guess I don't. *(Then, crossing to the counter-bar in the kitchen.)* Oh, what the heck. One for the breakup. *(Pouring whiskey into setup glass.)* Here's to the good times. We had some rocky ones, but we had some good ones, too. *(Walking to the chair opposite the sofa.)* Funny, for anyone as basically old-fashioned, filled-to-the-brim with the Puritan Ethic, you really do make the wildest—hugglebunnyburgers. *(Sits in the chair.)*

Jimmy: *(Laughing.)* Jesus, that is brutal. Who made that up? Did you?

Kate: No, my angel, you did. Actually, I've grown rather fond of it.

Jimmy: Hugglebunnyburgers! *(Then.)* Were they really that good?

Kate: Tops in town. Actually, I think that's what hooked me on you, least at first. I mean when we'd be out, you're so—oh, opening doors, Boy Scoutish, helping old women and blind people across streets, never giving a cab driver back any of the lip they give out. Then we'd get home and . . . Wow, it was like some dusty Italian workman.

Jimmy: *(After a long pause.)* Really?

Kate: Really. *(Then.)* Jimmy, all those unuttered opinions were uttered . . . because I care about you. Don't you know that?

Listen, I realize it's a sore point, but I hope you'll get back
to your book. It was so good.

Jimmy: To start all over again! It's hard to get steam up.

Kate: But please don't give up on it, just because—

Jimmy: *(Reaching for her hand.)* Listen, you can move your
things back to your place, but—why don't we spend New
Year's together? I'll call Claire up and tell her I can't make
it.

Kate: No, I can't, Jimmy. Honestly, I—if I'd known that all this,
I mean—but it was agreed we'd spend New Year's apart
and—well, I made other... plans.

The following is the monologue created from the previous
scene.

KATE (to JIMMY), age 20s to 30s.
pp. 18–22 (SAMUEL FRENCH, INC.)

Jimmy, it's rotten that you were fired from the play. And I
thought they were just writing you out of the soap opera
while the play was out of town. And that's kaput! I thought
you signed a three-year contract? If it can be canceled
every thirteen weeks, how can it be a three-year contract?
Ohh! Acting—what a tacky business!

Jimmy, I picked tonight to leave you because I knew
you'd be at Claire's, also because I thought you'd be so
tied up with the play it wouldn't matter that much. Oh,
Jimmy, it's not as if it were news. We both knew it was
coming. We said we'd skip New Year's. I wasn't going to sit
around again with that back-biting aunt of yours and watch
her dangle you on a string! "You're my only family, Jimmy,
and when I die..." and on and on. Promises, promises.
Wind the Aunt Claire doll up and it promises to die—but
doesn't! And you know it. You know what the annoying
thing is about you? You're thirty-eight years old and maybe
you're really a good actor—I mean, could be. But you play
it so almighty safe! All right, I'm going to tell you something else. Two people were talking about you at a party
once, and one of them said, "That Jimmy Zoole, he's such
an attractive guy. Say, are his front teeth capped?" You
know what the other one said? "Jimmy Zoole's whole life is

capped!" You have absolutely no imagination, not a fresh idea in your head about how to present yourself. You're always so busy playing "Good Dog" for everybody. You roll over, sit up and bark! An actor? Honey... you conduct yourself like some dried-up ad agency squeak! You won't even take any chances. You cling to the safe things: that tired soap opera, your occasional summer tour in—God help us!—*Call Me Madam!* For God's sake, Jimmy, you're attractive, you're bright. And one more stupid thing: two consenting adults in 1978 keeping separate apartments. And don't think I don't know why—Aunt Claire would have changed her will if we had lived together.... Oh, what the heck. Here's to the good times. We had some rocky ones, but we had some good ones, too. Funny, for anyone as basically old-fashioned, filled-to-the-brim with the Puritan Ethic, you really do make the wildest hugglebunnyburgers. I didn't make up the word. You did. And they were the tops in town. Actually, I think that's what hooked me on you, least at first. I mean when we'd be out, you're so—oh, opening doors, Boy Scoutish, helping old women and blind people across streets, never giving a cab driver back any of the lip they give out. Then we'd get home and... wow, it was like some dusty Italian workman... Jimmy, all those unuttered opinions were uttered... because I care about you. Don't you know that? Listen, I realize it's a sore point, but I hope you'll get back to your book. It was so good.... Now it was agreed we'd spend New Year's apart and—well, I made other... plans.

You must not play this piece without the love that you *still* feel for Jimmy. I mean really being in love with him! You are fighting for him to change. You still want him to assert himself in all areas of his life and take risks and chances. You are hoping for his sake that he does this for himself after you are out of his life. But what you want more is for him to right now with you right here with him, give you a strong enough sign that he will change. Because if he could and would change, you would not break up with him. Yes, there has been damage done to your feelings for him. But his more adult and assertive behavior could easily mend those feelings. There is still so much love for him within you. It could still become a wonderful relationship and might be everlasting. This is what you are fighting for.

P. S. YOUR CAT IS DEAD!
by James Kirkwood

pp. 54–58 (SAMUEL FRENCH, INC.)

Vito: *(After a beat, looking* JIMMY *directly in the eye.)* Makes me feel like a—crumb. Like a punk—yeah, a lousy little crumb. *(This reply throws* JIMMY *completely.)*

Jimmy: I—well...ah...

Vito: Heavy question, heavy answer! Hey, I'd loosen up a lot more if I had a little smoke, then I'd really talk. It's like truth serum. The stuff's in my knapsack over there on your bed.

Jimmy: Marijuana? I don't want some whacked-out zombie on my hands.

Vito: No, no...just opens me up. Come on, goddammit, you got a *depressed person* on your hands, and that don't make for good talk.

Jimmy: *(Yelling.)* *Depressed* person? What do you think this is—Pat Boone!

Vito: Well, we oughtta be able to come up with somethin'—if we ain't gonna smoke. *(Snapping his fingers.)* Hey, I got it, why don't we just—make it?

Jimmy: *(Unbelieving.)* Make it?

Vito: Yeah, you're here and I sure-in-the-fuck-am. Besides, you're humpy, in an off-beat sort of way.

Jimmy: You're calling *me* off-beat?

Vito: Yeah, you got this...something, like they just took the bandages off.

Jimmy: Cool it, cool it. Hey—if ripping people off makes you feel that rotten, why don't you get into another line of work?

Vito: I been all fouled up lately, account of personal tragedy which I had in my life. Tonight I needed bread to buy some presents for my daughter; I didn't get to see her over Christmas and—

Jimmy: Your daughter?

Vito: Yeah, Melody Antonucci, ain't that a pisser to hang on a kid? Not my idea, my wife's.

Jimmy: Your wife's—but what was that big pitch just now?

Vito: Listen, guy—gay, not gay, who's countin'. Who gives a rat's ass anymore. I was married at sixteen, got a daughter nine, so don't give me that oh-my-shocked-ass-you're-queer bit. Double-gaited, okay. Versatile—definitely! So . . . what about you? You gay?

Jimmy: No.

Vito: Ever been married?

Jimmy: No.

Vito: *(Slyly.)* Mmn . . . And thirty-eight, too. Just haven't found the right girl yet, huh?

Jimmy: Hey, who's interviewing who? Just remember I'm making the rules here.

Vito: Yeah, well, I got a rule for you. Like I said before, give me my smoke. No smokee, no talkie! *(Punches buttons, turning off cassette.* JIMMY *goes to his bed, gets the dope out of the airline bag and brings it to* VITO.*)*

Jimmy: Okay, okay . . . smoke your lungs out, see if I care. But talk.

Vito: Hey . . . how about a little fuego, too?

Jimmy: Fuego?

Vito: Fire . . . fire! Jesus. *(Foraging in the plastic bag for a rolled joint which he takes out.)* Hey—you know how to circumcise an Italian baby? *(Making chopping gesture with one hand.)* Wop! *(*JIMMY *lights a match and holds it while* VITO, *taking his time, wets the cigarette by sticking it in his mouth, rolling it, looking at it, then sticking it in smoking position, looking at* JIMMY, *as if to say: okay, now you can light it.* VITO *takes a deep drag, speaks while holding the smoke down.)* Wanna hit? *(Punches the cassette on again.)*

Jimmy: *(Stepping back away from him.)* Naw, naw . . . it doesn't work for me.

Vito: Oh, one of those! You gimme a kick. C'mon, guy, just take a little toke.

Jimmy: Uh-uh, I've tried it three, four times—nothing.

Vito: Bat-shit! You'd get a kick outta this. This stuff's guaranteed to make a chihuahua snap at a bulldog's ass. Oh, I get it, you're scared.

Jimmy: No, I'm not.

Vito: Yes, you are. You're afraid if you got high, you'd let me up.

Jimmy: Oh, no, I wouldn't.

Vito: I think Kate was right about you. Chicken, chicken, chicken! *(Imitating a chicken.)* Puck-puck-pa-kaw!

Jimmy: After everything that's gone down today and tonight— you think I'm scared of you or that dumb little cigarette? *(VITO does another chicken imitation as if Clara Cluck were debating the issue: puck-puck-pa-kawing.)* You've got to be kidding. Here, gimme that. *(Grabs joint, takes a quick puff and hands it back.)* There—nothing. *(Turns away.)*

Vito: Guy, you smoke like Pat Boone! Here, watch— *(Taking a deep "toke.")* You take it way in, suck it down . . . *(Talking while holding the smoke down.)* Let the goodies do their work, leave the gates of Heaven open, let that Senegalese Thunderfuck work its magic spell, hold it down with all you got—just like you was holding back a fart in an elevator. *(Finally expelling smoke.)*

Jimmy: You're a regular poet.

Vito: *(Holding out joint to JIMMY.)* Yeah. Here, make Daddy proud of you. Go on, go on . . . *(JIMMY takes a deep drag, holds it down for a second or two, then blows it out.)* Look, guy, you gotta—

Jimmy: Wait a minute, that was just a rehearsal. I was just rehearsing. *(As VITO stashes baggie on shelf below, JIMMY takes a deep "toke" and holds it down.)*

Vito: That's a good boy. Good, hold it down now. Good! You're gonna get a *Gold Star*, and if you're extra good—you're gonna get to stay after school and do naughties with the teacher.

The following is the monologue created from the previous scene.

VITO (to JIMMY), age 20s to 30s.
pp. 54–58 (SAMUEL FRENCH, INC.)

You know how it makes me feel to break into another man's home and clean him out? Makes me feel like a—crumb. Like a punk—yeah, a lousy little crumb. Hey, I'd loosen up a lot more if I had a little smoke, then I'd really talk. It's like truth serum. Come on, goddammit, you got a *depressed person* on your hands, and that don't make for good talk. Well, we oughtta be able to come up with somethin'—if we ain't gonna smoke. Hey, I got it, why don't we just—make it? Yeah, you're here and I sure-in-the-fuck-am. Besides, you're humpy, in an off-beat sort of way. Yeah, you got this . . . something, like they just took the bandages off.

I been all fouled up lately, account of personal tragedy which I had in my life. Tonight I needed bread to buy some presents for my daughter. I didn't get to see her over Christmas. Melody Antonucci, ain't that a pisser to hang on a kid? Not my idea, my wife's. Listen, who gives a rat's ass anymore. I was married at sixteen, got a daughter nine, so don't give me that oh-my-shocked-ass-you're-queer bit. Double-gaited, okay. Versatile—definitely! So . . . what about you? You gay? Ever been married? *(Slyly.)* Mmn . . . and thirty-eight, too. Just haven't found the right girl yet, huh? Yeah, well, I got a rule for you. Like I said before, give me my smoke. No smokee, no talkie! *(Has been handed a joint by* JIMMY.*)* Hey . . . how about a little fuego, too? Fire . . . fire! Jesus.

Hey—you know how to circumcise an Italian baby? *(Making chopping gesture with one hand.)* Wop! *(Takes a deep drag, speaks while holding the smoke down.)* Wanna hit? C'mon, guy, just take a little toke. You'd get a kick outta this. This stuff's guaranteed to make a chihuahua snap at a bulldog's ass. Oh, I get it, you're scared. You're afraid if you got high, you'd let me up. I think Kate was right about you. Chicken, chicken, chicken! *(Imitating a chicken.)* Puck-puck-pa-kaw!

*(*JIMMY *is now smoking joint.)* Guy, you smoke like Pat Boone! Here, watch. You take it way in, suck it down. Let the goodies do their work, leave the gates of heaven open, let that Senegalese Thunderfuck work its magic spell, hold it down with all you got—just like you was holding back a fart in an elevator. Here, make Daddy proud of you. Go on, go on. . . . That's a good boy. Good, hold it down now. Good! You're gonna get a Gold Star, and if you're extra good—you're gonna get to stay after school and do naughties with the teacher.

As you know (by reading the play), Vito has broken into Jimmy's apartment three times and finally has been caught and is now being held down by neckties to the sink. For the purposes of this monologue there is no need to stage yours this way. You certainly may move your arms and legs.

Now why would you, Vito, go back to the same apartment three times to rob it? Is it because there were still more goodies left for the taking? No. Of course, you must make a choice that you went back a third time because you became compelled and obsessed. You couldn't get the apartment out of your mind. You couldn't get Jimmy out of your mind. You had seen photographs of him in the apartment. You even took some. You looked into his drawers and saw the kind of underwear he wears. You smelled his cologne. You took some of his personal things. You wanted to meet him in person. You wanted to know him. You wanted to get caught! This is not in the play. At least not on the pages. But for this monologue, make choices like these to give yourself a strong background that includes him. Now you are tied up and you certainly are frightened, and rightly so. But at the same time, you are excited. Don't expect to get this from the playwright. This is your play within his play. These choices are from the opposites where the real truth so often lies. You are fighting for your life. He could kill you. You are fighting for his love. The words tell us that you go both ways sexually. You are very attracted to him. This you knew before you met him. He turns you on very much. Of course, it would be wonderful for you if he too went both ways and he was also attracted to you. It would be wonderful if he would love you.

P. S. YOUR CAT IS DEAD!
by James Kirkwood

pp. 74–79 (SAMUEL FRENCH, INC.)

Vito: Hey, let's have a little drink to celebrate, okay? *(Walking upstage right of the chair, taking the apartment in now that he's free, assuming his regular cockiness.)*

Jimmy: *(Looking at him, deciding.)*—Why the hell not? One for the road, Vito.

Vito: One for the road! I thought I was spending the night!

Jimmy: Vito, I have to be alone to figure out how I'm going to work this whole new plan of mine. I got a lot of thinking through to do.

Vito: *(Walking toward window upstage of bed.)* We had a goddam blizzard out!

Jimmy: *(Crossing to VITO, with two glasses.)* You'll survive it, Vito. You're a survivor if I ever met one. *(Hands VITO a glass; they clink them together.)* Here's to you, Vito.

Vito: Yeah . . .
Hail Mary Full of Grace
    Four balls, take a base!
(They drink; suddenly VITO gets an idea.) Hey, I gotcha. I can't go tonight. I got no pants. *(Struts to sofa.)* New Year's Day, stores all closed, you gotta put me up! *(Sits on sofa, puts legs on trunk, JIMMY goes to the closet, gets a suit on a hanger with extremely narrow lapels, brings it to VITO.)*

Jimmy: *(Presenting it to him.)* Here, Vito—Happy New Year from me to you!

Vito: The whole suit? I only need the pants.

Jimmy: *(Crossing back to closet.)* Take the suit, it's not exactly in style anyhow.

Vito: *(Holding the hanger up, sarcastic, putting him on.)* Oh, my goodness—how can you say that?

Jimmy: *(Taking an old-fashioned baggy pair of boxer shorts and tossing them at VITO.)* Here, take these!

181

Vito: (*Catching them, standing, holding them up.*) Oh, thanks—very racy!

Jimmy: (*Fishing in his pocket for money.*) Here, take some money for a hotel room.

Vito: (*Walking upstage toward bathroom door.*) No, I don't want any money from you.

Jimmy: You got to have some money.

Vito: So—I'll snatch a purse.

Jimmy: (*Following* VITO, *holding out bills.*) No, take it. Here's twelve dollars, I spent most of—

Vito: I ain't gonna take money from you!

Jimmy: (*Jamming the money into pocket of suit.*) Here, it's in here, you have to have some. (VITO *goes into the bathroom, shuts the door.* JIMMY *glances around, walks to coat-rack, picks up cat's scratching post, bowl, catnip toy, and a paper shopping bag, walks to trunk, sits on downstage end. Puts the things in the shopping bag—but holds the toy.*) Bobby Seale . . . I'm gonna miss the hell out of you. You were a rat to leave me. You punctuated the end of a whole era, but I just wish you'd stuck around for the new one. (*Gently drops toy mouse into bag.*)

Vito: (*Charging out of the bathroom, dressed in* JIMMY'S *pants which are too big for him.*) Okay, I got it! I got it!

Jimmy: Christ, what now?

Vito: (*Sits on sofa.*) Just do me a favor and listen! Look, I took the book, I fouled you up good, I know. Okay, you wanna write your book, how long would it take?

Jimmy: Vito!

Vito: How long?

Jimmy: Six, eight, ten months, but—I've got to live, I've got to eat. Vito—

Vito: So, two can live as cheap as one. I can get us another bed.

Jimmy: Another bed? (*A beat.*) Us? You mean—*you* and *me?* Together again?

Vito: Yeah—us. You and me.

Jimmy: (*Rising, walking to sink unit, grinning.*) Vito . . .

Vito: (*Standing, crossing over near him.*) It's okay, I got it, I got it. Look, I hate to wait tables. I'd rather train fleas. But I'll sign on at one of those pissy East Side restaurants where I'll make good tips. (*Cleans up trunk coffee-table, picks up glass, left-over napkin, etc.*) I pay the rent, buy the eats— (*Dusts off phone with napkin.*)—keep the place all douched up spic and span. All you gotta do is fly the fingers over the keys. *(Taking the stuff to the kitchen.)*

Jimmy: Do you really see us as a winning team?

Vito: What's to win, you won't win nothing, but you'll get your friggin' book written. You won't even have to cook. Did you know I'm a good cook?

Jimmy: No, I must have skipped that on your résumé.

Vito: Yeah, well, I am. I got sent to gourmet cooking school by Francine-from-Miami. Gorgeous red hair— *(Walking to* JIMMY.*)*—and so sophisticated she drove her car with her *legs crossed!*

Jimmy: *(Walking up to bed, to get* VITO's *bag.)* Vito, it just wouldn't work.

Vito: *(Running after him, digging in airline bag, taking out notebook.)* Here, look at this. *(Jamming notebook in* JIMMY's *hands.)* Ben's handwriting, lists of books and records for my reading and listening education. *(*JIMMY *walks downstage, sits on sofa, while* VITO *paces the room.)* The way Ben put it—so, okay, be a card, be the life of the party. *(Walking around sink unit.)* Great at twenty-six, twenty-seven, twenty-eight. But then you're gonna wake up one day and—flash, you're forty—*(Picks up paper hat, uses it as a megaphone.)* The Big Four-Oh! *(Puts hat down.)* Then you're gonna find out that what you are is just a dumb stupid schmuck that everyone's tired of, *and* your line of chatter *and* the buns have fallen, you can only get your dauber up when the moon's full. And suddenly people ain't knockin' you down and draggin' you home for patti-cakes. *(Sits on arm of chair, facing* JIMMY.*)* See, I'm not just doin' it for you, I'm doin' it for myself, too.

Jimmy: You really want to do something for me? *(Handing him the shopping bag.)* Take this down, throw it out with the trash when you go, and say goodnight.

Vito: *(Standing with the bag, walking away from him.)* Great! I work out this whole plan—it goes over like a pork roast at a Bar Mitzvah! *(Peers into the bag.)* Oh, the cat's—listen, keep 'em. I bet I could find another little kitty for you.

Jimmy: I don't want a cat.

Vito: You liked your cat.

Jimmy: I liked my cat because he kept hanging around my door and finally just moved in. I liked him, I—loved that cat, but

I don't like cats in general. *(Walks up to bed for* VITO's *jacket.)*

Vito: Okay, okay—what about a puppy? I'll bet I could get you a cute little puppy.

Jimmy: *(Crossing back with jacket.)* Why—you know a pet shop you could knock off?

Vito: Come on, guy. Level with me, and tell me why you're dumpin' cold water on my plan?

Jimmy: Because it's just too wild.

Vito: Wild for a writer should be good. What do you want—dull?

Jimmy: *(Holding open the jacket.)* Vito . . . !

Vito: *(Getting into it.)* Okay, okay, I can take a hint! *(Then, walking toward plastic bag on stool downstage sink.)* Oh, I left you the Thunderfuck. Want me to roll you a few joints?

Jimmy: *(Pulling him back, taking him toward the door.)* Thanks . . . thank you. *(Handing* VITO *his knitted cap.)*

Vito: *(Snapping his fingers.)* Oh, Christ—something I forgot to tell you!

Jimmy: What?

Vito: *(Big.)* I do floors and windows!

Jimmy: *(Hustling him toward entrance platform.)* Vito . . .

Vito: *(Putting on his knitted cap after he sets down bags.)* Listen, what the hell—we put in New Year's together. Would it be okay if I call or—drop in sometime? Just for old time's sake?

Jimmy: *(Smiling.)* Sure. Why not? *(Then looking at him in friendship.)* So long, Vito. Happy hunting.

Vito: Oh, yeah . . . uh—Happy New Year, guy! *(He goes to give* JIMMY *a quick embrace, but* JIMMY *blocks it with his hands.* VITO *quickly backs off, assumes a heavy jock attitude, hitching up his pants, smacking one fist into the other.)* Oh, that's right, I forgot, we're still playin' lumberjacks! *(Smacks fist again.)* Pow! Ey, so long, Mac—don't take any wooden nickels! *(Then—normal voice, walking to* JIMMY, *straightening his smoking jacket, picking piece of lint off.)* And-ah—whatever you do, don't take any chances. One of 'em might work out. *(*VITO *picks up all his things, walks to the door, turns around and gives* JIMMY *a long look.)* Hey, man, take care of yourself. Really! *(Opens door, is just about to go out, then:)*—Rotate your tires!

The following is the monologue created from the previous scene.

VITO (to JIMMY), age 20s to late 30s.
pp. 74–79 (SAMUEL FRENCH, INC.)

Hey, let's have a little drink to celebrate, okay?... One for the road! I thought I was spending the night. There's a goddam blizzard out there! I can't go tonight. I got no pants, New Year's Day, stores all closed, you gotta put me up! I don't want any money from you. I'll... snatch a purse. I ain't gonna take money from you! Just do me a favor and listen! You wanna write your book, how long would it take? Two can live as cheap as one. I can get us another bed. Yeah—us! You and me. It's okay, I got it, I got it. Look, I hate to wait tables. I'd rather train fleas. But I'll sign on at one of those pissy East Side restaurants where I'll make good tips. I pay the rent, buy the eats—keep the place all douched up spic and span. All you gotta do is fly the fingers over the keys. You won't win nothing, but you'll get your friggin' book written. You won't even have to cook. Did you know I'm a good cook? Yeah, well, I am. I got sent to gourmet cooking school by Francine-from-Miami. Gorgeous red hair—and so sophisticated she drove her car with her legs crossed! Here, look at this. Ben's handwriting, lists of books and records for my reading and listening education. The way Ben put it—so, okay, be a card, be the life of the party. Great at twenty-six, twenty-seven, twenty-eight. But then you're gonna wake up one day and—flash, you're forty—The Big Four-Oh! Then you're gonna find out that what you are is just a dumb stupid schmuck that everyone's tired of, and your line of chatter and the buns have fallen, you only get your dauber up when the moon's full. And suddenly people ain't knockin' you down and draggin' you home for patti-cakes. *(Negative response from JIMMY.)* Great! I work out this whole plan—it goes over like a pork roast at a Bar Mitzvah!... I bet I could find another little kitty for you. What about a puppy? I'll bet I could get you a cute little puppy. Come on, guy, level with me, and tell me why you're dumpin' cold water on my plan? Wild for a writer should be good. What do you want—dull? Okay, okay, I can take a

hint! Oh, Christ—something I forgot to tell you! I do floors
and windows! Listen, what the hell—we put in New Year's
together. Would it be okay if I call or—drop in sometime?
Just for old time's sake? Uh—Happy New Year, guy! . . . Pow!
Ey, so long, Mac—don't take any wooden nickels! And—
ah—whatever you do, don't take any chances! One of 'em
might work out. . . . Hey, man, take care of yourself. Really!
—Rotate your tires!

Vito is desperate. He has found a place, a home, a person
for himself. He is being rejected. He is fighting for his future
life. He wants to change his style of living. He's willing to do
things he's never wanted to do before. Just so he can live with
Jimmy and have what he perceives to be a secure place with
love. He's begging Jimmy to help him not be a loser. Jimmy
obviously doesn't respond well to this idea.

Keep fighting for what you need right up to the end of the
monologue. Even as you say good-bye, you must still be hoping
that Jimmy will accept your proposal. Don't forget the humor. I
know the piece is funny. But I said the humor! "And—ah—
whatever you do, don't take any chances!"

That line has a lot to do with Jimmy. Therefore, it is very
important that you read the entire play. You're being sarcastic
and ironic. Jimmy *never* takes chances. You are telling him to
once in his life, take a chance and see what happens. Stop
playing it safe! And as for yourself, you have never played it safe
and have always taken chances. And, of course, moving in with
him would be taking a chance, as it always is chance taking to
start a new relationship, but you *are* trying to get your life in
order. You are fighting for Jimmy's love so that he will want to be
in your life and the two of you will help each other.

SAME TIME, NEXT YEAR
by Bernard Slade

pp. 6–10 (Samuel French, Inc.)

George: Why do you have to look so luminous? It would make it a lot easier if you woke up with puffy eyes and blotchy skin like everyone else.

Doris: I guess God figured chubby thighs were enough.

George: Look, this is not just going to go away. We've got to talk about it.

Doris: Okay. *(She gets out of bed, the sheet around her, and starts for the bathroom.)*

George: Where are you going?

Doris: I'm going to brush my teeth.

George: Dorothy, please sit down. (DORIS *starts to speak.*) Please sit down and let me say this. *(She sits on the end of the bed.)* Dorothy, first of all, I want you to know last night was the most beautiful, wonderful, crazy thing that's ever happened to me and I'll never forget it—or you.

Doris: Doris.

George: What?

Doris: My name is Doris.

George: Your name is Doris. I've been calling you Dorothy all night. Why didn't you tell me earlier?

Doris: I didn't expect us to end up like we did. Then I did try to tell you but you weren't listening.

George: When?

Doris: Right in the middle of everything.

George: It was incredible, wasn't it?

Doris: It was—nice. Especially the last time.

George: I'm an animal. I don't know what got into me. What was the matter with the first two times?

Doris: What? Oh—well, the first time was kinda fast and the second—look, I feel funny talking about this.

187

George: It was a very beautiful thing, Doris. There was nothing disgusting or dirty in what we did.

Doris: Then how come you look so down in the dumps?

George: My wife is going to kill me.

Doris: How is she going to find out?

George: She knows.

Doris: You said she was in New Jersey.

George: It doesn't matter. She knows.

Doris: How?

George: Was it as incredible for you as it was for me?

Doris: Do all men like to talk about it a lot afterwards?

George: Why? You think I'm some sort of pervert or something?

Doris: No, I just wondered. See, I was a virgin when I got married. At least sort of.

George: Sort of?

Doris: Well, I was pregnant but I don't count that.

George: Doris, that counts.

Doris: I mean it was by the man I married.

George: Oh, I'm sorry.

Doris: *(She is putting on her blouse.)* That's okay. Harry and me would've gotten married anyway. It just speeded things up a bit. Turns out I get pregnant if we drink from the same cup. *(He looks at her.)* What's the matter?

George: It's okay. Trojans are very reliable.

Doris: Who are?

George: Never mind. I'm in a lot of trouble. I think I love you. It's crazy! It's really crazy! I don't even know if you've read "Catcher in the Rye."

Doris: I didn't graduate high school.

George: You see? I don't even care! Of course, I should've known this would happen. There's something about me I didn't tell you.

Doris: What? *(She puts on her skirt.)*

George: When it comes to life I have a brown thumb.

Doris: What do you mean?

George: Nothing I do ever turns out right. Ever. The first time I had sex I was eighteen years old. We were in the back seat of a parked 1938 Dodge sedan. Right in the middle of it we were rear ended.

Doris: Gee, that's terrible. Did you have insurance?

George: You know the song they were playing on the juke box last night when we met?

Doris: No?

George: "If I Knew You Were Coming I'd've Baked A Cake"!

Doris: So?

George: So that's going to be "our song"! Other people would get "Be My Love" or "Hello Young Lovers." Me—I get "If I Knew You Were Coming I'd've Baked A Cake"!

Doris: You're very romantic. I like that.

George: I think I'm in love with you. Now you want to know the luck I have? I'm happily married!

Doris: Are you Jewish?

George: No.

Doris: Well, how come you're so guilty?

George: Don't you feel guilty?

Doris: Are you kidding? Half my high school became nuns.

George: Catholics have rules about this sort of thing.

Doris: We have rules about everything. That's what's so great about being Catholic. You always know where you stand.

George: I tell you, Doris, I feel like slitting my wrists.

Doris: Are you Italian?

George: What's with you and nationalities?

Doris: You're so emotional.

George: I happen to be a C.P.A. I can be as logical as the next person.

Doris: You don't strike me as an accountant type.

George: It's very simple. My whole life has been a mess. Figures always come out right. I like that. What are you?

Doris: I'm Italian.

George: Why aren't you more emotional?

Doris: When you grow up in a large Italian family, it's enough to turn you off emotion for life.

George: I wondered why you weren't crying or yelling.

Doris: I did before in the bathroom.

George: Crying?

Doris: Yelling.

George: I didn't hear you.

Doris: I stuffed a towel in my mouth.

George: I'm sorry.

Doris: That's all right. There's no sense crying over spilt milk.

George: You're right.

Doris: Then how come we feel so terrible?

George: Because we're two decent, honest people and this thing is tearing us apart. I mean I know it wasn't our fault but I keep seeing the faces of my children and the look of betrayal in their eyes. I keep thinking of our marriage vows, the trust my wife has placed in me, the experiences we've shared together. And you know the worst part of it all? While I'm thinking of all these things, I have this fantastic hard on.

Doris: I really wish you hadn't said that.

George: I'm sorry. I just feel we should be totally honest with each other.

Doris: No, it's not that. I have to go to confession.

George: We're both crazy! I mean this sort of thing happens to millions of people every day. We're just normal, healthy human beings who did a perfectly healthy, normal thing. You don't use actual names in confession, do you?

The following is the monologue created from the previous scene.

GEORGE (to DORIS), age 20s to 40s.
pp. 6–10 (SAMUEL FRENCH, INC.)

Why do you have to look so—so luminous? I mean it would make everything so much easier if you woke up with puffy eyes and blotchy skin like most women. . . . Look, this thing is not just going to go away. We've got to talk about it. First of all, I want you to know last night was the most beautiful, fantastic, wonderful crazy thing that's ever happened to me and I'll never forget it—or you. It was incredible wasn't it? . . . I'm an animal! I don't know what got into me. It was a very beautiful thing, Doris. There was nothing disgusting or dirty in what we did. And my wife is going to *kill* me! We're in a lot of trouble, Doris. I think I love you. It's crazy! It's really crazy! I mean I don't even know if you like *Catcher in the Rye*. I have this test for people. If they don't like *Catcher in the Rye* or *Death of a Salesman* I won't even date them! With you I don't even *care!* And I'm really a *snob* about education! Of course, I should've known this would happen. You see there's something I didn't tell you about me, Doris. When it comes to life, I have a brown thumb. I mean nothing goes right. Ever. Let me think of something that will give you the picture. Okay. I was eighteen when I first had sex. It was in the backseat of a parked 1938 Dodge sedan. Right in the middle of it—we were rear ended. And take last night. You know what they were playing on the juke box when we met? "If I Knew You Were Coming I'd've Baked a Cake"! So that's going to be "our song"! Other people would get "Be My Love" or "Hello, Young Lovers." Me—I get "If I Knew You Were Coming I'd've Baked a Cake"! I think I've fallen in love with you, Doris. Now you want to know the luck I have? I'm happily married! I tell you, Doris, I feel like slitting my wrists. We're both decent, honest people and this thing is tearing us apart. I mean I know it wasn't our fault but I keep seeing the faces of my children and the look of betrayal in their eyes. I keep thinking of the trust my wife has placed in me. The times we've shared together. Our wedding vows. And you know the worst part of it all? Right at this moment, while I'm thinking all these things, I have this fantastic hard-on. I'm sorry. I just feel we should be totally honest with each other. We're both crazy! I mean this sort of thing happens to millions of people every day. We're just normal, healthy human beings who did a perfectly healthy, normal thing. . . . You don't use actual names in confession, do you?

Well, George, you certainly are trying to talk yourself into this affair. All that guilt! Oh, it's there, all right. But stronger than anything are your intense feelings toward Doris. And you've got to do and say anything to justify going to bed with her again. So what is it that you are fighting for from her? What is it that she and only she can give to you right now that will enhance your life? Not acceptance or approval or anything like that. You are fighting for her love. If she loves you, she will be so sensitive to you and will soothe, protect, and assure you. With her love, everything will be fine and good. Then your life will be perfect and perhaps she will help you to finally get rid of that "brown thumb" of yours once and for all!

SAME TIME, NEXT YEAR
by Bernard Slade

pp. 11–14 (SAMUEL FRENCH, INC.)

George: Doris, there's something I want to tell you.

Doris: What?

George: I know I must appear very smooth and glib—sexually. Well, I want you to know that since I've been married this is the very first time I've done this.

Doris: Don't worry, I could tell. Do you mind if I have some of your breakfast?

George: Go ahead. I'm not hungry. It's funny when I was single I was no good at quick, superficial affairs. I had to be able to really like the person before . . . What do you mean—you could tell? In what way could you tell?

Doris: What? Oh—I don't know—the way you tried to get your pants off over your shoes and then tripped and hit your head on the coffee table. Little things like that.

George: It's great to be totally honest with another person, isn't it?

Doris: It sure is.

George: I haven't been totally honest with you.

Doris: No?

George: No. I told you I was a married man with two children.

Doris: You're not?

George: No. I'm a married man with three children. I thought it would make me seem less married. Look, I just didn't think it through. Anyway, it's been like a lead weight inside me all morning. I mean denying little Debbie like that. I don't normally behave like this, I was under a certain stress. You understand?

Doris: Sure, we all do dopey things sometimes. How come your wife doesn't travel with you?

George: Phyliss won't get on a plane.

192

Doris: Is she afraid of flying?

George: Crashing.

Doris: *(Noticing that* GEORGE *is staring at her.)* Why are you looking at me like that?

George: I love the way you eat.

Doris: You wanta share some coffee with me?

George: No thank you. Doris, do you believe that two perfect strangers can look at each other across a crowded room and suddenly want to possess each other in every conceivable way possible?

Doris: No.

George: Then how did this whole thing start?

Doris: It started when you sent me over that steak in the restaurant.

George: They didn't serve drinks. They're known for their steaks.

Doris: Then when I looked over and you toasted me with your fork with a big piece of steak on it, that really made me laugh. I never saw anybody do that before. What made you do it?

George: Impulse. Usually I never do that sort of thing. I have a friend who says that life is saying "yes." The most I've ever been able to manage is "maybe."

Doris: So then why did you do it?

George: I was lonely and you looked so vulnerable. You had run in your stocking and your lipstick was smeared.

Doris: You thought I looked cheap?

George: I thought you looked beautiful.

Doris: I really should be going. The nuns will be wondering what happened to me.

George: Nuns?

Doris: Yeah. It didn't seem right to bring up when we met yesterday in the restaurant but I was on my way to retreat.

George: Retreat?

Doris: It's right near here. I go every year at this time when Harry takes the kids to Bakersfield.

George: What's in Bakersfield?

Doris: His mother. It's her birthday.

George: She doesn't mind that you don't go?

Doris: No, she hates me.

George: Why?

Doris: I got pregnant.

George: Her son had something to do with that.

Doris: She blocks that out of her mind. You see, he was in his first year of dental college and he had to quit and take a job selling waterless cooking. And so now every year on her birthday I go on retreat.

George: To think about God?

Doris: Well, Him too, sure. See, I have three little kids. I got pregnant the first time when I was eighteen and so I never really had any time to think about what I think. Never mind . . . sometimes I think I'm crazy.

George: Why?

Doris: Well, take my life. I live in a two-bedroom duplex in downtown Oakland, we have a 1948 Kaiser, a blond three-piece dinette set, Motorola TV, and we go bowling at least once a week. I mean what else could anyone ask for? But sometimes things get me down, you know? It's dumb!

George: I don't think it's dumb.

Doris: You don't? Boy, I can really talk to you. It's amazing I find myself saying things to you that I didn't know I thought. I noticed that yesterday right after we met in the restaurant.

George: We had instant rapport! Did you notice that too?

Doris: No, but I know we really hit it off. Harry's not much of a talker. How about your wife. Do you two talk a lot?

George: Doris, naturally we're both curious about each other's husband and wife. But rather than dwelling on it and letting it spoil everything, why don't we do this. I'll tell you two stories, one showing the best side of my wife and the other showing the worst. Then you do the same about your husband and then let's forget that. Okay?

Doris: Okay.

George: I'll go first. I'll start with the worst side. Phyliss knows about us.

The following is the monologue created from the previous scene.

GEORGE (to DORIS), age 20s to 40s.
pp. 11–14 (SAMUEL FRENCH, INC.)

Doris, there's something I want to tell you. You probably think I do this sort of thing all the time. I mean I know I must appear smooth and glib—sexually. Well, I want you

to know that since I've been married, this is the very first
time I've done this.... Do you believe me? It's funny,
even when I was single I was no good at quick, superficial
affairs. I had to be able to really *like* the person before—
It's great to be totally honest with another person, isn't it?
Doris, I haven't been totally honest with you. Okay—here
it comes—the big one. I told you I was a married man with
two children. I'm a married man with *three* children. I
thought it would make me seem less married. *(Becomes
agitated.)* I just didn't think it through. Anyway, it's been
like a lead weight inside me all morning. I mean denying
little Debbie like that. I'm sorry. I was under a certain
stress or I wouldn't have done it. Doris, I've been thinking. Sometimes if you *know* why something happened it
makes it easier to understand. Do you believe that two
total strangers can look across a room and both have this
sudden, overwhelming, totally irrational desire to possess
one another in every possible way? *(Puzzled.)* Neither do
I—so I guess that can't be it. Then how did this whole
thing start? Impulse. Usually I never do that sort of thing.
I have this—this friend who says that life is saying yes. The
most I can generally manage is maybe. I guess I was lonely
and you looked so—so vulnerable and—well, you had a
run in your stocking and your lipstick was smeared. I
thought you looked beautiful. We had instant rapport! Did
you notice that too? Doris, naturally we're both curious
about each other's husband and wife. But rather than
dwelling on it and letting it spoil everything, why don't we
do this. I'll tell you two stories, one showing the best side
of my wife and the other showing the worst. Then let's
forget that. Okay? I'll go first. I'll start with the worst side.
Phyliss knows about us.

Of course, George, you are not smooth and glib sexually!
You know that. But with Doris you feel better about yourself
sexually than you ever have felt. Having sex with her is the most
exciting experience in your life. Sex has never been this good.
Never with your wife or with anyone. Doris responds and
contributes so fully. She appreciates and communicates her
feelings to you. Therefore, you are beginning to feel more secure
about yourself as a man. Your attraction to flaws tells us so much
about who you are. And you are making discoveries about

yourself today. And you are sharing them with Doris. You are opening up yourself and exposing your vulnerability to her. You are trusting her. You need her to help you to be a happier person. You need her to love you and be in your life. Despite the fact that this relationship is an extramarital affair, it might be the healthiest one you have ever had. It is not just the sex. This is your life we are talking about. Everything said by you is very important. This is a comedy about very real and troubled feelings, needs, fears, guilt, and love.

SAME TIME, NEXT YEAR
by Bernard Slade

pp. 22–25 (SAMUEL FRENCH, INC.)

George: Don't you ever feel any guilt?

Doris: Sometimes.

George: You never say anything.

Doris: I just handle it in a different way.

George: How?

Doris: Privately.

George: I think in some ways men are more sensitive than women.

Doris: Would you like some more champagne, dear?

George: I mean women are more pragmatic than men.

Doris: What do you mean?

George: They adjust to rottenness quicker. Anyway, you have the Church.

Doris: The Church?

George: You're Catholic. You can get rid of your guilt all at one sitting. I have to live with mine.

Doris: There's a lot about being Catholic you don't understand.

George: I tell you, when she started talking about the tooth-fairy—well, it affected me in a very profound manner. On top of that I have indigestion you can't believe. It hit me hard, you know?

Doris: George, I have three children, too.

George: Sure, sure—I know. I don't mean that you don't understand. It's just that I think that my guilt is more acute than yours.

Doris: Honey, what do you want to do? Have a guilt contest? Will that solve anything?

George: What do you want me to do, Doris?

Doris: I think it might be a terrific idea if you stopped talking about it. It's only making you feel worse.

George: I couldn't feel worse. My little girl calls me on the

197

phone... that pure little voice saying... No, you're right. Forget it. Forget it. Talk about something else. Tell me the good story about Harry.

Doris: Okay. He went bankrupt.

George: How can anyone go bankrupt selling TV sets?

Doris: Harry has one failing as a salesman. It's a compulsion to talk his customers out of things they can't afford. He lacks the killer instinct. Actually, it's one of the things I like best about him. Anyway, he went into real estate. Your turn.

George: What?

Doris: Tell me your story about Helen.

George: I already did.

Doris: You just told me the bad one. Why do you always tell that one first?

George: It's the one I look forward to telling the most.

Doris: Tell me the good story about her.

George: Chris, our middle one, gashed his knee badly on the lawn sprinkler. Helen drove both of us to the hospital.

Doris: Both of you?

George: I fainted. The nice part was she never told anybody.

Doris: You faint often?

George: Only in emergencies.

Doris: Is it the sight of blood that—

George: Please, Doris! My stomach's already squeamish. Oh, listen, something just occurred to me. Instead of leaving at my usual time would you mind if I left a little earlier?

Doris: When did you have in mind?

George: Well, there's a plane in half an hour.

Doris: You want to leave twenty-three hours early?

George: Look, I know how you feel, I really do, and I wouldn't even suggest it if you weren't a mother. I mean I wouldn't even think of it if this crisis hadn't come up. (*He moves his suitcase to the bed and starts packing through the following.*) Oh, it's not just the tooth-fairy but she could have swallowed the tooth. It could be lodged God knows where. Now I know this leaves you up in the air but there's no reason for you to leave too. The room's all paid for—have you seen my hairbrush? Anyway, I'm probably doing you a favor. If I did stay I wouldn't be very good company. (DORIS *throws the hairbrush at him. It sails past his head and crashes into the wall. There is a pause.*) You feel somewhat rejected, right? I can understand that but I want you to know my leaving has nothing to do with you and me. Doris, I have a sick child at home. This is an emergency.

Doris: Will you stop it. It's got nothing to do with the goddam tooth-fairy. You're just feeling guilty and the only way you think you can deal with it is by getting as far away from me as possible.

George: Okay, I feel guilty. Is that so strange? Doris, we're cheating! Once a year we lie to our families and sneak off to a hotel in California and commit adultery. Not that I want to stop doing it! But yes, I feel guilt. I admit it.

Doris: You admit it! You take out ads. You probably stop strangers on the street. I'm surprised you haven't had a scarlet "A" embroidered on your jockey shorts. You think that by talking about it you can excuse what you're doing. So you wander around like an open nerve saying, "I'm cheating but look how guilty I feel so I must really be a nice guy"! And to top it all, you have the incredible arrogance to think you're the only one in the world with a conscience. Well, that doesn't make you a nice guy. You know what that makes you? A horse's ass.

George: You know something? I liked you a lot better before you joined the Book of the Month Club. Doris, it's not the end of the world. I'm not leaving permanently. I'll see you next year.

Doris: No, I don't think you will.

George: I don't believe this. Just because I have to leave early one year you're willing to throw away a lifetime of weekends? How can you be so *casual?*

Doris: I don't see any point in going on.

George: Oh, no. Don't do that to me, Doris. Don't try to manipulate me. I get enough of that at home. That's not what our relationship is about.

Doris: What is it about?

George: You don't know?

Doris: Yes. But it seems to be completely different from what you think it's about. That's why I think we should stop seeing each other.

George: You're serious.

Doris: George, what's the point of meeting in guilt and remorse? What joy is there in that?

George: Doris, I have a commitment there.

Doris: And you have none here?

George: Here? I thought our only commitment was to show up every year.

Doris: Just two friendly sex partners who meet once a year, touch and let go.

George: Okay. Maybe I was kidding myself. I'm human.

Doris: Well, so am I.

George: But you're different. Stronger. You always seem able to cope.

Doris: During the past year I picked up the phone and started to call you ten times. I couldn't seem to stop thinking about you. You kept slipping over into my real life and it bothered the hell out of me. More to the point I felt guilty. So I decided to stop seeing you. At first I wasn't going to show up at all but then I thought I at least owed you an explanation. So I came. When you walked in the door I knew I couldn't do it. That no matter what the price I'm willing to pay it.

George: Oh God, I feel so *guilty!*

Doris: I think you'd better leave, George.

George: Doris, I love you. I'm an idiot, I suspect I'm deeply neurotic, and I'm no bargain—but I do love you. Will you let me stay? (*She turns to him and smiles. They move into each other's arms.*) What are we going to do?

The following is the monologue created from the previous scene.

GEORGE (to DORIS), age 20s to 40s.
pp. 22–25 (SAMUEL FRENCH, INC.)

Don't you ever feel any guilt? You've never said anything. I don't know, maybe men are more—sensitive than women. Perhaps women are more pragmatic than men. They adjust to rottenness quicker. I mean they're more inclined to live for the moment. (*Offhandedly.*) Anyway, you have the Church. Well, you're Catholic, aren't you? You can get rid of all your guilt at one sitting. I have to *live* with mine. I don't mean that you don't understand. It's just that we're different people and your guilt is less—acute. Listen, something just occurred to me. Instead of my leaving at the usual time tomorrow night would you mind if I left a little earlier? There's a plane in half an hour. Look, I know how you feel—I really do—and I wouldn't even *suggest* leaving twenty-three hours early if I didn't think you'd understand the situation. Now I know this leaves you a bit—uh—at loose ends but there's no reason for you to leave too. The room's all paid up. Anyway, I'm probably doing you a favor. If I did stay I wouldn't be very good company. I want you to know my leaving has nothing to do with *you and me*! Doris, this is an *emergency*! I have a *sick child* at home. Okay, I feel guilty. Is that so strange? Doris, don't you understand? We're *cheating*! Once a year we lie to our families and sneak off to a hotel in California and commit adultery! Not that I want to stop doing it! But yes, I feel guilt. I admit it. Doris, it's not the end of the world. I'm not leaving you permanently. We'll see each other again next year. Just because I have to leave early one year you're willing to throw away a lifetime of weekends? How can you be so—so—*casual*? Don't try to manipulate me. I get enough of that at home. That's not what our relationship is about. Doris, I have a commitment there. I thought *our* only commitment was to show up every year. Okay—so maybe I was kidding myself. I'm human. But you're different. Stronger. You always seem able to—cope. Oh God, I feel so *guilty*! I love you, Doris. I'm an idiot. I suspect I'm deeply neurotic, and I'm no bargain—but I do love you. Will you let me stay? Doris, what are we going to do?

Poor George. Your guilt is really running at full-steam. You've got such a conflict. Never before have you been in the midst of such confusion. And it feels *great*! You don't want to leave. You want Doris to convince you to stay. Remember, do not fight to get away from the person to whom you are talking. Go to the opposites. You want her to do everything in her power to make you stay. You are, in fact, talking yourself into staying. But you've got to acknowledge that what you are doing is wrong. It makes you a nicer, more ethical person to be aware of the wrong that you do. Then you can enjoy doing the wrong. It then feels better. You are fighting to feel wonderful about yourself and to not be unloved by anyone in the world. But Doris is the most important person in your life even though you only spend one weekend a year with her and the rest with your wife and children.

SAME TIME, NEXT YEAR
by Bernard Slade

pp. 23–26 (SAMUEL FRENCH, INC.)

Doris: You want to leave twenty-three hours early?

George: Look, I know how you feel, I really do, and I wouldn't even suggest it if you weren't a mother. I mean I wouldn't even think of it if this crisis hadn't come up. *(He moves his suitcase to the bed and starts packing through the following.)* Oh, it's not just the tooth-fairy but she could have swallowed the tooth. It could be lodged God knows where. Now I know this leaves you up in the air but there's no reason for you to leave too. The room's all paid for—have you seen my hairbrush? Anyway, I'm probably doing you a favor. If I did stay I wouldn't be very good company. *(DORIS throws the hairbrush at him. It sails past his head and crashes into the wall. There is a pause.)* You feel somewhat rejected, right? I can understand that but I want you to know my leaving has nothing to do with you and me. Doris, I have a sick child at home. This is an emergency.

Doris: Will you stop it. It's got nothing to do with the goddam tooth-fairy. You're just feeling guilty and the only way you think you can deal with it is by getting as far away from me as possible.

George: Okay, I feel guilty. Is that so strange? Doris, we're cheating! Once a year we lie to our families and sneak off to a hotel in California and commit adultery. Not that I want to stop doing it! But yes, I feel guilt. I admit it.

Doris: You admit it! You take out ads. You probably stop strangers on the street. I'm surprised you haven't had a scarlet "A" embroidered on your jockey shorts? You think that by talking about it you can excuse what you're doing. So you wander around like an open nerve saying, "I'm cheating but look how guilty I feel so I must really be a nice guy"!

And to top it all, you have the incredible arrogance to think you're the only one in the world with a conscience. Well, that doesn't make you a nice guy. You know what that makes you? A horse's ass.

George: You know something? I liked you a lot better before you joined the Book of the Month Club. Doris, it's not the end of the world. I'm not leaving permanently. I'll see you next year.

Doris: No, I don't think you will.

George: I don't believe this. Just because I have to leave early one year you're willing to throw away a lifetime of weekends? How can you be so *casual?*

Doris: I don't see any point in going on.

George: Oh, no. Don't do that to me, Doris. Don't try to manipulate me. I get enough of that at home. That's not what our relationship is about.

Doris: What is it about?

George: You don't know?

Doris: Yes. But it seems to be completely different from what you think it's about. That's why I think we should stop seeing each other.

George: You're serious.

Doris: George, what's the point of meeting in guilt and remorse? What joy is there in that?

George: Doris, I have a commitment there.

Doris: And you have none here?

George: Here? I thought our only commitment was to show up every year.

Doris: Just two friendly sex partners who meet once a year, touch and let go.

George: Okay. Maybe I was kidding myself. I'm human.

Doris: Well, so am I.

George: But you're different. Stronger. You always seem able to cope.

Doris: During the past year I picked up the phone and started to call you ten times. I couldn't seem to stop thinking about you. You kept slipping over into my real life and it bothered the hell out of me. More to the point I felt guilty. So I decided to stop seeing you. At first I wasn't going to show up at all but then I thought I at least owed you an explanation. So I came. When you walked in the door I knew I couldn't do it. That no matter what the price I'm willing to pay it.

George: Oh God, I feel so *guilty!*

Doris: I think you'd better leave, George.

George: Doris, I love you. I'm an idiot, I suspect I'm deeply neurotic, and I'm no bargain—but I do love you. Will you let me stay? *(She turns to him and smiles. They move into each other's arms.)* What are we going to do?

Doris: Touch and hold on very tight . . . until tomorrow.

The following is the monologue created from the previous scene.

DORIS (to GEORGE), age 20s to 40s.
pp. 23–26 (SAMUEL FRENCH, INC.)

You want to leave *twenty-three hours early*? The only way you can deal with it is by getting as far away from me as possible? You probably take out ads and stop strangers on the street. It's a wonder you haven't hired a *skywriter!* I'm amazed you haven't had your shorts monogrammed with a scarlet *A* as a conversation starter! You think that by *talking* about it, by wringing your hands and beating your breast it will somehow excuse what you are doing? So you wander around like—like an open nerve saying, "I'm cheating but look how *guilty* I feel so I must really be a nice guy!" You know what it makes you? *A horse's ass.* There's not going to be a next year, George. I don't see any point in going on. The way I think about us seems to be completely different from how *you* think about us. That's why I think we should stop seeing each other. What's the point of going on if we're going to come to each other burdened down with guilt and remorse? What joy is there in that? You're supposed to have a commitment *here!* But with you it's nice and tidy, huh? Just two friendly sexual partners who meet once a year, touch, and let go. George, during the past year I picked up the phone and started to call you five times. I couldn't seem to stop thinking about you. You kept slopping over into my real life and it scared hell out of me. More to the point I felt *guilty.* So I decided to stop seeing you. At first I wasn't going to show up at all but then I thought I at least owed you an explanation. So I came. When you walked in the door I knew I couldn't do it. That despite the price it was all worth it. I think you'd better leave, George . . . or . . . we touch . . . and hold on very tight . . . until tomorrow.

You've made a commitment to this relationship and were under the impression that George was committed too. Now you are discovering that perhaps you were wrong. And it hurts so much. You are fighting for him to be the adult you thought he was so that he can handle the kind of relationship you both entered into. It truly takes a mature mind to be comfortable and secure with your arrangement. Don't give up on him. You love him so much. Fight like hell to make him know and understand what you know so that he can be open to give and receive love. Reach out emotionally and let him see how you feel about what he just told you. That he wants to leave early, very early. If he loved you enough, he would not allow his guilt to take over. Fight for that love even when you say to him, "I think you'd better leave, George." Allow yourself to get carried away with anger. Remember what anger is. Play off what caused the anger. The pain and rejection. Anger is loud pain. Don't rush through the piece. With high intensity and emotion, actors tend to rush. You want a sense of urgency but not at a galloping pace.

OH DAD, POOR DAD, MAMMA'S HUNG YOU IN THE CLOSET AND I'M FEELIN' SO SAD
by Arthur L. Kopit

pp. 25–27 (SAMUEL FRENCH, INC.)

Madame Rosepettle: Two warnings are enough for any man. Three are enough for any woman. The cuckoo struck three times and then a fourth and still she's here. May I ask why?

Rosalie: You've been listening at the keyhole, haven't you!

Madame Rosepettle: I'm talking to my son, harlot!

Rosalie: What did you say!

Madame Rosepettle: Harlot, I called you! Slut, scum, sleazy prostitute catching and caressing children and men. Stroking their hearts. I've seen you.

Rosalie: What are you talking about?

Madame Rosepettle: Blind man's buff with the children in the garden. The redheaded one—fifteen, I think. Behind the bush while the others cover their eyes. Up with the skirt, one-two-three and it's done. Don't try to deny it. I've seen you in action. I know your kind.

Rosalie: That's a lie!

Madame Rosepettle: Life is a lie, my sweet. Not words but Life itself. Life in all its ugliness. It builds green trees that tease your eyes and draw you under them. Then when you're there in the shade and you breathe in and say, "Oh God, how beautiful," that's when the bird on the branch lets go his droppings and hits you on the head. Life, my sweet, beware. It isn't what it seems. I've seen what it can do. I've watched you dance.

Rosalie: What do you mean by that?

Madame Rosepettle: Last night in the ballroom. I've watched you closely and I know what I see. You danced too near those men and you let them do too much. Don't try to deny it. Words will only make it worse. It would be best for all concerned if you left at once and never came again. Good day.

(MADAME ROSEPETTLE *turns to leave*. ROSALIE *does not move*.)

207

Rosalie: Why don't you let Jonathan out of his room?

Madame Rosepettle: Who?

Rosalie: Jonathan

Madame Rosepettle: Who?

Rosalie: Your son.

Madame Rosepettle: You mean Albert? Is that who you mean? Albert?

Jonathan: Pa-pa-please do-don't.

Madame Rosepettle: Is that who you mean, slut? H'm? Speak up. Is that who you mean?

Rosalie: I mean your son.

Madame Rosepettle: *I don't let him out because he is my son.* I don't let him out because his skin is as white as fresh snow and he would burn if the sun struck him. I don't let him out because outside there are trees with birds sitting on their branches waiting for him to walk beneath. I don't let him out because you're there, waiting behind the bushes with your skirt up. I don't let him out because he is *susceptible.* That's why. Because he is *susceptible.* Susceptible to trees and to sluts and to sunstroke.

Rosalie: Then why did you come and get me?

Madame Rosepettle: Because, my dear, my stupid son has been watching you through that stupid telescope he made. Because, in short, he wanted to meet you and I, in short, wanted him to know what you were really like. Now that he's seen, you may go.

Rosalie: And if I choose to stay?

(Pause.)

Madame Rosepettle: *(Softly; slyly.)* Can you cook?

Rosalie: Yes.

Madame Rosepettle: How well?

Rosalie: Fairly well.

Madame Rosepettle: Not good enough! My son is a connoisseur. A connoisseur, do you hear? I cook him the finest foods in the world. Recipes no one knows exist. Food, my sweet, is the finest of arts. And since you can't cook you are artless. You nauseate my son's aesthetic taste. Do you like cats?

Rosalie: Yes.

Madame Rosepettle: What kind of cats?

Rosalie: Any kind of cats.

Madame Rosepettle: Alley cats?

Rosalie: Especially alley cats.

Madame Rosepettle: I thought so. Go, my dear. Find yourself some weeping willow and set yourself beneath it. Cry of your lust for my son and wait, for a mockingbird waits above to deposit his verdict on your whorish head. My son is as white as fresh snow and you are tainted with sin. You are garnished with garlic and turn our tender stomachs in disgust.

Rosalie: Why did you come to Port Royale?

Madame Rosepettle: To find *you!*

Rosalie: And now that you've found me—?

Madame Rosepettle: I throw you out! I toss you into the garbage can! I heard everything, you know. So don't try to call. The phone is in my room—*and no one goes into my room but me. (She stares at* ROSALIE *for a moment, then exits with a flourish.* ROSALIE *and* JONATHAN *move slowly toward each other. When they are almost together,* MADAME ROSEPETTLE *reappears.)* One more thing. If, by some chance, the eleventh child named Cynthia turns out to be a Siamese cat, give it to me. I, too, pay well.

The following is the monologue created from the previous scene.

MADAME ROSEPETTLE (to ROSALIE), age 40s to 60s.
pp. 25–27 (SAMUEL FRENCH, INC.)

Two warnings are enough for any man. Three are enough for any woman. The cuckoo struck three times and then a fourth and still she's here. May I ask why? I'm talking to my son, harlot! Harlot, I called you! Slut, scum, sleazy prostitute catching and caressing children and men. Stroking their hearts. I've seen you. Blind man's buff with the children in the garden. The redheaded one—fifteen, I think. Behind the bush while the others cover their eyes. Up with the skirt, one-two-three and it's done. Don't try to deny it. I've seen you in action. I know your kind.

    Life is a lie, my sweet. Not words but Life itself. Life in all its ugliness. It builds green trees that tease your eyes and draw you under them. Then when you're there in the shade and you breathe in and say, "Oh God, how beautiful," that's when the bird on the branch lets go his droppings and hits you on the head. Life, my sweet, beware. It isn't what it seems. I've seen what it can do. I've watched you dance. Last night in the ballroom. I've watched you closely and I know what I see. You danced too near those men and you let them do too much. Don't try to deny it. Words will only make it worse. It would be best for all concerned if you left at once and never came again.

I don't let him out because he is my son. I don't let him out because his skin is as white as fresh snow and he would burn if the sun struck him. I don't let him out because outside there are trees with birds sitting on their branches waiting for him to walk beneath. I don't let him out because you're there, waiting behind the bushes with your skirt up. I don't let him out because he is susceptible. That's why. Because he is *susceptible*. Susceptible to trees and to sluts and to sunstroke. Because, my dear, my stupid son has been watching you through that stupid telescope he made. Because, in short, he wanted to meet you and I, in short, wanted him to know what you were really like.

Can you cook? Not good enough! My son is a connoisseur. A connoisseur, do you hear? I cook him the finest foods in the world. Recipes no one knows exist. Food, my sweet, is the finest of arts. And since you can't cook you are artless. You nauseate my son's aesthetic taste.

Do you like cats? Alley cats? I thought so. Go, my dear. Find yourself some weeping willow and set yourself beneath it. Cry of your lust for my son and wait, for a mockingbird waits above to deposit his verdict on your whorish head. My son is as white as fresh snow and you are tainted with sin. You are garnished with garlic and turn our tender stomachs in disgust. I throw you out! I toss you into the garbage can! I heard everything, you know. So don't try to call. The phone is in my room—*and no one goes into my room but me*. One more thing. If, by some chance, the eleventh child named Cynthia turns out to be a Siamese cat, give it to me. I, too, pay well.

Well, here we have the ultimate protective mother. You might say "monster mother"! But do not play her as you think of her when first reading this monologue. Do not play her as you think of her as actress when you read the entire play and make more discoveries about this woman. Get into her shoes and underwear. *You* may think she is a monster but *she* does not think she is one. Therefore, she is not! She seems strong and invincible. She is fighting like hell to protect her son from the cruel world. She knows only too well how cruel the world can be. She is actually very frightened for herself and for her son. She knows that she alone will never do harm to her son. But others will. And Rosalie will eventually. This Madame knows so she *must* protect her son. And she needs her son to be near her at all times. She is alone. She is very jealous of Rosalie or any woman who comes near her or her son. So she is not so strong and invincible.

Now, there is no love on these pages. So where are you going to find it? You need to have opposites. You are insulting her and demanding that she remove herself from your life and your son's life. You are communicating very strongly your contempt for her. You've got to find the love. I don't mean that the opposite of what you are saying is true. I mean that you are fighting for her to help you protect your son. You need her cooperation. She must not fight you on this. But you have to have opposite feelings for her other than all that contempt. She is young, pretty, and seems to care for your son. She is the object of your son's desire. It is of course threatening to you if he strongly desires a woman. His love and need for you *must* be stronger than his desire for a woman. With all your contempt for her, try to make her understand that you *must* protect your son. You are not going to *do* anything in your reading to indicate that you want her to understand and help you. But do incorporate these feelings into your choices for your character before you begin rehearsing out loud the actual monologue itself. Remember, the first part of each rehearsal deals with going through your history and background of yourself as character leading up to this confrontation. Formulate your choices and then begin the monologue itself.

This monologue is created from blocks of dialogue, which I do not normally believe in doing. I prefer one- or two-liners so that the dialogue is crisp and confrontational. Also, too often, blocks of dialogue are done and overdone. But this piece is not overdone and it is strong and confrontational material. Have fun with it.

OH DAD, POOR DAD...
by Arthur L. Kopit

pp. 30–36 (SAMUEL FRENCH, INC.)

The Commodore: How lovely it was this evening, madame, don't you think? (*She laughs softly and demurely and discreetly lowers her eyes. They waltz about the floor.*) How gentle the wind was, madame. And the stars, how clear and bright they were, don't you think? (*She turns her face away and smiles softly. They begin to whirl about the floor.*) Ah, the waltz. How exquisite it is, madame, don't you think? *One*-two-three, *one*-two-three, *one*-two-three. Ahhhhh, madame, how classically simple. How stark; how strong—how romantic—how sublime. (*She giggles girlishly. They whirl madly about the floor.*) Oh, if only madame knew how I've waited for this moment. If only madame knew how long. How this week, these nights, the nights we shared together on my yacht; the warm, wonderful nights, the almost-perfect nights, the would-have-been-perfect nights had it not been for the crew peeking through the portholes. Ah, those nights, madame, those nights; almost alone but never quite; but now, tonight, at last, we *are* alone. And now, madame, now we are ready for romance. For the night was made for love. And tonight, madame—we will love.

Madame Rosepettle: (*With the blush of innocence.*) Oh, Commodore, how you do talk.

(*They whirl about the room as the lilting rhythm of the waltz grows and sweeps on and on.*)

The Commodore: (*Suavely.*) Madame, may I kiss you?
Madame Rosepettle: Why?
The Commodore: (*After recovering from the abruptness of the question. With forced suaveness.*) Your lips . . . are a thing of beauty.

212

Madame Rosepettle: My lips, Commodore, are the color of blood. (*She smiles at him. He stares blankly ahead. They dance on.*) I must say, you dance exceptionally well, Commodore—for a man your age.

The Commodore: (*Bristling.*) I dance with *you*, madame. That is why I dance well. For to dance with you, madame—is to hold you.

Madame Rosepettle: Well, I don't mind your holding me, Commodore, but at the moment you happen to be holding me too tight.

The Commodore: I hold you too dear to hold you too tight, madame. I hold you close, that is all. And I hold you close in the hope that my heart may feel your heart beating.

Madame Rosepettle: *One*-two-three, *one*-two-three. You're not paying enough attention to the music, Commodore. I'm afraid you've fallen out of step.

The Commodore: Then lead me, madame. Take my hand and lead me wherever you wish. For I would much rather think of my words than my feet.

Madame Rosepettle: (*With great sweetness.*) Why certainly, Commodore. Certainly. If that is what you want—it will be my pleasure to oblige. (*They switch hands and she begins to lead him about the floor. They whirl wildly about, spinning faster than they had when* THE COMMODORE *led.*) Beautiful, isn't it, Commodore? The waltz. The Dance of Lovers. I'm so glad you enjoy it so much. (*With a gay laugh she whirls him around the floor. Suddenly he puts his arms about her shoulders and leans close to kiss her. She pulls back.*) Commodore! You were supposed to spin just then. When I squeeze you in the side it means *spin!*

The Commodore: (*Flustered.*) I—I thought it was a sign of affection.

(*She laughs.*)

Madame Rosepettle: You'll learn. (*She squeezes him in the side. He spins about under her arm.*) Ah, you're learning.

(*He continues to spin, around and around, faster and faster like a runaway top while* MADAME ROSEPETTLE, *not spinning at all, leads him about the floor, a wild smile of ecstasy spreading over her face.*)

The Commodore: Ho-ho, ho-ho. Stop. I'm dizzy. Dizzy.

Stop, please. Stop. Ho-ho. Stop. Dizzy. Ho-ho. Stop. Too
fast. Slow. Slower. Stop. Ho-ho. Dizzy. Too dizzy. Weeeeeeee!
*(And then, without any warning at all, she grabs him in the
middle of a spin, and kisses him. Her back is to the
audience, so* THE COMMODORE's *face is visible. At first he is
too dizzy to realize that his motion has been stopped. But
shortly he does, and his first expression is that of shock. But
the kiss is long and the shock turns into perplexity and then,
finally, into panic; into fear. He struggles desperately and
breaks free from her arms, gasping wildly for air. He points
weakly to his chest, gasping.)* Asthma. *(His chest heaves as
he gulps in air.)* Couldn't breathe. Asthmatic. Couldn't get
any air. *(He gasps for air. She starts to walk toward him,
slowly.)* Couldn't get any . . . air. *(She nears him. Instinctively
he backs away.)* You—you surprised me—you know. Out—of
breath. Wasn't—ready for that. Didn't—expect you to kiss me.

Madame Rosepettle: I know. That's why I did it. *(She laughs
and puts her arm tenderly about his waist.)* Perhaps you'd
prefer to sit down for a while, Commodore? Catch your
breath, so to speak. Dancing can be so terribly tiring—when
you're growing old. Well, if you like, Commodore, we could
just sit and talk. And perhaps—sip some pink champagne,
eh? Champagne?

The Commodore: Ah, champagne.

Madame Rosepettle: *(She begins to walk with him toward the
table.)* And just for the two of us.

The Commodore: Yes. The two of us. Alone.

Madame Rosepettle: *(With a laugh.)* Yes. All alone.

The Commodore: At last.

Madame Rosepettle: With music in the distance.

The Commodore: A waltz.

Madame Rosepettle: A *Viennese* waltz.

The Commodore: The Dance of Lovers.

Madame Rosepettle: *(She takes his hand, tenderly.)* Yes, Commodore. The Dance of Lovers. *(They look at each other in
silence.)*

The Commodore: Madame, you have won my heart. And
easily.

Madame Rosepettle: No, Commodore. You have lost it. *Easily.*
*(She smiles seductively. The room darkens till only a single
spot of light falls upon the table set in the middle of the
room. The waltz plays on.* MADAME ROSEPETTLE *nods to* THE

COMMODORE *and he goes to sit. But before he can pull his chair out, it slides out under its own power. He places himself and the chair slides back in, as if some invisible waiter had been holding it in his invisible hands.* MADAME ROSEPETTLE *smiles sweetly and, pulling out her chair herself, sits. They stare at each other in silence. The waltz plays softly.* THE COMMODORE *reaches across the table and touches her hand. A thin smile spreads across her lips. When finally they speak, their words are soft; the whispered thoughts of lovers.)* Champagne?

The Commodore: Champagne.

Madame Rosepettle: Pour?

The Commodore: Please.

(She lifts the bottle out of the ice bucket and pours with her right hand, her left being clasped firmly in THE COMMODORE'S *passionate hands. They smile serenely at each other. She lifts her glass. He lifts his. The music swells.)*

Madame Rosepettle: A toast?

The Commodore: To you.

Madame Rosepettle: No, Commodore, to you.

The Commodore: No, madame. To us.

Madame Rosepettle and The Commodore: *(Together.)* To us. *(They raise their glasses. They gaze wistfully into each other's eyes. The music builds to brilliance.* THE COMMODORE *clicks his glass against* MADAME ROSEPETTLE'S *glass. The glasses break.)*

The Commodore: *(Furiously mopping up the mess.)* Pardon, madame! Pardon!

Madame Rosepettle: *(Flicking some glass off her bodice.)* Pas de quoi, monsieur.

The Commodore: J'etais emporte par l'enthousiasme du moment.

Madame Rosepettle: *(Extracting pieces of glass from her lap.)* Pas de quoi. *(She snaps her fingers gaily. Immediately a* WAITER *appears from the shadows with a table in his hands. It is already covered with a table cloth, two champagne glasses, two candelabra [the candles already flickering in them], and a vase with one wilting rose protruding and whisks the wet table away. The new table is placed. The* WAITERS *disappear into the shadows.* MADAME ROSEPETTLE *lifts the bottle of champagne out of the ice bucket.)* Encore?

The Commodore: S'il vous plaît. *(She pours. They lift their glasses in toast. The music swells again.)* To us.

Madame Rosepettle: To us, Monsieur—Commodore. *(They clink their glasses lightly.* THE COMMODORE *closes his eyes and sips.* MADAME ROSEPETTLE *holds her glass before her lips, poised but not touching; waiting. She watches him. Softly.)* Tell me about yourself.

The Commodore: My heart is speaking, madame. Doesn't it tell you enough?

Madame Rosepettle: Your heart, monsieur, is growing old. It speaks with a murmur. Its words are too weak to understand.

The Commodore: But the feeling, madame, is still strong.

Madame Rosepettle: Feelings are for animals, monsieur. Words are the specialty of Man. Tell me what your heart has to say.

The Commodore: My heart says it loves you.

Madame Rosepettle: And how many others, monsieur, has your heart said this to?

The Commodore: None but you, madame. None but you.

Madame Rosepettle: And pray, monsieur, just what is it that I've done to make you love me so?

The Commodore: Nothing, madame. And that is why. You are a strange woman, you see. You go out with me and you know how I feel. Yet, I know nothing of you. You disregard me, madame, but never discourage. You treat my love with indifference—but never disdain. You've led me on, madame. This is what I mean to say.

Madame Rosepettle: I've led you to my room, monsieur. That is all.

The Commodore: To me, that is enough.

Madame Rosepettle: I know. That's why I did it.

(The music swells. She smiles distantly. There is a momentary silence.)

The Commodore: *(With desperation.)* Madame, I must ask you something. Why are you here? *(Short pause.)*

Madame Rosepettle: Well, I have to be somewhere, don't I?

The Commodore: But why here, where I am? Why in Port Royale?

Madame Rosepettle: You flatter yourself, monsieur. I am in Port Royale only because Port Royale was in my way. . . . I think I'll move on tomorrow.

The Commodore: For—home?

Madame Rosepettle: *(Laughing slightly.)* Only the very young and the very old have homes. I am neither. So I have none.

The Commodore: But—surely you must come from somewhere.

Madame Rosepettle: Nowhere you've ever been.

The Commodore: I've been many places.

Madame Rosepettle: *(Softly.)* But not many enough. *(She picks up her glass of champagne and sips, a distant smile on her lips.)*

The Commodore: *(With sudden, overwhelming and soul-rending passion.)* Madame, don't go tomorrow. Stay. My heart is yours.

Madame Rosepettle: How much is it worth?

The Commodore: A fortune, madame.

Madame Rosepettle: Good. I'll take it in cash.

The Commodore: But the heart goes with it, madame.

Madame Rosepettle: And you with the heart, I suppose?

The Commodore: Forever.

The following is the monologue created from the previous scene.

THE COMMODORE (to MADAME ROSEPETTLE), age 40s to 60s. pp. 30–36 (SAMUEL FRENCH, INC.)

How lovely it was this evening, madame, don't you think? How gentle the wind was, madame. And the stars, how clear and bright they were, don't you think? And the moon, madame, shining across the water, lighting the yachts, anchored, so silent and white and clean, waiting for the wind to come and fill their great, clean, white sails again. How poetic it was. How pure, madame. How innocent... don't you think? Ah, the waltz. How exquisite it is, madame; don't you think? One-two-three, one-two-three, one-two-three. Ahhhh, madame, how classically simple. How mathematically simple. How stark; how strong... how romantic... how sublime. Oh, if only madame knew how I've waited for this moment. If only madame knew how long. How this week, these nights, the nights we shared together on my yacht; the warm, wonderful nights, the almost-perfect nights, the would-have-been-perfect nights had it not been for the crew peeking through the portholes. Ah, those nights, madame, those nights; almost alone but never quite; but now, tonight at last, we *are* alone. And now, madame, now we are ready for romance. For the night was made for love. And tonight,

madame ... we will love. Madame, may I kiss you? Your
lips ... are a thing of beauty. I dance with *you*, madame.
That is why I dance well. For to dance with you, madame—
is to hold you. I hold you too dear to hold you too tight,
madame. I hold you close, that is all. And I hold you close
in the hope that my heart may feel your heart beating.
Lead me, madame. Take my hand and lead me wherever
you wish. For I would much rather think of my words than
my feet. The two of us. Alone. At last. A waltz. The Dance
of Lovers. Madame, you have won my heart. And easily.
My heart is speaking, madame. My heart says it loves you.
My heart has said this to none but you. Many have loved
me. Too many, madame. You alone ... do I love. You have
done nothing to make me love you so. And that is why I
do. You are a strange woman, you see. You go out with me
and you know how I feel. Yet, I know nothing of you. You
disregard me, madame, but never discourage. You treat
my love with indifference ... but never disdain. You've led
me on, madame. That is what I mean to say. You've led me
to your room. To me, that is enough. Madame, don't go
tomorrow. Stay. My heart is yours. It is worth a fortune,
madame, in cash. But the heart goes with the cash,
madame. And I with the heart. Forever.

I think this piece speaks for itself. However, even though the
text is clear as to what you are fighting for from Madame, you
still must create a play within the play so that you have opposites. You certainly *must* read this entire play before you begin
working on this monologue to present to yourself the gifts the
playwright has put forth on those pages. All that Madame is, you
the Commodore do not know as yet in this scene. Obviously you
cannot play the piece with knowledge that you, the actor, possess.
Just fight like hell to get this beautiful, charming, sexy woman to
love you and be with you forever. You have never felt such
passion in your life.

OH DAD, POOR DAD, ...
by Arthur L. Kopit

pp. 37–39 (SAMUEL FRENCH, INC.)

Madame Rosepettle: *(Nonchalantly.)* Would you like to see him?

The Commodore: A snapshot?

Madame Rosepettle: No. My husband. He's inside in the closet. I had him stuffed. Wonderful taxidermist I know. H'm? What do you say, Commodore? Wanna peek? He's my very favorite trophy. I take him with me wherever I go.

The Commodore: *(Shaken. Not knowing what to make of it.)* Hah-hah, hah-hah. Yes. Very good. Very funny. Sort of a—um—*white elephant*, you might say.

Madame Rosepettle: *You* might say.

The Commodore: Well, it's—certainly very—courageous of you, a—a woman still in mourning, to—to be able to laugh at what most other women wouldn't find—well, shall we say—funny.

Madame Rosepettle: Life, my dear Commodore, is never funny. It's grim! It's there every morning breathing in your face the moment you open your red baggy eyes. Life, Mr. Roseabove, is a husband hanging from a hook in the closet. Open the door too quickly and your whole day's shot to hell. But open the door just a little ways, sneak your hand in, pull out your dress and your day is made. Yet he's still there, and waiting—and sooner or later the moth balls are gone and you have to clean house. Oh, it's a bad day, Commodore, when you have to stare Life in the face, and you find he doesn't smile at all; just hangs there—with his tongue sticking out.

The Commodore: I—don't find this—very funny.

Madame Rosepettle: Sorry. I was hoping it would give you a laugh.

219

The Commodore: I don't think it's funny at all. And the reason that I don't think it's funny at all is that it's not my kind of joke. One must respect the dead.

Madame Rosepettle: Then tell me, Commodore—why not the living, too? *(Pause. She lifts out the bottle of champagne and pours herself some more.)*

The Commodore: *(Weakly, with a trace of fear.)* How—how did he die?

Madame Rosepettle: Why, I killed him, of course. Champagne? *(She smiles sweetly and fills his glass. She raises hers in toast.)* To your continued good health. *(He stares at her blankly. The music swells in the background.)* Ah, the waltz, monsieur. Listen. The waltz. The Dance of Lovers. Beautiful— don't you think?

(She laughs and sips some more champagne. The music grows to brilliance. THE COMMODORE *starts to rise from his chair.)*

The Commodore: Forgive me, madame. But—I find I must leave. Urgent business calls. Good evening. *(He tries to push his chair back, but for some reason it will not move. He looks about in panic. He pushes frantically. It does not move. It is as if the invisible waiter who had come and slid the chair out when he went to sit down, now stood behind the chair and held it in so he could not get up. And as there are arms on the chair,* THE COMMODORE *cannot slide out at the sides.* MADAME ROSEPETTLE *smiles.)*

Madame Rosepettle: Now you don't *really* want to leave—do you, Commodore? After all, the night is still so young—and you haven't even seen my husband yet. Besides, there's a little story I still must tell you. A bedtime story. A fairy-tale full of handsome princes and enchanted maidens; full of love and joy and music; tenderness and charm. It's my very favorite story, you see. And I never leave a place without telling it to at least one person. So please, Commodore, won't you stay? . . . *Just for a little while?* *(He stares at her in horror. He tries once more to push his chair back. But the chair does not move. He sinks down into it weakly. She leans across the table and tenderly touches his hand.)* Good. I knew you'd see it my way. It would have been such a shame if you'd had to leave. For you see, Commodore, we are, in a way, united. We share something in common—you and I.

We share desire. For you desire me, with love in your heart. While I, my dear Commodore—desire your heart.

The following is the monologue created from the previous scene.

MADAME ROSEPETTLE (to THE COMMODORE), age 40s to 60s. pp. 37–39 (SAMUEL FRENCH, INC.)

Would you like to see my husband? He's inside in the closet. I had him stuffed. Wonderful taxidermist I know. H'm? What do you say, Commodore? Wanna peek? He's my very favorite trophy. I take him with me wherever I go.

Life, my dear Commodore, is never funny. It's grim! It's there every morning breathing in your face the moment you open your red baggy eyes. Life, Mr. Roseabove, is a husband hanging from a hook in the closet. Open the door too quickly and your whole day's shot to hell. But open the door just a little ways, sneak your hand in, pull out your dress and your day is made. Yet he's still there and waiting—and sooner or later the mothballs are gone and you have to clean house. Oh, it's a bad day, Commodore, when you have to stare Life in the face, and you find he doesn't smile at all; just hangs there—with his tongue sticking out. I hope you find this funny. I was hoping it would give you a laugh. Why must we only respect the dead. Why not the living, too? I killed him, of course. Champagne? To your continued good health. Ah, the waltz, monsieur. Listen. The waltz. The Dance of Lovers. Beautiful—*don't you think?*

Now you don't *really* want to leave—do you, Commodore? After all, the night is still so young—and you haven't even seen my husband yet. Besides, there's a little story I still must tell you. A bedtime story. A fairy tale full of handsome princes and enchanted maidens; full of love and joy and music; tenderness and charm. It's my very favorite story, you see. And I never leave a place without telling it to at least one person. So please, Commodore, won't you stay? . . . Good. I knew you'd see it my way. It would have been such a shame if you'd had to leave. For you see, Commodore, we are, in a way, united. We share something in common—you and I. We share desire. For you desire me, with love in your heart. While I, my dear Commodore—desire your heart.

You are toying with him. You are flirting. You are trying to shock him. You are not saying anything to him that is not true. So as actress, what kind of character are you playing? Is she a devil; a witch; a very, very disturbed woman? Once you get into her shoes and underwear, you will never think of yourself as any of these things. You are a woman who lives her life as she so wishes. And if she wants to stuff her husband and hang him in the closet, that's her choice. She explains why. Seduce him with all your might. Fight for his love. Fight for your life.

OH DAD, POOR DAD...
by Arthur L. Kopit

pp. 50–58 (SAMUEL FRENCH, INC.)

Rosalie: Do you know why I had this key made? Do you know why I'm wearing this new dress?

Jonathan: She tells me I'm brilliant. She makes me read and re-read books no one's ever read. She smothers me with blankets at night in case of a storm. She tucks me in so tight I can't even get out till she comes and takes my blankets off.

Rosalie: Try and guess why I'm all dressed up.

Jonathan: She says she loves me. Every morning, before I even have a chance to open my eyes, there she is, leaning over my bed, breathing in my face and saying, "I love you, I love you."

Rosalie: Jonathan, isn't my dress pretty?

Jonathan: But I heard everything tonight. I heard it all when she didn't know I was here. (*He stares off into space, bewildered.*)

Rosalie: What's the matter? (*He does not answer.*) Jonathan, what's the matter?

Jonathan: But she must have known I was here. She *must* have known! I mean—where could I have gone? (*Pause.*) But—if that's the case—*why did she let me hear?*

Rosalie: Jonathan, I do wish you'd pay more attention to me. Here, look at my dress. You can even touch it if you like. Guess how many crinolines I have on. Guess why I'm wearing such a pretty, new dress. *Jonathan!*

Jonathan: (*Distantly.*) Maybe—it didn't make any difference to her—whether I heard or not. (*He turns suddenly to her and hugs her closely. She lets him hold her, then she steps back and away from him. Her face looks strangely old and determined under her girlish powder and pinkness.*)

Rosalie: Come with me.

223

Jonathan: What?

Rosalie: Leave and come with me.

Jonathan: *(Fearfully.)* Where?

Rosalie: Anywhere.

Jonathan: Wha'—wha'—what do you mean?

Rosalie: I mean, let's leave. Let's run away. Far away. Tonight. Both of us, together. Let's run and run. Far, far away.

Jonathan: You—mean, leave?

Rosalie: Yes. Leave.

Jonathan: Just like that?

Rosalie: Just like that.

Jonathan: But—but—but—

Rosalie: You want to leave, don't you?

Jonathan: I—I don't—don't know. I—I—

Rosalie: What about the time you told me how much you'd like to go outside, how you'd love to walk by yourself, anywhere you wanted?

Jonathan: I—I don't—know.

Rosalie: Yes, you do. Come. Give me your hand. Stop trembling so. Everything will be all right. Give me your hand and come with me. Just through the door. Then we're safe. Then we can run far away,' somewhere where she'll never find us. Come, Jonathan. It's time to go.

Jonathan: There are others you could take.

Rosalie: But I don't love them.

(Pause.)

Jonathan: You—you *love* me?

Rosalie: Yes, Jonathan. I love you.

Jonathan: Wha-wha-why?

Rosalie: Because you watch me every night.

Jonathan: Well—can't we stay here?

Rosalie: No!

Jonathan: Wha—wha—whhhhy?

Rosalie: *Because I want you alone.* (JONATHAN *turns from her and begins to walk about the room in confusion.*) I want you, Jonathan. Do you understand what I said? *I want you for my husband.*

Jonathan: I—I—can't, I mean, I—I want to go—go with you very much but I—I don't think—I can. I'm—sorry. *(He sits down and holds his head in his hands, sobbing quietly.)*

Rosalie: What time will your mother be back?

Jonathan: Na—not for a while.

Rosalie: Are you sure?

Jonathan: Ya—yes.

Rosalie: Where is she?

Jonathan: The usual place.

Rosalie: What do you mean, "the usual place"?

Jonathan: *(With a sad laugh.)* The beach. (ROSALIE *looks at* JONATHAN *quizzically.*) She likes to look for people making love. Every night at midnight she walks down to the beach searching for people lying on blankets and making love. When she finds them she kicks sand in their faces and walks on. Sometimes it takes her as much as three hours to chase everyone away. (ROSALIE *smiles slightly and walks toward the master bedroom.* JONATHAN *freezes in fear. She puts her hand on the door knob.*) WHAT ARE YOU DOING!? *(She smiles at him over her shoulder. She opens the door.)* STOP!! You can't go in there!!! STOP!!

Rosalie: *(She opens the door completely and beckons him to come.)* Come.

Jonathan: Close it. Quickly!

Rosalie: Come, Jonathan. Let's go inside.

Jonathan: Close the door!

Rosalie: *(With a laugh.)* You've never been in here, have you?

Jonathan: No. And you can't go in, either. No one can go in there but Mother. It's her room. Now close the door!

Rosalie: *(She flicks on the light switch. No lights go on.)* What's wrong with the lights?

Jonathan: There are none. Mother's in mourning. (ROSALIE *walks into the room and pulls the drapes from off the windows. Weird colored lights stream in and illuminate the bedroom in wild, distorted, nightmarish shadows and lights. They blink on and off, on and off. It's all like some strange, macabre fun house in an insane amusement park. Even the furniture in the room seems grotesque and distorted. The closet next to the bed seems peculiarly prominent. It almost seems to tilt over the bed. Still in the main room.*) What have you done!? (ROSALIE *walks back to the door and smiles to him from within the master bedroom.*) What have you done?

Rosalie: Come in, Jonathan.

Jonathan: GET OUT OF THERE!

Rosalie: Will you leave with me?

Jonathan: I can't!

Rosalie: But you want to, don't you?

Jonathan: Yes, yes, I want to, but I told you—I—I—I can't. I can't! Do you understand? I can't! Now come out of there.

Rosalie: Come in and get me.

Jonathan: Rosalie, *please*.

Rosalie: (*Bouncing on the bed*.) My, what a comfortable bed.

Jonathan: GET OFF THE BED!!!

Rosalie: What soft, fluffy pillows. I think I'll take a nap.

Jonathan: Rosalie, *please listen to me*. Come out of there. You're not supposed to be in that room. Please come out. Rosalie, *please*.

Rosalie: Will you leave with me if I do?

Jonathan: Rosalie—? I'll—I'll show you my stamp collection if you'll promise to come out.

Rosalie: Bring it in here.

Jonathan: Will you come out then?

Rosalie: Only if you bring it in here.

Jonathan: But I'm not allowed to go in there.

Rosalie: (*Poutingly*.) Then I shan't come out!

Jonathan: You've got to!

Rosalie: Why?

Jonathan: Mother will be back.

Rosalie: She can sleep out there. (ROSALIE *yawns*.) I think I'll take a little nap. This bed is so comfortable. Really, Jonathan, you should come in and try it.

Jonathan: MOTHER WILL BE BACK SOON!!

Rosalie: Give her your room then if you don't want her to sleep on the couch. I find it very nice in here. Good night.

(Pause.)

Jonathan: If I come in, will you come out?

Rosalie: If you don't come in I'll never come out.

Jonathan: And if I do?

Rosalie: Then I may.

Jonathan: What if I bring my stamps in?

Rosalie: Bring them and find out.

Jonathan: (*He goes to the dresser and takes out the drawer of stamps. Then he takes out the drawer of coins*.) I'm bringing the coins, too.

Rosalie: How good you are, Jonathan.

Jonathan: *(He takes a shelf full of books.)* My books, too. How's that? I'll show you my books and my coins and my stamps. I'll show you them all. Then will you leave?

Rosalie: Perhaps. *(He carries them all into the bedroom and sets them down next to the bed. He looks about fearfully.)* What's wrong?

Jonathan: I've never been in here before.

Rosalie: It's nothing but a room. There's nothing to be afraid of.

Jonathan: *(He looks about doubtfully.)* Well, let me show you my stamps. I have one billion, five—

Rosalie: Later, Jonathan. We'll have time. Let me show you something first.

Jonathan: What's that?

Rosalie: You're trembling.

Jonathan: What do you want to show me?

Rosalie: There's nothing to be nervous about. Come. Sit down.

Jonathan: What do you want to show me?

Rosalie: I can't show you if you won't sit down.

Jonathan: I don't want to sit down!

(She takes hold of his hand. He pulls it away.)

Rosalie: Jonathan!

Jonathan: You're sitting on Mother's bed.

Rosalie: Then let's pretend it's my bed.

Jonathan: It's not your bed!

Rosalie: Come, Jonathan. Sit down here next to me.

Jonathan: We've got to get out of here. Mother might come.

Rosalie: Don't worry. We've got plenty of time. The beach is full of lovers.

Jonathan: How do you know?

Rosalie: I checked before I came.

(Pause.)

Jonathan: Let—let me show you my coins.

Rosalie: Why are you trembling so?

Jonathan: Look, we've got to get out! Something terrible will happen if we don't.

Rosalie: Then leave with me.

Jonathan: The bedroom?

Rosalie: The hotel. The island. Your mother. Leave with me, Jonathan. Leave with me now, before it's too late.

Jonathan: I—I—I—

Rosalie: I love you, Jonathan, and I won't give you up. I want you . . . all for myself. Not to share with your mother, but for me, alone—to love, to live with, to have children by. I want you, Jonathan. You, whose skin is softer and whiter than anyone's I've ever known. Whose voice is quiet and whose love is in every look of his eye. I want you, Jonathan, and I won't give you up.

(Short pause.)

Jonathan: *(Softly, weakly.)* What do you want me to do?

Rosalie: Forget about your mother. Pretend she never existed and look at me. Look at my eyes, Jonathan; my mouth, my hands, my skirt, my legs. Look at me, Jonathan. Are you still afraid?

Jonathan: I'm not afraid. *(She smiles and starts to unbutton her dress.)* What are you doing!? No!

Rosalie: *(She continues to unbutton her dress.)* Your mother is strong, but I am stronger. *(She rises and her skirt falls about her feet. She stands in a slip and crinolines.)* I don't look so pink and girlish anymore, do I? *(She laughs.)* But you want me anyhow. You're ashamed but you want me anyhow. It's written on your face. And I'm very glad. Because I want you. *(She takes off a crinoline.)*

Jonathan: PUT IT ON! *Please*, put it back on!

Rosalie: Come, Jonathan. *(She takes off another crinoline.)* Lie down. Let me loosen your shirt.

Jonathan: No . . . NO . . . NO! STOP! *Please*, stop!

(She takes her last crinoline off and reaches down to take off her socks. The lights outside blink weirdly. Wild, jagged music with a drum beating in the background is heard.)

Rosalie: Don't be afraid, Jonathan. Come. Lie down. Everything will be wonderful. *(She takes her socks off and lies down in her slip. She drops a strap over one shoulder and smiles.)*

Jonathan: Get off my mother's bed!

Rosalie: I want you, Jonathan, all for my own. Come. The bed is soft. Lie here by my side. *(She reaches up and takes his hand. Meekly he sits down on the edge of the bed. The closet door swings open suddenly and the corpse of Albert Edward Robinson*

Rosepettle III tumbles forward stiffly and onto the bed, his stone-stiff arms falling across ROSALIE's *legs, his head against her side.* JONATHAN, *too terrified to scream, puts his hand across his mouth and sinks down onto the bed, almost in a state of collapse. Outside the music screams.)* Who the hell is this!?

Jonathan: It-it-it-it—it—it's—

Rosalie: What a stupid place to keep a corpse. *(She pushes him back in the closet and shuts the door.)* Forget it, Jonathan. I put him back in the closet. Everything's fine again.

Jonathan: It's—it's—it's my—my—my—

Rosalie: *(Kneeling next to him on the bed and starting to unbutton his shirt.)* It's all right, Jonathan. It's all right. Sshh. Come. Let me take off your clothes.

Jonathan: *(Still staring dumbly into space.)* It's—it's my—fffather.

(The closet door swings open again and the corpse falls out, this time his arms falling about ROSALIE's *neck.* JONATHAN *almost swoons.)*

Rosalie: Oh, for God's sake. *(She pushes him off the bed and onto the floor.)* Jonathan . . . ? LISTEN TO ME, JONATHAN! STOP LOOKING AT HIM AND LOOK AT ME! *(He looks away from his father, fearfully, his mouth open in terror.)* I love you, Jonathan, and I want you *now*. Not later and not as partner with your mother but now and by myself. I want you, Jonathan, as my husband. I want you to lie with me, to sleep with me, to be with me, to kiss me and touch me, to live with me, *forever*. Stop looking at him! He's dead! Listen to me. I'm alive. I want you for my husband! Now help me take my slip off. Then you can look at my body and touch me. Come, Jonathan. Lie down. I want you forever.

Jonathan: Ma-mother was right! You *do* let men do anything they want to you.

Rosalie: Of course she was right! Did you really think I was that sweet and pure? Everything she said was right. *(She laughs.)* Behind the bushes and it's done. One-two-three and it's done. Here's the money. Thanks. Come again. Hah-hah! Come again! *(Short pause.)* So what!? It's only you I love. They make no difference.

Jonathan: You're dirty! *(He tries to get up but can't, for his father is lying in front of his feet.)*

Rosalie: No, I'm not dirty. I'm full of love and womanly feelings. I want children. Tons of them. I want a husband. Is that dirty? Take off your clothes.

The following is the monologue created from the previous scene.

ROSALIE (to JONATHAN), age 20s to early 30s.
pp. 50–58 (SAMUEL FRENCH, INC.)

Do you know why I had this key made? Do you know why I'm wearing this new dress? Try and guess why I'm all dressed up. Stop talking and pay attention to me! Jonathan, isn't my dress pretty? You can even touch it if you like. Guess how many crinolines I have on. *Jonathan!* Let's run away. Far away. Tonight. Let's run and run. Far, far away. *Leave.* Just like that. You want to leave, don't you? What about the time you told me how much you'd like to go outside, how you'd love to walk by yourself, anywhere you wanted? Come. Give me your hand. Stop trembling so. Everything will be all right. Give me your hand and come with me. Just through the door. Then we're safe. Then we can run far away, somewhere where she'll never find us. Come, Jonathan. It's time to go. I've put on a new dress just for the occasion. I even had a key made so I could come and get you. I love you. I want you alone. Do you understand what I said? *I want you for my husband....* What time will your mother be back? Let's go inside. Will you leave with me? You want to, don't you? There's nothing to be afraid of. Let me show you something. There's nothing to be nervous about. I want you all for myself. Not to share with your mother, but for me, alone... to love, to live with, to have children by. You, whose skin is softer and whiter than anyone's I've ever known; whose voice is quiet and whose love is in every look of his eye. I want you, Jonathan, and I won't give you up. Forget about your mother. Pretend she never existed and look at me. Look at my eyes, Jonathan; my mouth, my hands, my skirt, my legs. Look at me, Jonathan. Are you still afraid? Your mother is strong, but I am stronger. I don't look so pink and girlish any more, do I? But you want me anyhow. You're ashamed but you want me anyhow. It's written on your face. And I'm very glad. Because I want you. Don't be afraid, Jonathan. Come. Lie down. Everything will be wonderful. Your mother was right! Did you really think I was that sweet and pure? Everything she said was right. Behind the bushes and it's done. One-two-three and it's done. Here's the money. Thanks. Come again. Hah-hah! Come again! So what!? It's only you I love. They make no difference. I'm not dirty. I'm full of love and womanly feelings. I want children. Tons of them. I want a husband. Is that dirty? Take off your clothes.

By reading the play, you will discover that you are no different from Jonathan's mother. By not reading this play and doing this monologue anyway, you are cheating your character and yourself.

You are fighting for Jonathan's love and to own him. You are alone and you have intense feelings for Jonathan. It is him and only him whom you crave and desire. As far as you are concerned you love him very much. Everything will be just wonderful if he is firmly ensconced in your life. Without him, there is nothing for you. You are fighting for the rest of your life.

PLAZA SUITE
by Neil Simon

pp. 37–40 (SAMUEL FRENCH, INC.)

Sam: Why do you always start the most serious discussions in our life when I'm halfway out the door?

Karen: If that's what you want, just tell me straight out. Just say, "Karen, there's no point in going on." I'd rather hear it from you personally, than get a message on our service.

Sam: Look, we'll talk about it when I get back, okay? *(He starts out again.)*

Karen: *(Can no longer contain herself. There is none of that "playful, toying" attitude in her voice now. Jumping up.)* No, God dammit, we'll talk about it now! I'm not going to sit around a hotel room half the night waiting to hear how my life is going to come out . . . If you've got something to say, then have the decency to say it before you walk out that door.

(There is a moment's silence while they try to compose themselves. SAM turns back into the room and closes the door.)

Sam: Is there any coffee left?

Karen: It's that bad, huh? . . . All right, sit down, I'll get you some coffee. *(She starts to cross to table and stops, looking at her hands.* SAM *crosses to sofa. Puts down attaché case by coffee table and sits.)* Look at this. I'm shaking like a leaf. Pour it yourself. I have a feeling in a few minutes I'm not going to be too crazy about you. (KAREN *crosses and sits on ottoman next to sofa, hands clasped together.)*

Sam: *(He finds it difficult to look at her.)* No matter what, Karen, in twenty-three years my feelings for you have never changed. You're my wife, I still love you.

Karen: Oh, God, am I in trouble.

232

Sam: It has nothing to do with you. It's something that just happened... It's true, I am having an affair with her... (SAM *waits for* KAREN *to react. She merely sits and looks at her hands.*) It's been going on for about six months now... I tried stopping it a few times, it didn't work... After a couple of days I'd start it again... And then—well, what's the point in going on with this? You wanted honesty, I'm giving it to you. I'm having an affair with Jean, that's all there is to it.

Karen: (*Looks up.*) Who's Jean?

Sam: Jean! Miss McCormack.

Karen: Oh. For a minute I thought there were two of them.

Sam: I'm not very good at this. I don't know what I'm supposed to say now.

Karen: Don't worry about it. You're doing fine. (*She gets up and moves to table.*) You want that coffee now? I just stopped shaking.

Sam: ...What are we going to do?

Karen: (*Turns back to* SAM.) Well, you're taken care of. You're having an affair. I'm the one who needs an activity.

Sam: Karen, I'll do whatever you want.

Karen: Whatever *I* want?

Sam: I'll leave. I'll get out tonight... Or I'll stop seeing her. I'll get rid of her in the office. I'll try it any way you want.

Karen: (*Moves to sofa.*) Oh. Okay. I choose "Stop Seeing Jean"... Gee, that was easy. (*Snaps her fingers.*) Now we can go back to our old normal life and live happily ever after. (*Starts to pour coffee, but stops and puts pot down.*) It's not my day. Even the coffee's cold.

Sam: Oh, come on, Karen, don't play "Aren't we civilized?" Call me a bastard. Throw the coffee at me.

Karen: You're a bastard. You want cream and sugar?

Sam: It's funny how our attitudes have suddenly changed. What happened to "I think a man of your age *should* have an affair"?

Karen: It looked good in the window but terrible when I got it home.

Sam: If it's any solace to you, I never thought it would go this far. I don't even remember how it started...

Karen: Think, it'll come back to you.

Sam: Do you know she worked for me for two years and I never batted an eye at her?

Karen: Good for you, Sam.

Sam: *(Angry.)* Oh, come on. *(Crosses to bedroom, and stretches out across bed.)*

Karen: *(She follows him into bedroom.)* No, Sam, I want to hear about it. She worked for you for two years and you didn't know her first name was Jean. And then one night you were both working late and suddenly you let down your hair and took off your glasses and she said, "Why, Mr. Nash, you're beautiful."

Sam: *(Takes pillow and places it over his head.)* That's it, word for word. You must have been hiding in the closet.

Karen: *(Tears the pillow away and throws it back down on bed.)* All right, you want to know when I think the exact date your crummy little affair started? I'll tell you. It was June nineteenth. It was your birthday and you just turned fifty years old. Five oh, count 'em, folks, and you were feeling good and sorry for yourself. Right?

Sam: Oh, God, here comes Doctor Franzblau again.

Karen: And the only reason you picked on Miss McCormack was because she was probably the first one you saw that morning... If she was sick that day, this affair very well could have been with your elevator operator.

Sam: Wrong. He's fifty-two and I don't go for older men.

Karen: *(Breaks away and crosses to living room.)* You were right before, Sam. Let's discuss this later tonight.

Sam: *(Sitting up on side of bed.)* No, no. We've opened this up, let's bring it all out. I've told you the truth, I'm involved with another woman. I'm not proud of it, Karen, but those are the facts. Now what am I supposed to do about it?

Karen: *(Moves back to bedroom doorway.)* Well, I *would* suggest committing suicide but I'm afraid you might think I meant *me* ... *(Goes back to living room.)* I have one other suggestion. Forget it.

Sam: *(Sharply.)* Forget it?

Karen: *(Pacing above sofa.)* I understand it, Sam. It's not your fault. But maybe I can live with it until it's over. What else can I do, Sam? I'm attached to you. So go out, have a good time tonight and when you come home, bring me the Daily News, I'm getting sick of the Post. *(Sits on sofa.)*

Sam: If I lived with you another twenty-three years, I don't think I'd ever understand you.

Karen: If that's a proposition, I accept.

Sam: *(Gets up and moves to* KAREN.*)* Dammit, Karen, stop accepting everything in life that's thrown at you. Fight back once in a while. Don't understand me. Hate me! I am *not* going through a middle-aged adjustment. I'm having an affair. A cheating, sneaking, sordid affair.

Karen: If it helps you to romanticize it, Sam, all right. I happen to know better.

Sam: *(Crossing above sofa to fireplace.)* You don't know better at all. You didn't even know I was having an affair.

Karen: I suspected it. You were working three nights a week and we weren't getting any richer.

Sam: *(Leaning on mantlepiece.)* I see. And now that you know the truth I have your blessings.

Karen: No, just my permission. I'm your wife, not your mother.

Sam: That's indecent. I never heard such a thing in my life. For crying out loud, Karen, I'm losing all respect for you.

The following is the monologue created from the previous scene.

SAM (to KAREN), age 40s to 60s.
pp. 37–40 (SAMUEL FRENCH, INC.)

Why do you always start the most serious discussions in our life when I'm halfway out the door?... No matter what, Karen, in twenty-three years my feelings for you have never changed. You're my wife, I still love you. It has nothing to do with you. It's something that just happened. . . . It's true, I am having an affair with her. . . . It's been going on for about six months now. . . . I tried stopping it a few times, it didn't work. . . . After a couple of days I'd start it again . . . and then—well, what's the point in going on with this? You wanted honesty, I'm giving it to you. I'm having an affair with Jean, that's all there is to it. I'm not very good at this. I don't know what I'm supposed to say now. . . . What are we going to do? Karen, I'll do whatever you want. I'll leave. I'll get out tonight . . . or I'll stop seeing her. I'll get rid of her in the office. I'll try it any way you want. If it's any solace to you, I never thought it would go this far. I don't even remember how it started. . . . Do you know she worked for me for two years and I never batted an eye at her? I've told you the truth, I'm involved with another woman. I'm not proud of it, Karen, but those are the facts. Now what am I supposed to do about it? Forget it?? If I lived with you another twenty-three years, I don't think I'd ever understand you. Dammit, Karen, stop accepting everything in life that's thrown at you. Fight back once in a while. Don't understand me. Hate me! I am *not* going through a middle-aged adjustment. I'm having an affair. A cheating, sneaking, sordid affair. And now that you know the truth I have your blessings! That's indecent. I never heard such a thing in my life. For crying out loud, Karen, I'm losing all respect for you!

This man is tormented. A married man having an affair *should* be tormented! He loves his wife but is not happy with her as the one and only woman in his life. It's been a very long time that they've been together. She is a good woman, a good wife, a good mother, with humor, compassion, intelligence, and love for her husband. So why would a man want to risk losing such a woman who provides everything for his comfort and life? Of course, the problem lies with him, not with her. He is having trouble with getting old. He is the one who needs new thrills with new women. He is the weak one. On the other hand, some would say it is an act of courage to take a risk and, as John Wayne said, "A man's gotta do what a man's gotta do."

You must make very strong choices to love Karen very much. Because whether you know it or not, you do love her but you *feel* love for the other woman. And what we are talking about is sex. Now when Karen obviously doesn't fall down the steps screaming and yelling and cursing, you are devastated! *This* is not the proper response or behavior! You are mortified! You must appreciate the vast humor in this piece to successfully perform it. Irony abounds. You are really fighting for Karen to love you. You make the discovery that *she* might not love *you* anymore! *That* you didn't count on. That was *not* in Sam's script. This is not what he expected at all.

When you read the play, you will see that he leaves her. Do not play that end with this monologue. Do not play that end if you are ever in performance with the entire play until you get to that event. For the purpose of the monologue, play that you want Karen to do everything to keep you here with her and that you actually told her about the affair to once and for all get it out so that she knows and you will *have* to end the affair. As Sam, you might not even be so aware that this is really what you have in mind. But as actor, please know this.

PLAZA SUITE
by Neil Simon

pp. 38–43 (SAMUEL FRENCH, INC.)

Karen: Don't worry about it. You're doing fine. (*She gets up and moves to table.*) You want that coffee now? I just stopped shaking.

Sam: . . . What are we going to do?

Karen: (*Turns back to* SAM.) Well, you're taken care of. You're having an affair. I'm the one who needs an activity.

Sam: Karen, I'll do whatever you want.

Karen: Whatever *I* want?

Sam: I'll leave. I'll get out tonight . . . Or I'll stop seeing her. I'll get rid of her in the office. I'll try it any way you want.

Karen: (*Moves to sofa.*) Oh. Okay. I choose "Stop Seeing Jean" . . . Gee, that was easy. (*Snaps her fingers.*) Now we can go back to our old normal life and live happily ever after. (*Starts to pour coffee, but stops and puts pot down.*) It's not my day. Even the coffee's cold.

Sam: Oh, come on, Karen, don't play "Aren't we civilized?" Call me a bastard. Throw the coffee at me.

Karen: You're a bastard. You want cream and sugar?

Sam: It's funny how our attitudes have suddenly changed. What happened to "I think a man of your age *should* have an affair"?

Karen: It looked good in the window but terrible when I got it home.

Sam: If it's any solace to you, I never thought it would go this far. I don't even remember how it started . . .

Karen: Think, it'll come back to you.

Sam: Do you know she worked for me for two years and I never batted an eye at her?

Karen: Good for you, Sam.

Sam: (*Angry.*) Oh, come on. (*Crosses to bedroom, and stretches out across bed.*)

238

Karen: *(She follows him into bedroom.)* No, Sam, I want to hear about it. She worked for you for two years and you didn't know her first name was Jean. And then one night you were both working late and suddenly you let down your hair and took off your glasses and she said, "Why, Mr. Nash, you're beautiful."

Sam: *(Takes pillow and places it over his head.)* That's it, word for word. You must have been hiding in the closet.

Karen: *(Tears the pillow away and throws it back down on bed.)* All right, you want to know when I think the exact date your crummy little affair started? I'll tell you. It was June nineteenth. It was your birthday and you just turned fifty years old. Five oh, count 'em, folks, and you were feeling good and sorry for yourself. Right?

Sam: Oh, God, here comes Doctor Franzblau again.

Karen: And the only reason you picked on Miss McCormack was because she was probably the first one you saw that morning. . . If she was sick that day, this affair very well could have been with your elevator operator.

Sam: Wrong. He's fifty-two and I don't go for older men.

Karen: *(Breaks away and crosses to living room.)* You were right before, Sam. Let's discuss this later tonight.

Sam: *(Sitting up on side of bed.)* No, no. We've opened this up, let's bring it all out. I've told you the truth, I'm involved with another woman. I'm not proud of it, Karen, but those are the facts. Now what am I supposed to do about it?

Karen: *(Moves back to bedroom doorway.)* Well, I *would* suggest committing suicide but I'm afraid you might think I meant *me* . . . *(Goes back to living room.)* I have one other suggestion. Forget it.

Sam: *(Sharply.)* Forget it?

Karen: *(Pacing above sofa.)* I understand it, Sam. It's not your fault. But maybe I can live with it until it's over. What else can I do, Sam? I'm attached to you. So go out, have a good time tonight and when you come home, bring me the Daily News, I'm getting sick of the Post. *(Sits on sofa.)*

Sam: If I lived with you another twenty-three years, I don't think I'd ever understand you.

Karen: If that's a proposition, I accept.

Sam: *(Gets up and moves to* KAREN.) Dammit, Karen, stop accepting everything in life that's thrown at you. Fight back once in a while. Don't understand me. Hate me! I am *not* going through a middle-aged adjustment. I'm having an affair. A cheating, sneaking, sordid affair.

Karen: If it helps you to romanticize it, Sam, all right. I happen to know better.

Sam: *(Crossing above sofa to fireplace.)* You don't know better at all. You didn't even know I was having an affair.

Karen: I suspected it. You were working three nights a week and we weren't getting any richer.

Sam: *(Leaning on mantlepiece.)* I see. And now that you know the truth I have your blessings.

Karen: No, just my permission. I'm your wife, not your mother.

Sam: That's indecent. I never heard such a thing in my life. For crying out loud, Karen, I'm losing all respect for you.

Karen: What's the matter, Sam, am I robbing you of all those delicious guilt feelings? Will you feel better if I go to pieces and try to lash back at you?

Sam: *(Crosses below sofa.)* At least I would understand it. It's normal. I don't know why you're not having hysterics and screaming for a lawyer.

Karen: *(Getting up to confront him.)* All right, Sam, if it'll make you happier . . . I think you stink. You're a vain, self-pitying, deceiving, ten-pound box of rancid No-Cal cottage cheese. How'm I doing?

Sam: Swell. Now we're finally getting somewhere.

Karen: Oh, you like this, don't you? It makes everything nice and simple for you. Now you can leave here the martyred, misunderstood husband. Well, I won't give you the satisfaction. I take it back, Sam. *(Sits on sofa. Pleasantly, with great control.)* You're a pussycat. I'll have milk and cookies for you when you get home.

Sam: *(Sits on ottoman.)* No, no. Finish what you were saying. Get it off your chest, Karen. It's been building up for twenty-three years. I want to hear everything. Vain, self-pitying, what else? Go on, what else?

Karen: You're adorable. Eat your heart out.

Sam: *(Furious.)* Karen, don't do this to me.

Karen: I'm sorry, I'm a forgiving woman. I can't help myself.

Sam: *(Gets up, takes case and crosses to door.)* You're driving me right out of here, you know that, don't you?

Karen: There'll always be room for you in my garage.

Sam: If I walk out this door now, I don't come back.

Karen: I think you will.

Sam: What makes you so sure?

Karen: You forgot to take your eye drops.

Sam: *(He storms to coffee table, snatches up drops and crosses back to door. Stops.)* Before I go I just want to say one thing. Whatever you think of me is probably true. No, not probably, *definitely*. I have been a bastard right from the beginning. I don't expect you to forgive me.

Karen: But I do.

Sam: *(Whirling back to her.)* Let me finish. I don't expect you to forgive me. But I ask you with all conscience, with all your understanding, not to blame Jean for any of this.

Karen: *(Collapses on couch. Then pulling herself together.)* I'll send her a nice gift.

Sam: *(Puts down case beside sofa.)* She's been torturing herself ever since this started. *I'm* the one who forced the issue.

Karen: *(Moving away from him on sofa, mimics* JEAN.*)* "It didn't show up on the 1400 but I rechecked it with my own files and made the correction on the 640."... You know as well as I do that's code for "I'll meet you at the Picadilly Hotel."

Sam: *(Kneeling beside sofa.)* You won't believe me, will you? That she's a nice girl.

Karen: Nice for you and nice for me are two different things.

Sam: If it's that Sunday supplement psychology you're using, Karen, it's backfiring because you're just making it easier for me.

Karen: Well, you like things easy, don't you? You don't even have an affair the hard way.

Sam: Meaning what?

Karen: *(Getting up.)* Meaning you could have at least taken the trouble to look outside your office for a girl... *(Picks up imaginary phone.)* "Miss McCormack, would you please come inside and take an affair!"... Honestly, Sam. *(Moves above sofa.)*

Sam: Karen, don't force me to say nice things about her to you.

Karen: I can't help it. I'm just disappointed in you. It's so damned unoriginal.

Sam: What did you want her to be, a fighter pilot with the Israeli Air Force?

Karen: *Everyone* cheats with their secretary. I expected more from *my* husband!

Sam: *(Shaking his head.)* I never saw you like this. You live with a person your whole life, you don't really know them.

Karen: *(Crossing below sofa to bedroom.)* Go on, Sam, go have your affair. You're fifty-one years old. In an hour it may be too late. *(Sits at dresser, and brushes hair.)*

Sam: *(Getting up and crossing to her in bedroom.)* By God, you are something. You are really something special, Karen. Twenty-three years I'm married to you and I still can't make you out. You don't look much different than the ordinary woman but I promise you there is nothing walking around on two legs that compares in any way, shape or form to the likes of you.

Karen: *(Drops brush and turns to him. Laughing.)* So if I'm so special, what are you carrying on with secretaries for?

Sam: I'll be God-damned if I know . . .

(They look at each other. He turns and starts to front door, taking attaché case.)

Karen: *(Following him into living room.)* Sam! (SAM *stops.)* Sam . . . do I still have my two choices? *(He turns and looks at her.)* Because if I do . . . I choose "Get rid of Miss McCormack." *(He looks away.)* I pick "Stay here and work it out with me, Sam." (KAREN *turns her back to him and leans against the arm of the sofa.)* Because the other way I think I'm going to lose. Don't go to the office tonight, Sam . . . Stay with me . . . Please.

Sam: *(Leaning on console table, looks at her.)* I swear, I wish we could go back the way it was before. A couple of years ago, before there were problems.

Karen: Maybe we can, Sam. We'll do what you said before. We'll lie. We'll tell each other everything is all right . . . There is nothing wrong in the office tonight, there is no Miss McCormack and I'm twenty-seven God-damned years old . . . What do you say, Sam?

The following is the monologue created from the previous scene.

KAREN (to SAM), age 40s to 60s.
pp. 38–43 (SAMUEL FRENCH, INC.)

You're doing fine. You're taken care of. You're having an

affair. I'm the one who needs an activity. If you'll try it the way I want, I choose "Stop Seeing Jean." . . . Gee, that was easy. Now we can go back to our old normal life and live happily ever after. . . . I want to hear about it. She worked for you for two years and you didn't know her first name was Jean. And then one night you were both working late and suddenly you let down your hair and took off your glasses and she said, "Why, Mr. Nash, you're beautiful." All right, you want to know when I think the exact date your crummy little affair started? I'll tell you. It was June nineteenth. It was your birthday and you just turned fifty years old. Five-oh, count 'em, folks, and you were feeling good and sorry for yourself. Right? And the only reason you picked on Miss McCormack was because she was probably the first one you saw that morning. . . . If she was sick that day, this affair very well could have been with your elevator operator. Well, I would suggest committing suicide but I'm afraid you might think I meant me . . . I have one other suggestion. Forget it. I understand it, Sam. It's not your fault. But maybe I can live with it until it's over. What else can I do, Sam? I'm attached to you. So go out, have a good time tonight and when you come home, bring me the *Daily News*, I'm getting sick of the *Post*. I suspected it. You were working three nights a week and we weren't getting any richer. What's the matter, Sam, am I robbing you of all those delicious guilt feelings? Will you feel better if I go to pieces and try to lash back at you? All right, Sam, if it'll make you happier . . . I think you stink. You're a vain, self-pitying, deceiving, ten-pound box of rancid No-Cal cottage cheese. How'm I doing? You like this, don't you? It makes everything nice and simple for you. Now you can leave here the martyred, misunderstood husband. Well, I won't give you the satisfaction. I take it back, Sam. You're a pussycat. I'll have milk and cookies for you when you get home You're adorable. Eat your heart out. I'm sorry, I'm a forgiving woman. I can't help myself. There'll always be room for you in my garage. I forgive you. And she's a nice girl. I'll send her a nice gift. Well, you like things easy, don't you? You don't even have an affair the hard way. You could have at least taken the trouble to look outside your office for a girl . . . *(Picks up imaginary phone.)* "Miss McCormack, would you please come inside and take an affair!"... Honestly, Sam. I'm disappointed in you. It's so damned unoriginal. *Everyone* cheats with their secretary. I expected more from *my* husband! Go on, Sam, go have your affair. You're fifty-one years old. In an hour it may be too late...

Sam! Sam... do I still have my two choices? Because if I do... I choose "Get rid of Miss McCormack." I pick "Stay here and work it out with me, Sam." Because the other way I think I'm going to lose.... Please. We'll do what you said before. We'll lie. We'll tell each other everything is all right.... There is nothing wrong in the office tonight, there is no Miss McCormack and I'm twenty-seven goddamned years old.... What do you say, Sam?

You are fighting to save your life. Sam *is* your life! Your humor has kept you going in tight spots throughout your life. But this is the tightest spot of all. Be aware that you are a funny person and don't abandon the humor just because you feel yourself losing everything. It is precisely at a time like this when you need your humor. Then suddenly, get rid of the opposites and play exactly what is on the page with the last paragraph. Totally expose your vulnerability, fear, anxiety, pain, and love for him. The more you communicate to the other character, the more you give to the auditors.

THE WEST SIDE WALTZ
by Ernest Thompson

pp. 50–52 (SAMUEL FRENCH, INC.)

Robin: Did I ask you to pimp for me?

Margaret Mary: I beg your pardon?

Robin: *(A careful warning.)* You better stop trying to manipulate me.

Margaret Mary: Hmm?

Robin: Margaret Mary, the manipulator, that's you.

Margaret Mary: What are you saying?

Robin: I'm saying you should behave yourself. Let people alone. I don't go out and arrange things for you. I don't go meeting men on buses and set them up with you. I've had enough men to last me, believe me. I went on a great binge when Peter Pan flew away, and what did it prove? Every man *stunk*. Who needs 'em? Maybe someday when I'm feeling charitable I'll go out and get one, and it ain't going to be a librarian. *(She glares at* MARGARET MARY.*)* I'm mad at you, Margaret Mary.

Margaret Mary: You seem mad.

Robin: I'm just trying to *live* my *life*, but, oh, no, that would be asking too much. There's always a mother popping up to make sure I don't get too good at it. I left one in Brooklyn, and I divorced another one. I don't *need* any more mothers. *Mothers* are *mothers! (She stands fuming at* MARGARET MARY, *who considers what she's said.)*

Margaret Mary: You should listen to yourself sometime. You're starting to sound like Mr. Goo. *(The doorbell rings.* ROBIN *stalks to the door, throws it open to reveal* SERGE.*)*

Robin: Not now, Serge! *(She slams the door.)*

Serge: *(Offstage.)* I understand.

Robin: *(Marching back to* MARGARET MARY.*)* Look, I don't have to stay here, you know. I can *quit*.

Margaret Mary: *(Taken aback.)* I know that, of course.

Robin: So what if I like to read newspapers and clip things out and put off my acting career for a little while and not waste time crapping around with my dorko friends? So what? So what?

Margaret Mary: *(Reasonably.)* So. It doesn't seem very realistic to me, that's all.

Robin: Oh, is that right?

Margaret Mary: It's just that I find you a very unusual girl and I would love to see you challenge yourself a little bit. Realize some of your potential. And not . . . sort of avoid reality.

Robin: You don't think I'm realistic, huh?

Margaret Mary: Um. Well, no.

Robin: *(Stung, she counterattacks.)* Do you think *you're* realistic?

Margaret Mary: What?

Robin: Holing up in this mausoleum apartment, never talking to anybody you don't feel like talking to . . . *(Shouting.)* That ain't realistic, it's bulltinky! *You* should be like *me*. At least I'm honest. At least I *honestly* know I'm screwing up.

Margaret Mary: What the hell are you talking about, Robin?

Robin: You know what you are? You're a user! You can't push me around like you do Cara. That makes you mad, doesn't it?

Margaret Mary: You're behaving like a real mutt, aren't you?

Robin: Well, shit. Excuse me. You're selfish, Margaret Mary. You're too selfish to reach out very far to anybody. You'd rather pay for it. Well, groovy for you. You can buy me for fifty dollars a week, and I can be bought, because I don't know what I'm doing maybe, but you don't own me, see, you only rent me, and you're not allowed to try to change me, that's not in the contract. So there! What do you think of that? I'll quit!

Margaret Mary: So what do you think of this? I'll fire you.

Robin: Fine. Good. As you wish. (MARGARET MARY *turns, trips on her walker, and falls in an awful heap.* ROBIN *rushes to help her, but* MARGARET MARY *pushes her away.* ROBIN *storms through the hall door, as* MARGARET MARY *pulls herself up. After a moment, the entrance door opens and* CARA *enters, looking very downcast.)*

Cara: Hello. (MARGARET MARY *doesn't answer.* ROBIN *marches in, wearing a coat.* MARGARET MARY *watches her.)* Hello. *(She smiles at* ROBIN, *who walks right past her, scowling at*

MARGARET MARY.) Hello. (ROBIN *doesn't answer. She heads for the entrance door.*)

Margaret Mary: Where are you going?

Robin: I'm going *out*. Is that all right? Should I turn in my key?

The following is the monologue created from the previous scene.

ROBIN (to MARGARET MARY), age 20s to 30s.
pp. 50–52 (SAMUEL FRENCH, INC.)

Did I ask you to pimp for me? You better stop trying to manipulate me. Margaret Mary, the manipulator, that's you. I'm saying you should behave yourself. Let people alone. I don't go out and arrange things for you. I don't go meeting men on buses and set them up with you. I've had enough men to last me, believe me. I went on a great binge when Peter Pan flew away, and what did it prove? Every man *stunk*. Who needs 'em? Maybe someday when I'm feeling charitable I'll go out and get one, and it ain't going to be a librarian. I'm mad at you, Margaret Mary. I'm just trying to *live* my *life*, but, oh, no, that would be asking too much. There's always a mother popping up to make sure I don't get too good at it. I left one in Brooklyn, and I divorced another one. I don't *need* any more mothers. *Mothers* are *mothers*!

Look, I don't have to stay here, you know. I can *quit*. So what if I like to read newspapers and clip things out and put off my acting career for a little while and not waste time crapping around with my dorko friends? So what? So what? You don't think I'm realistic, huh? Do you think *you're* realistic? Holing up in this mausoleum apartment, never talking to anybody you don't feel like talking to . . . (*Shouting.*) That ain't realistic, it's bulltinky! *You* should be like *me*. At least I'm honest. At least I *honestly* know I'm screwing up. You know what you are? You're a user! You can't push me around like you do Cara. That makes you mad, doesn't it? Well, shit. Excuse me. You're selfish, Margaret Mary. You're too selfish to reach out very far to anybody. You'd rather pay for it. Well, groovy for you. You can buy me for fifty dollars a week, and I can be bought, because I don't know what I'm doing maybe, but you don't own me, see, you only rent me, and you're not allowed to try to change me, that's not in the contract. So there! What do you think of that? I'll quit!

I'm going *out*. Is that all right? Should I turn in my key?

I've created this monologue not only because it is a good one but to show you the alternative to the "obvious" one recommended up to now. Naturally, the other one is a memory piece made up of a couple of blocks of dialogue. The "other" one is on pages 24 and 25 of the Samuel French edition of the play. Read Robin's two speeches and compare them to this piece.

Robin, you are complaining to Margaret Mary about her mothering you too much. You've had it with mothers, you say. You want to make your own choices, right or wrong. You want to live your own life your way without anyone meddling. Okay. So far so good. But you *also love* the fact that she is meddling! I know, this is not on the pages. Put it in. Because a part of this is true. Mothers may be mothers, as you say. But the love that goes with their interfering is nice. It's a pain in the butt. But it feels nice to be loved. You need love. You are feeling a certain kind of alienation. You've had a bad marriage. Your career has not taken off. Here you are, a paid companion to Margaret Mary, a very motherly person. You ran from your own mother because she was overbearing. It's the overbearing that you don't want, but it's the love that you *do* want. You are asking her to butt out. But you don't want her to stop loving you. Because you should realize that what she is doing, right or wrong, is being done with love. And you love her. And you do not want to move out and leave her. And you do not want her to tell you to leave. You don't want to deal with another good-bye. You are also trying to help her. She has cut herself off from the entire outside world. *She* needs as much or more guidance than even you do. And you can help her to open up her life more so she won't have time to deal with what's wrong with your life but just love you, appreciate you, and allow you to grow and change as you will.

BAD HABITS
by Terrence McNally

pp. 33–39 (Samuel French, Inc.)

April: Hi, April James. Nice to see you.

Dr. Pepper: April James?

April: It's my professional name.

Roy: You see that, honey? Even with these things on he recognized us.

Dr. Pepper: And what do *you* do, Mrs. Pitt?

April: What do you mean, "What do I do?" I'm an actress. Thanks a lot, buddy.

Roy: She's an actress.

April: I don't even know you but I really needed that little ego boost.

Roy: Honey, of course he recognized me. My movie was on the Late Show last night. "Cold Fingers." He probably caught it.

April: God knows you did.

Roy: It's the power of the medium! You know that kind of exposure.

April: "Cold Fingers" should have *opened* on the Late Show.

Roy: Now don't start with me.

April: Boy, I really needed that little zap.

Roy: He's a dummy.

April: You must have seen me in something. How about "Journey Through Hell" for Christ's sake! You didn't see me in "Journey Through Hell"?

Dr. Pepper: Were you in that?

Roy: That was my beautiful April all right!

April: You bet your sweet ass it was!

Dr. Pepper: That was a wonderful movie, Mrs. Pitt.

April: You see that? Another zap?

Roy: April wasn't in the movie. She created the role off-Broadway . . . didn't get the film version!

April: Boy, this is really my day!

Roy: She was brilliant in that part.

April: I know. Too bad the play didn't support me.

Dr. Pepper: I enjoyed the film, too.

April: I bet you did.

Roy: Hey. Try to cool it with her, will you?

April: Try *Random Thoughts and Vaguer Notions*, why don't you?

Roy: That one was on Broadway. April was one of the stars.

Dr. Pepper: I wasn't able to catch it.

April: It ran nearly eighty performances. You didn't exactly have to be a jackrabbit.

Roy: April!

April: Before you zap me again, I didn't do the movie of that one, either.

Roy: You never read notices like she got for that one. Show 'em to him, honey.

April: They're in the car. I break my balls trying to make that piece of garbage work and they sign some WASP starlet for the movie version thinking she's going to appeal to that goddamn Middle American drive-in audience.

Roy: I don't really think you can call Googie Gomez a WASP starlet.

April: White bread! That's all she is, white bread!

Roy: (*Calling down the aisle.*) Hey, that court's taken, Buddy. We got it reserved.

April: You heard him!

Dr. Pepper: I think that's the ground keeper.

Roy: That's okay, Mac! Sorry! Hang in there!

April: Hi! April James! Nice to see you!

Roy: Hi! Roy Pitt! Nice to see you! Ssh! Sssh!

April: What is it?

Roy: I thought I heard our phone.

April: Way out here? What are you? The big ear?

Roy: You sure you told the service where I'd be?

April: Of course I did. I might be getting a call, too, you know.

Roy: I'm expecting an important call from the coast. I'm not usually this tense.

April: Hah!

Roy: This could be the big one, April.

April: Almost anything would be bigger than "Cold Fingers."
(OTTO *has appeared.*)

Roy: *(Starting to do push-ups.)* You got one hell of a thirsty star
out here, waiter.

April: Two thirsty stars.

Otto: I am not a waiter. My name is Otto.

Roy: Hi, Otto. Roy Pitt, nice to see you.

April: Hi, Otto. April James, nice to see you.

Roy: *(Now he is doing sit-ups.)* What are you having, honey?

April: A screwdriver.

Roy: I'll have some Dom Perignon. The champagne.

April: Roy!

Roy: It's included.

April: Eighty-six the screwdriver. I'll have the same.

Otto: The Fraulein would like a nice rubdown, maybe?

April: From you?

Roy: Just bring the Dom Perignon, will you?

Dr. Pepper: Oh, and Otto! *(He holds up his glass.)*

Otto: Jawohl. *(He goes.)*

April: *(Sits, and looks at* DR. PEPPER'S *wheelchair for the first
time.)* I want to apologize for earlier when we yelled at you
for the ball. We didn't realize you were . . . like that.

Dr. Pepper: Half the time I don't realize it myself.

April: We do lots of benefits, you know.

Roy: April's been asked to do the Mental Health and Highway
Safety Telethons two years straight.

April: Easter Seals wanted me last month but they weren't
paying expenses.

Roy: Nobody's blaming you, honey.

April: I mean there's charity and then there's charity. I mean
you gotta draw the line somewhere, right? What am I?
Chopped liver?

Roy: Easter Seals wouldn't even send a limousine for her! Our
agent told them they could take their telethon and shove it.
(ROY is opening up a sun reflector.)

April: What are you doing?

Roy: You don't mind if we don't play tennis for a while? I want
to get some of the benefits.

April: There's not enough sun for a tan.

Roy: That's what you think. It's a day like this you can really
bake yourself. Just because the sky's grey doesn't mean

those rays aren't coming through. Make love to me, soleil, make love to me.

April: *(She is sitting near* DR. PEPPER. ROY *is sprawled out with his reflector under his chin. He just loves lying in the sun like this.)* What are you in for?

Dr. Pepper: The usual.

April: A bad marriage, huh? That's too bad. You're probably wondering what we're doing here. I know on the surface it must look like we got a model marriage. But believe me, we got our little problems, too. Don't look so surprised. Roy's got an ego on him you could drive a Mack truck with. Show biz marriages ain't nothing to write home about. Half our friends are divorced and the other half are miserable. Naturally, they don't think we're going to make it. Think. They *hope*. But we're going to show them. Right, honey?

Roy: Right.

April: Have you had a session with Dr. Pepper yet?

Dr. Pepper: Many. *(He picks up the book he took from* DOLLY *and opens it.)*

April: Is he all he's cracked up to be?

Dr. Pepper: I think so, but of course I'm prejudiced. *(He smiles at* APRIL *and begins to read.)*

April: He's gonna have his hands full with that one.

Dr. Pepper: *(Looking up.)* I'm sorry . . . ?

April: Skip it. (DR. PEPPER *returns to his book.* APRIL *silently mouths an obscenity at him and turns her attention to* ROY.)

Roy: Honey! You're blocking my sun.

April: You're just gonna lie there like that?

Roy: Unh-hunh.

April: So where's my reflector?

Roy: I told you to pack it if you wanted it.

April: I want it.

Roy: You said you didn't want to get any darker.

April: I'm starting to fade.

Roy: No, you're not.

April: It's practically all gone. Look at you. You're twice as dark!

Roy: It's not a contest, honey.

April: I mean what's the point of getting a tan if you don't maintain it? Roy!

Roy: *(For* DR. PEPPER's *benefit, but without looking up from the reflector.)* Do you believe this? I was with my agents all

day and I'm supposed to be worried about a goddamn
reflector!

April: Just give me a couple of minutes with it.

Roy: It's the best sun time now.

April: You know I've got that audition Wednesday.

Roy: No. N. O. (APRIL *gives up, gets the tin of cocoa butter off
the cart and begins applying it.*) April's up for another new
musical. They were interested in us both, actually, but I've
got these film commitments.

April: Tentative film commitments.

Roy: You're getting hostile, honey.

April: What's hostile is you not packing my reflector.

Roy: *I* was busy with my agents. *You* are getting hostile.

April: I've got a career, too, you know.

Roy: (*Sitting up, he drops the reflector and motions for quiet.*)
Ssshh!

April: (*Grabbing the reflector.*) Hello? Yes, we're checking on
the availability of Roy Pitt for an Alpo commercial!

Roy: Shut up, April! (*He listens, disappointed.*) Shit. (*Then he
sees* APRIL.) Hold it. Stop it! (*He grabs the reflector and lies
back.*)

April: Roy!

Roy: After that? You've gotta be kidding! I wouldn't give you
this reflector if you whistled "Swanee River" out of your ass.

April: I can, too.

Roy: I know. I've heard you.

April: Just lie there and turn into leather.

Roy: I will.

April: There are other things in the world more important than
your sun tan, you know.

Roy: Like yours?

April: For openers.

Roy: Like your career?

April: Yes, as a matter of fact.

Roy: Will you stop competing with me, April? That's one of the
reasons we came here. I can't help it if I'm hotter than you
right now.

April: That could change, Roy. Remember "A Star Is Born."

Roy: Well, until it does, love me for what I am: Roy Pitt, the
man. But don't resent me for my career.

April: I know, Roy.

Roy: I love you for what you are: April James, the best little actress in New York City.

April: What do you mean, "best little actress"?

Roy: I'm trying to make a point, honey!

April: As opposed to what? A dwarf?

Roy: If we're going to have a good marriage and, April, I want that more than anything...!

April: More than you wanted the lead in "Lenny"?

Roy: I didn't want "Lenny."

April: He would've crawled through broken glass for that part!

Roy: I didn't want "Lenny." Now goddammit, shut up!

April: I can't talk to you when you get like that.

Roy: Get like what? You haven't laid off me since we got in the car.

April: You know I'm upset.

Roy: We've all been fired from shows.

April: Before they went into rehearsal? I'm thinking of slitting the *two* wrists this time, Roy!

Roy: Actually, Heather MacNamara isn't a bad choice for that part.

April: She's the pits!

Roy: We're the Pitts! *(Breaking himself up, then ...)* We liked her in "The Seagull."

April: You liked her in "The Seagull." I'd like her in her coffin.

Roy: Obviously they're going ethnic with it.

April: She isn't even ethnic. She's white bread. I'm ethnic. I want a hit, Roy. I need a hit. I'm going crazy for a hit. I mean, when's it my turn?

Roy: Honey, you're making a shadow.

April: I'm sorry.

Roy: That's okay. Just stick with me, kid. We're headed straight for the top.

April: Roy?

Roy: What, angel?

April: Your toupee is slipping. (ROY *clutches at his hairpiece.*) Roy wears a piece.

Roy: It's no secret. I've never pretended. It's not like your nose job!

April: Don't speak to me. Just lie there and turn into Naugahyde like your mother!

Roy: Honey! I almost forgot. Your agent called! They're interviewing hostesses for Steak & Brew.

April: Give him skin cancer, God, give him skin cancer, please!

Dr. Pepper: Excuse me, I know it's none of my business, but how long have you two been married?

April: Three months.

Roy: And you were right the first time, it's none of your business.

April: But we lived together a long time before we did.

Roy: Not long enough.

April: Eight *centuries* it felt like!

Roy: Do you have to cry on the world's shoulder, April?

April: I want us to work, Roy! I love you.

Roy: I know. I love you, too, April.

April: You're the best.

Roy: *We're* the best.

April: You really think this Pepper fellow can help us?

The following is the monologue created from the previous scene.

APRIL (to ROY and DR. PEPPER), age 20s to 30s.
pp. 33–39 (SAMUEL FRENCH, INC.)

Hi, April James. Nice to see you. It's my professional name. What do you mean, "What do I do?" I'm an actress. Thanks a lot, buddy. I don't even know you but I really needed that little ego boost. Boy, I really needed that little zap. You must have seen me in something. How about *Journey through Hell* for Christ's sake! You didn't see me in *Journey through Hell*? You see that? Another zap? I was brilliant in that part. Too bad the play didn't support me. Try *Random Thoughts and Vaguer Notions*, why don't you? That one was on Broadway. I was one of the stars. It ran nearly eighty performances. You didn't exactly have to be a jackrabbit to catch it. Before you zap me again, I didn't do the movie of that one, either. I break my balls trying to make that piece of garbage work and they sign some WASP starlet for the movie version thinking she's going to appeal to that goddamn Middle American drive-in audience. White bread! That's all she is, white bread!

I want to apologize for earlier when we yelled at you for the ball. We didn't realize you were . . . like that. *(He is*

in a wheelchair.) We do lots of benefits, you know. Easter
Seals wanted me last month but they weren't paying
expenses. I mean there's charity and then there's charity. I
mean you gotta draw the line somewhere, right? What am
I? Chopped liver? Easter Seals wouldn't even send a
limousine for me! Our agent told them they could take
their telethon and shove it. . . . What are you in for? You're
probably wondering what we're doing here. I know on the
surface it must look like we got a model marriage. But
believe me, we got our little problems, too. Don't look so
surprised. Roy's got an ego on him you could drive a Mack
truck with. Show biz marriages ain't nothing to write home
about. Half our friends are divorced and the other half are
miserable. Naturally, they don't think we're going to make
it. Think. They *hope*. But we're going to show them. *(To*
ROY.) Right, honey? You're just gonna lie there like that?
So where's my reflector? I'm starting to fade. It's practically all gone. Look at you. You're twice as dark! I mean
what's the point of getting a tan if you don't maintain it?
Roy! You know I've got that audition Wednesday. *You've*
got *tentative* film commitments. I'm not getting hostile.
What's hostile is you not packing my reflector. I've got a
career, too, you know. Just lie there and turn into leather.
There are other things in the world more important than
your suntan, you know. Like my career! You may be hotter
than me right now but that could change, Roy. Remember
A Star Is Born. Roy? Your toupee is slipping. Roy wears a
piece. Don't speak to me. Just lie there and turn into
Naugahyde like your mother! Give him skin cancer, God,
give him skin cancer, please! *(To* DR. PEPPER.) You really
think this Pepper fellow can help us?

Do not be fooled by all the rage and bitterness displayed by
April toward Roy. She loves him and needs him. You (April) are
going through a very bad time. Your career is at a low ebb and
Roy seems to be doing better than you are. You two are surely
extremely competitive. You *both* have egos a Mack truck could
drive through. Not just Roy. You are fighting for him to love you
so much that he can pamper you like the baby you are. You as
April are not aware that you are acting like a very spoiled little
girl. As actress you must understand this. Roy can prove his love
to you by sacrificing everything for you. I'm sure even if he

shared with you that would not be enough. You would always be expecting more. As a matter of fact, no matter what he does for you it will not be enough. Which is good for you as actress. Keep fighting for his love like a wild animal.

This is a comedy. But there is nothing funny about not being cast in a play or film. There is nothing funny about not doing a benefit unless you are paid for it and given the use of a limo. There is nothing funny about two people fighting and hurting each other. The humor is situational and behavioral. Their marriage is an absurd one. Their relationship could set back the concept of marriage by one hundred years. But, they *enjoy* what they are doing to each other. It is their very harsh behavior toward one another that allows them to go on. And indeed, here they are in an institution where they can perhaps receive help to continue their relationship. Which means there is love there. Dr. Pepper is their audience. They function very well when there is someone to play to. Which is what they are doing. The whole world is their audience. They are playacting their life before anyone who happens to be there. I bet when they're alone, they become more subdued and congenial. They are not onstage as much as they want to be so they create their stage wherever they go and they perform their hearts out and love it!

SCENES

Drama

THE CHILDREN'S HOUR
by Lillian Hellman

pp. 18–21 (DRAMATISTS PLAY SERVICE, INC.)

Mrs. Mortar: *I* was asked to leave the room. (MARTHA *pays no attention.*) It seems that I'm not wanted in the room during the examination. It was a deliberate snub.

Martha: *(Over her shoulder.)* I don't think so.

Mrs. Mortar: *(Crosses to below R. end of sofa.)* I say it was a deliberate snub. Isn't it natural that the child should have me with her? Isn't it natural that an older woman should be present at a physical examination? *(No answer.)* Very well, if you are so thick-skinned that you don't resent these things— *(Sits R. end of sofa.)*

Martha: What are you talking about? Why in the name of heaven should *you* be with her?

Mrs. Mortar: I have been to good doctors in my better days. I say it's customary to have an older woman present.

Martha: *(Laughs.)* Tell that to Joe. Maybe he'll give you a job as duenna for his office.

Mrs. Mortar: *(Reminiscently.)* It was I who saved Delia Lampert's life the time she had that heart attack in Buffalo, right on the stage without losing a line. Poor Delia! She married Robert Laffonne in London after he found there was no soap with me. Not nine months later he left her and ran away with Eve Cloun, who had made a great hit playing the Infant Phenomenon when she was forty-seven, the British don't care about age. Delia's heart attack came afterwards——

Martha: *(Sharply.)* Yes. If you've seen one heart attack, you've seen them all.

Mrs. Mortar: So you don't resent your aunt being snubbed and humiliated?

Martha: Oh, Aunt Lily!

Mrs. Mortar: Karen is rude to me, and you know it.

Martha: *(Turns to* MRS. MORTAR.*)* I know that she is very kind to you, and—what's even harder—very patient.

Mrs. Mortar: Patient with me? I have worked my fingers to the bone to help you both——

Martha: *(Turns to papers.)* Don't tell yourself that too often, Aunt Lily; you'll come to believe it.

Mrs. Mortar: I know it's true. Where could you have gotten a woman of my reputation to give these children voice lessons, elocution lessons? Patient with me? Here I've donated my services——

Martha: You are being paid.

Mrs. Mortar: That small thing? I used to earn twice that for one performance.

Martha: No wonder the theater's in trouble. It was very extravagant of them to pay you so much. *(Suddenly tired of the whole thing.)* You've never been happy here, Aunt Lily.

Mrs. Mortar: Satisfied enough, I guess, for a poor relation.

Martha: You don't like the school or the farm or——

Mrs. Mortar: I told you at the beginning you shouldn't have bought a place like this. Burying yourself on a farm! Meeting no men! You'll regret it. (MARTHA *rises, taking papers with her. Crosses above sofa to L. of* MRS. MORTAR.*)*

Martha: We like it here. *(After a moment, leans over sofa to* MRS. MORTAR.*)* Aunt Lily, you've talked about London for a long time. Would you like to go over?

Mrs. Mortar: *(With a sigh.)* It's been twenty years. I shall never live to see it again.

Martha: You can go any time you like. We can spare the money now, and it will do you a lot of good. You pick out the boat and I'll get the passage. *(She has been talking rapidly, anxious to end the whole thing. Crosses L. to above desk.)* Now that's all fixed. You'll have a grand time seeing all your old friends, and if you live sensibly I ought to be able to let you have enough to get along on. *(Puts papers in desk drawer.)*

Mrs. Mortar: *(Slowly.)* So you want me to leave?

Martha: *(Gently.)* Aunt Lily, you've wanted to go ever since I can remember.

Mrs. Mortar: You're trying to get rid of me.

Martha: That's it. We don't want you around when we dig up the buried treasure.

Mrs. Mortar: So? You're turning me out? At my age! Nice, grateful girl you are!

Martha: *(Angrily, crosses to below L. end of sofa.)* How can anybody deal with you? You're going where you want to go, and we'll be better off alone. That suits everybody. You complain about the farm, you complain about the school, you complain about Karen, and now you have what you want and you're still looking for something to complain about.

Mrs. Mortar: *(Rises. With dignity.)* Please do not raise your voice.

Martha: Be glad I don't do worse.

Mrs. Mortar: I'm not going to England. I refuse to let you ship me off any place you like. I shall go back to the stage. I'll write to my agents tomorrow, and just as soon as they have something for me I'll be out of here. *(Moves away R.)*

Martha: The truth is I'd like you to leave soon. We can't live together, and it doesn't make any difference whose fault it is.

Mrs. Mortar: *(Turns to* MARTHA.*)* You wish me to go tonight?

Martha: Oh, stop it, Aunt Lily. *(Moves up C.)* Go as soon as you've found a place you like. I'll put the money in the bank for you tomorrow.

Mrs. Mortar: You think I'd take your money? I'd rather scrub floors first.

Martha: You'll change your mind after the first floor. *(Crosses to below desk.)* I've done the best I could by you for years, Aunt Lily. Your coming here wasn't ever thought of as a permanent arrangement. You knew that. You'll be happier——

Mrs. Mortar: *(Laughs knowingly. Moves up to R. of sofa.)* I should have known by this time that the wise thing is to stay out of your way when *he's* in the house.

Martha: What are you talking about now?

Mrs. Mortar: *(Crosses D. R.).* Never mind. I should have known better. You always take your spite out on me.

Martha: Spite? *(Crosses up R. of desk to above desk. Impatiently.)* Oh, don't let's have any more of this today. I'm tired. I've been working since six o'clock this morning.

Mrs. Mortar: Any day that he's in the house is a bad day.

Martha: *(Crosses to C.)* When *who* is in the house?

Mrs. Mortar: *(Crosses up to R. of sofa.)* Don't think you're fooling me, young lady. I wasn't born yesterday. And I didn't meet you last month.

Martha: *(Crosses R. to above C. of sofa.)* I don't know what you're talking about. But I do know that the amount of disconnected nonsense in your head tires me, and always has. Now go take your nap.

Mrs. Mortar: *(Crosses to* MARTHA.*)* I know what I know. Every time that man comes into this house, you're in a bad humor. *(Crosses L. upstage of* MARTHA *to above chair R. of desk.)* It seems like you just can't stand the idea of them being together. God knows what you'll do when they get married. You're jealous, that's what it is.

Martha: *(Her voice is tense and previous attitude of good-natured irritation is gone, turns to* MRS. MORTAR.*)* I'm very fond of Joe, and you know it.

Mrs. Mortar: *(Crossing to C.)* I don't know who you're fond of. I've never understood you. *(*MARTHA *moves away upstage.)* You'd better get a beau of your own. That's what you need. Every woman, no matter what she says, is jealous when another woman gets a husband. You'd just better set your cap for what comes along now——

Martha: *(Comes back to above L. end of sofa. Very sharply.)* Aunt Lily, please stop that talk. I had too much of it for too many years. I can't take any more.

Mrs. Mortar: *(Crosses to* MARTHA.*)* You've always had a jealous and possessive nature. Even as a child. *(*MARTHA *turns away.)* If you had a friend, you always got mad if she liked anybody else. That's what's happening now. And it's unnatural. Just as unnatural as it can be. I say you need a man of your own, and——

The following is the monologue created from the previous scene.

MRS. MORTAR (to MARTHA), age 45 to 65.
pp. 18–21 (DRAMATISTS PLAY SERVICE, INC.)

I was asked to leave the room. It seems that I'm not wanted in the room during the examination. It was a deliberate snub. Isn't it natural that the child should have me with her? Isn't it natural that an older woman should be present at a physical examination? If you are so thin-skinned that you don't resent these things... I have been to good doctors in my better days. I say it's customary to have an older woman present. *(Reminiscently.)* It was I who saved Delia Lampert's life the time she had the heart attack in Buffalo, right on the stage without losing a line. Poor Delia! She married Robert Laffonne in London after he found there was no soap with me. Not nine months later he left her and ran away with Eve Cloun, who had made a great hit playing the Infant Phenomenon when she was forty-seven. The British don't care about age. Delia's heart attack came afterwards... so anyway, you don't resent your aunt being snubbed and humiliated? Karen is rude to me and you know it. I have worked my fingers to the bone to help you both. Where could you have gotten a woman of my reputation to give these children voice lessons, elocution lessons? I've donated my services. I used to earn twice that for one performance. I suppose I should be satisfied, I guess, for a poor relation. I told you at the beginning you shouldn't have bought a place like this. Burying yourself on a farm! Meeting no men! You'll regret it. So now you want me to leave! You're trying to get rid of me. You're turning me out? At my age! Nice, grateful girl you are! I'm not going to England. I refuse to let you ship me off any place you like. I shall go back to the stage. I'll write to my agents tomorrow, and just as soon as they have something for me I'll be out of here. Unless you wish me to go tonight! I won't take your money! I'd rather scrub floors first. I should have known by this time that the wise thing is to stay out of your way when *he's* in the house. I should have known better. You always take your spite out on me. Any day that he's in the house is a bad day. Don't think you're fooling me, young lady. I wasn't born yesterday. And I didn't meet you last month. I know what I know. Every time that man comes into this house, you're in a bad humor. It seems like you just can't stand the idea of them being together. God knows what you'll do when they get married. You're jealous, that's what it is. I don't know who you're fond of. I've never understood you. You'd better get a beau of your own. That's what you need. Every woman, no matter what she says, is jealous when another woman gets a husband. You'd just better set your cap for what comes along now. You've always had a jealous and possessive nature. Even as a child. If you had a friend, you always got mad if she liked anybody else. That's what's happening now. And it's unnat-

ural. Just as unnatural as it can be. I say you need a man of
your own.

There appears to be no love in the words. Indeed you are
what appears to be an embittered, complaining, accusative woman. So be it. This is the result of frustrations and disappointments
in your life. The playwright gives us a bit of your background.
Actually, Ms. Hellman has supplied you with a great deal of
history and background leading up to today's confrontation. A
former actress. Time spent in Europe. Perhaps friends and lovers
abroad. But you wound up teaching in your niece's school in a
small town. You receive very little pay for your efforts. Did you
ever marry? Did you really say "no soap" to Robert Laffonne? Or
did he actually dump you? Did you get along well with people?
You, as Mrs. Mortar, would, of course, deny any existence of
antagonistic, uncongenial, or catty behavior—now or in the past.
But as actress, you are well aware that your character is not
behaving well. Get right into character. Do not stand on the
outside and judge her. Start making choices immediately and fill
in what the playwright has not given to you regarding your past.
Perhaps you lost the man you wanted more than once. Perhaps
you were rejected for many parts in plays. Perhaps all your
women friends were having wonderful relationships with men
and getting married and you were always left behind. Time went
by and now here you are. So you are frightened that you will be
all alone again. Your niece, who is the only person you've got in
your life, doesn't seem to want you to continue teaching and
living in the school. You strike out at her. She is going to be left
behind when her best friend and coteacher marries Joe. You
identify with her. Out of your hurt and feelings of rejection,
you strike out at what you know will hurt her. It is yourself that
you are talking about. You are fighting for your life and Martha's
love so that you can be wanted and needed and loved and safe.

THE CHILDREN'S HOUR
by Lillian Hellman

pp. 45–49 (Dramatists Play Service, Inc.)

Karen: I tried to reach you. I tried and tried. Hasn't she told you?

Cardin: Nobody's told me anything. I haven't heard anything but wild talk. What is it, Karen? *(She starts to speak, then dumbly shakes head.)* What's happened, Martha?

Martha: *(Violently.)* An insane asylum has been let loose. How do we know what's happened?

Cardin: What was it?

Karen: We didn't know what it was. Nobody would talk to us, nobody would tell us anything.

Cardin: *(With anger.)* Stop it. Tell me what's happened.

Martha: *(Moves to above L. end of love-seat.)* See if you can make any sense out of it. At dinner-time Mrs. Munn's chauffeur arrived and said that Evelyn must be sent home right away. At half-past seven Mrs. Burton came to tell us that she wanted Helen's things packed immediately and that she'd wait outside because she didn't want to enter a place like ours. Five minutes later the Wellses' butler came for Rosalie.

Cardin: Why? Why?

Martha: It was a madhouse. People rushing in and out, the children being pushed into cars, Karen and I begging people to tell us, nobody answering us——

Karen: *(Quiet now, takes his hand.)* Mrs. Rogers finally told us.

Cardin: What?

Karen: That—that Martha and I have been—have been lovers. Mrs. Tilford told them.

Cardin: *(For a moment stands staring at her incredulously. Then finally turns to* MRS. TILFORD, *stares at her a moment.)* Did you tell them that?

Mrs. Tilford: Yes.

Cardin: Are you sick? Are you a sick woman?

Mrs. Tilford: You know I'm not sick.

Cardin: (*Snapping the words out.*) Then what did you do it for?

Mrs. Tilford: (*Slowly.*) Because it's true.

Karen: (*Incredulously. Crosses to below R. love-seat.*) You think it's true, then?

Martha: You crazy, crazy, crazy old woman!

Karen: You mean you did say it? You knew what you were saying? You——

Mrs. Tilford: (*Crosses to* KAREN.) Yes. I knew what I was saying. I don't think you should have come here.

Martha: (*Crossing L. to above L. love-seat.*) You damned, vicious——

Mrs. Tilford: (*Crosses to* MARTHA. *Quietly.*) I shall not call you names, and I will not allow you to call me names. You should not have come here. I don't trust myself to talk about it with you now or ever.

Karen: What's she talking about, Joe? What's she mean? What is she trying to do to us? What did she do it for? (CARDIN *goes to* KAREN *and puts his arms around her.*)

Martha: (*Softly, as though to herself.*) We're being pushed around by a crazy woman. (*Shakes herself slightly.*) That's an awful thing. And we're standing here——We're standing here taking it. Didn't you know we'd come here? (*Suddenly, with violence.*) Were we supposed to lie down and smile while you took up a gun and looked around for people to kill?

Mrs. Tilford: This can't do any of us any good, Miss Dobie.

Martha: "This can't do any of us any good." Listen, listen! You're not playing with paper dolls. We're human beings, see? We're people. It's our lives you're playing with. *Our* lives. That's serious business for us. Can you understand that?

Mrs. Tilford: (*For the first time she speaks angrily.*) I can understand that, and I understand a lot more. *You've* been playing with a lot of children's lives, and that's why I stopped you. (*More calmly.*) I know how serious this is for you, how serious it is for all of us.

Cardin: (*Bitterly.*) I don't think you do know. I don't think so. (CARDIN *crosses R. below* KAREN *to R. end of love-seat.*)

Mrs. Tilford: I wanted to avoid this meeting because it can't do any good. You came here to find out if I had made the charge. You've found out. Let's end it there. *I don't want you in this house. (Turns to* CARDIN.) I'm sorry this had to be done to you, Joseph.

Cardin: Don't talk to me like that, Amelia, *please.*

Mrs. Tilford: *(Comes D. C.)* Very well. There's nothing I mean to do, nothing I want to do. There's nothing anybody can do.

Cardin: *(Carefully.)* You have done a terrible thing.

Mrs. Tilford: I have done what I had to do. What they are may possibly be their own business. It becomes a great deal more than that when children are concerned in it. Children——

Karen: *(Wildly.)* It's not true! Not a word of it is true; can't you understand that? (CARDIN *sits on R. end of love-seat.)*

Mrs. Tilford: There won't be any punishment for either of you. But there mustn't be any punishment for me, either—and that's what this meeting is. *(Moves L., sits in L. end of L. love-seat.)* This—this thing is your own. Go away with it. I don't understand it and I don't want any part of it. Take it out of here.

Martha: *(Slowly.)* So you think we should go away?

Mrs. Tilford: I think that's best for you.

Martha: *(Moves upstage.)* There must be something we can do to you, and, whatever it is, we must find it.

Mrs. Tilford: That will be very unwise.

Cardin: Do you know what's wise? *(Violently.)* You are an irresponsible old woman, that's all.

Karen: *(Crosses to R. of L. love-seat.)* It makes me dirty and sick to stand here and defend myself—and against what? Against a lie. A great, awful lie.

Mrs. Tilford: I'm sorry that I can't believe that.

Karen: There isn't a single word of truth in anything you said. *(Waits, then.)* Damn you. (KAREN *crosses U. R. to sideboard.)*

Cardin: They've worked eight long years to save enough money to buy that farm, to start that school. They did without everything that young people ought to have. You wouldn't know about that. That school meant things to them: self-respect, and bread and butter, and honest work. Do you know what it is to try so hard for anything? Well, now it's gone. What the hell did you do it for?

Mrs. Tilford: *(Softly. Rises.)* It had to be done.

Cardin: *(Rises.)* Righteousness is a great thing.

Mrs. Tilford: *(Gently.)* I know how you must feel about me.

Cardin: You don't know anything about how I feel.

Mrs. Tilford: *(Crosses to C.)* I've loved you as much as I loved my own boys. I wouldn't have spared them; I couldn't spare you.

Cardin: *(Fiercely.)* I believe you. *(Moves away U. R.)*

Martha: What is there to do to you? What can we do to you? There must be something—something that makes you feel the way we do tonight. *(Comes down to L. of* MRS. TILFORD.*)* You don't want any part of this, you said. But you'll get a part. More than you bargained for. *(Suddenly.)* Are you willing to stand by everything you've said tonight? *(*KAREN *comes down to above armchair.)*

Mrs. Tilford: Yes.

Martha: All right. That's fine. But don't get the idea we'll let you whisper this lie: you made it and you'll come out with it. Shriek it to your town of Lancet. We'll *make* you shriek it—and we'll make you do it in a court room. Tomorrow, Mrs. Tilford, you will have a libel suit on your hands.

Mrs. Tilford: *(Turns to* MARTHA.*)* Miss Dobie, don't do that.

Karen: It's your turn to be frightened.

Mrs. Tilford: It is you I am thinking of. I am frightened for you. It was wrong of you to brazen it out here tonight; it would be criminally foolish of you to brazen it out in public. That can bring you nothing but pain. I am an old woman, Miss Dobie, and I have seen too many people act in pride and anger. In the end they punish themselves.

Martha: *(With great anger.)* We'll take our own way.

Cardin: *(Comes down to R. at R. love-seat.)* So you took a child's word for it?

Martha: *(Looks at him, shakes head.)* Yes. That's what she did.

Karen: That is really where you got it? I can't believe—it couldn't be. Why, she's a child.

Martha: She's not a child.

Karen: Oh, my God, it all fits so well now. That girl has hated us for a long time. We never knew why, we never could find out. There didn't seem to be any reason——

Martha: There wasn't any reason. She hates everybody and everything.

Karen: Your Mary's a strange girl. A dark girl. There's something very awful the matter with her.

Mrs. Tilford: *(Crosses to below R. love-seat.)* I was waiting for you to say that, Miss Wright.

Karen: *(Crosses D. R., goes to* MRS. TILFORD.*)* I'm telling you the truth. We should have told it to you long ago. *(Stops, crosses to* MARTHA.*)* It's no use.

Cardin: Where is she?

Mrs. Tilford: You cannot see her.

Cardin: Where is she?

Mrs. Tilford: I won't have that, Joseph.

Cardin: I'm going to talk to her.

Mrs. Tilford: *I won't have her go through with that again.* (*To* KAREN *and* MARTHA.*)* You came here demanding explanations. It was I who should have asked them from you. You attack me, you attack Mary. I've told you I didn't mean you any harm. I still don't. You claim that it isn't true; it may be natural that you should say that, but I *know* that it is true. No matter what you say, you know very well that I wouldn't have acted until I was sure. All I wanted was to get those children away. That has been done. There will be nothing else. And there won't be any talk about it or about you—I'll see to that. You have been in my house long enough. Get out.

Karen: Let's go home. *(Starts to go,* MARTHA *stops her.)*

The following is the monologue created from the previous scene.

MARTHA or KAREN (To Mrs. Tilford) age 20s to 40. You may be either character.
pp. 45–49 (DRAMATISTS PLAY SERVICE, INC.)

I tried to reach you. An insane asylum has been let loose. We didn't know what it was. Nobody would talk to us. Nobody would tell us anything. See if you can make any sense out of it. At dinnertime, Mrs. Munn's chauffeur arrived and said that Evelyn must be sent home right away. At half-past seven, Mrs. Burton came to tell us that she wanted Helen's things packed immediately and that she'd wait outside because she didn't want to enter a place like ours. Five minutes later the Wellses' butler came for Rosalie. It was a madhouse. People rushing in and out. The children being pushed into cars, Karen [or Martha] and I begging people to tell us, nobody answering us. Mrs. Rogers finally told us. That—that Karen [or Martha] and I have been—have been—lovers! *You* told them! You think it's true? You crazy, crazy, crazy old woman! You really did say it? You knew what you were saying? You damned, vicious— We're being pushed around by a crazy woman. That's an awful thing. And we're standing here. We're standing here taking it. Didn't you know we'd come here? Were we supposed to lie down and smile while you took up a gun and looked around for people to kill? Listen, listen! You're not playing with paper dolls. We're human beings, see? We're people. It's our lives you're playing with. *Our* lives. That's serious business for us. Can you understand that? *(Wildly.)* It's not true! Not a word of it is true; can't you understand that? There must be something we can do to you, and, whatever it is, we must find it. It makes me dirty and sick to stand here and defend myself—and against what? Against a lie. A great, awful lie. There isn't a single word of truth in anything you said. Damn you. What is there to do to you? Don't get the idea we'll let you whisper this lie; you made it and you'll come out with it. Tomorrow, Mrs. Tilford, you will have a libel suit on your hands. It's your turn to be frightened. You took a child's word for it! *That* is really where you got it! Oh, my God, it all fits so well now. That girl has hated us for a long time. We never knew why, we never could find out. There didn't seem to be any reason. There *wasn't* any reason! She hates everybody and everything. Your Mary's a strange girl. A dark girl. There's something very awful the matter with her. I'm telling you the truth. I should have told it to you long ago. . . . I'm going home . . .

You see how you are fighting for the rest of your life? Your reputation, career, security, relationships, and your name are on the line. You are living through a nightmare. You feel lost, betrayed, frightened. You are in deep pain and anguish. Be very careful with Ms. Hellman's work. If you do not include the humor (the irony and absurdity of this situation), your performance will be melodramatic and pre-Stanislavsky!

Fight for the love. Fight for Mrs. Tilford to care about you, feel sorry for you, sorry for what she has done, sorry for believing Mary. Fight for her to love you. Fight for no less! I'm not saying that you feel love for her because you certainly could not possibly feel that at this time. But deal with the word and emotion *love*! Deal with how unloving and cruel she and Mary are being toward you. Fight to regain what you know you deserve and want and need so desperately. The rage and fury that you feel are because of what has been done to you and how it will affect your future. Anger and rage are loud pain, loud vulnerability. Play that. Not the anger itself.

THE CHILDREN'S HOUR
by Lillian Hellman

pp. 64–67 (Dramatists Play Service, Inc.)

Martha: *(Goes to lamp on D. L. table, lights it.)* It gets dark so early now. *(Crosses to desk, puts down tray, empties ashtray into it.)* Cooking always makes me feel better. I found some purple scylla for the table. Remember! They were the first things we planted here. And I made a small cake. Know what? I found a bottle of wine. We'll have a good dinner. *(Crosses to below R. end of sofa, picks newspaper up from floor. No answer. She crosses back to above desk.)* Where's Joe?

Karen: Gone.

Martha: *(Puts newspaper on desk.)* A patient? Will he be back in time for dinner?

Karen: No.

Martha: *(Watching her.)* We'll wait dinner for him, then. Karen! What's the matter?

Karen: *(In a dull tone.)* He won't be back.

Martha: *(Speaking slowly, carefully.)* You mean he won't be back anymore tonight? *(Slowly crossing L. above desk.)*

Karen: He won't be back at all.

Martha: *(Quickly, walks to R. of* KAREN.*)* What happened? *(*KAREN *shakes head.)* What happened, Karen?

Karen: He thought we had been lovers.

Martha: *(Tensely.)* I don't believe you. I don't believe it. What kind of awful talk is that? I don't believe you. *I don't believe it*.

Karen: All right, all right.

Martha: Didn't you tell him? For God's sake, didn't you tell him it wasn't true?

Karen: Yes.

Martha: He didn't believe you?

Karen: I guess he believed me.

Martha: (*Moves U. S. angrily.*) Then what have you done? It's all wrong. It's crazy. I don't understand what you've done. You "guess" that he believed you. (*Comes back to R. of* KAREN.) There's no guessing about it. Why didn't you——?

Karen: I don't want ever to talk about it, Martha.

Martha: (*Sits in chair L. of desk.*). Oh God, I wanted that for you so much!

Karen: Don't carry on. I don't feel well.

Martha: What's happened to us? What's really happened to us?

Karen: I don't know. I think I'll make a cup of tea and go to bed now.

Martha: Whatever happened, go back to Joe. It's too much for you this way.

Karen: (*Irritably.*) Stop talking about it. Let's pack and get out of here. Let's take the train in the morning.

Martha: The train to where?

Karen: I don't know. Some place; any place.

Martha: A job? Money!

Karen: In a big place we could get something to do.

Martha: They'd know about us. We've been in the headlines. We're very famous.

Karen: A small town, then.

Martha: They'd know more about us, I guess.

Karen: We'll find a place to go.

Martha: I don't think we will. Not really. I feel as if I couldn't move, and what would be the use? It seems to me I'll be sitting the rest of my life, wondering what happened. It's a bad night, tonight, but we might as well get used to it. They'll all be like this.

Karen: (*Gets up, goes to stove. Hands in front of it, warming herself.*) But it isn't a new sin they tell us we've done. Other people aren't destroyed by it.

Martha: They are the people who believe in it, who want it, who've chosen it for themselves. That must be very different. We aren't like that. We don't love each other. We don't love each other. We've been close to each other, of course. I've loved you like a friend, the way thousands of women feel about other women.

Karen: (*Turns her back to stove.*) I'm cold.

Martha: You were a dear friend who was loved, that's all. Certainly there's nothing wrong with that. It's perfectly natural that I should be fond of you. Why, we've known each other since we were seventeen and I always thought——

Karen: *(As if she were tired.)* Why are you saying all this?

Martha: Because I love you.

Karen: *(Sits on D. L. chair.)* Yes, of course. I love you, too.

Martha: But maybe I love you *that* way. The way they said I loved you. I don't know——Listen to me.

Karen: What?

Martha: *(Kneels down next to* KAREN.*)* I have loved you the way they said.

Karen: *(Idly.)* Martha, we're both so tired. Please don't——

Martha: There's always been something wrong. Always—as long as I can remember. But I never knew it until all this happened.

Karen: *(For first time looks up, horrified, turns to* MARTHA.*)* Stop that crazy talk——

Martha: You're afraid of hearing it; I'm more afraid than you.

Karen: *(Turns away, hands over her ears.)* I won't listen to you.

Martha: You've got to know it. I can't keep it to myself any longer. I've got to tell you that I'm guilty.

Karen: *(Deliberately.)* You are guilty of nothing.

Martha: I've been telling myself that since the night we heard the child say it. I lie in bed night after night praying that it isn't true. But I know about it now. It's there. I don't know how. I don't know why. But I did love you. I do love you. I resented your marriage; maybe because I wanted you; maybe I wanted you all these years; I couldn't call it by a name but maybe it's been there ever since I first knew you——

Karen: *(Tensely, grips arms of chair.)* It's not the truth. Not a word of it. We never thought of each other that way.

Martha: *(Bitterly.)* No, of course *you* didn't. But who says I didn't? I never felt that way about anybody but you. I've never loved a man—— *(Stops. Softly.)* I never knew why before. Maybe it's that.

Karen: *(Carefully.)* You are tired and sick.

Martha: *(As though talking to herself.)* It's funny. It's all mixed up. There's something in you and you don't do anything about it because you don't know it's there. Suddenly a little girl gets bored and tells a lie—and there, that night, you see it for the first time, and you say it yourself, did she see it, did she sense it——?

Karen: *(Turns to* MARTHA. *Desperately.)* What are you saying?

You know it could have been any lie. She was looking for
anything——

Martha: Yes, but why this one? She found the lie with the
ounce of truth. I guess they always do. I've ruined your life
and I've ruined my own. I swear I didn't know it, I swear I
didn't mean it——(*Rises, crosses U. L. In a wail.*) Oh, I feel
so God-damned sick and dirty—I can't stand it anymore.

The following is the monologue created from the previous
scene.

MARTHA (to KAREN), age 20s to 40.
pp. 64–67 (DRAMATISTS PLAY SERVICE, INC.)

It gets dark so early now. Cooking always makes me feel
better. I found some purple scylla for the table. Remember! They were the first things we planted here. And I
made a small cake. Know what? I found a bottle of wine.
We'll have a good dinner. Where's Joe? Will he be back in
time for dinner? We'll wait dinner for him. Karen! What's
the matter? What happened? What happened, Karen? . . . He
thought we had been lovers? I don't believe you. I don't
believe it. What kind of awful talk is that? Didn't you tell
him? For God's sake, didn't you tell him it wasn't true? It's
all wrong. It's crazy. Oh God, I wanted that for you so
much! What's happened to us? What's really happened to
us? Go back to Joe. It's too much for you this way. I've
loved you like a friend, the way thousands of women feel
about other women. You were a dear friend who was
loved, that's all. Certainly there's nothing wrong with that.
It's perfectly natural that I should be fond of you. Why,
we've known each other since we were seventeen and I
always thought . . . I'm saying this . . . because I love you . . .
but maybe I love you *that* way! The way they said I love
you. I don't know. Listen to me. *I have loved you the way
they said!* There's always been something wrong. Always—
as long as I can remember. But I never knew it until all
this happened. You're afraid of hearing it; I'm more afraid
than you. You've got to know it. I can't keep it to myself
any longer. I've got to tell you that I'm guilty. I've been
telling myself that since the night we heard the child say

it. I lie in bed night after night praying that it isn't true. But I know about it now. It's there. I don't know how. I don't know why. But I did love you. I do love you. I resented your marriage; maybe because I wanted you; maybe I wanted you all these years; I couldn't call it by a name but maybe it's been there ever since I first knew you. I never felt that way about anybody but you. I've never loved a man. I never knew why before. Maybe it's that. It's funny. It's all mixed up. There's something in you and you don't do anything about it because you don't know it's there. Suddenly a little girl gets bored and tells a lie—and there, that night, you see it for the first time, and you say it yourself, did she see it, did she sense it? She found the lie with the ounce of truth. I guess they always do. I've ruined your life and I've ruined my own. I swear I didn't know it. I swear I didn't mean it. Oh, I feel so goddamned sick and dirty. I can't stand it anymore.

When you are adapting, creating, and developing your monologues, always make a strong effort to have your character respond to the other character's nonverbal reactions. You don't want to hesitate between your lines to allow the other character (in your mind's eye) to speak a line of dialogue to you. Not even to answer a question asked by you. Questions put forth by you should be rhetorical, for the most part. There can be exceptions, of course. Perhaps there is simply no way for you to eliminate a line spoken by the other character. It is essential to the heart of the relationship and important event at hand.

Such is the case in this monologue when Martha says, "He thought we had been lovers?" It is that discovery that sets the tone for the rest of the monologue.

As you can see by reading the scene as written by the playwright, liberties galore were taken! (I do urge you to read the scenes as written by the playwright and if you are not familiar with the play, to read it in its entirety!)

This piece is about discoveries. You are finally able to openly admit to yourself and to Karen that you have loved her romantically and sexually. But do not play the end of the scene until you get there.

As you make each discovery, communicate strongly that indeed as you are saying the words, it is for the very first time clear to you. Even though as part of your preparation you make choices as Martha that since you've known Karen you have felt an extra warm loving feeling for her like you've never felt for anybody else. You know that you really have never lusted after men. You also must know that you have fantasized about Karen. You have daydreamed about her. You have dreamed in your sleep of her. These are choices that the playwright has not given to you. This is your inner life. The playwright doesn't give you that. You must do that for yourself. The stronger, more interesting, and more erotic it is, the better your performance will be. Just be honest about the way your mind works with all its intricacies and quirks and indeed embarrassing thoughts that you wouldn't necessarily want to share with the outside world. It is these thoughts and feelings that you should be creating for your character. You will not be contradicting anything on the page. You will be adding the honesty, humanity, and vulnerability, which precipitate the words you are saying aloud. You will be creating a full, rich, and honest character. We will believe you. You will get the call-back!

THE CHILDREN'S HOUR
by Lillian Hellman

pp. 68–70 (Dramatists Play Service, Inc.)

Mrs. Tilford: Let me come in, please.

Mrs. Mortar: *(Crosses to her, tries to block her way.)* I say you can't come in. You...

Mrs. Tilford: *(Crosses down to L. of sofa.)* Move away, please. Karen, I've something to say to you. You must hear me. *(MRS. MORTAR goes U. L., leans against bookcase, facing upstage.)*

Karen: Why have you come here?

Mrs. Tilford: I had to come. I've been outside all day.... I've been at the door.... I've been phoning you.... I tried to speak to Joe, but he won't talk to me. I've been waiting for you to come out. Then I thought I heard a shot, or something, but...

Karen: Get out of here.

Mrs. Mortar: *(Turns to MRS. TILFORD.)* You bad, bad woman. You have no right in this house. You don't know what you've done.

Mrs. Tilford: Please be still. *(MRS. MORTAR, her face in her hands, exits L. down hall.)* Karen, you must let me speak. I know it wasn't true. I found out it wasn't true. Mrs. Wells came to me today with...

Karen: *(Stares at her, shudders.)* You know it wasn't true, do you? I don't care what you know. If that's what you had to say, you've said it. Go away.

Mrs. Tilford: *(Moves to below L. end of sofa.)* I've got to tell you.

Karen: I don't want to hear you.

Mrs. Tilford: Mrs. Wells found a bracelet in Rosalie's room. The bracelet had been hidden for several months. She found out that Rosalie had taken the bracelet from another girl,

280

and that Mary— (*Closes her eyes.*) that Mary knew that and used it to force Rosalie into saying that she had seen you and Miss Dobie together. I—I've talked to Mary. I found out.

Karen: (*In a loud voice.*) Go away, Mrs. Tilford. Get out of here.

Mrs. Tilford: I have only a little more to say. I've talked to Judge Potter. He has made all arrangements. There will be a public apology and an explanation. The damage suit will be paid to you in full and—and any more that you will be kind enough to take from me. He's waiting to talk to you. We will do whatever you say.

Karen: Martha is dead. (MRS. TILFORD *gasps, shakes head, very slowly, sits L. end of sofa, covers face.* KAREN *watches her.*) So last night you found out you had done wrong to us. And now you have to right that wrong or you can't rest your head again. Well, don't rest it. I won't be your confessor. Take your conscience some place else, get somebody else to help you be a "good" woman again. (*Smiles.*) You told us that night you had to do what you did. Now you have to do this. A public apology and money paid and you can sleep and eat again. You and all those who always know how right they are. What's somebody else's life to you? A way to show your own righteousness. And if you happen to be wrong, (*Shrugs.*) then you can always put it right some other day. (*Quietly.*) I have a dead friend. Get out of here and be noble on the street.

Mrs. Tilford: (*Slowly shakes head.*) There is no relief for me, and there never will be again. I didn't come here for that. I swear to God I did not. But what I am or why I came doesn't make any difference. Doesn't matter. All that matters is you and—— You now. Help me, Karen.

Karen: (*Smiles.*) Help you?

Mrs. Tilford: Let me do whatever I can do. Take whatever I can give. It won't bring me peace, and you don't think it will. I'm too old to recover, too narrow to forgive myself.

Karen: (*After a pause.*) Yes. I believe you. You will have a hard time ahead.

Mrs. Tilford: I will.

Karen: Mary?

Mrs. Tilford: I don't know. I don't know what to do. People say——I've read—but I can't believe or understand it. I—I'll just——I don't know.

Karen: She's yours. (*Smiles.*) Blood of your blood, the result of you. Yes, it will be hard for a woman like you. She's harmed us both, but she did you the most harm. *(Softly.)* I guess I'm even sorry.

Mrs. Tilford: You will try for yourself?

Karen: *(Wearily.)* Yes, I will.

Mrs. Tilford: Come away now. You can't stay with——

Karen: No, I don't want to go.

Mrs. Tilford: You'll be all right?

Karen: *(Slowly rises, crosses to above chair U. L. of D. R. table. Looks out window.)* Yes. Good-bye, now. I don't want to see you again.

Mrs. Tilford: *(Slowly rises, crosses U. C. Turns to* KAREN.*)* But you'll let me help you? You'll let me try?

Karen: If it will make you feel better.

Mrs. Tilford: Yes, yes, yes. Will you write to me some time?

Karen: *(Not turning from window.)* If I ever have anything to say.

Mrs. Tilford: You will have something to say. Good-bye, my dear child.

The following is the monologue created from the previous scene.

MRS. TILFORD (to KAREN), age 60 or older.
pp. 68–70 (DRAMATISTS PLAY SERVICE, INC.)

Let me come in please. Karen, I've something to say to you. You must hear me. I had to come. I've been outside all day. I've been at the door. I've been phoning. I tried to speak to Joe, but he won't talk to me. I've been waiting for you to come out. Then I thought I heard a shot or something. Karen, you must let me speak. I know it wasn't true. I found out it wasn't true. Mrs. Wells came to me today. Mrs. Wells found a bracelet in Rosalie's room. The bracelet had been hidden for several months. She found out that Rosalie had taken the bracelet from another girl, and that Mary knew that and used it to force Rosalie into saying that she had seen you and Miss Dobie together. I've been talking to Mary. I found out. I have only a little more to say. I've talked to Judge Potter. He has made all the arrangements. There will be a public apology and an explanation. The damage suit will be paid to you in full and any more that you will be kind enough to take from me. He's waiting to talk to you. We will do whatever you say. There is no relief for me and there never will be again. I didn't come here for that. I swear to God I did not. But what I am or why I came doesn't make any difference. Doesn't matter. All that matters is you. Help me, Karen. Let me do whatever I can do. Take whatever I can give. It won't bring me peace, I know. I'm too old to recover, too narrow to forgive myself. I will have a hard time ahead. Please try for yourself. You'll be all right? You'll let me help you? Please let me try! It will make me feel better. Will you write to me some time? You will have something to say. Good-bye, my dear child.

The torment and remorse is on the page in the words. You don't have to search for it. By reading the entire play, you certainly can understand what you as Mrs. Tilford are going through right now. Remember every scene is about love and you are always fighting for your life. You are in great pain because of your guilt over how you've done so much damage to two innocent women. This is indeed the most important day in your life. Fight for Karen to forgive and love you. Fight for her to save you. This is a living nightmare you are now going through. Fight for the help *she* can give to *you*. Make this monologue all about *you* and *your* life. Your feelings and needs. The way in which you will have to continue your life knowing and remembering this tragedy and your part in it.

ORPHANS
by Lyle Kessler

pp. 28–32 (SAMUEL FRENCH, INC.)

Harold: *(Smiling, simply.)* I'm an admirer of Houdini's, real name was Erich Weiss. Yiddish boy, Houdini, don't let the Italian flavor fool you, born Erich Weiss, east side of New York.

Phillip: What am I gonna say to Treat?

Harold: Let me take care of that.

Phillip: He's gonna slap me around.

Harold: He's not going to touch you.

Phillip: He's not?

Harold: You think I would let him touch you!

Phillip: You wouldn't?

Harold: He's not going to lay a hand on you.

Phillip: How can you stop him?

Harold: I have my ways.

Phillip: Treat's got a violent temper.

Harold: I love violent tempers.

Phillip: He see you over there he's gonna go crazy.

Harold: I'm not going to be over here.

Phillip: *(Startled.)* Where you gonna be!

Harold: I'm going to be sitting on the couch probably, sitting reading the Philadelphia Inquirer.

Phillip: You are?

Harold: Uh huh. You have the Inquirer?

Phillip: Yes.

Harold: I'm going to be reading the Financial section probably, or maybe even the Sports section, depends on when he comes home. What's your name?

Phillip: Phillip.

Harold: Phillip, mine's Harold. Pleased to meet you. (HAROLD *stands tied to the chair, wiggles his fingers.*)

284

Phillip: I better not.

Harold: You don't want to shake?

Phillip: Treat said not to touch you.

Harold: Not ever?

Phillip: I don't know.

Harold: Or did he mean just now, just today?

Phillip: I didn't ask him.

Harold: Because that would be a shame if we could never touch. I mean, if I could never put my arm around your shoulders and give them an encouraging squeeze. How come you walk around with your shoes untied?

Phillip: I don't know how to lace 'em.

Harold: You don't know how to tie a knot?

Phillip: I try, but they get all tangled up. They get impossible to unknot.

Harold: That's no crime. Man doesn't have to know how to tie a knot. Didn't you ever hear of loafers?

Phillip: Loafers?

Harold: You have no need of laces with loafers. Didn't anyone ever tell you that?

Phillip: No.

Harold: You're a deprived person, Phillip. Here I am talking to a deprived person. You don't know the principle behind electricity, do you?

Phillip: No.

Harold: But you can turn on a light. Don't need to learn how to tie laces either, wear loafers instead. No one'll know the difference. What color you like?

Phillip: Wadaya mean?

Harold: What color loafer?

Phillip: I don't know. Green?

Harold: Green's no good. Don't go with your personality. What about pale yellow?

Phillip: Pale yellow's okay.

Harold: I'm going to buy you a pair of pale yellow loafers.

Phillip: You are?

Harold: That's not the half of it, going to buy you a lot of things, going to buy you a whole new wardrobe, make you presentable, going to teach you how to behave in company.

Phillip: I don't know how to behave.

Harold: You'll learn. Going to teach you etiquette, teach you the proper way to cut your meat, knife in the right hand, not in the left. Fuck laces, you're going to be wearing loafers from now on in. This is a real tragic situation I've wandered into, one boy's a delinquent, in and out of the House of Detention, the other boy's shoulders just dying for a gentle encouraging squeeze.

Phillip: They are?

Harold: Anybody ever give your shoulders an encouraging squeeze?

Phillip: I don't think so.

Harold: That's a tragedy. Every young man's shoulders need an encouraging squeeze now and then.

Phillip: Treat never did that.

Harold: I imagine not. What about your father?

Phillip: I don't know. He ran away from home when I was small.

Harold: He deserted the family?

Phillip: Yes.

Harold: Well, I know shoulders, Phillip. If I know anything, I know about shoulders. (*His arm comes out, free.*) You want me to give them a squeeze, try it out, see how it feels?

Phillip: (*Hesitantly.*) I don't know.

Harold: You don't have to touch me. I'll touch you.

Phillip: Well, maybe that would be all right.

Harold: That would be fine. Come on over here. Come on. (*Puts his arm around* PHILLIP's *shoulders, long pause.*) How's that feel?

Phillip: Feels okay.

Harold: Feels good?

Phillip: Yes.

Harold: Feels real good?

Phillip: Yes, feels real good.

Harold: Feels encouraging, huh?

Phillip: Uh huh.

Harold: Makes you feel there's hope.

Phillip: Yes.

Harold: (*Squeezing.*) This is what you missed.

Phillip: Yes.

Harold: That feeling.

Phillip: I missed that.

Harold: You got it now.

Phillip: I do?

Harold: Forever and ever, Phillip. I would never leave you.

Phillip: You wouldn't?
Harold: No.
Phillip: What will Treat say?
Harold: Treat doesn't have anything to do with it.
Phillip: He might not like it.
Harold: Let me worry about Treat. You got an intellect, you know that, Phillip.
Phillip: I do?
Harold: Positively. Don't let anyone tell you any different. Never came out, that's all, you never let it out.

The following is the monologue created from the previous scene.

HAROLD (to PHILLIP), age 40 to 60s.
pp. 28–32 (SAMUEL FRENCH, INC.)

I'm an admirer of Houdini's, real name was Erich Weiss. Yiddish boy, Houdini, don't let the Italian flavor fool you, born Erich Weiss, east side of New York. Let me take care of what you're gonna say to Treat. He's not going to touch you. You think I would let him touch you! He's not going lay a hand on you. I can stop him. I have my ways. Let him have a violent temper. I love violent tempers. I'm going to be sitting on the couch probably, sitting reading *The Philadelphia Inquirer*. You have *The Inquirer*? I'm going to be reading the financial section probably, or maybe even the sports section, depends on when he comes home. What's your name? Phillip, mine's Harold. Pleased to meet you. You don't want to shake? Not ever? Because that would be a shame if we could never touch. I mean, if I could never put my arm around your shoulders and give them an encouraging squeeze. How come you walk around with your shoes untied? You don't know how to tie a knot? That's no crime. Man doesn't have to know how to tie a knot. Didn't you ever hear of loafers? You have no need of laces with loafers. Didn't anyone ever tell you that? You're a deprived person, Phillip. Here I am talking to a deprived person. You don't know the principle behind electricity, do you? But you can turn on a light. Don't need to learn how to tie laces either, wear loafers instead. No one'll know the difference. What color you like? What color loafer? Green's no good. Don't go with your personality. What about pale yellow? I'm going to buy you a pair of pale yellow loafers. That's not the half of it, going to buy you a lot of things, going to buy you a whole new wardrobe, make you presentable, going to teach you how to behave in company. You'll learn. Going to teach you etiquette, teach you the proper way to cut your meat, knife in the right hand, not in the left. Fuck laces, you're going to be wearing loafers from now on in. This is a real tragic situation I've wandered into, one boy's a delinquent, in and out of the House of Detention, the other boy's shoulders just dying for a gently encouraging squeeze. Anybody ever give your shoulders an encouraging squeeze? That's a tragedy. Every young man's shoulders need an encouraging squeeze now and then. I imagine Treat never did that. What about your father? He deserted the family? Well, I know shoulders, Phillip. If I know anything, I know about shoulders. You want me to give them a squeeze, try it out, see how it feels? You don't have to touch me. I'll touch you. That would be fine. Come on over here. This is what you missed. Feeling of encouragement. Feeling that there's hope. Those feelings. You got it now. Forever and ever, Phillip. I would never leave you. Treat doesn't have anything to do with it. Let me worry about him. You got an intellect, you know that, Phillip. Positively. Don't let anyone tell you any different. Never came out, that's all, you never let it out.

It is very important that you read this play so that you will be able to take advantage of the background and events leading up to this confrontation. Use what the playwright has given to you. It is strong material. He is the professional writer, not you. Let him write the play. After reading it, you then have the right to substitute, add to or delete regarding what came before.

What are you fighting for from Phillip? You need him to trust you, to believe in you, to need you. In other words you are fighting for his love. His love will give you power and safety. Also make a choice that you feel for him and want very much to make him into a functioning young man. Perhaps he is the younger brother or son you never had. It is the rest of your life that you are fighting for right now.

ORPHANS
by Lyle Kessler

pp. 36–43 (SAMUEL FRENCH, INC.)

Harold: You're a Dead End Kid, though, aren't you?

Treat: No.

Harold: I don't mean a real Dead End Kid, for Christ sake, I don't mean a literal Dead End Kid, never take me literally, Treat, you're going to have to learn not to take me literally or you're going to end right up the garden path. How the hell could you be a Dead End Kid, you would have to be 60, 70 years of age, for Christ sake. *(Crosses to pantry, pours himself a drink.)* I mean, those Dead End Kids are old now, they've aged! Some of them are dead, others are suffering from debilitating illnesses, unrecognizable! We're talking about life and death, Treat, mortality! The human condition! You remind me of a Dead End Kid, that's why I came home with you and that's why I'm going to give you everything I have . . . I mean that, son, you name it, it's yours.

Phillip: Did'ja hear that, Treat!

Treat: Shut up!

Harold: It was a lucky thing me meeting up with you in that downtown Philly bar. This is the first good thing that's ever happened to me in Philadelphia.

Treat: What kind of friends you have!

Harold: What do you mean?

Treat: I made some calls.

Harold: You have my wallet.

Treat: That's right. I called up some people.

Harold: What did you say?

Treat: I told them I had you.

Harold: What did they say?

Treat: They wouldn't believe me. They thought it was some kind of a joke. They thought you put me up to it.

289

Harold: I'm not surprised.

Treat: I told them I was serious. I said I want ransom. I told them to get it together, a million bucks!

Harold: What did they do?

Treat: They laughed in my face. I said who the fuck you laughing at! I told them I'd send a piece of you back to them to prove it. I said, "How would you like to receive a finger or two in the mail as proof positive? How would you like to receive his ring finger with the ring still on it!" They said they would love to receive it. They said if it's a nice ring they would melt it down and get a few bucks for it in the open market.

Harold: That sounds like them.

Treat: Another guy cursed me, he cursed you. They hung up on me.

Harold: I could have told you that if you asked.

Treat: Told me what?

Harold: Not to call those fellows up.

Treat: Who should I call up!

Harold: For ransom?

Treat: Yeah!

Harold: Well, you might try those orphans, they're the only family I ever had. Problem is most of them are dead now: TB, polio, hunger, poverty, violence. On second thought I wouldn't bother with those orphans.

Treat: What about your business acquaintances?

Harold: What business acquaintances?

Treat: The people whose names you got in your wallet. The people who you do business with!

Harold: I wouldn't exactly call them acquaintances, Treat. I hope you didn't give them your name and address.

Treat: I didn't give them no fucking name and address.

Harold: That's good.

Treat: Wadaya think I am, stupid?

Harold: Absolutely not.

Treat: I'm calling up people asking for ransom, I'm gonna give my fuckin' name and address!

Harold: You're interested in money, huh?

Treat: Wadya think?

Harold: I think so.

Treat: I figured we could hold you here for a nice size ransom.

Harold: The best laid plans of mice and men.

Treat: Don't give me any of that shit!

Harold: William Shakespeare.

Treat: Don't give me any of that Shakespeare shit!

Harold: How would you like to work for me?

Treat: For you?

Harold: Yes, good pay, pleasant working conditions.

Treat: You must be kidding!

Harold: No, I'm serious.

Treat: This guy's unbelievable!

Harold: You can be my personal bodyguard. You have a streak of violence in you, Treat. I like that.

Treat: I'm not interested.

Harold: I'm offering you five hundred a week, all expenses paid.

Treat: Shove it!

Harold: I'm offering you seven hundred and fifty a week. You like women?

Treat: Sure I like women.

Harold: I'm offering you seven hundred and fifty dollars, plus all the women you can handle.

Treat: Where you gonna get 'em!

Harold: I got a little black book. *(Takes out a black book from his sock.)* See this little book, worth a fortune! You talking about money, I'm showing you money right here.

Treat: I'm self-employed.

Harold: You talking about your work?

Treat: That's right!

Harold: You talking about those lousy nickel and dime stick-ups!

Treat: I don't work for no one! I ain't got the temperament.

Harold: How come?

Treat: It never works out.

Phillip: I told him you were a delinquent.

Treat: You shut the fuck up!

Harold: We're going to get along real well, Treat. I'm willing to take all this into consideration. You can still be your own man.

Treat: Forget it!

Harold: I'm offering you a thousand a week. *(TREAT stares at him.)* That comes to fifty-two thousand a year. That's not peanuts. And I'm talking about a position where there's room for advancement.

Treat: How I know you're not bullshitting me!

Harold: Cross my heart and hope to die.

Treat: I think you're full of shit.

Harold: Here's your first month's salary in advance. Four thousand dollars. Count it!

Treat: Bring that here, Phillip. (PHILLIP *brings it over.*) Where d'ja get that?

Harold: My armpit.

Treat: I got your wallet.

Harold: I don't carry all my money in my wallet, Treat, just in case I get robbed. I carry money in my armpit, my money belt, my hat, anywhere but in my wallet.

Treat: How much you got on you?

Harold: Quite a bit, Treat, and access to much more. (TREAT *locks the front door.*) What do you say? Is it a deal?

Treat: No deal.

Harold: One thousand dollars, that's my final offer.

Treat: I don't take orders.

Harold: I'm easy to get along with.

Treat: I kidnapped you! Who's in control here!

Harold: That depends.

Treat: I'm in control. This is my house, you're my kidnap victim!

Harold: I understand that.

Treat: Don't you go offering me anything, empty out your pockets, Mister!

Harold: That's a mistake.

Treat: That's no mistake! Mistake was offering me a job, the mistake was showing me your money!

Harold: I'm offering you security for life. I'm offering you a job with a pension plan. I'm not just talking about the money I have on me. What the hell good is that! Don't you want to advance in the world!

Treat: I'm happy where I am. Empty out your pockets.

Harold: I can't do that.

Treat: You can't do that!

Harold: It's against my principles! (TREAT *takes out his knife and opens it.*)

Treat: I'll cut out your fucking heart, Mister!

Phillip: Do what he says, Harold!

Treat: Whoa! What are you, on a first name basis?

Harold: Phillip and I have an understanding. He calls me Harold. I call him Phillip.

Treat: I don't work for nobody, you understand me! They tried to get me to work in a department store once, only trouble is I burned it down.

Harold: You're violent.

Treat: Fuckin' A, Mister!

Harold: I like it.

Treat: You don't hand over that money, I'm gonna cut out your heart, I swear to God!

Phillip: He's not kidding!

Harold: I'll give you money, Treat. I told you that. I'll give you way more than what I have on me, you work for me.

Treat: I just want what you got on you. Ain't interested in anything else. You ain't gonna do anyone any good, Mister. No one wants you! I called them fucking numbers in your wallet, no one's interested in you! I don't want you either, Mister. I'm a lone operator, Phillip can tell you, strictly on my own. I don't work for no one! I don't take no orders!

Harold: I'll make you a bet you're going to work for me.

Treat: This guy's crazy.

Phillip: He's well intentioned, Treat.

Treat: He don't hear what I'm saying.

Harold: I'm going to take on the two of you, as a matter of fact. I don't intend to leave Phillip out of the picture. I'm going to work out a package deal.

Treat: Give me your money, Mister!

Harold: *(Continuing.)* I'm talking about new clothes, fine food, fancy women! You like cashmere?

Phillip: I like cashmere.

Harold: I'm talking about only the best!

Phillip: Maybe we should do it, Treat.

Treat: You're not doing nothing! You ain't goin' nowhere! This guy is dangerous, he's putting ideas in your head, making you think you can go out there like the rest of us. I don't want you dropping dead!

Phillip: I'm not gonna drop dead!

Treat: I got the responsibility to take care of you. I don't want your tongue and throat swelling up and you gasping for breath!

Phillip: I won't gasp for breath.

Harold: Good boy!

Treat: I kidnapped this fucking guy!

Harold: Seventeen hundred and fifty a week for the two of you,

for the first six months, and a nice healthy bonus later on.
I'm talking about redheaded women, Treat, redheaded,
freckled women, Phillip. You like breasts?

Phillip: I like breasts!

Harold: I got just the girl for you.

The following is the monologue created from the previous
scene.

HAROLD (to TREAT), age 40 to 60s.
pp. 36–43 (SAMUEL FRENCH, INC.)

You're a Dead End Kid, aren't you? I don't mean a real
Dead End Kid, for Christ sake, I don't mean a literal Dead
End Kid, never take me literally, Treat, you're going to
have to learn not to take me literally or you're going to end
right up the garden path. How the hell could you be a
Dead End Kid, you would have to be sixty, seventy years
of age, for Christ sake, I mean, those Dead End Kids are
old now, they've aged! Some of them are dead, others are
suffering from debilitating illnesses, unrecognizable! We're
talking about life and death, Treat, mortality! The human
condition! You remind me of a Dead End Kid, that's why I
came home with you and that's why I'm going to give you
everything I have . . . I mean that, son, you name it, it's
yours. It was a lucky thing me meeting up with you in that
downtown Philly bar. This is the first good thing that's ever
happened to me in Philadelphia. You interested in money?
I think so. How would you like to work for me? Good pay,
pleasant working conditions. I'm serious. You can be my
personal bodyguard. You have a streak of violence in you,
Treat. I like that. I'm offering you five hundred a week, all
expenses paid. I'm offering you seven hundred and fifty a
week. You like women? I'm offering you seven hundred
and fifty dollars, plus all the women you can handle. I got
a little black book. See this little book, worth a fortune!
You talking about money, I'm showing you money right
here. I know you're self-employed. Lousy nickel-and-dime
stick-ups. We're going to get along real well, Treat. I'm
willing to take all this into consideration. You can still be
your own man. I'm offering you a thousand a week. That

comes to fifty-two thousand a year. That's not peanuts. And I'm talking about a position where there's room for advancement. I'm not bullshitting you. Cross my heart and hope to die. Here's your first month's salary in advance. Four thousand dollars. Count it! I don't carry all my money in my wallet, Treat, just in case I get robbed. I carry money in my armpit, my money belt, my hat, anywhere but in my wallet. I've got quite a bit, Treat, and access to much more. One thousand dollars, that's my final offer. I'm easy to get along with. I'm offering you security for life. I'm offering you a job with a pension plan. I'm not just talking about the money I have on me. What the hell good is that! Don't you want to advance in the world! You're violent. I like it. I'll give you money, Treat. I told you that. I'll give you way more than what I have on me, you work for me. I'll make you a bet you're going to work for me. I'm going to take on the two of you, as a matter of fact. I don't intend to leave Phillip out of the picture. I'm going to work out a package deal. I'm talking about new clothes, fine food, fancy women! You like cashmere? I'm talking about only the best! Seventeen hundred and fifty a week for the two of you, for the first six months, and a nice healthy bonus later on. I'm talking about redheaded women, Treat, redheaded, freckled women, Phillip. You like breasts? I got just the girl for you.

This of course is a three-character scene. Try if you can to turn three-character scenes into two-character ones. It's easier for you to perform a two-character scene for a monologue. The third character can get in your way. You're dividing up your sense of importance, which should be concentrated on one person. What is actually important is to try not to have to address the third person unless it adds to the sense of importance and immediacy. This scene really deals with Treat more than Phillip so it works.

I do not include Harold's speech that follows this dialogue because even though it is good material, it is a speech written by the playwright. Therefore, it probably will be done too much. You don't want to be one of the many who might be doing it.

ORPHANS
by Lyle Kessler

pp. 46–50 (SAMUEL FRENCH, INC.)

Treat: I had a fabulous day! What are you drinking, Harold? (TREAT *is at the side table with the liquor.*)

Harold: I'm having bourbon and water.

Treat: (*Mixing.*) Bourbon and water coming up!

Harold: Only constant thing in my life, Treat. Everything else is in flux, the whole goddamn universe is in flux except for this one constant . . . whenever liquor makes an appearance you can bet your bottom dollar, old Harold is sure to order bourbon and water.

Treat: (*Stirring drink.*) That's good to know.

Harold: These are the facts of life, Treat, memorize them.

Treat: They're memorized! (TREAT *offers* HAROLD *his drink and takes his own.* HAROLD *sits on the couch.*) Wadaya think of this fit, Harold?

Harold: It's a perfect fit.

Treat: It ain't too tight in the crotch?

Harold: The crotch is fine.

Treat: You like this suit as much as you like the beige one?

Harold: I like it even more.

Treat: No kidding! Even more than the beige! (*Admiring himself in mirror.*) I'll tell you something, Harold, I can really get into this shit! You don't mind if I hold on to your American Express card a few more days?

Harold: Be my guest. (TREAT *holds up the American Express card.*)

Treat: This little bastard is changing my life! The reason I wanna hold on to it, Harold, is I seen this real sharp navy blue suit in the window at Bonwit's. I realize I got the beige suit and this here baby, plus a few sport jackets and slacks, but there are seven days in the week, Harold, seven fucking days!

296

Harold: And on the seventh day we rest, Treat.

Treat: I don't mind resting, Harold, as long as I'm resting in one of these here Pierre Cardin suits.

Harold: You're developing a sense of style, Treat, that's fine . . . but remember, please, everything in moderation.

Treat: I don't know much about moderation, Harold.

Harold: I can see that, Treat. Did you pick up my paper?

Treat: I sure did, Harold. I stopped off at the out-of-town newsstand.

Harold: Let's have it. (TREAT *hands the paper to* HAROLD. *He opens it.*) I appreciate that, Treat. I have a terrible nostalgia for Chicago. (HAROLD *takes out a Tiparillo.* TREAT *lights it.* TREAT *sits on the other end of the couch and takes out his own Tiparillo. They both sit in the same position, smoking.*)

Treat: You know, Harold, it's a real pleasure picking up your Chicago Tribune and mixing you them bourbon and waters, but when are you gonna send me out on a real assignment?

Harold: Whenever you're ready, Treat.

Treat: I'm ready, Harold. I've taken good care of you, haven't I?

Harold: I have no complaints.

Treat: Nobody's laid a hand on you, have they?

Harold: Nobody.

Treat: Not even a finger.

Harold: Not a finger.

Treat: Not even a fucking mosquito bite. Am I right?

Harold: You're right.

Treat: What about cold symptoms?

Harold: None.

Treat: Not even a sniffle.

Harold: Not a sniffle. Is that because of you, Treat?

Treat: Fucking A, Harold! No goddamn bacteria gettin' their foot in the door while I'm around! Why, if one of those fellows from Chicago was to point a gun at you, Harold, I'd place myself between your body and that bullet.

Harold: You'd have to move awfully fast to do that, Treat.

Treat: I can move fast, Harold.

Harold: You'd do that for me?

Treat: Absolutely.

Harold: You'd sacrifice yourself?

Treat: Whatever it takes.

Harold: This is amazing, Treat.

Treat: So how 'bout it, Harold. What about a little more responsibility! Send me out on an assignment. I'm sitting here on pins and needles. *(Indicates pins and needles.)* Ohhh! Ahhh! *(Laughs.)* I got my whole new wardrobe selected.

Harold: There's more to it than that, Treat.

Treat: What else is there?

Harold: There's your feelings.

Treat: What's the matter with my feelings?

Harold: They're still uncontrollable.

Treat: *(Angry; hits couch.)* Who says so!

Harold: What happened at Broad and Olney the other night?

Treat: That was a week ago, Harold. I've changed since then.

Harold: What happened?

Treat: I was crossing the street.

Harold: Go on!

Treat: I was standing alongside of you, Harold, minding my own business, standing waiting for the red light to turn green.

Harold: I remember.

Treat: When this big, fat son of a bitch walks up to me and scuffs my shoe.

Harold: It was an accident, Treat.

Treat: It was my brand new alligator shoes, Harold.

Harold: There's no justice.

Treat: What's that supposed to mean?

Harold: If you're looking for justice, you're living in the wrong century. This is the 20th century.

Treat: I don't know if I agree with you there, Harold. Do you mind if we have a slight difference of opinion?

Harold: I don't mind.

Treat: Good, 'cause when we crossed the street, I just happened to stretch out my right leg covered over by my brand new Pierre Cardin trousers and that s.o.b. happened to trip over it and land on his big fat fucking face. *(Pause.)* So you see, Harold, sometimes, every so often, there is justice.

Harold: You believe in an eye for an eye, in other words.

Treat: I don't know, Harold, I got these feelings! Some s.o.b. comes along and scuffs my shoe, these feelings rise up in me. What am I supposed to do with them!

Harold: Did you ever try counting to ten?

Treat: Counting to ten? (PHILLIP *enters carrying the loafers.*)

Harold: You know, one, two, three, four, et cetera...

Treat: You must be kidding.

Harold: I'm serious. It's a first step. It gives your emotions time to settle down.

Treat: I can see if you tell me to count to a thousand or maybe even ten thousand, that way the cock sucker is outta sight. If I count to a million, he's outta the fucking country!

The following is the monologue created from the previous scene.

TREAT (*to* HAROLD), age 20s.
pp. 46–50 (SAMUEL FRENCH, INC.)

I had a fabulous day! Wadaya think of this fit, Harold? It ain't too tight in the crotch? You like this suit as much as you like the beige one? I'll tell you something, Harold, I can really get into this shit! You don't mind if I hold on to your American Express card a few more days? This little bastard is changing my life! The reason I wanna hold on to it, Harold, is I seen this real sharp navy blue suit in the window at Bonwit's. I realize I got the beige suit and this here baby, plus a few sport jackets and slacks, but there are seven days in the week, Harold, seven fucking days! I don't mind resting on the seventh day, Harold, as long as I'm resting in one of these here Pierre Cardin suits. I don't know much about moderation, Harold.

I stopped off at the out-of-town newsstand and picked up your paper. You know, Harold, it's a real pleasure picking up your *Chicago Tribune* and mixing you them bourbon and waters, but when are you gonna send me out on a real assignment? I'm ready, Harold. I've taken good care of you, haven't I? Nobody's laid a hand on you, have they? Not even a finger. Not even a fucking mosquito bite. Am I right? What about cold symptoms? Not even a sniffle. Fucking A, Harold! No goddamn bacteria gettin' their foot in the door while I'm around! Why, if one of those fellows from Chicago was to point a gun at you, Harold, I'd place myself between your body and that bullet. I can move fast, Harold. I would do that for you. I would sacrifice myself. Whatever it takes. So how 'bout it,

Harold. What about a little more responsibility! Send me out on an assignment. I'm sitting here on pins and needles. I got my whole new wardrobe selected. My feelings are not uncontrollable anymore. What happened at Broad and Olney was a week ago, Harold. I've changed since then. I was crossing the street. I was standing alongside of you, Harold, minding my own business, standing waiting for the red light to turn green. When this big, fat son of a bitch walks up to me and scuffs my shoe. It was my brand new alligator shoes, Harold. When we crossed the street, I just happened to stretch out my right leg covered over by my brand new Pierre Cardin trousers and that s.o.b. happened to trip over it and land on his big fat fucking face. So you see, Harold, sometimes, every so often, there is justice. I got these feelings! Some s.o.b. comes along and scuffs my shoe, these feelings rise up in me. What am I supposed to do with them! Count to ten? You must be kidding. I can see if you tell me to count to a thousand or maybe even ten thousand, that way the cocksucker is outta sight. If I count to a million, he's outta the fucking country!

You've succumbed to Harold. You are working for him after all. And are you living it up with his charge card and the money he gives you! You've never felt so important in your life. You're working hard at controlling your feelings despite what occurred at Broad and Olney. That couldn't have been avoided. The guy was asking for it! Sure! And you know that as long as you still have a way to go with your feelings being kept under control, Harold is not going to allow you to do the most important things for him. Which is what you need to do because although you feel important it is not enough. It's better than ever before. But you need more. More to do for him. More trust from him. More love from him. If he loved you, he would be more sensitive to your feelings and the way you react to situations. He would admire you for not being a coward but for standing up when you're under attack and fighting back. Just like that s.o.b.—he attacked you; you had no choice. Fight for Harold to see it your way. You know you're right. Make him know what you already know, try to change him, and win him over completely. This is your life you are fighting for.

'NIGHT, MOTHER
by Marsha Norman

pp. 16–24 (DRAMATISTS PLAY SERVICE, INC.)

Jessie: I don't want anybody else over here. Just you and me. If Dawson comes over it'll make me feel stupid for not doing it ten years ago.

Mama: I think we better call the doctor. Or how about the ambulance. You like that one driver, I know. What's his name, Timmy? Get you somebody to talk to.

Jessie: (*Going back to her chair.*) I'm through talking, Mama. You're it. No more.

Mama: We're just going to sit around like every other night in the world and then you're going to kill yourself? (JESSIE *doesn't answer.*) You'll miss. (*Again, there is no response.*) You'll just wind up a vegetable. How would you like that? Shoot your ear off? You know what the doctor said about getting excited. You'll cock the pistol and have a fit.

Jessie: I think I can kill myself, Mama.

Mama: You're not going to kill yourself, Jessie. You're not even upset! (*And* JESSIE *smiles, or laughs quietly, and* MAMA *tries a different approach.*) People don't really kill themselves, Jessie. No, Mam, doesn't make sense, unless you're retarded or deranged and you're as normal as they come, Jessie, for the most part. We're all *afraid* to die.

Jessie: I'm not, Mama. I'm cold all the time anyway.

Mama: That's ridiculous.

Jessie: It's exactly what I want. It's dark and quiet.

Mama: So is the back yard, Jessie! Close your eyes. Stuff cotton in your ears. Take a nap! It's quiet in your room. I'll leave the TV off all night.

Jessie: So quiet I don't know it's quiet. So nobody can get me.

Mama: You don't know what dead is like. It might not be quiet at all. What if it's like an alarm clock and you can't wake up so you can't shut it off. Ever.

Jessie: Dead is everybody and everything I ever knew, gone. Dead is dead quiet.

Mama: It's a sin. You'll go to hell.

Jessie: Uh-huh.

Mama: You will.

Jessie: Jesus was a suicide, if you ask me.

Mama: You'll go to hell just for saying that. Jessie!

Jessie: *(Genuine surprise.)* I didn't know I thought that.

Mama: Jessie! (JESSIE *doesn't answer. She puts the now loaded gun back in the box and crosses to the kitchen. But* MAMA *is afraid she is headed for the bedroom.* MAMA, *in panic.)* You can't use my towels! They're my towels. I've had them for a long time. I like my towels.

Jessie: I asked you if you wanted that swimming towel and you said you didn't.

Mama: And you can't use your father's gun either. It's mine now too. And you can't do it in my house.

Jessie: Oh come on.

Mama: No. You can't do it. I won't let you. The house is in my name.

Jessie: I have to go in the bedroom and lock the door behind me so they won't arrest you for killing me. They'll probably test your hands for gunpowder anyway, but you'll pass.

Mama: Not in my house!

Jessie: If I'd known you were going to act like this, I wouldn't have told you.

Mama: How am I supposed to act? Tell you to go ahead? O.K. by me, sugar. Might try it myself. What took you so long?

Jessie: There's just no point in fighting me over it, that's all. Want some coffee?

Mama: Your birthday's coming up, Jessie. Don't you want to know what we got you?

Jessie: You got me dusting powder, Loretta got me a new housecoat, pink probably and Dawson got me new slippers, too small, but they go with the robe, he'll say. (MAMA *cannot speak.)* Right? *(Apparently* JESSIE *is right.)* Be back in a minute. (JESSIE *takes the gun box, puts it on top of the stack of towels and garbage bags and takes them into her bedroom.* MAMA, *alone for a moment, goes to the phone, picks up the receiver, looks toward the bedroom, starts to dial and then replaces the receiver in its cradle as* JESSIE *walks back into the room.* JESSIE *wonders, silently. They have lived*

*together for so long, there is very rarely any reason for one
to ask what the other was about to do.)*

Mama: I started to, but I didn't. I didn't call him.

Jessie: Good. Thank you.

Mama: *(Starting over, a new approach.)* What's this all about,
Jessie?

Jessie: About? (JESSIE *now begins the next task she had "on the
schedule," which is refilling all the candy jars, taking the
empty papers out of the boxes of chocolates, etc.* MAMA
generally snitches when JESSIE *does this. Not tonight, though.
Nevertheless,* JESSIE *offers.)*

Mama: What did I do?

Jessie: Nothing. Want a caramel?

Mama: *(Ignoring the candy.)* You're mad at me.

Jessie: Not a bit. I am worried about you, but I'm going to do
what I can before I go. We're not just going to sit around
tonight. I made a list of things.

Mama: What things?

Jessie: How the washer works. Things like that.

Mama: Did you grow up wearing dirty clothes?

Jessie: No.

Mama: I know how the washer works. You put the clothes in.
You put the soap in. You turn it on. You wait.

Jessie: You do something else. You don't just wait.

Mama: Whatever else you find to do you're still mainly waiting. The waiting's the worst part of it. The waiting's what
you pay somebody else to do, if you can.

Jessie: *(Nodding.)* O.K. Where do we keep the soap?

Mama: I could find it.

Jessie: See?

Mama: If you're mad about doing the wash, we can get Loretta
to do it.

Jessie: Oh now, that might be worth staying to see.

Mama: She'd never in her life, would she?

Jessie: Nope.

Mama: What's the matter with her?

Jessie: She thinks she's better than we are. She's not.

Mama: Maybe if she didn't wear that yellow all the time.

Jessie: The washer repair number is on a little card taped to
the side of the machine.

Mama: Loretta doesn't ever have to come over here again.
Dawson can just leave her at home when he comes. And we

won't ever see Dawson either if he bothers you. Does he bother you?

Jessie: Sure he does. Be sure you clean out the lint tray every time you use the dryer. But don't ever put your house shoes in, it'll melt the soles.

Mama: What does Dawson do, that bothers you?

Jessie: He just calls me Jess like he knows who he's talking to. He's always wondering what I do all day. I mean, I wonder that myself, but it's my day, so it's mine to wonder about, not his.

Mama: Family is just accident, Jessie. It's nothing personal, hon. They don't mean to get on your nerves. They don't even mean to be your family, they just are.

Jessie: They know too much.

Mama: About what?

Jessie: They know things about you, and they learned it before you had a chance to say whether you wanted them to know it or not. They were there when it happened and it don't belong to them, it belongs to you, only they got it. Like my mail order bra got delivered to their house.

Mama: By accident!

Jessie: All the same . . . they opened it. They saw the little rosebuds on it. (*Offering her another candy.*) Chewy mint?

Mama: (*Shaking her head no.*) What do they know about you? I'll tell them never to talk about it again. Is it Ricky or Cecil or your fits or your hair is falling out or you drink too much coffee or you never go out of the house or what?

Jessie: I just don't like their talk. The account at the grocery is in Dawson's name when you call. The number's on a whole list of numbers on the back cover of the phone book.

Mama: Well! Now we're getting somewhere. They're none of them ever setting foot in this house again.

Jessie: It's not them, Mother. I wouldn't kill myself just to get away from them.

Mama: You leave the room when they come over, anyway.

Jessie: I stay as long as I can. Besides, it's you they come to see.

Mama: That's because I stay in the room when they come.

Jessie: It's not them.

Mama: Then what is it?

Jessie: (*Checking the list on her notepad.*) The grocery won't deliver on Saturday anymore. And if you want your order the same day, you have to call before 10. And they won't deliver less than 15 dollars' worth. What I do is tell them what we need and tell them to add on cigarettes until it gets to 15 dollars.

Mama: It's Ricky. You're trying to get through to him.

Jessie: If I thought I could do that, I would stay.

Mama: Make him sorry he hurt you, then. That's it, isn't it?

Jessie: He's hurt me, I've hurt him. We're about even.

Mama: You'll be telling him killing is O.K. with you, you know. Want him to start killing next? Nothing wrong with it. Mom did it.

Jessie: Only a matter of time anyway, Mama. When the call comes, you let Dawson handle it.

Mama: Honey, nothing says those calls are always going to be some new trouble he's into. You could get one that he's got a job, that he's getting married, or how about he's joined the army, wouldn't that be nice?

Jessie: If you call The Sweet Tooth before you call the grocery, that Susie will take your fudge next door to the grocery and it'll all come out together. Be sure you talk to Susie, though. She won't let them put it in the bottom of a sack like that one time, remember?

Mama: Ricky could come over, you know. What if he calls us?

Jessie: It's not Ricky, Mama.

Mama: Or anybody could call us, Jessie.

Jessie: Not on Saturday night, Mama.

Mama: Then what is it? Are you sick? If your gums are swelling again, we can get you to the dentist in the morning.

Jessie: No. Can you order your medicine or do you want Dawson to? I've got a note to him. I'll add that to it if you want.

Mama: Your eyes don't look right. I thought so yesterday.

Jessie: That was just the ragweed. I'm not sick.

Mama: Epilepsy is sick, Jessie.

Jessie: It won't kill me. *(A pause.)* If it would, I wouldn't have to.

Mama: You don't *have* to.

Jessie: No, I don't. That's what I like about it.

Mama: Well, I won't let you!

Jessie: It's not up to you.

Mama: Jessie!

Jessie: I want to hang a big sign around my neck, like Daddy's on the barn. Gone Fishing.

Mama: You don't like it here.

Jessie: *(Smiles.)* Exactly.

Mama: I meant here in my house.

Jessie: I know you did.

Mama: You never should have moved back in here with me. If you'd kept your little house or found another place when Cecil left you, you'd have made some new friends at least. Had a life to lead. Had your own things around you. Give Ricky a place to come see you. You never should've come here.

Jessie: Maybe.

Mama: But I didn't force you, did I?

Jessie: If it was a mistake, we made it together. You took me in. I appreciate that.

Mama: You didn't have any business being by yourself right then, but I can see how you might want a place of your own. You could be as close or as far away as you wanted. A grown woman should . . .

Jessie: Mama . . . I'm just not having a very good time and I don't have any reason to think it'll get anything but worse. I'm tired. I'm hurt. I'm sad. I feel used.

Mama: Tired of what?

Jessie: It all.

Mama: What does that mean?

Jessie: I can't say it any better.

Jessie: Well, you'll have to say it better because I'm not letting you alone til you do. What were those other things. Hurt . . . *(Before* JESSIE *can answer.)* You had this all ready to say to me, didn't you? Did you write this down? How long have you been thinking about this?

Jessie: Off and on, ten years. On all the time, since Christmas.

Mama: What happened at Christmas?

Jessie: Nothing.

Mama: So why Christmas?

Jessie: That's it. On the nose. *(A pause.* MAMA *knows exactly what* JESSIE *means. She was there, too, after all.* JESSIE, *putting the candy sacks away.)* See where all this is? Red hots up front, sour balls and horehound mixed together in this one sack. New packages of toffee and licorice right in back there.

Mama: Go back to your list. You're hurt by what?

Jessie: *(*MAMA *knows perfectly well.)* Mama . . .

Mama: O.K. Sad about what? There's nothing real sad going on right now. If it was after your divorce or something, that would make sense.

Jessie: *(Looks at her list, then opens the drawer.)* Now, this drawer has everything in it that there's no better place for. Extension cords, batteries for the radio, extra lighters, sand paper, masking tape, Elmer's glue, thumbtacks, that kind of stuff. The mousetraps are under the sink, but you call Dawson if you've got one and let him do it.

Mama: Sad about what?

Jessie: The way things are.

Mama: Not good enough. What things?

Jessie: Oh, everything from you and me to Red China.

Mama: I think we can leave the Chinese out of this.

Jessie: *(Crosses back into the living room.)* There's extra lightbulbs in a box in the hall closet. And we've got a couple of packages of fuses in the fuse box. There's candles and matches in the top of the broom closet, but if the lights go out, just call Dawson and sit tight. But don't open the refrigerator door. Things will stay cool in there as long as you keep the door shut.

Mama: I asked you a question.

Jessie: I read the paper. I don't like how things are. And they're not any better out there than they are in here.

Mama: If you're doing this because of the newspapers, I can sure fix that!

Jessie: There's just more of it on TV.

Mama: *(Kicks the television.)* Take it out then!

Jessie: You wouldn't do that.

Mama: Watch me.

Jessie: What would you do all day?

Mama: *(Desperate.)* Sing. *(JESSIE laughs.)* I would too. You want to watch? I'll sing til morning to keep you alive, Jessie, please!

Jessie: No. *(Then affectionately.)* It's a funny idea, though. What do you sing?

Mama: *(Has no idea how to answer this.)* We've got a good life here!

Jessie: *(Going back into the kitchen.)* I called this morning and cancelled the papers, except for Sunday, for your puzzles, you'll still get that one.

Mama: Let's get another dog, Jessie! You liked a big dog, didn't you, that King dog, didn't you?

Jessie: *(Washing her hands.)* I did like that King dog, yes.

Mama: I'm so dumb. He's the one run under the tractor.

Jessie: That makes him dumb, not you.

Mama: For bringing it up.

Jessie: It's O.K. Handi-wipes and sponges under the sink.

Mama: We could get a new dog and keep him in the house. Dogs are cheap!

Jessie: *(Now getting big pill jars out of the cabinet.)* No.

Mama: Something for you to take care of.

Jessie: I've had you, Mama.

Mama: *(Frantically starts filling pill bottles.)* You do too much for me. I can fill pill bottles all day, Jessie, and change the shelf-paper and wash the floor when I get through. You just watch me. You don't have to do another thing in this house if you don't want to. You don't have to take care of me, Jessie.

The following is the monologue created from the previous scene.

MAMA (to JESSIE), age 40s to 60s.
pp. 16–24 (DRAMATISTS PLAY SERVICE, INC.)

We're just going to sit around like every other night in the world and then you're going to kill yourself? You'll miss. You'll just wind up a vegetable. How would you like that? Shoot your ear off? You'll cock the pistol and have a fit. You're not going to kill yourself, Jessie. You're not even upset! People don't really kill themselves, Jessie. No, Mam, doesn't make sense, unless you're retarded or deranged and you're as normal as they come, Jessie, for the most part. We're all *afraid* to die. Close your eyes. Stuff cotton in your ears. Take a nap! It's quiet in your room. I'll leave the TV off all night. You don't know what dead is like. It might not be quiet at all. What if it's like an alarm clock and you can't wake up so you can't shut it off. Ever. It's a sin. You'll go to hell. And you can't use your father's gun either. It's mine now too. And you can't do it in my house. I won't let you. The house is in my name. How am I supposed to act? Tell you to go ahead? Okay by me, sugar. Might try it myself. What took you so long? Your birthday's coming up, Jessie. Don't you want to know what we got you? What is it? Are you sick? If your gums are swelling

again, we can get you to the dentist in the morning. Your
eyes don't look right. You don't have to kill yourself. I
won't let you! You never should have moved back in here
with me. If you'd kept your little house or found another
place when Cecil left you, you'd have made some new
friends at least. Had a life to lead. Had your own things
around you. Give Ricky a place to come see you. You
never should've come here. I didn't force you, did I? You
had this all ready to say to me, didn't you? Did you write
this down? How long have you been thinking about this?
There's nothing real sad going on right now. If it was after
your divorce or something, that would make sense. We've
got a good life here! Let's get another dog, Jessie! You
liked a big dog, didn't you, that King dog, didn't you? I'm
so dumb. He's the one run under the tractor. We could get
a new dog and keep him in the house. Dogs are cheap!
Something for you to take care of. You do too much for me.
I can fill pill bottles all day, Jessie, and change the shelf paper
and wash the floor when I get through. You just watch me.
You don't have to do another thing in this house if you
don't want to. You don't have to take care of me, Jessie.

Fighting for your daughter's life is the same as fighting for
your own life. This is a living nightmare. Your child tells you she
plans to shoot herself. She no longer wants to live. Don't forget
the humor! Yes, humor! There is nothing funny about this situation. But there is humor here. You need it desperately. It's in the
words. Be aware of it. Don't allow this to be a soap-opera
performance.

What you are going through is pure hell. This is the very
worst event of your life. What you are fighting for is to stop your
daughter from killing herself. It is a positive thing to fight for. So
be aware of the negatives but work off your positives. You are
indeed coming up with all those nice positive solutions. Another
dog. Relieving Jessie of doing things for you. See the future as
being much improved for Jessie and play off this wonderful
future you are planning for her. It is not just her life that will be
over. If she dies, *you* will be alone. *You* will be the one left
behind. You have depended on Jessie in your life. She has needed
you. You cannot give that up. You are fighting for *your* life.

'NIGHT, MOTHER
by Marsha Norman

pp. 21–26 (DRAMATISTS PLAY SERVICE, INC.)

Jessie: I want to hang a big sign around my neck, like Daddy's on the barn. Gone Fishing.

Mama: You don't like it here.

Jessie: *(Smiles.)* Exactly.

Mama: I meant here in my house.

Jessie: I know you did.

Mama: You never should have moved back in here with me. If you'd kept your little house or found another place when Cecil left you, you'd have made some new friends at least. Had a life to lead. Had your own things around you. Give Ricky a place to come see you. You never should've come here.

Jessie: Maybe.

Mama: But I didn't force you, did I?

Jessie: If it was a mistake, we made it together. You took me in. I appreciate that.

Mama: You didn't have any business being by yourself right then, but I can see how you might want a place of your own. You could be as close or as far away as you wanted. A grown woman should . . .

Jessie: Mama . . . I'm just not having a very good time and I don't have any reason to think it'll get anything but worse. I'm tired. I'm hurt. I'm sad. I feel used.

Mama: Tired of what?

Jessie: It all.

Mama: What does that mean?

Jessie: I can't say it any better.

Mama: Well, you'll have to say it better because I'm not letting you alone til you do. What were those other things. Hurt . . . *(Before* JESSIE *can answer.)* You had this all ready to

310

say to me, didn't you? Did you write this down? How long have you been thinking about this?

Jessie: Off and on, ten years. On all the time, since Christmas.

Mama: What happened at Christmas?

Jessie: Nothing.

Mama: So why Christmas?

Jessie: That's it. On the nose. *(A pause.* MAMA *knows exactly what* JESSIE *means. She was there, too, after all.* JESSIE, *putting the candy sacks away.)* See where all this is? Red hots up front, sour balls and horehound mixed together in this one sack. New packages of toffee and licorice right in back there.

Mama: Go back to your list. You're hurt by what?

Jessie: *(*MAMA *knows perfectly well.)* Mama . . .

Mama: O.K. Sad about what? There's nothing real sad going on right now. If it was after your divorce or something, that would make sense.

Jessie: *(Looks at her list, then opens the drawer.)* Now, this drawer has everything in it that there's no better place for. Extension cords, batteries for the radio, extra lighters, sand paper, masking tape, Elmer's glue, thumbtacks, that kind of stuff. The mousetraps are under the sink, but you call Dawson if you've got one and let him do it.

Mama: Sad about what?

Jessie: The way things are.

Mama: Not good enough. What things?

Jessie: Oh, everything from you and me to Red China.

Mama: I think we can leave the Chinese out of this.

Jessie: *(Crosses back into the living room.)* There's extra lightbulbs in a box in the hall closet. And we've got a couple of packages of fuses in the fuse box. There's candles and matches in the top of the broom closet, but if the lights go out, just call Dawson and sit tight. But don't open the refrigerator door. Things will stay cool in there as long as you keep the door shut.

Mama: I asked you a question.

Jessie: I read the paper. I don't like how things are. And they're not any better out there than they are in here.

Mama: If you're doing this because of the newspapers, I can sure fix that!

Jessie: There's just more of it on TV.

Mama: *(Kicks the television.)* Take it out then!

Jessie: You wouldn't do that.

Mama: Watch me.

Jessie: What would you do all day?

Mama: (*Desperate.*) Sing. (JESSIE *laughs.*) I would too. You want to watch? I'll sing til morning to keep you alive, Jessie, please!

Jessie: No. (*Then affectionately.*) It's a funny idea, though. What do you sing?

Mama: (*Has no idea how to answer this.*) We've got a good life here!

Jessie: (*Going back into the kitchen.*) I called this morning and cancelled the papers, except for Sunday, for your puzzles, you'll still get that one.

Mama: Let's get another dog, Jessie! You liked a big dog, didn't you, that King dog, didn't you?

Jessie: (*Washing her hands.*) I did like that King dog, yes.

Mama: I'm so dumb. He's the one run under the tractor.

Jessie: That makes him dumb, not you.

Mama: For bringing it up.

Jessie: It's O.K. Handi-wipes and sponges under the sink.

Mama: We could get a new dog and keep him in the house. Dogs are cheap!

Jessie: (*Now getting big pill jars out of the cabinet.*) No.

Mama: Something for you to take care of.

Jessie: I've had you, Mama.

Mama: (*Frantically starts filling pill bottles.*) You do too much for me. I can fill pill bottles all day, Jessie, and change the shelf-paper and wash the floor when I get through. You just watch me. You don't have to do another thing in this house if you don't want to. You don't have to take care of me, Jessie.

Jessie: I know that. You've just been letting me do it so I'll have something to do, haven't you?

Mama: (*Realizing this was a mistake.*) I don't do it as well as you, I just meant if it tires you out or makes you feel used...

Jessie: Mama, I know you used to ride the bus. Riding the bus and it's hot and bumpy and crowded and too noisy and more than anything in the world you want to get off and the only reason in the world you don't get off is it's still 50 blocks from where you're going? Well, I can get off right now if I want to, because even if I ride 50 more years and get off then, it's the same place when I step down to it. Whenever

I feel like it, I can get off. As soon as I've had enough, it's my stop. I've had enough.

Mama: You're feeling sorry for yourself!

Jessie: The plumber's helper is under the sink, too.

Mama: You're not having a good time! Whoever promised you a good time? Do you think I've had a good time?

Jessie: I think you're pretty happy, yeah. You have things you like to do.

Mama: Like what?

Jessie: Like crochet.

Mama: I'll teach you to crochet.

Jessie: I can't do any of that nice work, Mama.

Mama: Good times don't come looking for you, Jessie. You could work some puzzles or put in a garden or go to the store. Let's call a taxi and go to the A & P.

Jessie: I shopped you up for about two weeks already. You're not going to need toilet paper til Thanksgiving.

Mama: (Interrupting.) You're acting like some little brat, Jessie. You're mad and everybody's boring and you don't have anything to do and you don't like me and you don't like going out and you don't like staying in and you never talk on the phone and you don't watch TV and you're miserable and it's your own sweet fault.

Jessie: And it's time I did something about it.

Mama: Not something like killing yourself. Something like . . . buying us all new dishes! I'd like that. Or maybe the doctor would let you get a driver's license now, or I know what let's do right this minute, let's rearrange the furniture.

Jessie: I'll do that. If you want. I always thought if the TV was somewhere else, you wouldn't get such a glare on it during the day. I'll do whatever you want before I go.

Mama: (Badly frightened by those words.) You could get a job!

Jessie: I took that telephone sales job and I didn't even make enough money to pay the phone bill, and I tried to work at the gift shop at the hospital and they said I made people real uncomfortable smiling at them the way I did.

Mama: You could keep books. You kept your Dad's books.

Jessie: But nobody ever checked them.

Mama: When he died, they checked them.

Jessie: And that's when they took the books away from me.

Mama: That's because without him there wasn't any business, Jessie!

Jessie: (Puts the pill bottles away now.) You know I couldn't work. I can't do anything. I've never been around people my whole life except when I went to the hospital. I could have a seizure any time. What good would a job do? The kind of job I could get would make me feel worse.

Mama: Jessie!

Jessie: It's true!

Mama: It's what you think is true!

Jessie: *(Struck by the clarity of that.)* That's right. It's what I think is true.

Mama: *(Hysterical.)* But I can't do anything about that!

Jessie: *(Quietly.)* No. You can't. (MAMA *slumps, if not physically, at least emotionally.*) And I can't do anything either, about my life, to change it, make it better, make me feel better about it. Like it better, make it work. But I can stop it. Shut it down, turn it off like the radio when there's nothing on I want to listen to. It's all I really have that belongs to me and I'm going to say what happens to it. And it's going to stop. And I'm going to stop it. So. Let's just have a good time.

Mama: Have a good time.

Jessie: We can't go on fussing all night. I mean, I could ask you things I always wanted to know and you could make me some hot chocolate. The old way.

The following is the monologue created from the previous scene.

JESSIE (to MAMA), age 30 to late 40s.
pp. 21–26 (DRAMATISTS PLAY SERVICE, INC.)

I want to hang a big sign around my neck, like Daddy's on the barn: Gone Fishing. Mama...I'm just not having a very good time and I don't have any reason to think it'll get anything but worse. I'm tired. I'm hurt. I'm sad. I feel used. I'm tired of it all. I can't say it any better. I've been thinking about this off and on, ten years. On all the time, since Christmas. I read the paper. I don't like how things are. And they're not any better out there than they are in here.

Mama, I know you used to ride the bus. Riding the bus and it's hot and bumpy and crowded and too noisy and more than anything in the world you want to get off and the only reason in the world you don't get off is it's still fifty blocks from where you're going? Well, I can get off right now if I want to, because even if I ride fifty more years and get off then, it's the same place when I step down to it. Whenever I feel like it, I can get off. As soon as I've had enough, it's my stop. I've had enough. I think you're pretty happy, yeah. You have things you like to do. Like crochet. I can't do any of that nice work, Mama. I took that telephone sales job and I didn't even make enough money to pay the phone bill, and I tried to work at the gift shop at the hospital and they said I made people real uncomfortable smiling at them the way I did. I kept Dad's books. When he died, they checked them. And that's when they took the books away from me. You know I couldn't work. I can't do anything. I've never been around people my whole life except when I went to the hospital. I could have a seizure any time. What good would a job do? The kind of job I could get would make me feel worse. It's true! And I can't do anything either, about my life, to change it, make it better, make me feel better about it, like it better, make it work. But I can stop it—shut it down, turn it off like the radio when there's nothing on I want to listen to. It's all I really have that belongs to me and I'm going to say what happens to it. And it's going to stop. And I'm going to stop it. So. Let's just have a good time. We can't go on fussing all night. I mean, I could ask you things I always wanted to know and you could make me some hot chocolate. The old way.

What are you desperately fighting for from your mother? Do you need her permission to kill yourself? Do you need her approval? Do you need her acceptance? The answer is a huge no! These choices are not big enough for you to make and play off. First of all you are fighting for her love. You may think this is silly. After all, she is your mother. She loves you. But what you are communicating to her now is something very powerful and epic. She may not ever be able to love you enough to condone what you are about to do. But you are still fighting for just this. Fight for what you wish to get, not what you have to settle for. Fight through your fantasies. You are going to go through with your plan no matter how she tries to stop you. It is the first time in your life that you have control over your fate. This is important. You mean to do away with yourself. You've got to know that she will not crumble and fall apart and die herself. This too is important to you. You certainly want to try to explain to her why you are going to kill yourself, to share your feelings with her so that she will see that you have thought this out and you know you are right. All of this is true—*and* you want her to convince you *not* to kill yourself! You do not get this from the playwright. She may or may not have thought of this or even now believe that this could be true. But it is for you, the actress, to create opposites for yourself. It's not in the dialogue. But it does not negate one thing on the page. This choice will simply help you to have a stronger emotional reach-out to Mama. You will be communicating with another layer. You will be exposing more of your humanity. It will be more of a life-and-death performance. Yes, you are fighting for your life. You have not given up hope. Not until the moment you pull the trigger. If you do! Because at this time, you do not know if you will or will not. You are only planning to do it. You are fighting for a miracle. Why not!

'NIGHT, MOTHER
by Marsha Norman

pp. 47–49 (Dramatists Play Service, Inc.)

Mama: Everything you do has to do with me, Jessie. You can't do *anything*, wash your face or cut your finger, without doing it to me. That's right! You might as well kill me as you, Jessie, it's the same thing. This has to do with me, Jessie.

Jessie: Then what if it does! What if it has everything to do with you! What if you are all I have and you're not enough? What if I could take all the rest of it if only I didn't have you here? What if the only way I can get away from you for good is to kill myself? What if it is? I can *still* do it!

Mama: (*In desperate tears.*) Don't leave me, Jessie! (JESSIE *stands for a moment, then turns for the bedroom.*) No! (MAMA *grabs her arm.*)

Jessie: (*Carefully takes her arm away.*) I have a box of things I want people to have. I'm just going to go get it for you. You . . . just rest a minute. (*And* JESSIE *is gone and* MAMA *heads for the telephone, but she can't even pick up the receiver this time, and instead, stoops to clean up the bottles that have spilled out of the tray.* JESSIE *returns carrying a box that groceries were delivered in. It probably says Hershey Kisses or Starkist Tuna.* MAMA *is still down on the floor cleaning up, hoping that maybe if she just makes it look nice enough,* JESSIE *will stay.*)

Mama: Jessie, how can I live here without you? I need you! You're supposed to tell me to stand up straight and say how nice I look in my pink dress and drink my milk. You're supposed to go around and lock up so I know we're safe for the night, and when I wake up, you're supposed to be out there making the coffee and watching me get older every day and you're supposed to help me die when the time comes. I can't do that by myself, Jessie. I'm not like you, Jessie. I hate the quiet and I don't want to die and I don't want you to go, Jessie. How can I . . . (*Has to stop a moment.*) How can I get up every day knowing you had to kill yourself to make it stop hurting and I was here all the time and I never even saw it. And then you gave me this chance to make it better, convince you to stay alive and I couldn't do it. How can I live with myself after this, Jessie?

Jessie: I only told you so I could explain it, so you wouldn't blame yourself, so you wouldn't feel bad. There wasn't anything you could say to change my mind. I didn't want you to save me. I just wanted you to know.

Mama: Stay with me just a little longer. Just a few more years. I don't have that many more to go, Jessie. And as soon as I'm dead, you can do whatever you want. Maybe with me gone, you'll have all the quiet you want, right here in the house. And maybe one day you'll put in some begonias up the walk and get just the right rain for them all summer. And Ricky will be married by then and he'll bring your grandbabies over and you can sneak them a piece of candy when their Daddy's not looking and then be real glad when they've gone home and left you to your quiet again.

Jessie: Don't you see, Mama, everything I do winds up like this. How could I think you would understand? How could I think you would want a manicure? We could hold hands for an hour and then I could go shoot myself? I'm sorry about tonight, Mama, but it's exactly why I'm doing it.

Mama: If you've got the guts to kill yourself, Jessie, you've got the guts to stay alive.

The following is the monologue created from the previous scene.

MAMA (to JESSIE), age 40s to 60s.
pp. 47–49 (DRAMATISTS PLAY SERVICE, INC.)

Everything you do has to do with me, Jessie. You can't do *anything*, wash your face or cut your finger, without doing it to me. That's right! You might as well kill me as you, Jessie, it's the same thing. This has to do with me, Jessie. Don't leave me, Jessie! Jessie, how can I live here without you? I need you! You're supposed to tell me to stand up straight and say how nice I look in my pink dress and drink my milk. You're supposed to go around and lock up so I know we're safe for the night, and when I wake up, you're supposed to be out there making the coffee and watching me get older every day and you're supposed to help me die when the times comes. I can't do that by myself, Jessie. I'm not like you, Jessie. I hate the quiet and I don't want to die and I don't want you to go, Jessie. How can I . . . how can I get up every day knowing you had to kill yourself to make it stop hurting and I was here all the time and I never even saw it? And then you gave me this chance to make it better, convince you to stay alive and I couldn't do it. How can I live with myself after this, Jessie? Stay with me just a little longer. Just a few more years. I don't have that many more to go, Jessie. And as soon as I'm dead, you can do whatever you want. Maybe with me gone, you'll have all the quiet you want, right here in the house. And maybe one day you'll put in some begonias up the walk and get just the right rain for them all summer. And Ricky will be married by then and he'll bring your grandbabies over and you can sneak them a piece of candy when their Daddy's not looking and then be real glad when they've gone home and left you to your quiet again. If you've got the guts to kill yourself, Jessie, you've got the guts to stay alive.

Of course, you are fighting for your daughter's life. You must stop her from wanting to kill herself. You can't imagine what your life would be like if she were to actually take her own life. Or for that matter, what it would be like if she died from natural causes. Just having her dead and gone is too much to bear. But at least now you can stop her. If you can just find the right combination of words. If you can convince her somehow by finding the magic words. And then of course, if Jessie really loved you, she would not do such a thing—make you suffer through a tragedy like this. And you would have to live without her, knowing you were unable to stop her. So what are you fighting for? For Jessie's love. If she really loved you, she would be more sensitive to you and not do this to *you*! You love and need her. She is there for you. You depend on her. She is part of you. She is part of your life and very being. She *is* you! You are fighting for the rest of your life. She is trying to kill *you*!

THE RAINMAKER
by N. Richard Nash

pp. 38–43 (Samuel French, Inc.)

Starbuck: *(Steps onto the threshold. He hears* Jim's *line about the wind.)* Wind?—did you say wind? There's not a breath of wind anywhere in the world!

Noah: Who are *you?*

Starbuck: The name's Starbuck! Starbuck is the name! *(He espies* Lizzie *and his whole manner changes. He doffs his hat and his bow is part gallantry, part irony. Crosses to her.)* Lady of the house—*hello!*

Lizzie: *(Involuntarily.)* Hello.

Starbuck: ¨That's a mighty nice dress—it oughta go to a party!

Lizzie: *(Not charmed.)* Don't you knock on a door before you come in?

H.C.: *(R. C.)* What is it? What can we do for you?

Starbuck: *(L. C.)* You're askin' the wrong question. The question is what can I do for you?

Noah: I don't remember we called for anybody to do anything.

Starbuck: You should have, Mister—you sure should have! You need a lot of help! You're in a parcel of trouble. You lost twelve steers on the north range and sixty-two in the gully. The calves are starvin' and the heifers are down on their knees.

Jim: *(Up R. C.)* You know a heckuva lot about our herd!

Starbuck: *(Noticing* Jim's *black eye.)* Man, that sure is a shiner! *(To* H.C.*)* Your ranch, Mister?

Noah: He owns it—I run it.

Starbuck: *(To* Noah.*)* Well, I guess I'll talk to *you.* You got a look of business about you, Mister. You got your feet apart—and you stand solid on the ground! That's the kind of a man I like to talk to! Well, what are you gonna do about them cattle?

320

Noah: If you know we lost the cattle, you oughta know what killed them. Drought! Ever hear of it?

Starbuck: Hear of it! That's *all* I hear! Wherever I go, there's drought ahead of me! But when I leave—behind me there's rain—*rain!*

Lizzie: *(On step L.)* I think this man's crazy!

Starbuck: *(Crosses down L.)* Sure!—that's what I am!—crazy! I woke up this mornin'—I looked at the world and I said to myself: "The world's gone completely out of its mind! And the only thing that can set it straight is a first class, A-number-one lunatic!" Well, here I am, folks—crazy as a bedbug! Did I introduce myself? The name is Starbuck—*Rainmaker!*

H.C.: *(Doubtfully.)* I've heard about rainmakers. *(Offers C. chair, then lights lamp above sofa.)*

Noah: I read about a rainmaker—I think it was Idaho.

Starbuck: What'd you read, Mister?

Noah: I can't remember whether they locked him up or ran him out of town.

Starbuck: *(Sits C. chair. Laughing goodnaturedly.)* Might be they strung him up on a sycamore tree.

Noah: *(Sits R. of table.)* Look, fella, the idea is—we don't believe in rainmakers.

Starbuck: What *do* you believe in, Mister—dyin' cattle?

Jim: You really mean you can bring rain?

Lizzie: He talks too fast—he can't bring anything!

Jim: *(Sits on hassock.)* I asked *him.* Can you bring rain?

Starbuck: It's been done, brother—it's been done!

Jim: *(Excitedly.)* Where? How?

(LIZZIE lights hanging lamp up C.)

Starbuck: *(Rises. With a flourish of his stick.)* How? Sodium chloride!—pitch it up high—right up to the clouds! Electrify the cold front! Neutralize the warm front! Barometricize the tropopause! Magnetize occlusions in the sky! *(Crosses R. to door.)*

Lizzie: *(Confronting him quietly.)* In other words—bunk!

Starbuck: *(Realizing he will have to contend with LIZZIE and NOAH, he suddenly and shrewdly reverses his field—he agrees with her.)* Lady, you're right! You know why that sounds like bunk? Because it is bunk! Bunk and hokey pokey! And I tell you, I'd be ashamed to use any of those methods!

Jim: What method do you use?

Starbuck: *(To up L. C.)* My method's like my name—it's all my own! You want to hear my deal?

Lizzie: We're not interested.

Noah: Not one bit!

H.C.: *(Crosses C.)* What is it?

Noah: Pop, you're not listenin' to this man—?!

H.C.: *(Crosses to* STARBUCK. *Quietly.)* Any charge for listenin'?

Starbuck: No charge—free!

H.C.: *(Crosses; sits on chest R. C.)* Go ahead. What's the deal?

Starbuck: *(C.)* One hundred dollars in advance—and inside of twenty-four hours you'll have rain!

Jim: *(In a dither.)* You mean it? Real rain?

Starbuck: Rain is rain, brother! It comes from the sky! It's a wetness known as water! Aqua pura! Mammals drink it, fish swim in it, little boys wade in it, and birds flap their wings and sing like sunrise! Water! *(L. C.; pours water from pitcher over his head.)* I recommend it!

Jim: *(Convinced, crosses to* NOAH.*)* Pay him the hundred, Noah!

Lizzie: *(Up L. C.)* Noah, don't be a chump!

Noah: Me?—don't worry—I won't!

Jim: We got the drought, Noah! It's rain, Lizzie—we need it!

Lizzie: We won't get a drop of it!—not from him!

H.C.: *(Quietly.)* How would you do it, Starbuck?

Starbuck: Now don't ask me no questions.

Lizzie: Why? It's a fair question! How will you do it?

Starbuck: *(L. C.)* What do you care how I do it, sister, as long as it's done! But I'll tell you how I'll do it! I'll lift this stick and take a long swipe at the sky and let down a shower of hailstones as big as canteloupes! I'll shout out some good old Nebraska cusswords and you turn around and there's a lake where your corral used to be! Or I'll just sing a little tune maybe and it'll sound so pretty and sound so sad you'll weep and your old man will weep and the sky will get all misty-like and shed the prettiest tears you ever did see! How'll I do it?! Girl, I'll just do it!

Noah: Where'd you ever bring rain before?

Lizzie: What town? What state?

Starbuck: Sister, the last place I brought rain is now called Starbuck—they named it after me! Dry? I tell you, those people didn't have enough damp to blink their eyes! So I get out my big wheel and my rolling drum and my yella hat with the three little feathers in it! I look up at the sky and I say: "Cumulus!" I say: "Cumulo-nimbus! Nimbulo-cumulus!" And pretty soon—way up there—there's a teeny little cloud the size of a mare's tail—and then over there—there's another cloud lookin' like a white-washed chicken house! And then I look up and all of a sudden there's a herd of white buffalo stampedin' across the sky! And then, sister-of-all-good-people, down comes the rain! *(Crosses to door R.)* Rain in buckets, rain in barrels, fillin' the lowlands, floodin' the gullies! And the land is as green as the valley of Adam! And when I rode out of there I looked behind me and I see the prettiest colors in the sky—green, blue, purple, gold— colors to make you cry! And me?! I'm ridin' right through that rainbow!—Well, how about it? Is it a deal? *(To C.)*

H.C.: Well—

Lizzie: *(Seeing her father's indecision.)* Pop—no! He's a liar and a con man!

H.C.: *(Reluctantly.)* Yep, that's what he is all right—a liar and a con man!

Starbuck: *(Gets hat.)* Hurts me to hear you say that, Mister! Well, so long to you—so long for a sorry night! *(He starts for the door.)*

H.C.: Wait a minute!

Starbuck: *(R. C.)* You said I was a con man!

H.C.: *(To L. of him.)* You're a liar and a con man—but I didn't say I wouldn't take your deal!

Lizzie: Pop—

H.C.: *(Quickly, to LIZZIE.)* I didn't say I *would,* neither!

Noah: Pop, you ain't gonna throw away a hundred bucks! How do I write it in the books?!

H.C.: Write it as a gamble, Noah! I've lost more'n that in poker on a Saturday night!

Lizzie: *(Sits on sofa.)* You get an even chance in poker!

H.C.: Lizzie, I knew an old fella once—and he had the asthma. He went to every doctor and still he coughed and still he wheezed. Then one day a liar and a con man come along and took the old man for fifty dollars and a gold-plated watch! But a funny thing——! After that con man left, the old boy never coughed one minute until the day he was kicked in the head by a horse!

Lizzie: That's a crazy reason!

Starbuck: I'll give you better reasons, Lizzie-girl! *(Crosses L. C.)* You gotta take my deal because once in your life you gotta take a chance on a con man! You gotta take my deal because there's dyin' calves that might pick up and live! Because a hundred bucks is only a hundred bucks—but rain in a dry season is a sight to behold! You gotta take my deal because it's gonna be a hot night—and the world goes crazy on a hot night—and maybe that's what a hot night is for!

H.C.: *(R. C.)* Starbuck, you got you a deal!

Starbuck: *(With a sudden smile.)* Tell you: I knew I had a deal the minute I walked into this house!

Jim: How'd you know that?

Starbuck: I see *four* of you and *five* places set for supper! And I says to myself: "Starbuck, your name's written right on that chair!" *(Picks up C. chair.)*

The following is the monologue created from the previous scene.

STARBUCK (to LIZZIE and H.C.), age mid-20s to 40.
pp. 38–43 (SAMUEL FRENCH, INC.)

Wind? Did you say wind? There's not a breath of wind anywhere in the world! The name's Starbuck! Starbuck is the name! Lady of the house—hello! That's a mighty nice dress—it oughta go to a party!

You sure should have called me. You're in a parcel of trouble. You lost twelve steers on the north range and sixty-two in the gully. The calves are starvin' and the heifers are down on their knees. *(To H.C.)* Your ranch, Mister? Well, I guess I'll talk to you. You got a look of business about you, Mister. You got your feet apart—and you stand solid on the ground! That's the kind of a man I like to talk to! Well, what are you gonna do about them cattle? Wherever I go, there's drought ahead of me! But when I leave—behind me there's rain—*rain!*

I woke up this mornin'—I looked at the world and I said to myself, "The world's gone completely out of its mind! And the only thing that can set it straight is a first class, A-number-one lunatic!" Well, here I am, folks—crazy as a bedbug! Did I introduce myself? The name is Starbuck—

rainmaker! How? Sodium chloride! Pitch it up high—right up to the clouds! Barometricize the tropopause! Magnetize occlusions in the sky! You know why that sounds like bunk? Because it is bunk! Bunk and hokey pokey! And I tell you, I'd be ashamed to use any of those methods! My method's like my name—it's all my own! You want to hear my deal? One hundred dollars in advance—and inside of twenty-four hours you'll have rain! It comes from the sky! It's a wetness known as water! Aqua pura! Mammals drink it, fish swim in it, little boys wade in it, and birds flap their wings and sing like sunrise! Water! *(To* LIZZIE.*)* I'll tell you, sister, how I'll do it! I'll lift this stick and take a long swipe at the sky and let down a shower of hailstones as big as canteloupes! I'll shout out some good old Nebraska cusswords and you turn around and there's a lake where your corral used to be! Or I'll just sing a little tune maybe and it'll sound so pretty and so sad you'll weep and your old man will weep and the sky will get all mistylike and shed the prettiest tears you ever did see! How'll I do it? Girl, I'll just do it! Sister, the last place I brought rain is now called Starbuck—they named it after me! Dry? I tell you, those people didn't have enough damp to blink their eyes! So I get out my big wheel and my rolling drum and my yella hat with the three little feathers in it! I look up at the sky and I say: "Cumulus!" I say: "Cumulo-nimbus! Nimbulo-cumulus!" And pretty soon—way up there, there's a teeny little cloud the size of a mare's tail—and then over there there's another cloud lookin' like a white-washed chicken house! And then I look up and all of a sudden there's a herd of white buffalo stampedin' across the sky! And then, sister of all good people, down comes the rain! Rain in buckets, rain in barrels, fillin' the lowlands, floodin' the gullies! And when I rode out of there I looked behind me and I see the prettiest colors in the sky—green, blue, purple, gold—colors to make you cry! And me? I'm ridin' right through that rainbow! Well, how about it, Lizzie?

Well, how about it? Is it a deal? You gotta take my deal, Lizzie-girl, because once in your life you gotta take a chance on a con man! You gotta take my deal because there's dyin' calves that might pick up and live! Because a hundred bucks is only a hundred bucks—but rain in a dry season is a sight to behold! You gotta take my deal because it's gonna be a hot night—and the world goes crazy on a hot night—and maybe that's what a hot night is for! Tell you: I knew I had a deal the minute I walked into this house! I see *four* of you and *five* places set for supper! And I says to myself: "Starbuck, your name's written right on that chair!"

This is a piece full of rich imagery. When you are doing imagery work, pleasant or ugly imagery, you must be able to convey to us that you are actually seeing what it is you are describing or feeling or smelling or fearing or whatever. Take your time while you are talking about these things. Make us wait, but not too long. Don't say the words until you see the image. This, of course, is achieved through intense rehearsals where you will return to your beginning technique exercises, sense memory, and memory recall.

An example of the imagery is "It's a wetness known as water!" Before you say that line, smell fresh water, feel it falling on you, recall when you swam in a lake or the ocean on a hot day and how cool and refreshed you felt, remember how thirsty and hot and parched you felt and then drank a glass of fresh cold water. Bring these remembrances to the rehearsal stage so that you may bring them with you to the audition stage, which is really your performance stage for your first audience.

"Mammals drink it, fish swim in it, little boys wade in it, and birds flap their wings and sing like sunrise!" Before you say that line and before each image first see a deer drinking from a brook, see the fish swimming, see and hear little boys playing in water at a fire hydrant or at a fountain or in the shallow part of a pool (as you once did and had the time of your life—remember?), see birds in a birdbath or a puddle cooling themselves, washing themselves, flapping their wings; hear them singing with delight; and see that beautiful sunrise. (Surely you've seen one—if not, get out there tomorrow morning and see what you've been missing, you owe this to yourself.)

Do these exercises and all the rest for the entire monologue filled with imagery at the beginning of each rehearsal. Rehearse this monologue at least ten times. This monologue is longer than two minutes. Time it after you've rehearsed it at least four times and then begin to cut what you feel you can live without if you know the auditor will only let you go on for two minutes. Otherwise leave it alone and do it as it is.

Starbuck is as grand and splendid and noble as the sky itself. He sees, reacts to, and responds to the beauty around him. He also needs money very badly. He's sharp, clever, creative, poetic, romantic, dramatic, and a con man. He's the most charming man seen by just about all the folks he comes into contact with wherever he goes.

Make the choice that Lizzie is beautiful in a very different way from other women. You feel because of her that somehow today is going to be a very important day for you. Perhaps the most important day in your entire life. You sense there is magic here. You know it. She and her family do not. Today is the day you've got to change your life. You also want to believe in yourself. You usually take off with your money before they realize there will be no rain. You don't want that to happen today. You really must believe, yourself, that it *will* rain. Because of Lizzie. You've fallen in love with her already. She can help you to change your life.

So play off those wonderful words and imagery and play each event—and create your play within the play; all this is your inner life that will strengthen your performance and get you that call-back.

THE RAINMAKER
by N. Richard Nash

pp. 49–52 (SAMUEL FRENCH, INC.)

Starbuck: *(Tenses, then controls his anger.)* Lizzie, can I ask you a little question?

Lizzie: No!

Starbuck: I'll ask it anyway. Why are you fussin' at the buttons on your dress?

Lizzie: Fussing at the—! I'm not! *(And she stops doing it.)*

Starbuck: *(Evenly, gently.)* Let 'em alone. They're all buttoned up fine. *(Circles to L. of her.)* As tight as they'll ever get—And it's a nice dress too. Brand new, ain't it? You expectin' somebody?

Lizzie: None of your business.

Starbuck: A woman gets all decked out—she must be expectin' her beau. Where is he?—it's gettin' kinda late.

Lizzie: *(Breaking out.)* I'm not expecting anybody! *(To C.)*

Starbuck: *(Quietly.)* Oh, I see. You were—but now you ain't. Stand you up?

Lizzie: Mr. Starbuck, you've got more gall—! *(And she starts for the stairs. But he grabs her arm.)*

Starbuck: Wait a minute!

Lizzie: Let go of me!

Starbuck: *(Tensely.)* The question I really wanted to ask you before—it didn't have nothin' to do with buttons! It's this: The minute I walked into your house—you didn't like me! Why?!

Lizzie: I said let go!

Starbuck: *(Letting her go.)* You didn't like me—why? Why'd you go up on your hind legs like a frightened mare?!

Lizzie: I wasn't frightened, Mr. Starbuck! You paraded yourself in here—and you took over everything! I don't like to be taken by a con man!

Starbuck: *(Lashing out.)* Wait a minute! I'm sick and tired of this! I'm tired of you queerin' my work, callin' me out of my name!

Lizzie: I called you what you are—a big-mouthed liar and a fake!

Starbuck: *(With mounting intensity.)* How do you know I'm a liar? How do you know I'm a fake? Maybe I *can* bring rain! Maybe when I was born God whispered a special word in my ear! Maybe He said: "Bill Starbuck, you ain't gonna have much in this world! You ain't gonna have no wife and no kids—no green little house to come home to! But Bill Starbuck—wherever you go—you'll bring rain!" Maybe that's my one and only blessing!

Lizzie: *(To L. of sofa.)* There's no such blessing in the world!

Starbuck: *(C.)* I seen even *better* blessings, Lizzie-girl! I got a brother who's a doctor! You don't have to tell him where you ache or where you pain! He just comes in and lays his hand on your heart and pretty soon you're breathin' sweet again! And I got another brother who can sing—and when he's singin', that song is *there!*—and never leaves you! *(With an outcry.)* I used to think—why ain't *I* blessed like Fred or Arny? Why am I just a nothin' man, with nothin' special to my name? And then one summer comes the drought—and Fred can't *heal* it away and Arny can't *sing* it away! But me—I go down to the hollow and I look up and I say: "Rain! Dammit!—*please!*—bring rain!" And the rain came! And I knew—I knew I was one of the family!

(She sits, L. end of sofa.)

(Suddenly quiet, angry with himself.) That's a story. You don't have to believe it if you don't want to. *(He sits, R. end of sofa.)*

Lizzie: *(A moment. She is affected by the story—but she won't let herself be. She pulls herself together with some effort.)* I *don't* believe it!

Starbuck: You're like Noah! You don't believe in anything!

Lizzie: That's not true!

Starbuck: Yes it is. You're scared to believe in anything! You put the fancy dress on—and the beau don't come! So you're scared that *nothin'll ever come!* You got no faith!

Lizzie: *(Crying out.)* I've got as much as anyone!

Starbuck: You don't even know what faith is! And I'm gonna tell you! It's believin' you see white when your eyes tell you black! It's knowin'—with your heart!

Lizzie: And I know you're a fake.

Starbuck: *(In sudden commiseration.)* Lizzie, I'm sad about you. You don't believe in nothin'—not even in yourself! You don't even believe you're a woman. And if you *don't*—you're *not!* *(He turns on his heel and goes outdoors.)*

The following is the monologue created from the previous scene.

STARBUCK (to LIZZIE), age mid-20s to 40.
pp. 49–52 (SAMUEL FRENCH, INC.)

Lizzie, can I ask you a little question? Why are you fussin' at the buttons on your dress? Let 'em alone. They're all buttoned up fine. As tight as they'll ever get. And it's a nice dress too. Brand new, ain't it? You expectin' somebody? A woman gets all decked out—she must be expectin' her beau. Where is he? It's gettin' kinda late. Oh I see. You were—but now you ain't. Stand you up? The question I really wanted to ask you before—it didn't have nothin' to do with buttons! It's this: the minute I walked into your house—you didn't like me! Why?! Why'd you go up on your hind legs like a frightened mare?! I'm tired of you queerin' my work, callin' me out of my name! How do you know I'm a liar? How do you know I'm a fake? Maybe I *can* bring rain! Maybe when I was born God whispered a special word in my ear! Maybe He said, "Bill Starbuck, you ain't gonna have much in this world! You ain't gonna have no wife and no kids—no green little house to come home to! But, Bill Starbuck—wherever you go—you'll bring rain!" Maybe that's my one and only blessing! I seen even *better* blessings, Lizzie-girl! I got a brother who's a doctor. You don't have to tell him where you ache or where you pain! He just comes in and lays his hand on your heart and pretty soon you're breathin' sweet again! And I got another brother who can sing—and when he's singin', that song is *there*! And never leaves you! *(With an outcry.)* I used to think—why ain't I blessed like Fred or Arny? Why am I just a nothin' man, with nothin' special to my name? And then one summer comes the drought—and Fred can't *heal* it away and Arny can't *sing* it away! But me—I go down to the hollow and I look up and I say, "Rain! Dammit! —*please!*—bring rain!" And the rain came! And I knew—I knew I was one of the family! That's a story. You don't have to believe it if you don't want to. You're like Noah! You don't believe in anything! You're scared to believe in anything! You put the fancy dress on—and the beau don't come! So you're scared that *nothin'll ever come!* You got no faith! You don't even know what faith is! And I'm gonna tell you! It's believin' you see white when your eyes tell you black! It's knowin'—with your heart! Lizzie, I'm sad about you. You don't believe in nothing—not even in yourself! You don't even believe you're a woman. And if you *don't*— you're *not!*

You know what you're talking about. You've *got* to believe in yourself. You've gone through what Lizzie is going through: self-doubt, low self-esteem, feeling like a nothing. Teach her what you have learned, what you now know. Believing in yourself is the *most* important thing in the world. Then you can make things happen and only then. And you love Lizzie and want her but she's got to feel good about herself before she can feel good about you. And if you can help her, it will reaffirm your own beliefs, which you must constantly do. You're fighting for her to love you so you can have a better life.

THE RAINMAKER
by N. Richard Nash

pp. 61–74 (SAMUEL FRENCH, INC.)

Lizzie: *(With surface laughter, with bravura.)* Of course not. I'm perfect!—everybody knows I'm perfect! A very nice girl—good housekeeper, bright mind, very honest! So damn honest it kills me! How about a sandwich?

H.C.: *(Puzzled by her mood. More definitely than before.)* No, thanks.

Lizzie: *You gotta get a man like a man gets got!* That's what Noah said. *(Laughing.)* Now isn't that stupid? Why, it's not even good English!

H.C.: *(Soberly.)* Don't think about that, Lizzie. *(Sits R. of table.)*

Lizzie: *(Protesting too much.)* Think about it?—why, I wouldn't give it a second thought! *(Abruptly.)* Pop, do you know what that Starbuck man said to me?!

H.C.: *(Quietly.)* What, Lizzie?

Lizzie: No—why repeat it? A man like that—if you go repeating what people like that have to say—! *(Abruptly.)* Why doesn't it rain?! What we need is a flood— *(With sudden gaiety.)* —a great big flood—end of the world—ta-ta—goo'bye! *(Abruptly serious.)* Pop, can a woman take lessons in being a woman?

H.C.: You don't have to take lessons! You are one!

Lizzie: *(Here it is!—the outcry.)* Starbuck says I'm not!!!!

H.C.: *(A split second of surprise on H.C.'s part.)* —If Starbuck don't see the woman in you, he's blind!

Lizzie: Is File blind? *Are they all blind? (Then, with deepening pain.)* Pop, I'm sick and tired of *me!* I want to get out of *me* for a while—be somebody else!

H.C.: Go down to the Social Club and be Lily Ann Beasley—is that what you want to be?

Lizzie: Lily Ann Beasley knows how to get along!

332

H.C.: Then you better call her on the telephone—ask her to let you join up!

Lizzie: *(Defiantly.)* I will!—you see if I don't! And I'm going to buy myself a lot of new dresses—cut way down to here! And I'll get myself some bright lip rouge—and paint my mouth so it looks like I'm always whistling!

H.C.: Fine!—go ahead!—look like a silly little jackass!

Lizzie: It won't be *me* looking silly—it'll be somebody else! You've got to hide what you are! You can't be honest!

H.C.: *(Angrily.)* You wouldn't know how to be anything else!

Lizzie: Oh, wouldn't I?—wouldn't I?! You think it's hard?—it's easy! Watch me—it's easy—look at this! *(She crosses the room, swinging her hips voluptuously. When she speaks it is with a silly, giggling voice—imitating Lily Ann. She addresses her father as if he were Phil Mackie, the town oaf.)* "Why, Phil Mackie!—how goodie-good-lookin' you are! Such curly blond hair, such pearly white teeth! C'n I count your teeth? One—two—three—four—nah—nah, mustn't bite! And all those muscle-ie muscles! Ooh, just hard as stone, that's what they are, hard as stone! Oh dear, don't tickle—don't tickle— or little Lizzie's gonna roll right over and dee-I-die! *(She is giggling uproariously.)*

(As she continues this makeshow game, she carries herself into convulsions of laughter. And H.C., seeing that she has unintentionally satirized the very thing she proposes to emulate, has joined her laughter. While this has been going on, they haven't noticed that FILE has appeared in the open doorway—and has witnessed most of LIZZIE's improvisation.)

File: Good evening.

(The laughter in the room stops. LIZZIE, at L. is stock still in mortification.)

H.C.: *(Rises to C.)* Hello, File. Come in.

File: Kinda late. I hope I'm not disturbin' you.

H.C.: No—no! We were just—well, I don't know *what* we were doin'—but come on in!

File: *(Entering to C. Quietly.)* Hello, Lizzie.

Lizzie: Hello, File.

File: No—uh—no let-up in the drought, is there?

Lizzie: Just—none—at all.

File: *(Uncomfortably—to H.C.)* H.C., I got to thinkin' about the little fuss I had with Jimmy and—about his eye and—well—I wanted to apologize. I'm sorry.

H.C.: *(To L. of table, with a hidden smile.)* You said that this afternoon, File.

File: But I didn't say it to Jim.

H.C.: That's true—you didn't. *(With a quick look at* LIZZIE.*)* He's upstairs—I'll send him down.

(And quickly H.C. *starts up the stairs. But* LIZZIE, *seeing it is her father's plan to leave her alone with* FILE, *takes a quick step toward the stairs and, all innocence, calls up to* JIM.*)*

Lizzie: Oh, Jim—Jimmy—can you come down for a minute?

H.C.: *(With studied casualness.)* That's all right, Lizzie.—I was goin' up anyway.

(And giving her no choice, he disappears from sight upstairs. LIZZIE *and* FILE *are both aware of* H.C.'s *maneuver. They are both painfully embarrassed, unable to meet one another's glance.)*

Lizzie: *(Just to fill the silence.)* How about a cup of coffee?

File: No, thank you.—I already had my supper.

Lizzie: *(Embarrassed at the mention of "supper.")* Yes—yes of course.

File: *(Seeing her embarrassment.)* I didn't mean to mention supper—sorry I said it.

Lizzie: *(Up L. C.)* How about some nice cold lemonade?

File: No, thank you.

Lizzie: *(In agony—talking compulsively.)* I make lemonade with limes. I guess if you make it with limes you can't really call it *lemon*-ade, can you?

File: *(Generously—to put her at ease.)* You can if you want to. No law against it.

Lizzie: But it's really *lime*-ade, isn't it?

File: Yep—that's what it is, all right!

Lizzie: *(Taking his mannish tone.)* That's what it is, all right!

(An impasse—nothing more to talk about. At last JIM *appears. He comes down the steps quickly—and he is all grins that* FILE *is visiting.)*

Jim: You call me, Lizzie?—Hey, File.

File: Hello, Jim—My, that's a bad eye. I came around to say I'm sorry.

Jim: *(Delighted to have* FILE *here, he is all forgiveness. Crosses to him C. Expansively:)* Oh, don't think nothin' of it, File! Bygones is bygones!

File: Glad to hear you talk that way.

Jim: Sure—sure.

> *(An awkward silence.)*
>
> *(*JIM's *grin fills the whole room. He looks from one to the other, not knowing what to say, not knowing how to get out. Abruptly.)* Well—well! File's here, huh?
>
> *(Silence.)*
>
> *(On a burst of enthusiasm.)* Yessir—he certain'y is!
>
> *(And, in sheer happy animal spirits, he gives one loud whack at the drum—and races out R. He leaves a vacuum behind him.)*

File: Was that Jim's drum I been hearin'?

Lizzie: —Yes.

File: *(With a dry smile.)* Didn't know he was musical.

Lizzie: *(Smiling at his tiny little joke.)* Uh—wouldn't you like to sit down—or something?

File: No, thank you— *(Looking in the direction of* JIM *and* H.C.*)* I guess they both knew I was lyin'.

Lizzie: Lying? About what?

File: I didn't come around to apologize to Jim.

Lizzie: What did you come for, File?

File: To get something off my chest. *(His difficulties increasing.)* This afternoon—your father—he—uh— *(Diving in.)* Well, there's a wrong impression goin' on in the town—that I'm a widower. Well, I'm not!

Lizzie: *(Quietly—trying to ease things for him. To sofa; sits.)* I know that, File.

File: I know you know it—but I gotta say it! *(Blurting it out.)* I'm a divorced man!

Lizzie: You don't have to talk about it if you don't—

File: *(To L. C., interrupting roughly.)* Yes I do! I came to tell the truth! I've been denyin' that I'm a divorced man—well, now I admit it! That's all I want to say— *(Angrily.)* —and that squares me with everybody!

Lizzie: *(Soberly.)* Does it?

File: Yes it does! And from here on in—if I want to live alone—all by myself—it's nobody's business but my own!

(He has said what he thinks he came to say. And having said

*it, he turns on his heel and starts to beat a hasty retreat.
But* LIZZIE *stops him.)*

Lizzie: *(Sharply.)* Wait a minute! *(As he turns, she rises; to C. chair.)* You're dead wrong!

File: Wrong? How?

Lizzie: *(Hotly.)* It's everybody's business!

File: How do you figure that, Lizzie?

Lizzie: Because you owe something to people!

File: I don't owe anything to anybody!

Lizzie: Yes you do!

File: What?!

Lizzie: *(Inarticulate—upset.)* I don't know—friendship! If somebody holds out his hand toward you, you've got to reach! —and take it!

File: *(To up R. C.)* What do you mean I've got to?!

Lizzie: *(In an outburst.)* Got to! There are too many people alone—! And if you're lucky enough for somebody to want you—for a friend—! *(With a cry.)* It's an *obligation!*

(Stillness. He is deeply disturbed by what she has said; even more disturbed by her impassioned manner.)

File: This—this ain't something the two of us can settle by just talkin' for a minute.

Lizzie: *(Tremulously.)* No—it isn't.

File: *(A move toward her.)* It'll take some time.

Lizzie: —Yes. *(Sits on sofa.)*

(A spell has been woven between them. Suddenly it is broken by NOAH's *entrance. Coming in by way of the front door, he is surprised to see* FILE.)

Noah: Oh, you here, File?

File: Yeah, I guess I'm here.

Noah: *(Looking for an excuse to leave.)* Uh—just comin' in for my feed book.

(He gets one of his ledgers from cupboard and goes out the front door. It looks as though the charmed moment is lost between them.)

File: *(Going to the door.)* Well—

Lizzie: *(Afraid he will leave.)* What were we saying?

File: What were *you* sayin'?

Lizzie: *(Snatching for a subject that will keep him here.)* I—you were telling me about your divorce.

File: No—I wasn't— *(Then, studying her, he changes his mind.)* —but I will. *(As he moves a step back into the room.)* She walked out on me.

Lizzie: I'm sorry.

File: Yes—with a schoolteacher. He was from Louisville.

Lizzie: *(Helping him get it said.)* Kentucky? *(As he nods.)* Was she—I guess she was beautiful—?

File: *(A step toward her.)* Yes, she was.

Lizzie: *(Her hopes dashed.)* That's what I was afr— *(Catching herself.)* —that's what I thought.

File: Black hair.

Lizzie: *(Drearily, with an abortive little movement to her un-black hair.)* Yes—black hair's pretty, all right.

File: I always used to think: If a woman's got pitch black hair she's already half way to bein' a beauty.

Lizzie: *(Agreeing—but without heart.)* Oh yes—at least half way!

File: *(At C. chair. Suddenly, intensely, like a dam bursting.)* With a schoolteacher, dammit!—ran off with a schoolteacher!

Lizzie: —What was *he* like?

File: *(Moves chair L. and sits. With angry intensity.)* He had weak hands and nearsighted eyes!—and he always looked like he was about ready to faint!—and she ran off with *him!* And there *I* was—!

Lizzie: *(Gently.)* Maybe the teacher needed her and you didn't.

File: Sure I needed her!

Lizzie: Did you tell her so?

File: *(Raging.)* No I didn't! Why should I?!

Lizzie: *(Astounded.)* Why *should* you? Why *didn't* you?

File: Look here! There's one thing I've learned! *Be independent!* If you don't *ask* for things—if you don't let on you *need* things—pretty soon you *don't* need 'em!

Lizzie: *(Desperately.)* There are some things you *always* need!

File: *(Doggedly.)* I won't ask for anything!

Lizzie: But if you *had* asked her, she might have stayed!

File: I know darn well she mighta stayed! The night she left she said to me: "File, tell me not to go! Tell me don't go!"

Lizzie: *(In wild astonishment.)* And you didn't?!

File: I tried—I couldn't!

Lizzie: Oh, pride—!

File: Look, if a woman wants to go, let her go! If you have to hold her back—*it's no good!*

Lizzie: File, if you had to do it over again—

File: (*Interrupting, intensely.*) I still wouldn't ask her to stay! .

Lizzie: (*In a rage against him.*) Just *two words!*—"*don't go!*"—you wouldn't say them?

File: It's not the words! It's beggin'—and I won't beg!

Lizzie: You're a fool!

(*It's a slap in the face. A dreadful moment for an overly proud, stubborn man. A dreadful moment for* LIZZIE. *It is a time for drastic measures—or he will go. Having failed with* FILE *on an honest, serious level, she seizes upon flighty falsity as a mode of behavior. Percipitously, she becomes Lily Ann Beasley, the flibbertigibbet. He rises; to up L. C.) Chattering. With false, desperate. laughter.*) Whatever am I doing?—getting so serious with you, File! I shoulda known better—because whenever I do, I put my foot in it! Because bein' serious—that's not my nature! I'm really a happy-go-lucky girl—just like any other girl and I—would you like some grapes? (*R. of him, hands him bowl from table.*)

File: (*Quietly.*) No, thank you.

Lizzie: (*Giddily.*) They're very good! And so purply and pretty! We had some right after supper! Oh, I wish you'd been here to supper! I made such a nice supper! I'm a good cook—and I just love cookin'! I think there's only one thing I like better than cookin'! Readin' a book! (*Gets book from sofa.*) Do you read very much?

File: (*Watching her as if she were a strange specimen.*) No. Only legal circulars—from Washington.

Lizzie: (*L. of him. Seizing on any straw to engage him in the nonsensical chit-chat.*) Oh, Washington!—I just got through readin' a book about him! What a great man! Don't you think Washington was a great man?!

File: (*Drily.*) Father of our country. (*Puts bowl back on table.*)

Lizzie: Yes—exactly! (*More Lily Ann Beasley than ever.*) Oh my!—what a nice tie! I just die for men in black silk bow ties!

File: (*Quietly—getting angry.*) It ain't silk—it's celluloid!

Lizzie: No!—I can't believe it! It looks so real—it looks so real!

File: (*Significantly—like a blow.*) It ain't real—it's fake!

Lizzie: (*Unable to stop herself.*) And when you smile—you've got the strongest white teeth!

File: *(Angrily.)* Quit that!

Lizzie: *(Stunned.)* What—?

File: *(Raging.)* Quit it! Stop sashayin' around like a dumb little flirt!

Lizzie: *(With a moan.)* Oh no—

File: Silk tie—strong white teeth! What do you take me for? And what do you take yourself for?!

Lizzie: *(In flight, in despair.)* I was trying to—trying to—

File: Don't be so damn ridiculous! Be yourself!

(Saying which he leaves quickly. Alone, LIZZIE *is at her wits' end—humiliated, ready to take flight from everything, mostly from herself.* H.C. *enters.)*

H.C.: *(Enters from upstairs.)* What happened, Lizzie?

Jim: *(Rushes in R.)* What'd he do?—run out on you?! What happened?!

Noah: *(Comes hurrying in from R.)* I never seen a man run so fast! Where'd he go?

Lizzie: *(Berserk—to all of them.)* My God, were you watching a show? Did you think it was lantern slides?

Jim: What'd he say?

Noah: What'd *you* say?

Lizzie: I didn't say anything! Not one sensible thing! I couldn't even talk to him!

H.C.: But you were talkin'!

Lizzie: *(On floor, R. end of sofa.)* No! I was sashaying around like Lily Ann Beasley! I was making a fool of myself! Why can't I ever *talk* to anybody!?

H.C.: Lizzie, don't blame yourself! It wasn't your fault!

Noah: *(Savagely.)* No! It wasn't her fault—and it wasn't File's fault! *(Squaring off at his father.)* And you know damn well whose fault it was!

H.C.: *(On step L.)* You mean it was mine, Noah?

Noah: You bet it was yours!

Lizzie: *(Seeing a fight—trying to head it off.)* Noah—Pop—

H.C.: No! He's got to explain that!

(At this point, STARBUCK *appears at the R. doorway. He leans against the doorframe, silent, listening.)*

Noah: *(Accepting* H.C.'s *challenge.)* I'll explain it all right! You been building up a rosy dream for her—and she's got no right to hope for it!

H.C.: She's got a right to hope for anything!

Noah: No! She's gotta face the facts—and you gotta help her face them! Stop tellin' her lies!

H.C.: *(Crosses up R.)* I never told her a lie in my life!

Noah: You told her nothin' *but* lies. She's the smartest girl in the world! She's beautiful! And that's the worst lie of all! Because you know she's not beautiful! *She's plain!!*

Jim: Noah, you quit that!

Noah: *(Whirling on JIM, up L.)* And you go right along with him! *(Whipping around to LIZZIE.)* But you better listen to me! I'm the only one around here that loves you enough to tell you the truth! You're plain!

Jim: *(Violently.)* Dammit, Noah—you quit it!

Noah: *(To LIZZIE.)* Go look at yourself in the mirror—you're plain!

Jim: Noah!

(Saying which, JIM hurls himself at his brother. NOAH falls into chair L. of C. table. But the instant he gets to him, NOAH strikes out with a tough fist. It catches JIM hard and he goes reeling. He returns with murder in his eye, but NOAH slaps him across the face, grabs the boy and forces him back to the table. Meanwhile, a frenetic outburst from H.C. and LIZZIE:)

H.C. and Lizzie: Noah—Jim—stop it! Stop it, both of you—stop it!

(And simultaneously, STARBUCK rushes forward and breaks the two men apart. Out of NOAH's grip, JIM goes berserk, bent on killing NOAH. But STARBUCK holds him off.)

Jim: *(Through tears and rage.)* Let me go, Starbuck—let me go!

Starbuck: *(Holding JIM down C.)* Quit it, you damn fool—quit it!

Jim: *(With a cry.)* Let go!

Starbuck: Get outside! *(Letting him go.)* Now go on—get outside!

Jim: *(Weeping.)* Sure—I'll get outside! I'll get outside and never come back! *(And in an outburst of tears, JIM rushes out R.)*

(LIZZIE crosses to door R.)

Noah: The next time that kid goes at me, I'll—I'll—

Starbuck: The next time he goes at you, I'll see he has fightin' lessons!

Noah: Look, you—clear out of here!

Starbuck: No, I won't clear out! And while I'm here, you're gonna quit callin' that kid a dumbbell!—because he's not! He can take a lousy little hickory stick—and he can see magic in it! But you wouldn't understand that!—because it's not in your books!

Noah: (*To door R.*) I said clear out!

Starbuck: (*Above* LIZZIE. *He cannot be stopped.*) And while I'm here, don't you ever call her plain! Because you don't know what's plain and what's beautiful!

Noah: Starbuck, this is family—it's not your fight!

Starbuck: Yes it is! I been fightin' fellas like you all my life! And I always lose! But this time—by God, this time—!

(*He reins himself in, then hurries out R. We hear his voice calling "Jimmy!"* NOAH *breaks the stillness with quiet deliberateness:*)

Noah: (*To* LIZZIE *and* H.C.) I'm sorry I hit Jim—and I'll tell him so. But I ain't sorry for a single word I said to *her!*

H.C.: (*Angry.*) Noah, that's enough!

Noah: (*Intensely.*) No, it ain't enough! (*To* LIZZIE.) Lizzie, you better think about what I said. Nobody's gonna come ridin' up here on a white horse. Nobody's gonna snatch you up in his arms and marry you. *You're gonna be an old maid!* And the sooner you face it, the sooner you'll stop breakin' your heart. (*He goes upstairs.*)

(*Silence.*)

Lizzie: (*In doorway R. Dully—half to herself.*) Old maid—

H.C.: Lizzie, forget it. Forget everything he said. (*To L. of table.*)

Lizzie: No—he's right.

H.C.: (*With a plea.*) Lizzie—

Lizzie: He's right, Pop. I've known it a long time. But it wasn't so bad until he put a name to it. Old maid. (*With a cry of despair.*) Why is it so much worse when you put a name to it?

H.C.: Lizzie, you gotta believe me—

Lizzie: I don't believe you, Pop. You've been lying to me—
and I've been lying to myself!

H.C.: Lizzie, honey—please—

Lizzie: *(To chest.)* Don't—don't! I've got to see things the way
they are! And the way they will be! I've got to start thinking
of myself as a spinster! Jim will get married! And one of
these days, even Noah will get married! I'll be the visiting
aunt! I'll bring presents to their children—to be sure I'm
welcome! And Noah will say: "Junior, be kind to your Aunt
Lizzie—her nerves aren't so good!" And Jim's wife will say:
"She's been visiting here a whole week now—when'll she
ever go?!" *(With an outcry.)* Go where, for God's sake—go
where?!

H.C.: *(In pain for her.)* Lizzie, you'll always have a home. This
house'll be *yours*!

Lizzie: *(Crossing to stairs L. Hysterically.)* House—house—house!

H.C.: *(R. of her, trying to calm, to comfort her.)* Lizzie, stop it!

Lizzie: Help me, Pop—tell me what to do!—help me!

The following is the monologue created from the previous
scene.

LIZZIE (to H.C.), age 30 to mid-40s.
pp. 61–74 (SAMUEL FRENCH, INC.)

I'm perfect!—everybody knows I'm perfect! A very nice
girl—good housekeeper, bright mind, very honest! So
damn honest it kills me!

"You gotta get a man like a man gets got!" That's what
Noah said. *(Laughing.)* Now isn't that stupid? Why, it's not
even good English!

Pop, can a woman take lessons in being a woman?
Starbuck says I'm not! Pop, I'm sick and tired of *me*! I want
to get out of *me* for a while—be somebody else! Lily Ann
Beasley knows how to get along! *(Defiantly.)* I'm going to
buy myself a lot of new dresses—cut way down to here!
And I'll get myself some bright lip rouge—and paint my
mouth so it looks like I'm always whistling! It won't be *me*
looking silly—it'll be somebody else! You've got to hide
what you are! You can't be honest! Watch me—it's easy—
look at this! *(Silly, giggling voice.)* Why, Phil Mackie!—how

goodie-good-lookin' you are! Such curly blond hair, such pearly white teeth! C'n I count your teeth? One-two-three-four-nah-nah-mustn't bite! And all those muscle-ie muscles. Ooh, just as hard as stone, that's what they are, hard as stone! Oh dear, don't tickle—don't tickle—or little Lizzie's gonna roll right over and dee-I-die. *(Back to normal.)* Old maid. *(With a cry of despair.)* Why is it so much worse when you put a name to it? I've got to start thinking of myself as a spinster! Jim will get married! And one of these days, even Noah will get married! I'll be the visiting aunt! I'll bring presents to their children—to be sure I'm welcome! And Noah will say, "Junior, be kind to your Aunt Lizzie—her nerves aren't so good!" And Jim's wife will say, "She's been visiting here a whole week now—when'll she ever go?!" *(With an outcry.)* Go where, for God's sake—go where? Help me, Pop—Tell me what to do!—Help me!

You want so much to be loved as a man loves a woman, not only as a father loves a daughter. A father's love is your past. A lover's love is your future. Your future is your life. What's in store for you as you get older and when your father is gone and your brothers are married? You are now seeing your future. And it is a total disaster. Today is the day that you've *got* to do something about it so that you've got a shot for romance, marriage, children, and all the rest that goes with it. Your father is the most important person in your life. He loves you and thinks you are pretty. He's *got* to guide you toward what you so desperately want and need.

THE SHADOW BOX
by Michael Cristofer

pp. 23–27 (Samuel French, Inc.)

Mark: *(Shakes her hand.)* Yes. I figured it was you.

Beverly: You did?

Mark: Yes ... it wasn't hard.

Beverly: No, I guess not. *(She smiles.)* And you're ... uh ...

Mark: Yes.

Beverly: Yes. I figured.

Mark: Mark.

Beverly: Great. Well—

Mark: Well. *(Pause.)*

Beverly: Well, now that we know who we are ... how about a drink.

Mark: A what?

Beverly: A drink. A drink.

Mark: Oh, no.

Beverly: No?

Mark: No. We don't keep any liquor here. I could get you some coffee or some penicillin, if you'd like.

Beverly: No. No. *I* was inviting *you.* *(Out of her tote bag she pulls a half finished bottle of Scotch.)* I had an accident with the Scotch on the way out here. There's quite a dent in it. *(She laughs—*MARK *doesn't.)* Anyway, we both look like we could use a little. Hmn?

Mark: No. I don't drink.

Beverly: *(Rummaging in her bag.)* Ah, a dope man.

Mark: Neither. I like to avoid as much poison as possible.

Beverly: I see.

Mark: Anyway, it's really not the time or place, is it?

Beverly: Oh, I don't know.

Mark: Well, you go ahead. If you feel you have to.

Beverly: No. No, really. I don't *need* it. I mean, I'm not ... forget

344

it. (*She looks remorsefully at the bottle, takes off the cap, takes a swig, replaces the cap and puts the bottle back in the tote bag.* MARK *stares at her, obviously displeased by the action. There is a pause.* BEVERLY *smiles.* MARK *does not.*) So. How is he?

Mark: Dying. How are you?

Beverly: (*Taken aback.*) Ooooops. Let's start again. Is he feeling any pain?

Mark: Are you?

Beverly: Strike two. Well, I think we've got it all straight now. He's dying. I'm drunk. And you're pissed off. Did I leave anything out?

Mark: No, I think that just about covers it.

Beverly: Tell me. How is he?

Mark: Hard to say. One day he's flat on his ass, the next day he's running around like a two-year-old. But he is terminal—officially. They moved him down to these cottages because there's nothing they can do for him in the hospital. But he can't go home, either. There's some pain. But it's tolerable. At least he makes it seem tolerable. They keep shooting him full of cortisone.

Beverly: Ouch!

Mark: Yes. Ouch. You should be prepared, I guess.

Beverly: Prepared for what?

Mark: The cortisone.

Beverly: Why? They don't give it to the visitors, do they?

Mark: No. I mean it has side effects. It . . . well, you may not notice it, but the skin goes sort of white and puffy. It changed the shape of his face for a while, and he started to get really fat.

Beverly: His whole body?

Mark: Yes. His whole body.

Beverly: Charming.

Mark: Well, don't get too upset. A lot of it's been corrected, but he's still very pale. And he has fainting spells. They're harmless. Well, that's what they tell me. But it's embarrassing for him because he falls down a lot and his face gets a little purple for a minute.

Beverly: All the details. You're very graphic.

Mark: It happens a lot. The details aren't easy to forget.

Beverly: I guess not.

Mark: I just want you to know. If you're staying around. I mean, I think it would hurt him if people noticed.

Beverly: Well, if he turns purple and falls on the floor, it'd be sort of difficult not to notice, wouldn't it?

Mark: *(Taken aback.)* What?

Beverly: I mean, what do people *usually* do when it happens?

Mark: I don't know. I mean, there hasn't been anyone here except me and . . .

Beverly: And you have everything pretty much under control.

Mark: I do my best.

Beverly: I'm sure you do.

Mark: Look. I don't mean to be rude or stupid about this . . .

Beverly: Why not? I like people to be rude and stupid. It's one of the ways you can be sure they're still alive. Oh dear, I did it again, didn't I?

Mark: Yes. You have to understand—I mean, you will be careful, won't you?

Beverly: About what?

Mark: That's exactly what I mean. You're . . . I'm sorry, but you're very stoned, aren't you? And you're dressed in funny clothes, and you're saying a lot of funny things but I'm just not sure, frankly, what the fuck you're doing here.

Beverly: *(Still flip.)* Neither am I. You sure you wouldn't like a drink?

Mark: Positive. Look, please, don't you think it'd be better if you came back some other time, like tomorrow or next year or something?

Beverly: I'd just have to get drunk all over again.

Mark: I mean, it's sort of a delicate situation, right now. He's had a very bad time of it and any kind of, well, disturbance . . .

Beverly: Such as me? Oh, you'll get used to it. You just have to think of me as your average tramp.

Mark: . . . any disturbance might be dangerous, especially psychologically and . . . Shit! I sound like an idiot, the way I'm talking. But you don't seem to be understanding a goddamn word I'm saying!

Beverly: No. I am. I am. You know, you don't *look* like a faggot.

Mark: Oh, for Christ's sake!

Beverly: No, I mean it . . . I mean, I didn't expect . . .

Mark: Well, you'll get used to it. You just have to think of me as your average cocksucker. All right?

Beverly: Good. Now we're getting someplace. Are you sure you wouldn't like a drink?

Mark: *No!* I would not like a drink. *You* have a drink. Have two. Take off your clothes. Make yourself at home. *(He grabs his jacket and heads for the door.)* When you're ready to throw up, the bathroom is in there. *(He exits.)*

The following is the monologue created from the previous scene.

MARK (to BEVERLY), age 20s to 40.
pp. 23–27 (SAMUEL FRENCH, INC.)

I figured it was you. It wasn't hard. No. We don't keep any liquor here. I could get you some coffee or some penicillin, if you'd like. I don't drink. I like to avoid as much poison as possible. Anyway, it's really not the time or place, is it? You go ahead. If you feel you have to.

Brian is dying! How are you? One day he's flat on his ass, the next day he's running around like a two-year-old. But he is terminal—officially. They moved him down to these cottages because there's nothing they can do for him in the hospital. But he can't go home, either. There's some pain. But it's tolerable. At least he makes it seem tolerable. They keep shooting him full of cortisone. You should be prepared, I guess. I mean it has side effects. It . . . well, you may not notice it but the skin goes sort of white and puffy. It changed the shape of his face for a while, and he started to get really fat. Don't get too upset. A lot of it's been corrected, but he's still very pale. And he has fainting spells. They're harmless. Well, that's what they tell me. But it's embarrassing for him because he falls down a lot and his face gets a little purple for a minute. It happens a lot. The details aren't easy to forget. I just want you to know. If you're staying around. I mean, I think it would hurt him if people noticed. There hasn't been anyone here except me. I do my best. Look. I don't mean to be rude or stupid about this. You have to understand—I mean, you will be careful, won't you? I'm sorry, but you're very stoned, aren't you? And you're dressed in funny clothes, and you're saying a lot of funny things but I'm just not sure, frankly, what the fuck you're doing here. Don't you think it'd be better if you came back some other time, like tomorrow or next year or something? I mean, it's sort of a delicate situation, right now. He's had a very bad time of it and any kind of, well, disturbance, any disturbance might be dangerous, especially psychologically and . . . shit! I sound like an idiot, the way I'm talking. But you don't seem to be understanding a goddamn word I'm saying! Have a drink. Have two. Take off your clothes. Make yourself at home! When you're ready to throw up, the bathroom is in there.

First of all it is very important when you are announcing your name, the name of the play, and the name of your character, to tell the auditors that you are not doing the monologue they think you are doing. Put them at ease immediately. We are so completely tired of seeing that same monologue over and over again that appears on pages 68 to 71 of the Samuel French edition and also Beverly's monologue on pages 71 and 72 of the same edition.

Here is a monologue that deals with a third person. Brian is not in this play but he is the one you are talking about. Please remember, however, that the monologue is about you and the person to whom you are talking, not the person you are talking about. Therefore, give yourself a rich inner life of need for Beverly. It is her whom you need to help you, to tell you how wonderful you are for what you have been doing for Brian, to help you to care for him, to take your place in taking care of him, to love you. Yes, you are concerned about her drinking and joking around and rather frivolous behavior and you don't quite understand why she is even here in the first place. But how wonderful if she were here because she actually cares. That is what you wish for although you see no signs of it by her actions. But she was married to Brian at one time and surely she must know how wonderful a person he is and somewhere within her party-animal exterior, there *must* be some humanity! Shock it out of her. You are being flippant, sardonic, and mordant in describing Brian's condition. His condition is so horrendous and grim that underplaying the portrayal in the telling makes it that more terrible. Let it all out at the end. Really let her have it.

THE SHADOW BOX
by Michael Cristofer

pp. 39–43 (Samuel French, Inc.)

Brian: Pure and unadulterated masochism. No. It's just that
when they told me I was on the way out . . . so to speak . . . I
realized that there was a lot to do that I hadn't done yet. So
I figured I better get off my ass and start working.

Beverly: Doing what?

Brian: Everything! Everything! Everything! It's amazing what you can accomplish. Two rotten novels, twenty-seven boring stories,
several volumes of tortured verse—including twelve Italian
sonnets and one epic investigation of the Firth of Forth
Bridge . . .

Beverly: The what?

Brian: The bridge. The railroad bridge in Scotland. The one
Hitchcock used in 'The Thirty-Nine Steps.' You remember.
We saw the picture on our honeymoon.

Beverly: Oh, yes.

Brian: And I swore that one day I would do a poem about it.
Well, I've done it.

Beverly: Thank God.

Brian: Yes. Four hundred stanzas—trochaic hexameters with
rhymed couplets. (*He demonstrates the rhythm.*) Da-da-da,
Da-da-da, *Da*-da-da, *Da*-da-da, *Da*-da-da, *Da*-da-da, *Da*-da-
da-*Dee!* It's perfectly ghastly. But it's done. I've also completed nearly one hundred and thirty-six epitaphs, the largest contribution to the Forest Lawn catalogue since Edna St.
Vincent Millay, and I've also done four autobiographies.

Beverly: Four?!

Brian: Yes. Each one under a different name. There's a huge
market for dying people right now. My agent assured me.

Beverly: I don't believe it.

Brian: It's true. And then we thought we'd give them each one of those insipid dirty titles—Like 'Sex . . . And the Dying Man'!

Beverly: Or 'The Sensuous Corpse.'

Brian: Very good.

Beverly: *(Affectionately.)* You idiot. What else?

Brian: Not too much. For a while they were giving me this drug and my vision was doubled. I couldn't really see to write. So I started to paint.

Beverly: Paint?

Brian: Pictures. I did fourteen of them. Really extraordinary stuff. I was amazed. I mean, you know I can't draw a straight line. But with my vision all cockeyed—I could do a bowl of fruit that sent people screaming from the room.

Beverly: I can believe it. So now you're painting.

Brian: No, no. They changed the medication. Now all the fruit just looks like fruit again. But I did learn to drive.

Beverly: A car?

Brian: Yes.

Beverly: Good grief.

Brian: Not very well, but with a certain style and sufficient accuracy to keep myself alive—although that is beside the point, isn't it? Let's see, what else? I've become a master at chess, bridge, poker, and mah-jongg, I finally bought a television set, I sold the house and everything that was in it, closed all bank accounts, got rid of all stocks, bonds, securities, everything.

Beverly: What did you do with the money?

Brian: I put it in a sock and buried it on Staten Island.

Beverly: You did, didn't you?

Brian: Almost. I gave back my American Express card, my BankAmericard—severed *all* my patriotic connections. I even closed my account at Bloomingdale's.

Beverly: This is serious.

Brian: You're damn right it is. I sleep only three hours a day, I never miss a dawn or a sunset, I say and do everything that comes into my head. I even sent letters to everyone I know and told them exactly what I think of them . . . just so none of the wrong people show up for the funeral. And finally . . . I went to Passaic, New Jersey.

Beverly: For God's sake, why?!

Brian: Because I had no desire to go there.

Beverly: Then why did you go?

Brian: Because I wanted to be absolutely *sure* I had no desire to go there.

Beverly: And now you know.

Brian: Yes. I spent two weeks at a Holiday Inn and had all my meals at Howard Johnson.

Beverly: Jesus! You've really gone the limit.

Brian: Believe me, Passaic is beyond the limit. Anyway, that's what I've been doing. Every day in every way, I get smaller and smaller. There's practically nothing left of me.

Beverly: You're disappearing before my very eyes.

Brian: Good. You see, the only way to beat this thing is to leave absolutely nothing behind. I don't want to leave anything unsaid, undone . . . not a word, not even a lonely, obscure, silly, worthless thought. I want it all used up. All of it. That's not too much to ask, is it?

Beverly: No.

Brian: That's what I thought. Then I can happily leap into my coffin and call it a day. Lie down, close my eyes, shut my mouth and disappear into eternity.

Beverly: As easy as that?

Brian: Like falling off a log. (BRIAN *laughs.* BEVERLY *laughs. And then the laughter slowly dies.* BEVERLY *goes to him, takes his hands, holds them for a moment. Long pause.*) It shows. Doesn't it?

Beverly: You're shaking.

Brian: I can't help it. I'm scared to death.

Beverly: It's a lot to deal with.

Brian: No. Not really. It's a little thing. I mean, all this . . . this is easy. Pain, discomfort . . . that's all part of living. And I'm just as alive now as I ever was. And I *will* be alive right up to the last moment. *That's* the hard part, that last fraction of a second—when you know that the next fraction of a second—I can't seem to fit that moment into my life . . . You're absolutely alone facing an absolute unknown and there is absolutely nothing you can do about it . . . except give in. (*Pause.*)

The following is the monologue created from the previous scene.

BRIAN (to BEVERLY), age late 30s and older.
pp. 39–43 (SAMUEL FRENCH, INC.)

When they told me I was on the way out . . . so to speak . . . I realized that there was a lot to do that I hadn't done yet.

So I figured I better get off my ass and start working. It's amazing what you can accomplish. Two rotten novels, twenty-seven boring stories, several volumes of tortured verse—including twelve Italian sonnets and one epic investigation of the Firth of Forth Bridge. The railroad bridge in Scotland. The one Hitchcock used in *The Thirty-Nine Steps*. You remember. We saw the picture on our honeymoon. I swore that one day I would do a poem about it. Well, I've done it. Four hundred stanzas. It's perfectly ghastly. But it's done. I've also completed nearly one hundred and thirty-six epitaphs, the largest contribution to the Forest Lawn catalog since Edna St. Vincent Millay, and I've also done four autobiographies. Each one under a different name. There's a huge market for dying people right now. My agent assured me. And then we thought we'd give them each one of those insipid dirty titles—like *Sex . . . and the Dying Man*! For a while they were giving me this drug and my vision was doubled. I couldn't really see to write. So I started to paint pictures. I did fourteen of them. Really extraordinary stuff. I was amazed. I mean, you know I can't draw a straight line. But with my vision all cockeyed—I could do a bowl of fruit that sent people screaming from the room. They changed the medication. Now all the fruit just looks like fruit again. But I did learn to drive. Not very well, but with a certain style and sufficient accuracy to keep myself alive—although that is beside the point, isn't it? Let's see, what else? I've become a master of chess, bridge, poker, and mah-jongg; I finally bought a television set; I sold the house and everything that was in it and closed all bank accounts, got rid of all stocks, bonds, securities, everything. I put my money in a sock and buried it on Staten Island. Almost. I gave back my American Express card, my BankAmericard—severed all my patriotic connections. I even closed my account at Bloomingdale's. I sleep only three hours a day, I never miss a dawn or a sunset, I say and do everything that comes into my head. I even sent letters to everyone I know and told them exactly what I think of them . . . just so none of the wrong people show up for the funeral. And finally . . . I went to Passaic, New Jersey, because I had no desire to go there. I wanted to be absolutely *sure* I had no desire to go there. I spent two weeks at a Holiday Inn and had all my meals at Howard Johnson. That's what I've been doing. Every day in every way, I get smaller and smaller. There's practically nothing left of me. You see, the only way to beat this thing is to leave absolutely nothing behind. I don't want to leave anything unsaid, undone . . . not a word, not even a lonely, obscure, silly, worthless thought. I want it all used up. All of it. Then I can happily leap into my coffin and call it a day. Lie down, close my eyes, shut my mouth and disappear into eternity. Like falling off a log. *(Shaking.)* I'm scared to death. All this . . . this is easy. Pain, discomfort . . . that's all part of living. And I'm just as alive now as I ever was. And I *will* be alive right up to the last moment. *That's* the hard part, that last fraction of a second—when you know that the next fraction of a second—I can't seem to fit that moment into my life. . . . You're absolutely alone facing an absolute unknown and there is absolutely nothing you can do about it . . . except give in.

This is really a memory piece. The material that I have been saying all along not to use. However, I have decided to include this one. As I was converting the scene into a monologue, I realized that it deals with the past. But then I saw that it also deals with the here and now and the future. What we don't have in this piece is the feel for the other character. By reading the play you will know to whom Brian is talking. You must reach out to the other character and make strong connections. Make sure you react off the other person. You are fighting for his or her love. You need this person to help you slip away when the time comes. As you admitted, you are scared. You've done so much on your own to fill in the sparse places in your life so that when you die you will have done everything you had wanted to do. (Perhaps you did not do *everything* you said you did but it sure makes for good conversation.) We're dealing with life and death—yours. What can you use from your life that can help you to evoke feelings dealing with impending death? I assume you are not going to die in the near future from an illness, so how then will you know how Brian feels about this event? Do not play the dying. Play the living. This monologue is not about dying. It is about living. Fight for your life. Fight for the other person, a loved one, to help you to live. Even though you need her to be there for your death (this is not in the words, it is in your inner life). As you die, at death, and after, you have no further use for her!

THE SHADOW BOX
by Michael Cristofer

pp. 59–62 (Samuel French, Inc.)

Agnes: Yes. You see, it was after Claire died that Mama started to get sick. All of a sudden, she was 'old.' And she isn't, you know. But she just seemed to give up. I couldn't bring her out of it. Claire could have. But I couldn't. We lost the farm, the house, everything. One thing led to another. The letters... uh... It was after one of the last operations. Mama came home from the hospital and she seemed very happy. She was much stronger than ever. She laughed and joked and made fun of me, just like she used to... and then she told me she had written a letter while she was in the hospital... to Claire... and she said she was very nice to her and she forgave her for not writing and keeping in touch and she asked her to come home to visit and to bring her children... Claire had been dead for a long time then. I didn't know what to do. I tried to tell her... I tried... but she wouldn't listen... And, of course, no letter came. No reply. And Mama asked every day for the mail. Every day I had to tell her no, there wasn't any. Every day. I kept hoping she would forget, but she didn't. And when there wasn't any letter for a long time, she started to get worse. She wouldn't talk and when she did she accused me of being jealous and hiding the letters and sometimes... I didn't know what to do... So... *(Pause.)*

Voice of Interviewer: How long have you been writing these letters?

Agnes: Almost two years... You're not angry with me, are you?

Voice of Interviewer: No.

Agnes: It means so much to her. It's important to her. It's something to hope for. You have to have something. People *need* something to keep them going.

354

Voice of Interviewer: Do they?

Agnes: Yes. Sometimes I think, if we can wait long enough, something will happen. Oh, not that Mama will get better, but something... So I write the letters. I don't mind. It's not difficult. I read little things in books and newspapers and I make up what's happening. Sometimes I just write whatever comes into my head. You see, Mama doesn't really listen to them anymore. She used to. It used to be the only time I could talk to her. But now it doesn't matter what they say. It's just so she knows that Claire is coming.

Voice of Interviewer: What happens when Claire doesn't show up?

Agnes: Oh, but I don't think that will happen. I mean, Mama... well, she won't... I mean, even if...

Voice of Interviewer: You mean she'll probably die before she even finds out.

Agnes: *(Nods her head.)* Yes.

Voice of Interviewer: What will *you* do then, Agnes?

Agnes: *(Surprised by the question, she looks out at the* INTERVIEWER *for a long time. Then ...)* It makes her happy.

Voice of Interviewer: Does it?

Agnes: *(More confused.)* I don't know.

Voice of Interviewer: What about you, Agnes?

Agnes: Me?

Voice of Interviewer: Does it make you happy?

Agnes: Me?

Voice of Interviewer: Yes.

Agnes: *(She touches her head lightly.)* Please, I... I should be getting back.

Voice of Interviewer: Agnes?

Agnes: Sometimes she does things now, I don't know why... I... *(Trying to accuse the* INTERVIEWER.*)* The pain is much worse. This medicine you've given her... it doesn't help.

Voice of Interviewer: Yes, we know. It may be necessary to move her up to the hospital again.

Agnes: But you said before...

Voice of Interviewer: I know.

Agnes: And now?

Voice of Interviewer: It's hard to say.

Agnes: No.

Voice of Interviewer: I'm sorry.

Agnes: No, you're not sorry. You don't know anything about

sorry. You put her in some room. You do one more operation. You wrap her up in your machines. You scribble on her
chart. And then you go away. You don't know about sorry.

Voice of Interviewer: We had thought that it wouldn't go on
this long, but there's nothing we can do about it.

Agnes: *But I don't want it to go on.* You promised . . . it can't!
Even when she's asleep now, she has dreams. I can tell. I
hear them. You keep saying, a few days, a few days. But it's
weeks and months . . . all winter and now the spring . . .

Voice of Interviewer: She has a strong will.

Agnes: *(Almost laughs.)* Oh, yes. I know that.

Voice of Interviewer: Sometimes that's enough to keep a very
sick person alive for a long time.

Agnes: But why? Why? When it hurts so bad? Why does she
want to keep going like this? Why?

The following is the monologue created from the previous
scene.

AGNES (to VOICE OF INTERVIEWER), age 20s to 40.
pp. 59–62 (SAMUEL FRENCH, INC.)

It was after Claire died that Mama started to get sick. All
of a sudden, she was "old." And she isn't, you know. But
she just seemed to give up. I couldn't bring her out of it.
Claire could have. But I couldn't. We lost the farm, the
house, everything. One thing led to another. The letters. . . . It
was after one of the last operations. Mama came home
from the hospital and she seemed very happy. She was
much stronger than ever. She laughed and joked and made
fun of me, just like she used to . . . and then she told me
she had written a letter while she was in the hospital . . . to
Claire . . . and she said she was very nice to her and she
forgave her for not writing and keeping in touch and she
asked her to come home to visit and to bring her
children . . . Claire had been dead for a long time then. I
didn't know what to do. I tried to tell her . . . I tried . . . but
she wouldn't listen. . . . And, of course, no letter came. No
reply. And Mama asked every day for the mail. Every day
I had to tell her no, there wasn't any. Every day. I kept
hoping she would forget, but she didn't. And when there

wasn't any letter for a long time, she started to get worse. She wouldn't talk and when she did she accused me of being jealous and hiding letters and sometimes . . . I didn't know what to do . . . so . . . I've been writing these letters for two years. I hope you're not angry with me. It means so much to her. It's important to her. It's something to hope for. You have to have something. People *need* something to keep them going. Sometimes I think, if we can wait long enough, something will happen. Oh, not that Mama will get better, but something. . . . So I write the letters. I don't mind. It's not difficult. I read little things in books and newspapers and I make up what's happening. Sometimes I just write whatever comes into my head. You see, Mama doesn't really listen to them anymore. She used to. It used to be the only time I could talk to her. But now it doesn't matter what they say. It's just so she knows that Claire is coming. It doesn't matter that Claire won't show up. Mama will probably die before she finds out. Sometimes she does things now, I don't know why . . . I . . . the pain is much worse. This medicine you've given her . . . it doesn't help. You put her in some room. You do one more operation. You wrap her up in your machines. You scribble on her chart. And then you go away. You don't know about sorry. *But I don't want it to go on!* You promised . . . it can't! Even when she's asleep now, she has dreams. I can tell. I hear them. You keep saying, a few days, a few days. But it's weeks and months . . . all winter and now the spring. Why does she have such a strong will? Why? When it hurts so bad? Why does she want to keep going like this? Why?

I have seen this monologue being done many times. I have never seen it done well. That is why I am including it in this book. Everyone makes the weakest choices that can be made. Nobody has made the other character a part of this scene. First of all change the other character from the voice of the interviewer to your mother's doctor, or the head doctor of the hospital. Create a real person. One from your life. Perhaps a very attractive young (or not so young) man. Or a fatherly type man. This person to whom you are talking has to be the most important person in your life. Today is the day that you've *got* to get some change around here. Your mother is suffering and going on and on. You can't take it anymore. If she suffers, you suffer. It has come to the point where she should pass on and be out of her pain and suffering. Why can't they do something? Why do they keep telling you it will be soon and she still lives just to suffer? You are fighting for this person with power in this situation to *do* something! Your life is a living nightmare as long as she lives. You are ready to let her go. But she won't let go. Why? And why won't they help her to let go instead of wrapping her in their machines? Appeal to this person to whom you are talking. If he is attractive, allow yourself to see what it is you are missing in life. Meeting a nice man like this one. Getting on with your life. Having a relationship of your own. Being in love. Living! Being happy! Having someone who loves *you*!

Fight for what you are fighting for on two levels: an altruistic and a selfish need. Ask yourself, "What's in it for me?" Don't feel guilty because you are fighting for your *own* life while your mother suffers. You are *also* fighting for her life. Because of your love for her, you want her to die. And then you can also get on with your life, if there is to be one.

When reading the entire play you will learn that the mother favored Claire. Don't get into that for this monologue. It is not necessary to deal with that part of the play. You've got enough to do with this monologue. Don't complicate things by dealing with your jealousy. This monologue is about you and the man you are talking to. You desperately need his help. You are fighting for him to love you enough to help you so that your life can change. It is *now* that you want action and change. The here and now!

THE SHADOW BOX
by Michael Cristofer

pp. 76–79 (SAMUEL FRENCH, INC.)

Joe: It would have been nice.

Maggie: What?

Joe: A farm.

Maggie: We couldn't afford it.

Joe: Some place all our own.

Agnes: Something.

Maggie: Just to watch the sunset?

Joe: Every day a different job. Every day a different reason. Something grows. Something... all in a day.

Agnes: Something...

Maggie: It would have been nice.

Joe: Something to have.

Agnes: Something...

Joe: Jesus Christ, we built the house, and before we finish, fifteen years, and it's gone.

Maggie: We didn't need it. It was more work to keep up than it was worth.

Joe: Maybe... maybe it was. But it was *something*, wasn't it? Something to have. You put in one more fucking tree, you fix up another room, I kept seeing grandchildren. What the hell else was it for? Not right away, but someday, you figure, kids running around, falling down under it, when it's grown big enough to climb and you can chase them down, spend some time running around the goddamn house...

Maggie: *(Still detached.)* The apartment is nice. It was closer to work.

Joe: *(Starting to get really angry.)* Work? Shit. Fifty weeks a year in a flat-wire shop. Twenty-four years.

Maggie: We had the saloon in between. And the oil truck...

Joe: A bartender and a truck driver in between.

Maggie: We *owned* the bar. That was ours.

Joe: Gone.

Maggie: And the truck, we owned...

Joe: All gone. Christ, even the factory is gone.

Maggie: They couldn't get along without you.

Joe: Twenty-four years. Two weeks a year at the beach. One week off for Christmas... *(Pause.)* Talk to me, Maggie. Talk to me.

Maggie: What? What can I say?

Joe: I don't know. Somebody walks up one day, one day, somebody walks up and tells you it's finished. And me... all I can say is 'what?'... *what's* finished? What did I have that's finished? What?

Maggie: We give up too easy. We don't fight hard enough. We give up... too easy...

Joe: We got to tell him, Maggie. We got to face it and tell him. Some son of a bitch walks up one day and tells you it's finished. What? What did we have that's finished?

Maggie: *(Breaking down.)* Us. Us. For Christ's sake, don't make me say things I don't understand. I don't want to hear them. I shake all over when I think about them. How long? Two weeks? Three? A month? And then what? What have I got *then*? An apartment full of some furniture I can't even keep clean for company, a closet full of some old pictures, some curtains I made out of my wedding dress that don't even fit the windows... What? What do I do? Sit down with the TV set every night, spill my coffee when I fall asleep on the sofa and burn holes in the carpet, dropping cigarettes?

Joe: Maggie...

Maggie: No. I want you to come home. What is this place, anyway? They make everything so nice. Why? So you forget? I can't. I can't. I want you to come home. I want you to stay out four nights a week bowling, and then come home so I can yell and not talk to you, you son of a bitch. I want to fight so you'll take me to a movie and by the time I get you to take me I'm so upset I can't enjoy the picture. I want to get up too early, too goddamn early, and I'll let you know about it, too, because I have to make you breakfast, because you never, never once eat it, because you make me get up too early just to keep you company and talk to you, and it's cold, and my back aches, and I got nothing to say to you and we never talk and it's six-thirty in the morning, *every* morning, even Sunday morning and it's all right . . . it's all right . . . it's all right because I *want* to be there because you need me to be there because I want *you* to be there because I want you to come home.

Joe: Maggie . . .

Maggie: Come home, that's all. Come home.

Joe: I can't, Maggie. You know I can't.

Maggie: No, I don't know. I don't.

Joe: I can't.

Maggie: You can. Don't believe what they tell you. What do they know? We've been through worse than this. You look fine. I can see it.

Joe: No, Maggie.

Maggie: You get stronger every day.

Joe: It gets worse.

Maggie: No. I can see it.

Joe: Every day, it gets worse.

Maggie: We'll go home, tomorrow. I got another ticket. We can get a plane tomorrow.

Joe: Don't do this, Maggie.

Maggie: I put a new chair in the apartment. You'll like it. It's red. You always said we should have a big red chair. I got it for you. It's a surprise.

Joe: No! It won't work.

Maggie: We'll get dressed up. I'll get my hair done. We'll go out someplace. What do we need? A little time, that's all.

Joe: It's not going to change anything.

Maggie: No. It's too fast. Too fast. What'll I do? I can't remember tomorrow. It's no good. We'll look around. Maybe we *can* find a little place. Something we like.

Joe: No. This is all. This is all we got.

Maggie: No. Something farther out. Not big. Just a little place we like. All right, a farm, if you want. I don't care. Tomorrow.

Joe: *(Angry and frustrated.)* Tomorrow is nothing, Maggie! Nothing! It's not going to change. You don't snap your fingers and it disappears. You don't buy a ticket and it goes away. It's here. Now.

Maggie: No.

Joe: Look at me, Maggie.

Maggie: No.

Joe: *Look* at me. You want magic to happen? Is that what you want? Go ahead. Make it happen. I'm waiting. Make it happen!

The following is the monologue created from the previous scene.

JOE (to MAGGIE), age late 40s to 50s.
pp. 76–79 (SAMUEL FRENCH, INC.)

It would have been nice. A farm. Some place all our own. Every day a different job. Every day a different reason. Something grows. Something... all in a day. Something to have. Jesus Christ, we built the house, and before we finish, fifteen years, and it's gone. It was a lot of work but it was *something*, wasn't it? Something to have. You put in one more fucking tree, you fix up another room, I kept seeing grandchildren. What the hell else was it for? Not right away, but someday, you figure, kids running around, falling down under it, when it's grown big enough to climb and you can chase them down, spend some time running around the goddamn house... (*Really angry.*) Instead, an apartment close to work! Work! Shit. Fifty weeks a year in a flat-wire shop. Twenty-four years. A bartender and a truck driver in between. Gone. All gone. Christ, even the factory is gone. Twenty-four years. Two weeks a year at the beach. One week off for Christmas.... Somebody walks up one day, one day, somebody walks up and tells you it's finished. And me... all I can say is "What?".... *What's* finished? What did I have that's finished? What? What did we have that's finished? Now I can't go home with you, Maggie. You know I can't. It gets worse. Every day, it gets worse. It wouldn't change anything. No. This is all. This is all we got. Tomorrow is nothing, Maggie! Nothing! (*Angry and frustrated.*) It's not going to change. You don't snap your fingers and it disappears. You don't buy a ticket and it goes away. It's here. Now. *Look* at me. You want magic to happen? Is that what you want? Go ahead. Make it happen. I'm waiting. Make it happen!

*　　*　　*

That is exactly what you are fighting for: magic, from Maggie. You are bitter, angry, frustrated, and really in a rage. After all, you've been told you are dying. What makes it even worse is that you've wasted your life away by not going after what you really would have loved to have had and now it's too late. Other than Maggie, you've got nothing. Through her love, she *has* to make something good happen. This is not in the words, this is your wish, your fantasy, your dream. Don't fight for reality, for you, reality sucks.

THE SHADOW BOX
by Michael Cristofer

pp. 77–79 (SAMUEL FRENCH, INC.)

Maggie: *(Breaking down.)* Us. Us. For Christ's sake, don't make me say things I don't understand. I don't want to hear them. I shake all over when I think about them. How long? Two weeks? Three? A month? And then what? What have I got *then?* An apartment full of some furniture I can't even keep clean for company, a closet full of some old pictures, some curtains I made out of my wedding dress that don't even fit the windows... What? What do I do? Sit down with the TV set every night, spill my coffee when I fall asleep on the sofa and burn holes in the carpet, dropping cigarettes?

Joe: Maggie...

Maggie: No. I want you to come home. What is this place, anyway? They make everything so nice. Why? So you forget? I can't. I can't. I want you to come home. I want you to stay out four nights a week bowling, and then come home so I can yell and not talk to you, you son of a bitch. I want to fight so you'll take me to a movie and by the time I get you to take me I'm so upset I can't enjoy the picture. I want to get up too early, too goddamn early, and I'll let you know about it, too, because I have to make you breakfast, because you never, never once eat it, because you make me get up too early just to keep you company and talk to you, and it's cold, and my back aches, and I got nothing to say to you and we never talk and it's six-thirty in the morning, *every* morning, even Sunday morning and it's all right... it's all right... it's all right because I *want* to be there because you need me to be there because I want *you* to be there because I want you to come home.

Joe: Maggie...

Maggie: Come home, that's all. Come home.

364

Joe: I can't, Maggie. You know I can't.

Maggie: No, I don't know. I don't.

Joe: I can't.

Maggie: You can. Don't believe what they tell you. What do they know? We've been through worse than this. You look fine. I can see it.

Joe: No, Maggie.

Maggie: You get stronger every day.

Joe: It gets worse.

Maggie: No. I can see it.

Joe: Every day, it gets worse.

Maggie: We'll go home, tomorrow. I got another ticket. We can get a plane tomorrow.

Joe: Don't do this, Maggie.

Maggie: I put a new chair in the apartment. You'll like it. It's red. You always said we should have a big red chair. I got it for you. It's a surprise.

Joe: No! It won't work.

Maggie: We'll get dressed up. I'll get my hair done. We'll go out someplace. What do we need? A little time, that's all.

Joe: It's not going to change anything.

Maggie: No. It's too fast. Too fast. What'll I do? I can't remember tomorrow. It's no good. We'll look around. Maybe we *can* find a little place. Something we like.

Joe: No. This is all. This is all we got.

Maggie: No. Something farther out. Not big. Just a little place we like. All right, a farm, if you want. I don't care. Tomorrow.

The following is the monologue created from the previous scene.

MAGGIE (to JOE), age 30s to 50.
pp. 77–79 (SAMUEL FRENCH, INC.)

Don't make me say things I don't understand. I don't want to hear them. I shake all over when I think about them. How long? Two weeks? Three? A month? And then what? What have I got *then*? An apartment full of some furniture I can't even keep clean for company, a closet full of some old pictures, some curtains I made out of my wedding dress that don't even fit the windows. . . . What? What do I do? Sit down with the TV set every night, spill my coffee when I fall asleep on the sofa and burn holes in the carpet, dropping cigarettes? No! I want you to come home. What is this place anyway? They make everything so nice. Why? So you forget? I can't. I can't. I want you to come home. I want you to stay out four nights a week bowling, and then come home so I can yell and not talk to you, you son of a bitch. I want to fight so you'll take me to a movie and by the time I get you to take me, I'm so upset I can't enjoy the picture. I want to get up too early, too goddamn early; and I'll let you know about it, too, because I have to make you breakfast; because you never, never once eat it; because you make me get up too early just to keep you company and talk to you; and it's cold, and my back aches, and I got nothing to say to you and we never talk and it's six-thirty in the morning; *every* morning, even Sunday morning and it's all right . . . it's all right . . . it's all right because I *want* to be there because you need me to be there because I want *you* to be there because I want you to come home. Don't believe what they tell you. What do they know? We've been through worse than this. You look fine. I can see it. You get stronger every day. I can see it. We'll go home tomorrow. I got another ticket. We can get a plane tomorrow. I put a new chair in the apartment. You'll like it. It's red. You always said we should have a big red chair. I got it for you. It's a surprise. We'll get dressed up. I'll get my hair done. We'll go out someplace. What do we need? A little time, that's all. We'll look around. Maybe we *can* find a little place. Something we like. Something farther out. Not big. Just a little place we like. A farm, if you want. I don't care. Tomorrow!

Maggie is fighting for magic too. She does not want to believe that her husband is dying. Having him home with her and away from this place, removes him from the sickness. She needs to keep him in her life. She is lonely and afraid and depends on him even though he goes out without her four times a week and wakes her to make him a very early morning breakfast that he doesn't eat. But there is no death in that life. Only in this life where he stays here and she is home by herself. She is fighting for her life. Joe *is* her life. She has not done anything for herself so she depends on him for her very existence.

THE SHADOW BOX
by Michael Cristofer

pp. 84–87 (SAMUEL FRENCH, INC.)

Brian: *(Crossing to D. L. stool.)* People don't want to let go. Do they. They think it's a mistake. They think it's supposed to last forever...

Joe: *(At U. R.)* There's a few things—I could talk to you about them...

Brian: I suppose it's because...

Joe: ...you don't expect it to happen.

Brian: You don't expect it to happen to you.

Joe: But it happens anyway, doesn't it? It doesn't matter what you do, you can't stop it.

Brian: You try.

Mark: *(In the living room.)* You keep thinking, there's got to be some way out of this.

Brian: You want to strike a bargain... make a deal.

Mark: You don't want to give in.

Joe: You want to say no.

Maggie: *(At U. R.)*...no...

Mark: ...no...

Brian: Your whole life goes by—it feels like it was only a minute.

Beverly: *(Entering stage left and moving to the L. porch.)* You try to remember what it was you believed in.

Mark: What was so important?

Maggie: What was it?

Beverly: You want it to make a difference.

Maggie: You want to blame somebody.

Brian: You want to be angry.

Joe: You want to shout, 'Not me!'

Brian: Not me!

Maggie: Not me!

367

Felicity: What time is it, Agnes?

Agnes: I don't know, Mama.

Brian: And then you think, someone should have said it sooner.

Mark: Someone should have said it a long time ago.

Beverly: When you were young.

Brian: Someone should have said, this living...

Mark: ...this life...

Beverly: ...this lifetime...

Brian: It doesn't last forever.

Maggie: A few days, a few minutes... that's all.

Brian: It has an end.

Joe: Yes.

Mark: This face.

Beverly: These hands.

Mark: This word.

Joe: It doesn't last forever.

Brian: This air.

Mark: This light.

Brian: This earth.

Beverly: These things you love.

Maggie: These children.

Beverly: This smile.

Maggie: This pain.

Brian: It doesn't last forever.

Joe: It was never supposed to last forever.

Mark: This day.

Maggie: This morning.

Beverly: This afternoon.

Mark: This evening.

Felicity: What time is it, Agnes?

Agnes: I don't know, Mama. It's time to stop. Please, Mama. It's time to stop.

Brian: These eyes...

Mark: These things you see.

Maggie: It's pretty.

Joe: Yes.

Mark: Yes.

Brian: These things you hear.

Mark: This noise.

Beverly: This music.

Steve: I can play for you now. It's not good, but it's not bad either.

Maggie: Yes.

Beverly: Yes.

Brian: They tell you you're dying, and you say all right. But if I *am* dying . . . I must still be alive.

Felicity: What time is it?

Mark: These things you have.

Maggie: Yes.

Joe: This smell, this touch.

Mark: Yes.

Beverly: This taste.

Brian: Yes.

Maggie: This breath.

Steve: Yes.

Mark: Yes.

Brian: Yes.

Maggie: Yes.

Beverly: Yes.

Joe: Yes.

Brian: This moment. (*Long pause. Lights fade.*)

The following is the monologue created from the previous scene. In the play, this scene is spoken by BRIAN, JOE, MARK, MAGGIE, and BEVERLY. For the monologue, the character may be male or female.

MALE (OR FEMALE), age late 20s to 50s.
pp. 84–87 (SAMUEL FRENCH, INC.)

People don't want to let go. Do they? They think it's a mistake. They think it's supposed to last forever. . . . There's a few things—I could talk to you about them . . . I suppose it's because . . . you don't expect it to happen. You don't expect it to happen to you. But it happens anyway, doesn't it? It doesn't matter what you do, you can't stop it. You try. You keep thinking, there's got to be some way out of this. You want to strike a bargain . . . make a deal. You don't want to give in. You want to say no. No . . . no . . . your whole life goes by—it feels like it was only a minute. You try to remember what it was you believed in. What was so important? What was it? You want it to make a difference. You want to blame somebody. You want to be angry. You want to shout, "Not me!" And then you think, someone should have said it sooner. Someone should have said it a long time ago. When you were young. Someone should have said, this living... this life... this lifetime... it doesn't last forever. A few days, a few minutes... that's all. It has an end. Yes. This face. These hands. This word. It doesn't last forever. This air. This light. This earth. These things you love. These children. This smile. This pain. It doesn't last forever. It was never supposed to last forever. This day. This morning. This afternoon. This evening. These eyes... these things you see. It's pretty. Yes. These things you hear. This noise. This music. Yes. They tell you you're dying, and you say all right. But if I *am* dying... I must still be alive! These things you have. Yes. This smell, this touch. Yes. This taste. Yes. This breath. Yes. This moment.

You must decide to whom you are telling these things. Create a relationship. Don't allow this to just be a soliloquy. Why is it important to say these words to this person? What are you fighting for from this person? We are dealing with death. Your death! But you are talking about life and living and feeling and being. Do not forget the humor in this piece! Yes, humor! The irony! And what you are fighting for is positive. Do not play this in a maudlin way, turning it into melodrama. Be passionate in your discoveries and needs and regarding the circumstances of your life. Keep the emotional action moving. No long Pinter pauses in between sentences. But *do* take a breath a time or two for emotional reasons rather than needing the air. Fight like hell for the rest of your life. See two or three times what the other person's nonverbal reaction is to what you are saying. Respond to his or her reaction to your words. You know this person quite well so you are able to read his or her body and face language. You can tell what he or she would be saying to you. This day is indeed the most important day in your life. It is today that you must discover how to appreciate every drop of life you've got coming to you and this person *must* help you.

MRS. DALLY HAS A LOVER
by William Hanley

A ONE-ACT play.
pp. 73–75 (DRAMATISTS PLAY SERIVCE, INC.)

Mrs. Dally: *(After a pause.)* I told you a lie once, Frankie.

Frankie: *(Referring back, lightly.)* You mean you told me something you didn't mean?

Mrs. Dally: Oh, no. I never did that. . . . But I'm older than I said I was even. I'm thirty-eight years old.

Frankie: *(After a pause.)* Okay.

Mrs. Dally: And I love you, Frankie. *(She waits for him to speak, then turns to him.)* Stupid, huh? *(He still cannot answer, she moves D. L.)* Isn't it?

Frankie: *(Finally.)* Considering me, yeah. I mean, I don't know why anyone would wanta love *me*.

Mrs. Dally: You're a kind young man, Frankie.

Frankie: Why? I mean it.

Mrs. Dally: I know you do. That's why you're kind. If you said that and didn't mean it, you'd be polite, but not kind. . . . I shouldn't've told you, I know that. . . .

Frankie: Why?

Mrs. Dally: But once you feel it, you can only go so long before you have to say it. It's like waiting for the other shoe to drop.

Frankie: Why shouldn't you've told me?

Mrs. Dally: Because once you say it, it can change everything.

Frankie: *(Stands.)* It don't change anything.

Mrs. Dally: It isn't enough just to be loved, sweetheart. You have to know what to do with it.

Frankie: So what do I have to *do* with it?

Mrs. Dally: That's what I mean.

Frankie: *(Impatiently.)* What. *(She only smiles, ruefully.)* Well, don't look at me like I'm an idiot! What!

Mrs. Dally: No, no, no! I wasn't doing that. I wasn't. The thing is . . . I can't tell you what to do with it. Nobody can. *(Now he understands, pause.)* I've been good to you, haven't I, Frankie?

Frankie: Sure you have.

Mrs. Dally: I've given you a lot of things.

Frankie: Yes. You'll get it all back, too.

Mrs. Dally: From you? *(He nods.)* No. . . . But maybe someone else will . . . and that'll be just as good. *(Pause.)* It's like that game we used to play when I was a kid: Pass it on. You ever play that? You'd say something to the kid next to you, or do something and tell him to pass it on. Sometimes it was something nice, sometimes it was a punch in the arm. Being alive is a lot like that game.

Frankie: I played that when I was a kid.

Mrs. Dally: Don't stop.

Frankie: Unless it's a punch in the arm.

Mrs. Dally: No, you'll pass those on too. . . . You remember you asked me why I picked you and not somebody else?

Frankie: You said you couldn't say.

Mrs. Dally: No. But I know why I wanted you to come back after that first time . . . and all the times. You ever noticed that very often people got ways of talking to each other to avoid talking to each other?

Frankie: No . . . I don't think so.

Mrs. Dally: You listen, you'll see. But it was hardly ever like that with you and me. Every once in a while in this life, Frankie, somebody talks to somebody else. I mean, *talks.* It's sweet music, Frankie. And you listen for it, you hear? Always, your whole life, listen for it. *(Pause, he understands. She kisses him seriously.)* You'd better get outta here, it's almost time.

Frankie: That isn't what I want to do.

Mrs. Dally: What do you want to do? *(He smiles.)* Tomorrow's another day.

Frankie: It's nice they arranged it like that.

Mrs. Dally: Beat it, fresh kid. *(She goes to the door, unlocks it and looks into the hall, she closes the door, turns to him, holding his coat, waiting. He approaches and takes the coat from her.)*

Frankie: I'll see you tomorrow?

Mrs. Dally: I'll be here. *(Pause.)*

Frankie: Do you *really* love *me?*

Mrs. Dally: No, I don't really love you, you're not even good-looking. Why aren't you wearing a scarf or something, you'll catch cold going around like that. (*She embraces him fiercely and kisses him, pause.*) One of these days you'll say that and I won't.

Frankie: What?

Mrs. Dally: One of these days you'll say I'll see you tomorrow and I won't.

Frankie: Stop, will ya.

Mrs. Dally: Just remember what I said: listen to the sweet music... and pass it on.

The following is the monologue created from the previous scene.

MRS. DALLY (to FRANKIE), age late 30s to early 40s.
pp. 73–75 (DRAMATISTS PLAY SERVICE, INC.)

I told you a lie once, Frankie. I'm older than I said I was even. I'm thirty-eight years old. And I love you, Frankie.... stupid, huh?... Isn't it? You're a kind young man, Frankie. I know you don't believe that anyone would want to love you. I know you mean that. That's why you're kind. If you said that and didn't mean it, you'd be polite, but not kind.... I shouldn't've told you, I know that.... But once you feel it, you can only go so long before you have to say it. It's like waiting for the other shoe to drop. Once you say it, it can change everything. It isn't enough just to be loved, sweetheart. You have to know what to do with it. I can't tell you what to do with it. Nobody can... I've been good to you, haven't I, Frankie? I've given you a lot of things. I don't want any of it back... but maybe someone else will... and that'll be just as good. It's like that game we used to play when I was a kid: Pass It On. You ever play that? You'd say something to the kid next to you, or do something and tell him to pass it on. Sometimes it was something nice, sometimes it was a punch in the arm. Being alive is a lot like that game. If you played it as a kid, don't stop. And pass on the punch in the arm too.... You remember you asked me why I picked you and not somebody else? You ever noticed that very often people got ways of talking to each other to avoid talking to each other? You listen, you'll see. But it was hardly ever like that with you and me. Every once in a while in this life, Frankie, somebody talks to somebody else. I mean, *talks*. It's sweet music, Frankie. . . . And you listen for it, you hear? Always, your whole life, listen for it. . . . One of these days you'll say, "I'll see you tomorrow," and I won't. Just remember what I said: Listen to the sweet music . . . and pass it on.

So, Mrs. Dally, you know that nothing lasts—nothing. Everything changes—everything! But it's what we take with us from each experience that is so important. And Frankie is so young and nice and he will go on and have other relationships and you might not ever have another one. If he can take the good from what the two of you have had, you will be satisfied. If he can pass it on, the world will be a better place in which to live. Part of you will go with him. Part of you will remain with him forever. What is it that you are fighting for from him? What do you desperately need from him that only he can give to you that will enhance the rest of your life? Do you need for him to always remember you with kind feelings about how you "put out" for him? You didn't love his choice of words but he is young. He must learn how not to hurt. He must learn from you. He must want to keep you alive in his memories. He *must* need you all his life to live a kind life.